P9-AOF-038

WITHDRAWN

Gramley Library
Salem College
Winston-Salem, NC 27108

True Rites and Maimed Rites

True Rites and Maimed Rites

Ritual and Anti-Ritual in Shakespeare and His Age

EDITED BY

LINDA WOODBRIDGE

AND

EDWARD BERRY

University of Illinois Press
Urbana and Chicago

Gramley Library
Salem College
Winston-Salem, NC 27108

©1992 by the Board of Trustees of the University of Illinois
Manufactured in the United States of America
1 2 3 4 5 C P 5 4 3 2 1

This book is printed on acid-free paper.

Library of Congress Cataloging-in-Publication Data

True rites and maimed rites : ritual and anti-ritual in Shakespeare
and his age / edited by Linda Woodbridge and Edward Berry.
    p.   cm.
Includes bibliographical references and index.
ISBN 0-252-01897-4 (acid-free paper). — ISBN 0-252-06243-4 (pbk.
: acid-free paper)
    1. Shakespeare, William, 1564–1616 – Knowledge – Manners and
customs.   2. Rites and ceremonies – England – History – 16th century.
3. Rites and ceremonies in literature.   4. Ritual in literature.
I. Woodbridge, Linda, 1945–   II. Berry, Edward I.
PR3069.R55T78   1992
822.3'3 – dc20   91-30338
                                                                    CIP

> Caesar shall
> Have all true rites and lawful ceremonies.
> —*Julius Caesar*

> Who is this they follow?
> And with such maimed rites?
> —*Hamlet*

Contents

Introduction

In 1957, at the close of their history of literary criticism, William K. Wimsatt Jr. and Cleanth Brooks cast their eyes upon the contemporary critical scene. "Surely," they concluded, "the hugest cloudy symbol, the most threatening, of our last ten or fifteen years in criticism is the principle of criticism by myth and ritual origins" (733). Thirty years and many critical movements later, ritual criticism persists, and the anxious foreboding of Wimsatt and Brooks, with their fulminations about myth-and-ritual critics resembling "eighteenth-century Gothicists and Druidists" who "want to push us back into some prelogical and hence preliterary" age (741) seems oddly misplaced, especially since their portents of doom included such classics as Northrop Frye's *Anatomy of Criticism*. While the present collection of essays makes clear that ritual criticism continues to flourish, it also suggests that it has continued to change and develop.

Something of the change in the critical climate for this kind of study over the past thirty years becomes clear if we compare Robert Hapgood's survey of the field in 1962, "Shakespeare and the Ritualists," with the contents of the present collection. Hapgood, who wrote under the shadow of Wimsatt and Brooks, made general claims for the value of this approach that might be made by the editors of the present volume: "The myth and ritual approach has thrown light on Shakespeare's histories, comedies, tragedies, and romances, illuminating lines, scenes, characters, rhythms and patterns of action, plays, groups of plays, and his whole 'idea of theatre'" (111). Many of the studies he surveys, however, have no counterparts in the present collection. Our essayists make no mention of archetypes, for example, or of Jung, and invoke the ideas of Northrop Frye, if at all, only to supplant them. Christ figures appear rarely and only where sanctioned by allusion. Except in one essay, myth has been divorced from ritual, suggesting the dissolution of that critical joint stock company Myth-and-Ritual Criticism. Genres are not traced to specific ritual origins. No one uses ritual to chart Shakespeare's artistic development. Nor, with one exception, does an author explore in any detail the connections between ritual and theater. What most interests the present writers, with a few exceptions, is the relationship between Elizabethan ritualism, broadly conceived, and Shakespeare's plays.

Such shifts in focus are not unusual in the history of that heterogeneous cluster of approaches known as "ritual." A flurry of ritualism has occurred about once in each generation since Frazer — the Cornford/Murray/Harrison/ Weston generation, the Bodkin/Welsford/Cornford generation, the Fergusson generation, the Barber/Frye generation, the Lévi-Strauss~ and Van Gennep~influenced structuralist generation, the Turner/Douglas/Bakhtin/ Girard generation, and now the anthropologically influenced New Historicists. (Even where newly historicized critics are not explicitly addressing ritual, the major shift in literary criticism away from formalist approaches toward historicized, politicized reading, effected by thinkers from Gramsci to Foucault to Greenblatt, has inevitably affected the study of ritual.) Each generation has taken a different direction and provoked its own skeptics and scoffers. The "generations" of course overlap extensively; in the cases of Van Gennep and Bakhtin, a huge time lag intervened between time of writing and availability in English; for linguistic, political, and other reasons, these theorists' main influence was on a generation not their own. Other theorists' popularity has waxed and waned and waxed again, mingling the generations. Of this century's major critical schools loosely classifiable as "ritual," some are at present in nearly total eclipse; but many still appear in some form in the present collection, whatever sea change they have undergone. To help situate the present essays in a tradition of ritual criticism, we begin with a brief description of the ritual approaches most pertinent to this volume, introducing and commenting on the major proponents and opponents of such approaches.

Fertility Rites

Attempts to locate in ancient fertility ritual the origins and structure of literary forms, especially tragedy and comedy, began with classicists — Jane Harrison, Gilbert Murray, Francis Macdonald Cornford — and spread to the modern literatures (Murray himself made the leap from Orestes to Hamlet) where, thanks to the prestige of theorists like Northrop Frye, whose "fertility" theories of Shakespearean comedy remain influential to this day, the theory enjoyed a considerable vogue long after its complete demise among classicists. Classicist Gerald Else was incredulous and irate at finding, as late as 1965, critics of English literature still promulgating as fact Murray's theory of the origin of tragedy, demolished by Pickard-Cambridge in 1927. Classicists have heavily documented the scholarly crimes and logical lapses of Harrison, Cornford, and Murray, who were indeed overenthusiastic, mistaken about many details, naïve about the relation between rite and literature, reductive in tracing all dramas (even all myths) to a single archaic ritual (whose existence they failed to prove), led astray by Frazer's dubious anthropology. (For the case against Harrison, Murray, and Cornford, see Pickard-Cambridge, Else, Dover; for Frazer, see below.) By now, even English literary folk have largely given up on fertility rite. (Only occasionally does a modern critic, gingerly, essay a comment like Marjorie Garber's: "Whatever the merits of the claim for 'origins', the work of the Cambridge school . . . suggests a persuasive series of analogies between ritual behavior and dramatic action" [18].) But given the link between fertility and the female, it would be surprising if feminist critics did not begin to have another look at fertility rites. In the present volume, Jeanne Roberts, in "Shakespeare's Maimed Birth Rites," reopens the field, using recent work of Gerda Lerner and others to link fertility rite once again with myth and also with the now much more common preoccupation of ritual critics, rites of passage.

The Cambridge school foundered largely on the approach through ritual forms. Murray sought formal ritual in tragedies: a play, like a fertility rite, should contain a *threnos* or lamentation, and if the rite were absent, he sought vestiges of it with more ingenuity than persuasiveness. The school also stumbled because of its resolute structuralism: as Propp found a list of functions invariably occurring in the same order in folk tales, Murray found in tragedy and Cornford in comedy a fixed series of ritual forms—*agon, pathos, messenger, threnos, anagnorisis, theophany* in tragedy. But the school's critical antagonists showed that the plays do not display this series of forms and that no known Greek ritual did either, and mocked such absurdities as Murray's taking an earthquake for a vestigial *theophany* (see Pickard-Cambridge 188, 200).

But in retrospect it is a pity that the entire approach was abandoned because of its flawed methods. Shakespeare lived in the *beginning* of the era that witnessed Keith Thomas's "decline of magic," an age in which many relics of pagan fertility rites remained. The Swedish historian Olaus Magnus described in 1555 a traditional May 1 battle between cohorts representing summer and winter; a woodcut shows a joust wherein Summer— man and horse crowned with leaves and flanked by a leafy tree—pierces with a lance the horse of Winter, who wears a fur hat and is flanked by a leafless tree (503). In the Isle of Man, a mock battle between the forces of the Queen of May and the Queen of Winter (a man dressed in furs) persisted through the early modern period and indeed into the early nineteenth century (Train 118–20). The tug-of-war was a common early modern rural sport (see Bord's account of late survivals in Shropshire and Radnorshire on Shrove Tuesday [195–97]); that it was vestigially a winter-summer combat is suggested by ethnographic evidence further afield: an Inuit rite has two sides, "the ptarmigans . . . , those who were born in the winter, and the ducks . . . , or the children of summer. A large rope of sealskin is stretched out. One party takes one end of it and tries with all its might to drag the opposite party over to its side. The others hold fast to the rope. . . . If the ptarmigans give way the summer has won the game" and the winter will be mild (Boas 605). Calderon likens to winter/summer mock battles Ruthenian and Bulgarian pre-wedding-night mock battles: "this fighting [seems] to have a phallic significance, being intended to procure vigour for the male principle" (80). In a modern African fertility rite Turner calls "the fruitful contest of the sexes" (*Process* 77), in which men and women hurl insults at each other, combat leads to fruition; Cornford notes similar male/female slanging matches, fertility rites of the ancient world (110–11). Such cross-cultural parallels should be pursued with caution: anthropologists now use the pejorative label "butterfly collecting" for the Frazerian habit of amassing examples taken out of context from many disparate cultures, and the most we can safely claim for some cultural resemblances, in societies as remote in time and place from Shakespeare's as are Turner's Ndembu, is probably a suggestive analogy with early modern rites. But such analogies can indeed be suggestive;[1] and much evidence of lingering fertility ritual can be found in early modern Britain and northern Europe, without butterfly collecting in modern Africa. In the widespread pastoral debate, as Steven Marx shows, winter images attach to an old man, summer to a young; close links with winter/summer combat appear in the first surviving medieval eclogue, Alcuin's *Conflictus Veris et Heimis*, ninth century, a summer/winter combat. Debates addressed such diverse topics as hetero- versus homosexuality, thrift versus generosity, even lentil soup versus lentil puree, but the commonest topics were youth versus age and spring versus winter (Marx 153–54). Such a youth-age combat in a green world is clearly the war that paradoxically brings fertility, as in the ritual tug-of-war or the mummer's rivalry between young and old suitor—Turner's "fruitful contest." The Renaissance recognized the archaic nature of the pastoral debate: sixteenth-century Scaliger "saw in this bucolic convention a literary imitation of the verse debates of primitive peoples" (Marx 151-52).

In other rites, sterility is driven out: a killjoy is expelled, or (in saturnalian rites) revelry-dampening authority figures dethroned. Death's effigy may be carried out of town, and often as a complement to expulsion, a tree or a green man (crowned forest king) is brought in.[2] Phillip Stubbes's description of the pulling of a maypole into English villages — by thirty or forty yoke of oxen with nosegays of flowers on their horns — is familiar to many readers. The "foliate head" with features of foliage, or foliage springing from its mouth, is a familiar carving on late medieval Christian churches (see Basford), and English pubs to this day may be called The Green Man.

British culture offered a palimpsest of Mother Earth beliefs. Pre-Roman Celts worshipped a number of earth-goddesses, such as Rosmerta, related to the Greek Maia, and also a sky god, Taranis (see Webster). In pre-Christian Roman Britain these continued to be worshipped alongside Cybele, Atys, Isis, and Syrian sky gods imported by Roman soldiers (Green 53-59). Ernst Curtius argues that throughout the Middle Ages, "the pagan Natura" or Mother Earth "never entirely vanishes from consciousness"; in the twelfth-century writings of Bernard Silvestris on Natura, "as through an opened sluice, the fertility cult of the earliest ages flows once again into the speculation of the Christian West" (108, 123; see also Dieterich, Gill, Neumann). Mother Earth contributed to the cult of the Virgin Mary. Thomas Kuhn and others have insisted that the development of science cannot be neatly extricated from the history of magic, and early modern science was often piggy-backed on traditional beliefs, as when Copernicus spoke the language of sky god/mother earth: "The Earth conceives by the sun and becomes pregnant with annual offspring" (I.10.50). The concept of "the earth that's nature's mother" came naturally to Shakespeare: "from her womb children of divers kind / We sucking on her natural bosom find" (*Rom.* II.iii.9-12); the earth is "common mother, thou / Whose womb unmeasurable and infinite breast / Teems and feeds all" (*Tim.* IV.iii.177-79). Familiarity with ancient rite also appears in Shakespeare's surprisingly frequent use of blood sacrifice, mostly in imagery, occasionally as incident.

How consciously did Shakespeare and his contemporaries understand fertility ritual? The populace did practice vestigial fertility rites — May games, saturnalian Twelfth Night festivities, the mummer's play with its dying-and-reviving figures and ritual-linked Robin Hood, occasionally even blood sacrifice (Bord 130). One suggestive link between folk drama and high-culture drama is that like the "men's ceremonial" of mumming or sword dance, high drama was enacted by men; both the mummers' "betty" and *Twelfth Night*'s Viola were played by male actors. Some, such as Robert Weimann, regard mummings and May games as ceremonies clung to for community cohesion, to keep touch with the past in an age of great social change; ritual meanings, they think, had been largely forgotten by the twelfth century. Anthropologist Jack Goody thinks all rituals lose meaning over time, through forgetting and through the numbing effect of repetition, which makes response automatic and dulls meaning (32). Others maintain that as late as the seventeenth century, popular observances were consciously understood as remnants of ancient religious rite. Douglas Hewitt reminds us that Puritans opposed mummings, May games, and morris dances in the belief that they were remnants of a pagan religion. An early twentieth-century theory, that seventeenth-century witches were knowledgeable about ancient religions and practiced pagan fertility rites,[3] has long been out of favor, but received stunning support in Carlo Ginzburg's *Night Battles,* 1966 (in English, 1983), which draws on Inquisition archives to show the widespread existence until at least the late sixteenth century of *benandanti,* good witches, who as custodians of an ancient agrarian cult practiced fertility rites. They claimed their spirits left their bodies by night at solstices and equinoxes, to combat evil witches who harmed crops and children: "When the witches win, a great famine follows, and when the benandanti win, there is abundance" (103). Since Ginzburg's Italian finds, *benandanti* have been discovered across Europe; "what Ginzburg discovered . . . was only a small part of a phenomenon of European or even world dimensions" (Burke 33). In England, "beliefs in black witches and cunning men were integrally connected. . . . Contemporaries rightly called them both 'witches': 'The one twineth; the other untwineth,' said a Hampshire man in 1532. Ursula Kemp, hanged at Chelmsford for witchcraft in 1582, had protested that 'though she could unwitch, she could not witch,' while John Weemse later wrote that 'there are some witches which the common people call the loosing witches, who do no harm at all, but remove only that hurt which the binding witch lays on the sick person'" (Thomas, *Decline* 654).

Arne Runeberg compares early modern witchcraft as reported by inquisitors with sorcery beliefs in modern tribal Africa, again suggesting witchcraft beliefs as remnants of tribal religion (49–59). Many Renaissance charges against "bad" witches cast them as figures of sterility. They harmed crops, livestock, and babies: *Macbeth*'s witches ruin grain and kill swine

(IV.i.55, I.iii.ii), and witches took away nursing mothers' milk (Kittredge 166). They harmed human fertility by causing impotence. "Witches were characterized not in terms of crimes theologically defined, but rather in terms of the destruction they brought to the harvests and famine, and the sorcery they worked on children" (Ginzburg 27). They also affected the food supply by "frustrating such domestic operations as making butter, cheese or beer" (Thomas, *Decline* 519).

Whether or not the Renaissance was conscious of lingering pagan fertility rites, similar rites were accessible in Christianity. The Christian myth is of the same family as that of Dionysus or Osiris, a dying-and-reviving spring god restoring the earth, and Christian rite resembles other fertility rites. In fifteenth-century art, Jesus closely resembles a fertility god: in a painting a stalk of wheat and a grapevine grow from his body; in an altarpiece, Mary and the evangelists pour grain into a mill and crank out a wafer and Baby Jesus; in an embroidery, Christ is pressed under the crossbeam of a winepress, identified with the crucifixion cross; his blood is wine (Bynum, Plates 4, 1, 5). The Easter liturgy recalls the winter/summer combat: the atonement was "understood as an agon – a dramatic conflict between Christ and Satan culminating in the triumph of the Resurrection" (Hardison 82). Christ's death and descent into hell, ritualized in Holy Saturday liturgies dwelling on the harrowing of hell, recalls Persephone's underworld descent and annual resurrection, ritualized in Eleusinian mystery rites. Ritual copulation, Sky wedding Earth, lingers in rites attending the notion of the church as Christ's bride, reflecting the Christian myth of divine father impregnating human mother, Jehovah fathering Jesus upon Mary as Zeus fathered Dionysus upon Semele. The spring god's death and revival appear in rites like the medieval Maundy Thursday *tenebrae* service, a death ceremony (Hardison 117) followed by the Easter announcement of Christ's resurrection. Ancient rites of eating a slain god, a sacrifice to renew humanity, survive in the communion service, especially central at Eastertime: Maundy Thursday commemorates the institution of the Lord's Supper, and the elevation of the host is the climax of the Easter mass.

Though under heavy attack in the Reformation, fertility magic persisted: people recited "set prayers when planting and grafting"; "the medieval practice of reading the gospels in the corn fields survived in some areas until the Civil War"; " 'three parts at least of the people' were 'wedded to their old superstition still,' declared a Puritan document in 1584" (Thomas, *Decline* 71, 73, 84). The Shakespeare canon's deep concern with fertility and sterility may well reflect the ingrained mentality of the age. In

Shakespeare, winning and losing, surviving and perishing, are often articulated in a language of plants and seasons: tragedy *and* comedy cast goodness, happiness, triumph in terms of greenness, growth, fertility; both cast evil, misery, defeat in terms of sterility. Shakespearean tragedy pretends to no ritual efficacy; it repeatedly challenges the possibility of human control over events. But its language situates it within a discourse of fertility, casting what is desirable as organic, green, even explicitly rural. Such mental sets were bound to cause strain in an urbanizing culture.

Ritual studies related to fertility rites have long been out of fashion not only (one suspects) because the early theorists have been discredited. There is a gender issue here: though some cultures associate fertility with male deities, many others have worshipped female fertility gods, and Shakespeare's culture, true to its roots in the Celtic earth-mother tradition, largely linked fertility with the female principle. Studies of ritual tend to stratify along gender lines: "male" rites such as ceremonies of political power, male initiation, war, and ceremonies of international diplomacy draw most theorists' attention,[4] while "female" rites promoting human and agrarian fertility now languish in neglect,[5] after a period of virulent scholarly attacks. Those who write of political power are seldom attacked for their mere choice of subject matter, as are those who have opted for fertility; anything deeply involved with women seems automatically suspect. The exclusion of fertility from serious attention, the defining of ritual as rites of power, is the preference of a male-dominated society. Jeanne Roberts has done us a service in reopening the issue of fertility and linking it with a feminist exploration of patriarchal thinking.

One is bound to admit that overt fertility rites are, in the works of Shakespeare, almost entirely lacking. But fertility was a discourse, comprising in early modern Europe a complex semiotic system whose signs included hero combat, seasonal personifications, processions with greenery, blood sacrifice, harvest, water, food, babies, tug-of-wars, slanging matches: signs which abound in Shakespeare. Early modern readers may well have placed such signs much more readily than we do in the ritual discourse of fertility. Shakespeare's plays can be seen as at once deeply embedded in this archaic discourse, and (as products of a dawning rationalistic and antiritualistic age) shrewdly skeptical of the older magical thinking.

But should such material be called ritual, or included alongside other classes of ritual, such as rites of passage, whose ceremonies were still "alive" in Shakespeare's time? (The same question can be raised about scapegoating, which also occurs in Shakespeare largely without formal religious or magical ritual.) We retain the term "ritual" in this collection, even in the absence or paucity of formal rite, because it has come to be understood as referring to a mixed bag of phenomena — scapegoating, misrule, fertility, rites of passage — positioned at a crossroads where magic meets ceremony and literature meets anthropology.

Scapegoating

In his 1962 survey of approaches to Shakespeare, Hapgood found that the scapegoat interpretation stood out among them: "the association — not equation — of the death of the tragic hero with the sacrifice of the scape-goat king . . . [is] the soundest and most suggestive contribution which the ritualists have made" (120). In the best known scapegoat reading of Shakespeare, John Holloway in 1961 had seen tragedy's "vertebrate structure" as "human sacrifice" (98): Coriolanus is driven from his city like a classical scapegoat, his death a *sparagmos* ("tear him in pieces"); the hero goes "from being the cynosure of his society to being estranged from it; . . . what happens to him suggests the expulsion of a scapegoat, or the sacrifice of a victim" (135). Scapegoats have also been found in other genres. History-play kings "are loaded at their end with . . . collective respon-sibility for the many kinds of evil which have been freed (by whatever agency) during their reign" (Henn 84). Shylock and Antonio, *Merry Wives'* Falstaff, and Pericles have been called scapegoats (Girard, "To Entrap," Spens, Roberts's essays on *Merry Wives,* Barber [*Festive Comedy*], Thorne). C. L. Barber thinks fools act as scapegoats "to consolidate the hold of the serious themes by exorcising opposition" ([*Festive Comedy*] 232); Linda Woodbridge thinks the stage misogynist, "not unlike the classical pharmakos or scapegoat, [carries] doubts, fears, and antagonisms [toward women] out of the play with him" (*Women* 290). John-Pierre Guépin distinguishes tragic from comic scapegoats: in tragedy our sympathy is with the scapegoat, while in comedy we are distanced from him (116); if we apply Guépin's terms, René Girard's attempted compromise — that only the refined sympa-thize with scapegoat Shylock — creates a tragedy for the refined, a comedy for the vulgar ("Wisest" 109).

Though more frequently encountered these days than the fertility ritual school, the scapegoat interpretation has also been in at least partial eclipse for a generation, kept alive in the controversial work of René Girard more than in any other single critic. Critics of the scapegoat school have invited readers' distrust insofar as they have too frequently lacked a firm theoretical base. They bandy about the word "scapegoat" without definition, as if everyone knows what a scapegoat is, or breezily toss out an all-inclusive footnote to Sir James Frazer. Even the redoubtable Derrida, in "Plato's Pharmacy," relies almost exclusively on Frazer and Harrison, those elderly authorities, for information on scapegoats. Frazer's monumental *The Scapegoat*, part 6 of *The Golden Bough*, still casts its shadow over the field, and literary "scapegoat" critics often go no farther than to Frazer, despite the out-datedness of his work, which belongs, after all, to anthropology's infancy or at most adolescence. Northrop Frye's influential ritual approaches to literature are based on late nineteenth- and early twentieth-century work by Frazer and Cornford. But to read Frazer now is to confront stunning ethnocentricity. "It is hard to forgive Frazer for his complacency and undisguised contempt of primitive society," writes anthropologist Mary Douglas, concluding that "Frazer's influence has been a baneful one" (*Purity* 24, 28). There is still valuable information to be found in Frazer; his source authors do enjoy the irreplaceable advantage of having witnessed rites which have since died out. But can we trust his data? As his contemporaries showed, he misrepresented his sources (see Lang, Lyall): though his assembled mass of data can still be convenient, one should always check to make sure he has fairly used his sources. Some of his evidence is open to bias: many reports of guilt transfer Frazer took from missionaries (one eye-witness report of human sacrifice is from *The Gospel on the Banks of the Niger*), who may view a rite as sin transfer on the Hebrew scapegoat model, rather than seeking the African meaning. And as Girard notes, condescending ethnocentrism blinded Frazer to the fact that scapegoating can exist in a civilized, modern world: "He only saw an ignorant superstition that religious disbelief and positivism have . . . remove[d]" (*Scapegoat* 120).

Much evidence suggests that scapegoat thinking was alive in early modern England, not only as encoded in Christianity—Jesus' sacrificial death was itself a form of scapegoating—but in small magical rites of daily life. In a rite practiced in Shakespeare's time, a poor person was hired to attend a funeral and take on the deceased's sins, keeping the ghost from walking; sin was transferred via bread and beer, passed over the corpse and then consumed by the "sin-eater." The seventeenth-century historian John Aubrey, who details instances of the rite, likens it to "the Scapegoat in the old law," quoting Leviticus 16; "this custom (though rarely used in our days), yet by some people was observed even in the strictest time of the Presbyterian government" (35–36). Less formal scapegoating was also common: "At the local level the clergy did not hesitate to identify the scapegoat responsible for the community's sufferings. When 190 persons died of the plague at Cranbrook, Kent, in 1597–8, the vicar of St. Dunstan's church entered his diagnosis in the parish register: it was a divine judgement for the town's sins, and in particular for 'that vice of drunkenness which did abound here.' [He identified two culprits by name.] . . . At Hitchin the minister blamed the plague of 1665 on the local prostitute" (Thomas, *Decline* 100). Such blaming was natural to scapegoat thinking, to which transfer of evil is basic. In rural England, until quite recent times, illness was often transferred to plants, animals, or objects: folklore collectors have noted transfers of illness into rushes that are floated downstream (Thistleton-Dyer 163), into snails or tree trunks (Palmer 65), dogs, potatoes, or rings (A. R. Wright 70, 72). Warts were transferred to sticks; whoever picked them up got warts (ibid., 70). The many transference cures Palmer records in *The Folklore of Warwickshire* are late survivals of folk beliefs Shakespeare grew up with. Some early modern witchcraft charges arose from such cures: "The 'good' witch who . . . cured [a client] by transferring his disease to another person, might well be regarded as a 'bad' one by the injured party" (Thomas, *Decline* 520). But despite the availability of English material contemporary with Shakespeare, scapegoating's main theorists have drawn examples mostly from biblical, ancient Mediterranean, or modern African sources.

The most fashionable current scapegoat theorist, René Girard, writes of scapegoating's social dynamic, the therapeutic effect of deflecting violence onto a noncommunity member, thus protecting the community from its own innate violence. Girard has aroused mixed reactions, some strong: the innate violence of the academic community is perhaps being deflected onto him. Anthropologist Luc De Heusch dismisses him as a scribbling dilettante, who builds "a universal psychological theory of sacrifice out of thin air" and "misuses anthropology"; he scorns Girard's "strange psychological concept" of innate violence and its reduction of ritual sacrifice to crime prevention, and Girard's belief that with an effective judicial system, sacrifice will die out: how has he overlooked ancient Greece's complex sacrificial system, coexisting with a well established judicial system? (16). De Heusch's criticisms are persuasive, especially on ancient Greece; but classicist Helene Foley, whose book on ritual appeared the same year as De Heusch's, treats Girard with great respect.

Girard *is* more "modern" than Frazer; but his theories are to many unsatisfying. His forcing all phenomena into a procrustean bed of scape-

Gramley Library
Salem College
Winston-Salem, NC 27108

goats does violence to the complexity of sacrifice: De Heusch is not exaggerating when he says Girard "reduces all forms of sacrifice to a theory of the scapegoat" (17), for he reduces that and more: scapegoating is "the very basis of cultural unification, the source of all rituals and religion" (*Violence and the Sacred* 235, 302); "all human language, and other cultural institutions . . . originated in collective murder" (*Scapegoat* 193). Girard's tracing violence to loss of difference, blurred distinctions, resembles Mary Douglas's theory that danger inheres in the breakdown of categories; but Douglas's view that blurred distinctions result in pollution covers the data better than Girard's—that they result in violence. Girard's *The Scapegoat* offers some valuable insights, but its focus on mob violence ignores individual scapegoating. Viewing myths as relics of real events ("there must be a real victim behind the text"), Girard finds it "statistically inconceivable that all these texts could have been forgeries" (52), a startling notion of the fictive. To him, all myths are persecution stories: persecution, if absent, must have been suppressed after an early version. At this writing, scapegoating still lacks a theorist of real authority.

Despite the potential usefulness of scapegoating, then, contemporary critics shy away from it, probably because its theory is shaky and confusing. Among important issues still to be clarified concerning scapegoating is whether such a sacrificial victim must be innocent, like Romeo and Juliet, or whether a guilty victim like Richard III or Macbeth can serve as an efficacious scapegoat; another is the extent to which political assassinations can be regarded as displaying the "primitive" mentality of scapegoating. Those who use the notion of scapegoating most effectively tend to ground it in early modern European history, steering clear of Africa; they often assume an archaic mentality at work behind "civilized" events in which no *overt* scapegoat ritual is present. For example, Steven Mullaney has compared the scapegoating of Angelo in *Measure for Measure* with Cesare Borgia's scapegoating his lieutenant de Orco, whose bisected body was displayed, in 1502, in a province he had cruelly subdued. Knowing Borgia had ordered the oppressions, the people still accepted the body as "a convenient object for their hatred and fear, a much-desired catharsis that would 'purge their spirits'—a scapegoat who, like any scapegoat, is effective because he is at least a partial fiction, a symbolic object constituted as such by an entire community" (88–92). Other historical "scapegoatings" close to Shakespeare's time may well prove useful to Shakespeare critics: as Lacey Baldwin Smith notes, for example, Empson and Dudley "were sacrificed at the commencement of Henry VIII's reign because they seemed to personify the financial extortion of the government of the first Tudor," and "Cromwell suffered . . . because the king needed a scapegoat in 1540 for his discarded religious and foreign policies" (475, 477).

Two essays in the present volume, Naomi Liebler's "The Mockery King of Snow: Richard II and the Sacrifice of Ritual" and Mark Rose's "Conjuring Caesar: Ceremony, History, and Authority in 1599," show scapegoat readings still viable and vital. Both ground their work in the Elizabethan political moment, and both assume that the mentality of scapegoating can be in some way operative even without formal ritual, as for Rose, Caesar's death is both a political assassination and a "sacrificial death," a "kind of political Mass."

Carnival

One of the liveliest ritual approaches in recent years has been that of carnival and saturnalia. In Shakespeare studies the landmark study of carnival misrule, C. L. Barber's *Shakespeare's Festive Comedy* (1959), most memorable for linking Falstaff with the Lord of Misrule and the carnival spirit, has been supplemented in the last several decades by infusions of Bakhtinian theory. (Insofar as this involves substituting Bahktin's French materials for Barber's English materials, it may be something of a retrograde step for those seeking to ground Shakespearean ritual study securely in an Elizabethan and Jacobean context.) Since carnival's world-upside-down inverts hierarchies of class, gender, and age, and so does Shakespeare, the approach has been of great interest to Marxist, feminist, and social-history oriented readers.

The influence of the Roman holiday Saturnalia, inverting master and servant, appears in Roman New Comedy, whose clever servant, brighter than his master, directs the action (Mosca and Jeeves are his descendants); in Shakespeare, Armado's servant Moth essays this role in *Love's Labor's Lost*, and *Shrew* mimics saturnalia as Lucentio changes clothes and identities with his servant. In other saturnalian moments, Oswalt behaves insolently to Lear (I.iv); Caliban leads a servant revolt, to set up a butler as king; Bolingbroke, inverting relations with his king, inadvertently casts himself as a Lord of Misrule, a posture from which his regime never wholly recovers.

As for topsy-turviness of gender, Renaissance literature abounds in sonneteers who grovel before mistresses, shrews who dominate husbands; "carnival" interpretation can illuminate Kate, Adriana, the cross-dressing romantic heroines, the domineering women of the histories. Of the latter, one might invoke Victor Turner's theory of gender inversion during social crises: when structural superiors, through "dissensions over particularistic or segmented interests, have brought disaster on the local community, it is for structural inferiors . . . to set things right again, . . . by symbolically usurping for a short while the weapons, dress, accouterments, and behavioral style of structural superiors—i.e., men" (*Process* 184). The *Henry VI* plays, which riot in "dissensions over segmented interests," war abroad alternating with civil strife at home, bristle with warlike, "mankind" women: Joan of Arc, Constance, Margaret. When men have made a mess of things, "ladies and pale-visag'd maids / Like Amazons come tripping after drums, / Their thimbles into armed gauntlets change, / Their needles to lances" (*Jn.* V.ii.154–57); completing the inversion, males are often called effeminate: "Why stand we like soft-hearted women here, / Wailing our losses, whiles the foe doth rage?" (*3H6* II.iii.25–26). In its political dimension, gender saturnalia rubs shoulders with class inversion. Davis ("Women on Top") thinks the literary/festive tradition of the licensed scold helped legitimize real women's unruly political behavior, Woodbridge that the Renaissance feared that shrews, "armed with governing skills acquired in their own households, . . . might advance into the political arena" (*Women* 197).

Among many inversions (male/female, master/servant, human/animal) in broadsheet woodcuts of the "world-upside-down" type—a very saturnalian genre—age inversions are the most prominent: "the infant son beating his father and the infant daughter feeding the mother. . . . The aged couple [playing] with childish toys, and the child bigger than . . . the adult" (Kunzle 50). Age inversion is pervasive in Shakespeare. It is no accident that comedy's young folks often outwit the old in order to marry: ancient Saturnalia was a fertility rite, and Time's saturnalia, humbling the strong generation and elevating the weak, promotes the continuance of the species. The old in Shakespeare are often under the tutelage or leadership of the young, as Armado is rebuked as a "negligent student" by Moth, whose "true wit" is "offer'd by a child to an old man" (*LLL* III.i.33, V.i.58–59). The topsy-turviness of Falstaff under Hal's leadership parodies the political action, especially in *Part 1*, where two young men strive to come into their own. As Hal is ringleader of the old tavern reprobates, so he leads the forces at Shrewsbury, while older heads follow. Hotspur dominates his father, uncle, and other older relatives and allies; the play thrice repeats the youth-leading-age pattern. Natalie Davis's finding that the Lord of Misrule tradition grew ultimately out of carnivalesque youth groups ("Misrule") opens the possibility that age inversion provides a model for all such inversions, that the carnival impulse springs from the human experience of the generations changing places, stronger adults ultimately replaced by their weaker offspring. Carnival readings have as much to offer as Freudian readings to an understanding of the ubiquitous generational conflict in Shakespeare.

Whether it manifests itself as an inversion of class, gender, or age, the saturnalian impulse is basically a revolt against established power. The great unresolved question is whether carnival is subversive or conservative, a challenger of authority or an extension of ideological control. In *Carnival and Theater,* Michael Bristol sees in carnival's ritual inversions a conscious challenge to received hierarchies. To the lower classes, he argues, carnival *is* a world right-side-up; it is noncarnival seasons in which the world is upside down to the oppressed. A servant feels little relief as a saturnalian holiday ends. Christopher Hill calls upside down "a relative concept; the assumption that it means the wrong way up is itself an expression of the view from the top" (312); Louis Montrose thinks "what is being turned upside-down [in saturnalian festivities] is not everyday life at all, but rather an idealized or coercive hierarchical model" ("Purpose" 65). Bristol regards the saturnalian impulse as an active revolt against hierarchy and authority, citing Le Roy Ladurie's instances of carnival spawning peasant revolt in medieval France: Le Roy Ladurie holds that carnival was not "intended to justify the status quo.... It was a way to action, perhaps modifying the society as a whole in the direction of change and possible progress" (Bristol 292). Others argue that saturnalian rites both express and contain class tensions, by providing a regular outlet, harmless because understood to be temporary. This disagreement, which Jonathan Dollimore dubs the "subversion-containment debate" (12), is an old one: it divided Trotsky from Marx. Trotsky "regarded seasonal folk rebellions as steam valves preserving the established order and thereby hindering the emergence of a revolutionary consciousness. Marx ... regarded ritual rebellion ... as a significant step in the development of a revolutionary class consciousness. The occurrence of many actual rebellions, especially in the slave communities of the New World, during the Christmas and carnival seasons, would seem to confirm Marx's insight" (Babcock, *Reversible* 22-23). As evidence in favor of this view we might cite statutes of the reigns of Edward III, Richard II, Henry IV and V, banning Christmas mumming for fear of political unrest (Rodgers 71).

But did each revolt (medieval French peasants, New World slaves) advance revolutionary consciousness a little, or are such revolts, over the centuries, as seasonal as holidays? Shakespeare's one clear peasant revolt, Cade's rebellion, little advances revolutionary consciousness. Even assuming that the world's proletariat is marginally better off than in Shakespeare's day, which is debatable, did the carnival impulse help this process or hinder it? "Carnival, after all, is a *licensed* affair in every sense, a permissible rupture of hegemony, a contained popular blow-off as disturbing and relatively ineffectual as a revolutionary work of art. As Shakespeare's Olivia remarks, there is no slander in an allowed fool" (Eagleton 148). For a thorough and thoughtful account of recent debate on this question, see the introduction to Stallybrass and White's book; and Barbara Babcock's introduction to *The Reversible World* remains very useful.

Bristol objects to the "steam-valve" theory (the felicitous anthropological term for which is *Ventilsitten*) insofar as it assumes that upper classes *consciously* manipulate carnivalesque rites to maintain the status quo and keep lower classes in their place; such a programmatic theory of ruling-class action does smack of conspiracy theories of history. Could an entire class be organized enough to marshall carnival effectively to Machiavellian ends, century after century, even if they wanted to? But while not granting the ruling class too much credit for consciousness, others stress the complicity of oppressed groups in any hierarchical authority structure, a complicity fostered by indoctrination urging oppressed groups to stay in their place, but born of a very human desire for stability and predictability — even of an oppressive situation — which creates inertia against major social change. Bristol is right that "holiday, or holy-day, Carnival and misrule are not isolated episodes in a uniform continuum of regularly scheduled real-life: the experience of holiday pervades the year and defines its rhythm" (201), but others argue that this very fact shows how holiday and misrule have been co-opted, appointed a place in an annual cycle, which licenses them on condition that they remain temporary, isolated in calendric ghettoes. That carnival must give way to "laws and customs which subordinated plebeian to patrician" is "implicit in the very notion of a festive *calendar*" (Stallybrass, "Patrician" 234). School misrule, such as the barring-out of the master by pupils, had prescribed seasons: "the approach of Christmas, . . . Shrove Tuesday, Royal Oak Day, . . . St. Andrew's Day or the day of the mayoral election [were] traditional times of misrule" (Thomas, *Rule and Misrule* 29). Thomas concludes, "like other forms of misrule, barring-out [was] essentially an alternative to political activity rather than a positive agent of change" (34).

In the present collection Michael Bristol follows up his book on carnival with an essay on charivari and *Othello*. The charivari was carnivalesque in its inversion of youth and age as well as in its wild unruliness. But as Natalie Davis has shown, this "noisy, masked demonstration to humiliate some wrongdoer" worked "in the service of the village community, clarifying the responsibilities that the youth would have when they were married men and fathers, helping to maintain proper order within marriage" ("Misrule" 42, 54; see also Capp). Here again, misrule was a kind of rule. And "apprentice rioters did not indiscriminately run amok; they pulled down brothels" (Thomas, *Rule and Misrule* 32)—another "unruly" enforcement of conservative community standards.

Keith Thomas says of charivari: "This was a harshly intolerant popular culture, hostile to privacy and eccentricity, and relying on the sanction not of reason but of ridicule," adding of saturnalian abuse in general, "shocking though it seemed, the main drift of this laughter of burlesque and inversion was conventional enough. It reinforced accepted morality by mocking superiors by standards which they themselves upheld" ("Laughter" 78). The conservatism of festive abuse is often overlooked: many regard nose-thumbing at authority as tending naturally toward left-wing politics. Barber's hearing in the "satire of the period" the tone of "a Lord of Misrule's vaunting and abuse" (*Festive* 52) ignores the overwhelming conservatism of Renaissance satire, whose targets were not obnoxious authority or repressive convention but fops, usurers, extravagantly dressed women, smokers, lying travelers—those who *failed* to conform to repressive convention. The repressiveness, the nastiness, of saturnalian festivity is often ignored. Hardin notes that neither Margaret Mead nor Victor Turner "equates ritual with the festive spirit, as scholars do in studies that follow the lead of C. L. Barber's *Shakespeare's Festive Comedy*, where 'puritan' antiritualism is opposed to the natural impulse toward the celebrative and saturnalian. In the wake of the nostalgia for our primitive past developed by Mircea Eliade, Roger Caillois, and others, we should keep in mind that not all primitive people indulge in saturnalian release during festivals" (851). Or as we might modify this, not all that is saturnalian is "release." *Twelfth Night* shrewdly portrays authority-flouting festivity turning nasty (see Woodbridge, "Fire").

Peter Stallybrass writes insightfully about the Stuart "attempt to re-form popular festivities as a means of social control" ("Patrician" 237). Leah Marcus shows how James I and Charles I co-opted misrule: "By placing their official stamp of approval on the old pastimes, James and Charles I attempted to extend royal power into an area of ambivalence and instability, to channel the equivocal status of popular festival into what we can perhaps call an official 'paradox of state' – a condition of happy ambiguity in which the license and lawlessness associated with the customs could be interpreted as submission to authority. In his *Basilikon Doron,* even before he was anointed King of England, James had published his views as to the utility of the traditional customs in governing the lower orders" (3). Though favoring compromise between carnival as proto-revolution and as steam valve ("seemingly lawless topsy-turvydom can both undermine and reinforce – it can constitute a process of adjustment within a perpetuation of order"), Marcus does grant the establishment's power to put carnival to its own uses: "Neither James nor Charles I countenanced the riotous side of festival. . . . Pastimes had to be contained. . . . But their consistent position was that the customs, well managed, would serve to buttress authority by dissolving seditious impulses that might otherwise threaten church and state" (5~7). Of course, Stuart attempts to contain misrule were not wholly successful: "During and after the English Civil War, there was a resurgence of the threatening side of May Day and its age-old association with the 'misrule' of public mayhem. Among some radical groups, holiday mirth shook loose from the Stuart mechanisms that had contained it and reasserted itself as class violence. Indeed, the Civil War itself was commonly depicted as a 'world upside down' – a series of carnival inversions which were stampeding out of control" (ibid., 21). But the world came right-side-up, restoring the hierarchy, by 1688 – partly because even lower classes grew restive about its being upside down: Hill notes, "once it had been decided that there was to be no further social revolution, it was inevitable that those who had done well out of the civil war should seek to consolidate their position, . . . by compromise with their defeated enemies, even at the price of retaining or restoring much of the old order. The alternative of continuous revolution . . . was too frightening to contemplate" (278~79).

The civil war abetted the waning, during the seventeenth century, of "the ritual, spectacle, and carnival forms of folk culture, which became small and trivial" (Bakhtin, *Rabelais* 236). The Puritan attack on all forms of "pagan" saturnalian expression had long been growing – Boy Bishop festivities were abolished in 1541, and Puritans attacked lords of misrule, court jesters, barrings-out, the Oxford *terrae filius;* a cleric fumed of this last that it was "one of the grossest immoralities" that youths should "boldly and openly reproach, vilify, name and point at their superiors." Through Stuart times "the university authorities struggled to silence this licensed buffoon. They tried persuasion, threats, even bribery. One vice-chancellor called the troops in; another pulled the orator down with his own hands" (Thomas, "Laughter" 79). The "vices" Puritans attacked were largely elements of youth culture: holidays when youths were free from adult supervision, resorts of young people such as theaters, alehouses, and dances, and "all the annual rites of misrule when youth temporarily inverted the social order" (Thomas, "Age" 221).

Thomas sees pre-war unrest as a cause of anti-saturnalianism: "Religious and political discord made mockery and affront appear a threat to the social order, rather than a means of symbolic reinforcement. . . . So long as the social hierarchy itself went unchallenged, the rites of inversion could be safely tolerated. . . . But once men had begun to question the principles of that hierarchy, then an annual ritual which emphasized its arbitrary nature came to seem positively dangerous" ("Laughter" 79).

Again, tinder box and steam valve compromise: saturnalian rite *can* spark revolutionary impulse, but revolution destroys saturnalia. Anthropologist Max Gluckman's findings about the Zulu translate well into a Renaissance context: saturnalian "ritual rebellions proceed within an established and sacred traditional system, in which there is dispute about particular distributions of power, and not about the structure of the system itself. This allows for instituted protest, and in complex ways renews the unity of the system" ("Rebellion" 112). "Instituted protest" is that encouraged by the authorities, "seemingly against the established order, yet [aiming] to bless that order to achieve prosperity" (114). Because calendric saturnalian rite "occurs within an established and unchallenged social order," these African rites can "express, freely and openly, fundamental social conflicts" (126–27). In Zulu civil wars, "Contenders for power against established authority sought only to acquire the same positions of authority for themselves" (127), a situation like the Wars of the Roses. Saturnalian rites can exist here, as the saturnalian behavior of Hal and Falstaff befits English civil wars, because such wars actually strengthen a centralized government. In the multi-tribe Zulu nation, as in the Wars of the Roses when feudalism was giving birth to a nation state, the greatest danger is tribal secession and national disintegration: "Periodic civil wars thus strengthened the system by canalizing tendencies to segment, and by stating that the main goal of leaders was the sacred kingship itself" (130–31). The Puritan Civil War, however, differed fundamentally in replacing not monarch but monarchy; such a threat to the established order made saturnalian rites too dangerous to maintain. " 'Ritual rebellion' can be enjoyed by tradition, as a social blessing, in repetitive social systems, but not in systems where revolution is possible" (Gluckman, "Rituals" 135). And "just as a saturnalian reversal of social roles need not threaten the social structure, but can serve instead to consolidate it, so a temporary, playful reversal of sexual roles can renew the meaning of the normal relation. . . . With sexual as with other relations, it is when the normal is secure that playful aberration is benign" (Barber, *Festive* 245). "Normal" and "benign" suggest that Barber would find a departure from male dominance as abnormal and malign as Elizabethans did; otherwise, the point is well taken.

The rise of the middle classes, too, damaged carnival, because as Thomas notes, carnival as a class inverter works best in a two-class system: waning of such rites "reflected the growth of a more complex social structure. Lords and servants could exchange places, but for the middle classes, who had no polar opposite, role-reversal was impossible" ("Laughter" 79). The middle classes deconstructed the aristocrat/plebeian opposition on which saturnalian rites depended. Jonson's "To Penshurst" and the anonymous *Pasquil's Palinodia* blame on the middle classes the decay of "all good sports and merriments"; "royalist defense of sport was not intended to lift repression but to create an alliance between top and bottom against the growing power of the Puritans" (Stallybrass, "Patrician" 237–48).

Thus was saturnalia disabled. The rise of the middle classes destroyed the system's invertibility; Puritans dismantled ritual forms; political authorities co-opted what had not been dismantled; and revolutionary impulses sparked by saturnalian rites only abetted a war whose chaos caused all classes to lose their taste for carnival inversions. Carnival's power to question the status quo was lost; but how great this power ever was remains the great disputed question. "Although the world might appear to be turned upside down during the carnival season, the fact that Kings and Queens were chosen and crowned actually reaffirmed the *status quo*," maintain Sales (13) and other writers, while their opponents hold out for the possibility of subversion, and a range of other theorists imagine various degrees of compromise.

Carnival is a major concern of the present volume, where in addition to Bristol's essay on charivari, Michael Neill offers a vision of Renaissance comedy as carnivalized tragedy, Phyllis Gorfain explores in the context of *Measure for Measure* the folk genre of riddling, with its carnivalesque potential for weak outwitting strong (see also Gorfain's other articles on riddles), and Naomi Liebler shows Richard II creating carnival, turning himself into Misrule, in his image of becoming "a mockery king of snow."

Carnival is one site where the influence of the New Historicist emphasis on political power, patriarchal hegemony, and ideology is evident. Another is the study of rites of passage.

Rites of Passage

Although (like any rite) capable of subversion, rites of passage offer—more than other kinds of ritual—an apparent program of social control, and often appear as ideological tools perpetuating the status quo. Initiations define manhood as aggressive, womanhood reproductive; wedding sermons hammer home wifely subservience; graduations admit to the establishment those who can afford education; funeral processions put gentry and pauper where they belong. Accordingly, "Records of Tudor and Stuart village life leave [the impression]...of the tyranny of local opinion and the lack of tolerance displayed towards nonconformity or social deviation.... The customs of the countryside required joys and sorrows, weddings and funerals, to be shared with other members of the community; there was no idea of the holiday as 'getting away from it all,'...[no] challenge to the view that a man's most personal affairs were the legitimate concern of the whole community" (Thomas, *Decline* 629).

Other rites' ideology is more ambiguous: a beggar can be a scapegoat, to the approval of ideological conservatives; but if a king is a scapegoat, rite borders on revolution, expressing *resistance* to political authority. Whether the social, sexual, and age inversions of saturnalian rites are conservative or revolutionary is still an embattled question. But rites of passage are unalloyed ideology—one reason left-leaning readers delight in their disruption. Whether literature is by nature politically radical, or simply sensational and excitement-loving (or just mischievous), it relishes disruptions, rejoices in those who will not submerge individuality in the social order. A number of our contributors deal with rites of passage—birth (Roberts, Carroll), initiation into a trade (Gorfain), wedding (Bristol, Carroll), funeral (Neill, Carroll); and these essays find rites more often disrupted than completed, parodied than treated seriously. Many other studies have found "maimed" rites predominant: David Bevington notes that Shakespearean funerals are "almost always interrupted or otherwise maimed" (146); Lynda Boose writes of Lear's ultimate inability to give his daughter in marriage and let her go; Carol Neely has written a book on disrupted marital rites, *Shakespeare's Broken Nuptials*.

Such disruptions point to the question we encountered with carnival: is a potential for subversion built into such ideology-serving ritual? The state funeral procession, as Neill shows, was an instrument of political ideology: "Every detail, . . . from the display of knightly arms, banners, and heraldic devices to the arrangement of successive groups of paupers, yeomen, household servants, serving gentlemen, client gentry, and noble mourners with their followers, was designed to proclaim not just the power, wealth, and status of the dead man, but his place inside a fixed and unassailable social order, to which the rituals of the church gave ultimate sanction and the inscriptions and iconography of his tomb bore lasting testament. . . . [It was] a piece of propaganda—the symbolic celebration and justification of an entire social order, . . . political theater" ("Exeunt" 154–61). And yet, although the message that though the man dies the state goes on is not unlike comedy's vision, funerals are a hallmark of tragedy: "The final procession of mourners with its accompanying 'dead march' came to occupy in tragedy precisely the place accorded in comedy to wedding revels and the final dance"; if the comic dance suggests "seasonal rotation and renewal (appropriate to the marriage festivals of romantic comedy . . .), the funeral procession answers to the alternative sense of time as ineluctable linear process" (ibid., 163–64). Inscribed in tragedy, state funerals inevitably lose propaganda value: tragedy is inhospitable to state mystifications, and funerals' dramatic pageantry undercuts the icon of state power: the procession is "not simply an incarnation of earthly order, but an intimation of the process that will ultimately sweep that order away forever: against the elaborately arranged hierarchy of its processional form funeral sets the leveling anonymity of its mourning blacks. . . . The poignancy of funeral ceremony derives exactly from this sense that all its pompous ritual is only a mask for that procession to dusty death which haunts Macbeth's imagination" (ibid., 164).

Central to the study of rites of passage has been the work of Arnold Van Gennep who, struck by the continuity of personal with community rites, boldly synthesized the whole realm of ritual, drawing together personal and community rites (including seasonal ritual), structurally so similar: "For groups, as well as for individuals, . . . there are always new thresholds to cross: the threshold of summer and winter, of a season or a year, of a month or a night; the thresholds of birth, adolescence, maturity, and old age; the threshold of death and that of the afterlife" (190). Van Gennep describes three phases of rite: *séparation* or preliminal rites, *marge* or liminal (threshold) rites, and *agrégation* or postliminal incorporation rites, showing that this tripartite structure links public territorial-passage rites with personal rites of passage – initiations, marriages, funerals – the latter almost metaphors of the former. Each phase is marked by symbols and acts – *séparation* by death symbols like sacrifices and cutting emblems like knives, *marge* by inertness and indeterminacy symbols, *agrégation* by incorporation symbols: threshold crossing, food and lodging, shared meals, handclasps, kisses, sexual contact, gift exchange, encircling symbols like rings and crowns. His sweeping synthesis has stood the test of time much better than Frazer's. Shakespeare's works confirm his thesis repeatedly, especially in the swords, veils, rings, threshold-crossings, and other symbolism which Van Gennep posited as nearly universal tokens of the three-phase rite (see Van Gennep 130; Turner, *Process*).

Van Gennep noted that cultures take a special interest in liminal stages; Turner made an anthropological specialty of liminality. Metaphoric and physical thresholds are not thin lines but expanded zones; initiands may spend much time in liminal states – betrothal, the sequestered life of tribal adolescents awaiting initiation. Liminality involves namelessness, absence of property, nakedness or uniform clothing, transvestism, sexual continence, minimized distinctions of sex, rank, and wealth, humility, disregard for personal appearance, total obedience, sacredness, silence, sacred instruction, suspended kinship rights and obligations, invoking of mystical powers, foolishness, simplicity, acceptance of pain (Turner, *Process* 106–7). The fact that the world's pilgrimage sites are on margins or borders, not in main population centers, emphasizes the separation from the world of those liminal creatures, pilgrims (Turner, *Dramas* 195–96). Literary pilgrimages show liminal features: Helena's homeless anonymity (*AWW*), the *communitas* of Chaucer's pilgrims, the hero's spiritual instruction in *The Pilgrim's Progress*. Van Gennep's analogy between spatial journeys and life-phase journeys helps account for the ubiquity of the journey, in folk tale and literature, as an analogue of growing up.

Category-making, mental boundary-fixing, sets firm lines between classes. The ritual implications of such habits of thought have been brilliantly explored by anthropologist Mary Douglas. Deconstruction has illuminated ritual study as well, since it crosses or dismantles boundaries that in binary thinking fixed frontiers between male and female, Jew and Gentile, signifier and signified. Derrida's interest in intermediate states, such as "living on," which deconstructs the life/death boundary, is analogous with Turner's contemporaneous interest in liminality. Woodbridge's essay in this volume uses the concept of liminality, drawing on theories of Van

Gennep, Turner, Douglas, and Derrida to link literary patterns with cultural assumptions.

Louis Montrose argues that Shakespeare focuses the action of his plays "on points of transition in the life cycle—birth, puberty, marriage, death—where discontinuities arise, and where adjustments are necessary to basic interrelationships in the family and in society"; the actions of many plays "resemble rites of passage" ("Purpose" 62–63). In *Shakespeare's Comic Rites*, Edward Berry argues that the comedies are structured like Van Gennep's three-part rites, shipwrecks and banishments effecting *séparation*, the "dislocations and confusions of identity, the ordeals, and the education characteristic of the liminal phase" occurring in a green world like "the sacred forests of initiation," and the *agrégation* having "actual rites of incorporation prominent in Elizabethan weddings—the exchanging of rings and oaths, kissing, feasting, and dancing." Romantic heroines' cross-dressing, preceding marriage and adulthood, Berry thinks is "like the face-painting, masking, or sex reversal characteristic of novices during the liminal period"; disguised Rosalind "undergoes a comic ordeal that prepares her for marriage" (84, 18). Berry also sees disorientations—dream, error, madness, witchcraft, metamorphosis—as liminal (58; see also Falk); young men's conventional behavior—"writing of sonnets, wearing of love-locks, posturing in romantic attitudes—fulfills many of the conditions of a liminal experience" (30). Marjorie Garber notes language change, at maturity, in Romeo, Hal, and others (80–115); Brian Vickers notes shifts from prose to poetry at coming of age and onset of courtship (49, 53–54).

Coppélia Kahn thinks separation from family in a sea storm in *Errors*, *Twelfth Night*, *Pericles*, *Winter's Tale*, and *Tempest* suggests passage through both time and space: "the individual's passage from emotional residence within the family to independence and adulthood. . . . The tempest and shipwreck initiating the main action represent the violence, confusion, and even terror of passing from one stage of life to the next" (*Man's Estate* 194). Adelman and others have applied Freudian theory to comings-of-age, as in the initiatory moment when Coriolanus achieves his new name. The siege at Corioli (in the usual trope, the city is a woman threatened with rape) is a transformation "of the nightmare of oral vulnerability ('to th'pot' [I.iv.47], one of his soldiers says as he is swallowed up by the gates) into a phallic adventure. . . . But the dramatic action itself presents the conquest of Corioli as an image not of rape but of triumphant rebirth: after Coriolanus enters the gates of the city, he is proclaimed dead; . . . [he] miraculously reemerges, covered with blood (I.v.22) and is given a new

name. For the assault on Corioli is both a rape and a rebirth: the underlying fantasy is that intercourse is a literal return to the womb, from which
one is reborn" (134). Tribal initiatory thinking corresponds to Freud's
theory that boys establish identity by splitting off from the mother; C. L.
Barber reads Shakespeare's own Freudian history, noting in his early
career a triumph over engulfing females—Joan of Arc, the Countess of
Auvergne, Queen Margaret, Hippolyta, Adriana, *Shrew's* Kate ("Family").
The first tetralogy's dangerous women overcome, women largely disap-
pear from history plays, which then explore a post-initiatory realm where
power is male, the female ruthlessly suppressed (see Rackin).

Walter Ong ("Latin") shows that schooling resembled tribal male initiation rites: induction of youth into extra-familial life, separation from
females ("schools, including the universities, were male rendezvous strongly
reminiscent of male clubhouses in primitive societies" [108]), harsh physical ordeals like flogging, and a secret language, Latin. (With no native
speakers, Latin was for 1000 years exclusively a male language, and other
male languages developed simultaneously: Rabbinic Hebrew, Classical
Arabic, Sanskrit, Classical Chinese, Byzantine Greek [Ong, *Orality* 115];
these too must have had their initiatory purposes.) Ong thinks *periculo
facto* ("having undergone the [requisite] danger or trial") on university
diplomas reveals "the old feeling that education was an initiation" ("Latin"
107–9). Alan Sinfield says study of Shakespeare now "initiates[s] the
young into the mysteries of knowledge," a rite providing entry into the
adult middle class (143). Shakespeare is the new Latin. Berry thinks
imitating classical models was a way of effacing students' identity, as in
initiation's liminal stage. The implications for the few girls given a classical
education are bleak: as Valerie Wayne shows, educational tracts assumed
boys would eventually do their own thinking, find their own style, but
recommended *only* imitation for girls. Female students were arrested in
educational liminality, identity effaced. Female initiatory rites are just
beginning to be explored, but it is certainly possible to suggest that the
secret lore of spinning, sewing, food preparation, and home medical
remedies—a female lore often feared and suspected by men (see for
example Eliade 46; Bynum 189–90)—offer the female equivalent of the
lore and secret language of initiates which school and Latin language study
offered boys.

Elizabethan coming of age meant leaving home: some two-thirds of
adolescent boys, three-quarters of the girls, lived away from home (Berry
34): "To move from a small village to an apprenticeship in London, as

many young boys did, was to enter a world as bizarre and disorienting as the bush for an African novice. The same might be said of studying at Oxford, Cambridge, or the Inns of Court; of entering the service of the Queen; or of travelling abroad. Although not formal rites of initiation, these journeys served a ritual function and were framed by ceremonies; departures were ceremonious occasions, and returns . . . were marked by the rite of marriage" (ibid., 145). This custom helps account for Shakespeare's obsession with sundered families searching for each other, from *Errors* to *Pericles* (see Berry 41).

Berry corrects the frequent overemphasis, by those influenced by Barber, on the "time out" quality of comedic "holiday time," a notion that "does not suggest the extent of the change that takes place. Shakespeare's lovers do not merely return to the work-a-day world after their 'holiday' experience; they assume new identities as married adults. . . . What seems to be a period of stasis is actually a period of frantic, though invisible activity. The cocoon is inert; but inside, the larva is becoming a butterfly" (151).

In Shakespeare, identity emerges during pubescence: "individuation [is] . . . closely related to sexual maturity . . . as one grows in self-knowledge, one moves from the confused and mingled identity of twinship . . . toward productive courtship" (Garber 31–32). Separation from twinned states of intense adolescent friendship may mean insulting old friends as in tribal rite: Hermia and Helena, who as girls "grew together, / Like to a double cherry," during courtship call each other "cankerblossom," "vixen," "dwarf" (*MND* III.ii.208–328). By such rites, Renaissance literature propels girls out of a tomboy phase, boys out of a girl-hating phase into heterosexual adulthood (see Woodbridge, *Women* 291–94). Despite delightful variations, the stylized quality of such adulthood-achieving plots shows a debt to familiar rites of passage.

The commonest ritual in Renaissance drama, marital rites (a type of coming-of-age rite) involve both sexes (why Garber includes them among "Women's Rites" is a puzzle). Ritual is essential: "a daughter and a son are being incorporated into a new family unit, [which] . . . breaks down the boundaries of two previously existing families" (Boose, "Father" 326); Van Gennep and Douglas have shown the perils of boundary crossing. *Séparation* sees a break with parents and old friends. Courtship and betrothal are liminal; the wedding, incorporating the two among married adults, has special clothes, a name-change, and encircling symbols—rings, crowns (see *Tmp.* V.i.204–5).

The upsitting, the first official reception of company after childbirth, like other women's rites was frequently satirized in literature—gossips swarmed around the mother from the instant of birth, expecting fancy foods, swigging celebratory spirits. Churching, a Christian vestige of the Hebrew post-partem purification rite (see Leviticus 12), was also satirized, especially in the many imitations of and allusions to *Le Quinze Joyes de Mariage*; for many female literary figures it is an excuse to demand expensive new gowns. For women's rites, Renaissance literature (largely male authored) has a program of ridicule and satire. Shakespeare's treatment of women's birth-giving rites is on the whole less vicious than that of his contemporaries; he evokes sympathy for Hermione's bewildered indignation at her "child-bed privilege denied" (*WT* III.ii.103), and treats with a homely charm at least one father excluded from the birth chamber: in a long tradition of husbands who fret outside the room in which their wives are giving birth, Henry VIII, like countless television husbands after him, absentmindedly tries to play cards, breaking off with "my mind's not on 't" (V.i.57). Yet in her essay in the present volume, Jeanne Roberts teases out considerable subterranean anxiety attaching to the woman-centered rites of birth in Shakespeare.

Rites of installation into public office bring us back to the world of political power and state ideology; such rites have been much studied in recent criticism, often drawing on the work of historians such as Marc Bloch, who has shown that as the coronation rite evolved in Europe, Germanic belief in royal sacrality was intensified by adoption of Hebrew anointing rites, with their notions of royal sacredness (Bloch 35–41). (See for example the essays in David Bergeron's 1985 collection *Pageantry in the Shakespearean Theater.*)[6] Anthropologist Clifford Geertz, who writes of Elizabethan as well as Javanese ritual, says of coronation processions that "royal progresses (of which...coronation is but the first)...[stamp] a territory with ritual signs of dominance. When kings journey around the countryside...they mark it, like some wolf or tiger spreading his scent through his territory" (16). Choosing among the rich possibilities of royal ritual, one of our contributors, Deborah Willis, draws out the implications of the fact that despite Protestantism's attacks on ritual, Protestant monarchs continued the magical rite of touching for the king's evil.

Turner's account of installations suggests close affinities with initiation into adulthood. The ruler-to-be may endure enforced sojourn among lower classes, their powerless poverty reminding him of his pre-initiation youth; as authority figures then afflicted him with liminal ordeals, so now, in a saturnalian inversion typical of installation, future subjects abuse him. Elements of this account have applications to the careers of Hal and Lear.

Many writers have shown rites of passage a major current concern in Shakespeare. (In addition to those mentioned, see also, for example, essays by Arthur Holmberg, Margaret Loftus Ranald, Melita Schaum, and Louis Montrose ["Brother"].) This volume's opening section, "Rites of Passage," includes essays on rites of birth, initiation, marriage, and funeral. The concept of liminality has also become important for issues other than rites of passage, for example the position of the theater in early modern England. Steven Mullaney explores how Renaissance popular drama "dislocat[ed] itself from the confines of the existing social order and [took] up a place on the margins of society. . . . Erected outside the walls of early modern London in the 'licentious Liberties' of the city, the popular playhouses of Elizabethan England occupied a domain that had traditionally been reserved for cultural phenomena that could not be contained within the strict or proper bounds of the community" (vii). He sets in historical/ cultural context the plays' liminality: the Elizabethan sense of the marginal space occupied by theaters and drama was quite different from the ancient Athenians' sense that drama was as central to the culture as the theater was centrally located in Athens (7–8).

Permutations of Ritual

"Ritual" as Shakespeare scholars have used it is a term with a wealth of meanings ranging from the downright magical to the purely ceremonial; one would wish for a less all-encompassing term were it not for the peculiar indivisibility of many phenomena it embraces—often the ceremonial shades off into the magical, and the binary opposition between them proves impossible to maintain. For example, how can we be sure Shakespeare intended to demystify scapegoating and was not himself habituated to magical thinking? He lived, after all, in an age when sin could be transferred to a scapegoat from a dead body via bread and beer. Have we come to regard Shakespeare as our contemporary to the point of forgetting that magical thinking was much more viable in his age than in ours? (For that matter, our own political scapegoatings draw on a certain amount of magical thinking in the populace.) C. L. Barber poses the problem clearly with regard to one major scapegoating: regarding Falstaff's scapegoating as Shakespeare's rather than Hal's, he thinks the play fails in not demystifying Hal's ritual magic; the cynical, might-makes-right attitude is "too pervasive in the whole society of the play" to be banished "merely by getting rid of Falstaff"; elsewhere "Shakespeare typically uses ritual patterns of behavior and thought" to make clear that "rituals have no *magical* efficacy. The reason for his failure at the close of *Part Two* is that at this point he himself uses ritual, not ironically transformed into drama, but magically"; this is "a retreat into magic by the *dramatist*, as distinct from his characters" (*Festive* 217-19). But is this an isolated intrusion of magical thinking? The Henriad, one is bound to notice, is shot through with such thinking: to what extent *is* it demystified?

Shakespearean king-slaying has one foot in fertility rite, the other in politics; a king's magical powers may fail at the moment his political powers wax excessive: two Shakespearean leaders, Julius Caesar and Richard II, are slain for this double reason. Caesar is killed for being too weak and too powerful: too weak in that his fertility-guaranteeing power has failed (his wife's infertility is suggestive), and too powerful in that he grows tyrannous; the same pattern appears in *Richard II*. Exploring scapegoat theory will show that such duality is by no means anomalous: in tribal scapegoatings too, magic and politics are interwoven, and sacrifice cannot easily be distinguished from political assassination.

Some rites appear onstage in their ceremonial aspects: this is most true of rites of passage, especially betrothal, marriage, funeral processions. But in most cases, what critics call ritual occurs in plot structures, as traces of the archaic thinking of a deeply ritualized culture. This is true of fertility rite, which occurs mainly as a discourse of fertility permeating Shakespeare's figurative language; of scapegoat rite, which occurs not as formal ceremonial but as political assassination or blame-shifting with sacrificial implications; of carnival, which comprises inversions like Falstaff's world of Misrule; and even to a certain extent of rites of passage, whose phases of separation, liminality, and aggregation are reproduced (as Berry and others have argued) in the very structure of Shakespearean comedy. While some of our contributors discuss overtly ceremonial ritual (for example, Neill on funeral, Willis on the royal touch), the majority are more interested in the mental universe of a culture deep dyed in ritual: perhaps we should call this ritual thinking. We close our collection with Woodbridge's essay, which examines some such thinking through an anthropological lens.

On the Essays in this Collection

Our first section, "Rites of Passage," contains essays on birth, initiation, marriage, and death. Michael Neill surveys the comic exploitation of funeral motifs throughout the Elizabethan and Jacobean drama. Michael Bristol invites us to see behind the action of *Othello* a perverse or inverted rite of unmarrying, featuring the three principals of the charivari—a clownish bridegroom, a transvestite bride, and a "scourge of marriage." In her examination of riddling and ritual in *Measure for Measure*, Phyllis Gorfain uncovers in a textual crux a riddling ritual that initiates Pompey the bawd into the "mystery" of the hangman. In "Shakespeare's Maimed Birth Rites," Jeanne Addison Roberts finds in the surprising grimness of Shakespeare's allusions to birth reflections of male anxieties about female powers that seem characteristic of patriarchal society. Together, these four essays illuminate, often from unusual angles, Shakespeare's handling of the major rites in the life cycle of the individual.

The second section, "Rites of Rule," has two parts. In the first, "Authority and Grace," two essays deal with ritual means of securing or conferring different kinds of grace. Deborah Willis discusses the problematics of the ceremony for the healing of the king's evil in the reigns of Elizabeth and James and its implications for understanding *Macbeth* and *Pericles*. Bruce Young focuses on parental rather than political authority, examining the nature of the Elizabethan rite of parental blessings and its adaptations in three plays. The second part, "Monarchy and the Body Politic," includes four essays dealing with ritualistic connections between the monarch and the realm. William Carroll uncovers in Richard III's apparently radical subversion of ritual form an underlying conservatism that challenges audiences to question the value of ritual itself. Questions about Elizabethan attitudes towards political ritual are also explored in Naomi Liebler's essay, which responds sympathetically to Richard's ceremonialism, as an attempt to retain traditional values in an age bent on destroying them, and in Gillian Murray Kendall's essay, which argues that the false orderliness of the scripted language of trial by combat unmasks the cultural constructed-ness of rituals in general. The validity of ritual is at issue in Mark Rose's essay, which places *Julius Caesar* in the context of contemporary debates about religious ceremony and political authority; Rose argues that in its sacrificial treatment of Caesar the play registers a characteristically late Elizabethan ambivalence toward absolute authority. Finally, Linda Wood-bridge shows how several of Shakespeare's Roman works embody a distinctively Elizabethan anxiety linking political and sexual invasion. Although she does not examine specific Elizabethan rituals, Woodbridge uses the anthropological notions of marginality and liminality to explore what might be called ritualized cultural attitudes.

Reflecting the major emphasis of ritual readings in the 1980s, the majority of the essays deal with rites that relate to monarchical power or to ideologies that tend to derive from and support it. As recent critical debate on carnival/saturnalia and on rites of passage has frequently centered on the subversion/containment question, one finds woven throughout this collection an indirect debate over whether Shakespeare's theatrical use of ritual reproduces or subverts these dominant ideologies and structures of authority. As might be expected, the essays tend to avoid easy answers to this question. Some, such as Young's, imply that Shakespeare's use of such rituals as the parental blessing depends upon orthodoxies that are themselves not necessarily repressive. Others, such as Carroll and Willis, find in Shakespeare's use of ritual both a dependency upon and a questioning of orthodox values. Two of the essays, those by Bristol and Neill, explore a complex dialectic within plays between a dominant ritual form— for Bristol, marriage, for Neill, funerals—and their carnivalesque subversions. The essay by Rose sees in *Julius Caesar* a complex mediation of societal tensions centering on ritual and power, resulting in an attitude of "strategic ambivalence."

The attempt to situate Shakespeare's use of ritual politically raises broader questions in many of the essays about the role of ritual in Elizabethan society. Those that address such questions tend to focus on conflicts between different ritual modes or attitudes. The studies of the carnivalesque in Bristol and Neill, for example, explore the tension between an "official" ceremonialism, reflected preeminently in aristocratic rites of marriage and death, and a "popular," burlesque ceremonialism, reflected in such potentially subversive rites as the charivari. Other essays explore the conflicting attitudes toward ceremony brought on largely by religious discord. Puritan anticeremonialism, for example, features prominently in the essays by Rose and Willis. Rose finds in the language of the tribunes in *Julius Caesar* echoes of the hostility toward ritual expressed by contemporary Puritans. Willis, in her study of the curing of the king's evil, sets out very usefully three conflicting but contemporary attitudes toward the rite, which she characterizes as magical, orthodox, and theatrical. The increasing theatricalization of ceremonial practices in the sixteenth century provides a backdrop for Liebler's interpretation of Richard's commitment to ritual in *Richard II.*

In placing Shakespeare's ritualism in a cultural context, most of the essayists are acutely sensitive not only to conflicts within Elizabethan society but to the question of historical change. Several, for example, call attention to shifts in attitudes toward ritual beginning in the late Elizabethan and early Jacobean period. Neill suggests that the Jacobean decline in the comic exploitation of funeral motifs might reflect a corresponding decrease in the elaborateness of funerals. Woodbridge finds in the reigns of Elizabeth and James radically different attitudes toward the body politic. Many of the essays thus imply that Shakespeare's interest in ritual reflects dynamic tensions in ritual practice and belief that were profoundly revealing of society as a whole.

Two of our essays, those of Roberts and Woodbridge, foreground feminist issues. Roberts's view of Shakespeare's treatment of birth has disturbing implications for our understanding of Elizabethan patriarchy. Although Roberts views Shakespeare's representations of birth as reflections of an overarching patriarchal ideology, one would like to see that assumption tested against the works of other dramatists—against Webster's *Duchess of Malfi*, for example, which seems to celebrate motherhood even in the midst of a society that destroys it. Woodbridge's essay too raises questions for comparative study, especially in the contrast she draws between attitudes toward sexual and military invasion in the very different reigns of a virgin queen and a reputedly bisexual king. Although less explicitly concerned with feminist issues, several other essays have implications for our understanding of gender roles in Elizabethan society. Young, for example, argues for the importance of maternal as well as paternal blessings of children, a view that calls into question Lawrence Stone's attempt to explain the ritual as one of repressive patriarchal control. Gorfain includes a section on gender in her discussion of ritual riddling. Willis's study of the curing of the king's evil centers, interestingly, not on the kings in *Macbeth*, the play in which the ritual is most directly invoked, but on Marina in *Pericles*, in whose figure Shakespeare embodies some of the values most associated with the rite.

If feminist questions deserve somewhat more attention than they receive in this volume, so do those that center upon the relationship of ritual to theater. Several of our essays touch upon such questions, and in ways that invite further exploration. Gorfain discovered a riddling initiation rite in *Measure for Measure* in the process of trying to make sense of a textual crux for performance, and she explores imaginatively various ways in which this ritual moment can be realized on stage. In Rose's complex approach to the ritualization of Caesar's death in *Julius Caesar*, Shakespeare's tragedy becomes "a kind of political Mass" that both confirms and questions the legitimacy of the Tudor state. Rose's suggestion that the theatrical experience is itself akin to ritual prompts further questions along the lines of those explored in Mullaney's study of the liminal status of Elizabethan playhouses.

The variety of questions raised by the essays in this collection seems to the editors one measure of its success. The anthology, like the Shakespeare Association seminar in which it originated, is intended to be eclectic and exploratory; it offers neither a theoretical manifesto nor a definitive statement about Elizabethan ritual or Shakespeare. Individually, the essays illuminate many aspects of Shakespeare's treatment of ritual practices and attitudes. Collectively, they embody a wide variety of theoretical perspectives, ranging from formalism to feminism. The questions they raise suggest the need for further interdisciplinary collaboration — in particular, among cultural anthropologists, social historians, literary critics, and performers. As academic ritualists well know, much in our institutional and disciplinary practices inhibits such communal efforts. Ritual studies of Shakespeare lie at the margins of many fields, and margins are dangerous places, vulnerable to attack from many directions. We hope that these essays will remind us, however, that they can also be sources of power.

NOTES

1. Turner himself sometimes brought even his African findings to bear on Shakespeare and Elizabethan culture, for example in his remarks on court jesters in *Process*; he started out his academic career in English, and maintained a lifelong interest in literature. Barbara Babcock, who has written of Turner's literary interests (see her "Arts"), is herself an anthropologist who teaches in an English department; her fine work, elsewhere cited in this introduction, is eloquent testimony to the possibility of bringing anthropology fruitfully and sensitively to bear on literature.

2. In Russia a rag figure was thrown into the river (Calderon 80); at Eisenach a straw man representing Death was burned, a ribbon-decked tree brought in (Witzschel 192ff.).

3. See, for example Margaret Murray 172–85, on witches' rainmaking/fertility rites. In a 1489 woodcut, witches with snake, cock, and cauldron produce rain (Bord 117).

4. Even feminist criticism often focuses on political power, which means on Queen Elizabeth, an unfortunate narrowing. See Woodbridge's "Eventful History."

5. Recent exceptions to the general neglect are Steven Marx's *Youth Against Age*, and Linda Woodbridge's "Black and White and Red All Over."

6. Also useful is Bergeron's *English Civic Pageantry, 1558–1642.*

BIBLIOGRAPHY

Adelman, Janet. "'Anger's My Meat': Feeding, Dependency, and Aggression in *Coriolanus.*" *Representing Shakespeare: New Psychoanalytic Essays.* Ed. Murray M. Schwartz and Coppélia Kahn. Baltimore: Johns Hopkins University Press, 1980. 129–49.

Alford, Violet. *Sword Dance and Drama.* London: Merlin, 1962.

———. *The Hobby Horse and Other Animal Masks.* London: Merlin, 1978.

Aubrey, John. *Remains of Gentilism and Judaism.* Ed. James Britten. London: Satchell, Peyton, 1881. First published 1687.

Babcock, Barbara A. "'The Arts and All Things Common': Victor Turner's Literary Anthropology." *Comparative Criticism* 9 (1987): 39–46.

———, ed. *The Reversible World: Symbolic Inversion in Art and Society.* Ithaca: Cornell University Press, 1978.

Bakhtin, Mikhail. *Rabelais and His World.* Trans. Helene Iswolsky. Cambridge: MIT Press, 1965.

———. *The Dialogic Imagination.* Ed. Michael Holquist. Trans. Caryl Emerson and Michael Holquist. Austin: Texas University Press, 1981.

Barber, C. L. "The Family in Shakespeare's Development: Tragedy and Sacredness." *Representing Shakespeare: New Psychoanalytic Essays.* Ed. Murray M. Schwartz and Coppélia Kahn. Baltimore: Johns Hopkins University Press, 1980. 188–202.

———. *Shakespeare's Festive Comedy: A Study of Dramatic Form and Its Relation to Social Custom.* Cleveland: World, 1959.

Basford, Kathleen. *The Green Man.* Ipswich: D. S. Brewer, 1978.

Bergeron, David M. *English Civic Pageantry, 1558–1642.* Columbia: University of South Carolina Press, 1971.

———. *Pageantry in the Shakespearean Theater.* Athens: University of Georgia Press, 1985.

Berry, Edward. *Shakespeare's Comic Rites.* Cambridge: Cambridge University Press, 1984.

Bevington, David. *Action is Eloquence: Shakespeare's Language of Gesture.* Cambridge, Mass.: Harvard University Press, 1984.

Bloch, Marc. *The Royal Touch: Sacred Monarchy and Scrofula in England and France.* Trans. J. E. Anderson. London: Routledge and Kegan Paul; Montreal: McGill-Queen's University Press, 1973. First published in French, 1961.

Boas, Franz. *The Central Eskimo. Sixth Annual Report of the Bureau of Ethnology to the Secretary of the Smithsonian Institution, 1884–5.* Washington, D.C.: Government Printing Office, 1888.

Bock, Philip K. *Shakespeare and Elizabethan Culture: An Anthropological View.* New York: Schocken, 1984.

Bodkin, Maud. *Archetypal Patterns in Poetry: Psychological Studies of Imagination.* London: Oxford University Press, 1934.

Boose, Lynda E. "The Father and the Bride in Shakespeare." *PMLA* 97 (1982): 325–47.

Bord, Janet, and Colin Bord. *Earth Rites: Fertility Practices in Pre-Industrial Britain.* London: Granada, 1982.

Bourboule, Photeine. *Ancient Festivals of the "Saturnalia" Type.* Thessalonike, 1964.

Bristol, Michael D. *Carnival and Theater: Plebeian Culture and the Structure of Authority in Renaissance England.* New York: Methuen, 1985.

Brockbank, Philip. "Blood and Wine: Tragic Ritual from Aeschylus to Soyinka." *Shakespeare Survey* 36 (1983): 11–19.

Brody, Alan. *The English Mummers and Their Plays.* Philadelphia: University of Pennsylvania Press, 1969.

Bronowski, Jacob. "The Scapegoat King." *The Face of Violence.* Cleveland: World, 1967. 7–18.

Bryant, J. A., Jr. "Falstaff and the Renewal of Windsor." *PMLA* 89 (1974): 296–301.

Burke, Peter. "Good Witches." *New York Review of Books* 22 (28 Feb. 1985): 32–34.

Burkert, Walter, René Girard, and Jonathan Z. Smith. *Violent Origins: Ritual Killing and Cultural Formation.* Ed. Robert G. Hamerton-Kelly. Introduction by Burton Mack. Stanford: Stanford University Press, 1987.

——. "Greek Tragedy and Sacrificial Ritual." *Greek, Roman, and Byzantine Studies* 7 (1966): 87–121.

——. *Homo Necans: The Anthropology of Ancient Greek Sacrificial Ritual and Myth.* Trans. Peter Bing. Berkeley: University of California Press, 1983. First published in German, 1972.

Burland, C. A. *Echoes of Magic: A Study of Seasonal Festivals through the Ages.* Totowa, N. J.: Rowman and Littlefield, 1972.

Bynum, Caroline Walker. *Holy Feast and Holy Fast: The Religious Significance of Food to Medieval Women.* Berkeley: University of California Press, 1987.

Calderon, George. "Slavonic Elements in Greek Religion." *Classical Review* 27 (1913): 79–81.

Capp, Bernard. "English Youth Groups and *The Pinder of Wakefield.*" *Past and Present* 76 (1977): 127–33.

Chambers, E. K. *The English Folk-Play.* Oxford: Clarendon, 1933.

Copernicus, Nicolaus. *On the Revolutions of the Heavenly Spheres.* Trans. A. M. Duncan. New York: Barnes and Noble, 1976. First Latin edition 1543.

Cornford, Francis Macdonald. *The Origin of Attic Comedy.* Cambridge: Cambridge University Press, 1914.

Coursen, Herbert. *Christian Ritual and the World of Shakespeare's Tragedies.* Lewisburg: Bucknell University Press; London: Associated University Presses, 1976.

Curtius, Ernst Robert. *European Literature and the Latin Middle Ages.* Trans. Willard R. Trask. New York: Pantheon, 1953.

Davis, Natalie Zemon. "The Reasons of Misrule: Youth Groups and Charivaris in Sixteenth-Century France." *Past and Present* 50 (1971): 41–75.

———. "Women on Top: Symbolic Sexual Inversion and Political Disorder in Early Modern Europe." *The Reversible World*. Ed. Barbara A. Babcock. Ithaca: Cornell University Press, 1978.

De Gerenday, Lynn. "Play, Ritualization, and Ambivalence in *Julius Caesar.*" *Literature and Psychology* 24 (1974): 24–33.

De Heusch, Luc. *Sacrifice in Africa: A Structuralist Approach*. Trans. Linda O'Brien and Alice Morton. Manchester: Manchester University Press, 1985.

Derrida, Jacques. "Living On/Border Lines." Trans. James Hulbert. *Deconstruction and Criticism*. Ed. Geoffrey Hartman. New York: Continuum, 1984. 75–176.

———. *Of Grammatology*. Trans. Gayatri Chakravorty Spivack. Baltimore: Johns Hopkins University Press, 1974.

———. "Plato's Pharmacy." *Dissemination*. Trans. Barbara Johnson. Chicago: University of Chicago Press, 1981.

Dieterich, Albrecht. *Mutter Erde: Ein Versuch über Volksreligion*. Berlin-Leipzig, 1905.

Dollimore, Jonathan. *Radical Tragedy: Religion, Ideology and Power in the Drama of Shakespeare and his Contemporaries*. Chicago: University of Chicago Press; Brighton: Harvester, 1984.

Dorius, R. J. "A Little More Than a Little." *Shakespeare Quarterly* 11 (1960): 13–26.

Douglas, Mary. *Natural Symbols: Explorations in Cosmology*. New York: Pantheon, 1970.

———. *Purity and Danger: An Analysis of the Concepts of Pollution and Taboo*. London: Routledge and Kegan Paul, 1966.

Douglas, Wallace W. "The Meanings of 'Myth' in Modern Criticism." *Modern Philology* 50–51 (1952–54): 232–42.

Dover, K. J. "Greek Comedy." *Fifty Years (And Twelve) of Classical Scholarship*. Ed. Maurice Platnauer. New York: Barnes and Noble, 1968. 123–56.

Eagleton, Terry. *Walter Benjamin: Towards a Revolutionary Criticism*. London: Verso, 1981.

Eliade, Mircea. *Rites and Symbols of Initiation*. Trans. Willard R. Trask. Chicago: University of Chicago Press, 1956.

Else, Gerald F. *The Origin and Early Form of Greek Tragedy*. Cambridge, Mass.: Harvard University Press, 1965.

Elton, G. R. "Scapegoats." *New York Review of Books* 35 (19 Jan. 1989): 48–50.

Falk, Florence. "Dream and Ritual Process in *A Midsummer Night's Dream.*" *Comparative Drama* 14 (1980–81): 263–79.

Fergusson, Francis. *The Idea of a Theater*. Princeton: Princeton University Press, 1949.

Foley, Helene. *Ritual Irony: Poetry and Sacrifice in Euripides*. Ithaca: Cornell University Press, 1985.

Frankis, P. J. "The Testament of the Deer in Shakespeare." *Neuphilologische Mitteilungen* 59 (1958): 65–68.

Frazer, Sir James. *The Scapegoat*. Part 6 of *The Golden Bough*. Third edition. London: Macmillan, 1913. (First ed. of *Golden Bough*, 1890.)

——. *The Dying God*. Part 3 of *The Golden Bough*. London: Macmillan, 1911. (First ed. of *Golden Bough*, 1890).

Frost, William. "Shakespeare's Rituals and the Opening of *King Lear.*" *Hudson Review* 10 (1957–58): 577–85.

Frye, Northrop. *Anatomy of Criticism*. Princeton: Princeton University Press, 1957.

——. "Myth, Fiction, and Displacement." *Fables of Identity: Studies in Poetic Mythology.* New York: Harcourt, 1963. 21–38.

——. *A Natural Perspective: The Development of Shakespearean Comedy and Romance.* New York: Columbia, 1965.

Gallenca, C. "Ritual and Folk Custom in *The Merry Wives of Windsor.*" *Cahiers élisabéthains* 27 (1985): 27–41.

Garber, Marjorie. *Coming of Age in Shakespeare*. London: Methuen, 1981.

Geertz, Clifford. "Centers, Kings, and Charisma: Reflections on the Symbolics of Power." *Rites of Power: Symbolism, Ritual and Politics Since the Middle Ages.* Ed. Sean Wilentz. Philadelphia: University of Pennsylvania Press, 1985. 13–38.

Gill, Sam D. *Mother Earth*. Chicago: University of Chicago Press, 1987.

Ginzburg, Carlo. *The Night Battles: Witchcraft and Agrarian Cults in the Sixteenth and Seventeenth Centuries.* Trans. John and Anne Tedeschi. London: Routledge and Kegan Paul, 1983. First published in Italian, 1966.

Girard, René. " 'To Entrap the Wisest': A Reading of *The Merchant of Venice.*" *Literature and Society*. Ed. Edward W. Said. Baltimore: Johns Hopkins University Press, 1980. 100–119.

——. "Levi-Strauss, Frye, Derrida, and Shakespearean Criticism." *Diacritics* 3, iii (1973): 34–38.

——. "Myth and Ritual in Shakespeare: *A Midsummer Night's Dream.*" *Textual Strategies: Perspectives in Post-Structuralist Criticism*. Ed. Josué V. Harari. Ithaca: Cornell University Press, 1979. 189–212.

——. *The Scapegoat*. Trans. Yvonne Freccero. Baltimore: Johns Hopkins University Press, 1986.

——. *Violence and the Sacred*. Trans. Patrick Gregory. Baltimore: Johns Hopkins University Press, 1977.

Gluckman, Max. "*Les Rites de Passage.*" *Essays on the Ritual of Social Relations*. Ed. Max Gluckman. Manchester: Manchester University Press, 1962. 1–52.

——. "Rituals of Rebellion in South-East Africa." *Order and Rebellion in Tribal Africa*. London: Cohen and West, 1963.

Goody, Jack. "Against 'Ritual': Loosely Structured Thoughts on a Loosely Defined Topic." *Secular Ritual*. Ed. Sally F. Moore and Barbara G. Myerhoff. Assen: Van Gorcum, 1977.

Gorfain, Phyllis. "Remarks toward a Folklorist Approach to Literature: Riddles in Shakespearean Drama." *Southern Folklore Quarterly* 41 (1977): 143–57.

──────. "Riddles and Reconciliation: Formal Unity in *All's Well That Ends Well.*" *Journal of the Folklore Institute* 13 (1976): 263–81.

──────. "Riddles and Tragic Structure in *Macbeth.*" *Mississippi Folklore Register* 10 (1976): 187–205.

Green, Miranda. *A Corpus of Religious Material from the Civilian Areas of Roman Britain.* Oxford: British Archaeological Reports 24, 1976.

Greenblatt, Stephen. "Invisible Bullets: Renaissance Authority and Its Subversion, *Henry IV* and *Henry V.*" *Political Shakespeare: New Essays in Cultural Materialism.* Ed. Jonathan Dollimore and Alan Sinfield. Manchester: Manchester University Press, 1985. 18–47.

──────. *Renaissance Self-Fashioning: From More to Shakespeare.* Chicago: University of Chicago Press, 1980.

──────. "Shakespeare and the Exorcists." *Shakespeare and the Question of Theory.* Ed. Patricia Parker and Geoffrey Hartman. New York: Methuen, 1985. 163–87.

Guépin, Jean-Pierre. *The Tragic Paradox: Myth and Ritual in Greek Tragedy.* Amsterdam: Hakkert, 1968.

Hapgood, Robert. "Shakespeare and the Ritualists." *Shakespeare Survey* 15 (1962): 111–24.

Hardin, Richard F. " 'Ritual' in Recent Criticism: The Elusive Sense of Community." *PMLA* 98 (1983): 846–62.

Hardison, O. B. *Christian Rite and Christian Drama in the Middle Ages.* Baltimore: Johns Hopkins University Press, 1965.

Harrison, Jane. *Themis: A Study of the Social Origins of Greek Religion.* Cambridge: Cambridge University Press, 1912.

Hassel, R. Chris, Jr. *Renaissance Drama and the English Church Year.* Lincoln: University of Nebraska Press, 1979.

Helm, Alex. *The English Mummers' Play.* Woodbridge, Suffolk: Brewer, 1981.

Henn, Thomas Rice. *The Harvest of Tragedy.* London: Methuen, 1956.

Hewitt, Douglas. " 'The Very Pompes of the Divell'—Popular and Folk Elements in Elizabethan and Jacobean Drama." *Review of English Studies* 25 (1949): 10–23.

Hill, Christopher. *The World Turned Upside Down: Radical Ideas during the English Revolution.* London: Temple Smith, 1972.

Holland, Norman. "Macbeth as Hibernal Giant." *Literature and Psychology* 10 (1960): 37–38.

Holloway, John. *The Story of the Night.* London: Routledge and Kegan Paul, 1961.

Holmberg, Arthur. "*The Two Gentlemen of Verona*: Shakespearean Comedy as a Rite of Passage." *Queen's Quarterly* 90 (1983): 33–44.

Hulse, S. Clark. "Shakespeare's Myth of Venus and Adonis." *PMLA* 93 (1978): 95–105.

Kahn, Coppélia. *Man's Estate: Masculine Identity in Shakespeare.* Berkeley: University of California Press, 1981.

————. "The Rape in Shakespeare's *Lucrece.*" *Shakespeare Studies* 9 (1976): 45–72.

Kittredge, George Lyman. *Witchcraft in Old and New England.* Cambridge, Mass.: Harvard University Press, 1929.

Kuhn, Thomas S. *The Structure of Scientific Revolutions.* Second edition. Chicago: University of Chicago Press, 1970.

Kunzle, David. "World Upside Down: The Iconography of a European Broadsheet Type." *The Reversible World.* Ed. Barbara A. Babcock. Ithaca: Cornell University Press, 1978. 39–94.

Lang, Andrew. *Magic and Religion.* London: Longmans, Green, 1901.

Langman, F. H. "Comedy and Saturnalia: The Case of *TN.*" *Southern Review* (Australia) 7 (1974): 102–22.

Laroque, François. "Pagan Ritual, Christian Liturgy, and Folk Customs in *The Winter's Tale.*" *Cahiers élisabéthains* 22 (1982): 25–33.

Laslett, Peter. *The World We Have Lost.* London: Methuen, 1965.

Latimer, Kathleen. "The Communal Action of *The Winter's Tale.*" *The Terrain of Comedy.* Ed. Louise Cowan. Dallas: Dallas Institute of Humanities and Culture, 1984. 125–42.

Le Roy Ladurie, Emmanuel. *Les Paysons de Languedoc.* Paris: S.E.V.P.E.N., 1966.

Lerner, Gerda. *The Creation of Patriarchy.* New York: Oxford University Press, 1986.

Liebler, Naomi Conn. " 'Thou Bleeding Piece of Earth': The Ritual Ground of *Julius Caesar.*" *Shakespeare Studies* 14 (1981): 175–96.

Lyall, Alfred C. *Asiatic Studies Religious and Social.* London: Murray, 1899.

Magnus, Olaus. *Historia de Gentibus Septentrionalibus.* Ed. John Granlund. Copenhagen: Rosenkilde and Bagger, 1972. First published 1555.

Marcus, Leah. *The Politics of Mirth: Jonson, Herrick, Milton, Marvell, and the Defense of Old Holiday Pastimes.* Chicago: University of Chicago Press, 1986.

Marienstras, Richard. *New Perspectives on the Shakespearean World.* Trans. Janet Lloyd. Cambridge: Cambridge University Press, 1985. First published in French, 1981.

Marx, Steven. *Youth against Age: Generational Strife in Renaissance Poetry, with special reference to Edmund Spenser's "The Shepheardes Calendar."* New York: Peter Lang, 1985.

Montrose, Louis Adrian. "The Elizabethan Subject and the Spenserian Text." *Literary Theory/Renaissance Texts.* Ed. Patricia Parker and David Quint. Baltimore: Johns Hopkins University Press, 1986. 303–40.

————. " 'The Place of a Brother' in *AYL*: Social Process and Comic Form." *Shakespeare Quarterly* 32 (1981): 28–54.

————. "The Purpose of Playing: Reflections on a Shakespearean Anthropology." *Helios* 7 (1980): 51–74.

Mullaney, Steven. *The Place of the Stage: License, Play, and Power in Renaissance England.* Chicago: University of Chicago Press, 1988.

Murray, Gilbert. "Hamlet and Orestes." *The Classical Tradition in Poetry.* London: Oxford University Press, 1927. 205–40. First published 1914.

Murray, Margaret Alice. *The Witch-Cult in Western Europe.* Oxford: Clarendon, 1921.

Neely, Carol Thomas. *Broken Nuptials in Shakespeare's Plays.* New Haven: Yale University Press, 1985.

Neill, Michael. "'Exeunt with a Dead March': Funeral Pageantry on the Shakespearean Stage." *Pageantry in the Shakespearean Theater.* Ed. David M. Bergeron. Athens: University of Georgia Press, 1985. 153–93.

Neumann, Erich. *The Great Mother: An Analysis of the Archetype.* Trans. Ralph Manheim. New York: Pantheon, 1955.

Novy, Marianne. "Patriarchy, Mutuality, and Forgiveness in *King Lear.*" *Southern Humanities Review* 13 (1979): 281–92.

Ong, Walter J. "Latin Language Study as a Renaissance Puberty Rite." *Studies in Philology* 56 (1959): 103–24.

———. *Orality and Literacy: The Technologizing of the Word.* London: Methuen, 1982.

Ovid (P. Ovidius Naso). *Fasti.* Ed. and trans. Sir James Frazer. London: Heinemann; New York: Putnam, 1931.

Palmer, Roy. *The Folklore of Warwickshire.* London: Batsford, 1976.

Parfitt, G. A. E. "Renaissance Wombs, Renaissance Tombs." *Renaissance and Modern Studies* 15 (1971): 23–33.

Pickard-Cambridge, A. W. *Dithyramb Tragedy and Comedy.* Oxford: Clarendon, 1927.

Propp, Vladimir. *Morphology of the Folktale.* Trans. Lawrence Scott. Ed. Svatana Pirkova-Jakobson. Bloomington: Publications of the Indiana Research Center in Anthropology, Folklore, and Linguistics, 1958.

Rackin, Phyllis. "Anti-Historians: Women's Roles in Shakespeare's Histories." *Theatre Journal* 37 (1985): 329–44.

Ranald, Margaret Loftus. "The Degradation of Richard II: An Inquiry into the Ritual Backgrounds." *English Literary Renaissance* 7 (1977): 170–96.

Roberts, Jeanne Addison. "Falstaff in Windsor Forest: Villain or Victim?" *Shakespeare Quarterly* 26 (1975): 8–15.

———. "*The Merry Wives of Windsor* as a Hallowe'en Play." *Shakespeare Survey* 25 (1972): 107–12.

———. *Shakespeare's English Comedy: "The Merry Wives of Windsor" in Context.* Lincoln: University of Nebraska Press, 1979.

Rodgers, Edith C. *Discussion of Holidays in the Late Middle Ages.* New York: Columbia University Press, 1940.

Runeberg, Arne. *Witches, Demons and Fertility Magic.* Helsingfors: Centraltryckeri Och Bokbinderi Ab, 1946.

Sales, Roger. *English Literature in History 1780–1830: Pastoral and Politics.* London: Hutchinson, 1983.

Schanzer, Ernest. "The Tragedy of Shakespeare's Brutus." *ELH* 22 (1955): 1–15.

Schaum, Melita. "The Social Dynamic: Separation, Liminality and Reaggregation in *King Lear.*" *Aligarh Journal of English Studies* 9 (1984): 148–54.

Sinfield, Alan. "Give an account of Shakespeare and Education, showing why you think they are effective and what you have appreciated about them. Support your comments with precise references." *Political Shakespeare.* Ed. Jonathan Dollimore and Alan Sinfield. Manchester: Manchester University Press, 1985: 130–57.

Smith, Lacey Baldwin. "English Treason Trials and Confessions in the Sixteenth Century." *Journal of the History of Ideas* 15 (1954): 471–98.

Spens, Janet. *An Essay on Shakespeare's Relation to Tradition.* Oxford: Blackwell, 1916.

Stallybrass, Peter. "Patriarchal Territories: The Body Enclosed." *Rewriting the Renaissance: The Discourses of Sexual Difference in Early Modern Europe.* Ed. Margaret W. Ferguson, Maureen Quilligan, and Nancy J. Vickers. Chicago: University of Chicago Press, 1986. 123–42.

————. "'Wee feaste in our Defense': Patrician Carnival in Early Modern England and Robert Herrick's 'Hesperides.'" *English Literary Renaissance* 16 (1986): 234–52.

————, and Allon White. *The Politics and Poetics of Transgression.* Ithaca: Cornell University Press, 1986.

Still, Colin. *The Timeless Theme.* Folcroft, Pa.: Folcroft Press, 1973. First published 1936.

Stirling, Brents. *Unity in Shakespearian Tragedy.* New York: Columbia University Press, 1956.

Stubbes, Phillip. *The Anatomy of Abuses.* New York: Garland, 1973. First published 1583.

Thistleton-Dyer, Rev. T. F. *Domestic Folk-Lore.* London, Paris, and New York: Cassell, Petter, Galpin, ca. 1881.

Thomas, Keith. "Age and Authority in Early Modern England." *Proceedings of the British Academy* 62 (1976): 205–48.

————. *Man and the Natural World: Changing Attitudes in England 1500–1800.* London: Allen Lane, 1983.

————. "The Place of Laughter in Tudor and Stuart England." *Times Literary Supplement* 21 (Jan. 1977): 77–81.

————. *Religion and the Decline of Magic.* Harmondsworth: Penguin, 1973. First published 1971.

————. *Rule and Misrule in the Schools of Early Modern England.* The Stenton Lecture, 1975. Reading: University of Reading Press, 1976.

Thorne, William B. "*Pericles* and the Incest-Fertility Opposition." *Shakespeare Quarterly* 22 (1971): 43–76.

Tiddy, R. J. E. *The Mummers' Play.* Oxford: Clarendon, 1923.

Tinkler, F. C. "The Winter's Tale." Scrutiny 5 (1937): 343–64.

Train, Joseph. An Historical and Statistical Account of the Isle of Man. Vol. 2. Isle of Man: Douglas, 1845.

Turner, Victor. "Color Classification in Ndembu Ritual." The Forest of Symbols. Ithaca: Cornell University Press, 1967.

——. Dramas, Fields, and Metaphors: Symbolic Action in Human Society. Ithaca: Cornell University Press, 1974.

——. The Ritual Process: Structure and Anti-Structure. Chicago: Aldine, 1969.

Van Gennep, Arnold. The Rites of Passage. Trans. Monika B. Vizedom and Gabrielle L. Caffee. London: Routledge and Kegan Paul, 1960. First published in French, 1908.

Vickers, Brian. "Rites of Passage in Shakespeare's Prose." Jahrbuch der Deutschen Shakespeare-Gesellschaft West (1986): 45–67.

Vickery, John B., ed. The Scapegoat: Ritual and Literature. Boston: Houghton Mifflin, 1972.

Vizedom, Monika. Rites and Relationships: Rites of Passage and Contemporary Anthropology. Beverly Hills: Sage, 1976.

Watts, Harold. "Myth and Drama." Cross Currents 5 (1955): 154–70.

Wayne, Valerie. "Some Sad Sentence: Vives' Instruction of a Christian Woman." Silent But for the Word. Ed. Margaret Patterson Hannay. Kent, Ohio: Kent State University Press, 1985. 15–29.

Webster, Graham. The British Celts and Their Gods under Rome. London: Batsford, 1986.

Weimann, Robert. Shakespeare and the Popular Tradition in the Theatre. Ed. Robert Schwartz. Baltimore: Johns Hopkins University Press, 1978. First published in German, 1967.

Welsford, Enid. The Fool: His Social Literary History. Gloucester, Mass.: Peter Smith, 1935.

Weston, Jessie. From Ritual to Romance. Cambridge: Cambridge University Press, 1920.

Wimsatt, William K., Jr., and Cleanth Brooks. Literary Criticism: A Short History. London: Routledge and Kegan Paul, 1957.

Wincor, Richard. "Shakespeare's Festival Plays." Shakespeare Quarterly 1 (1950): 219–42.

Witzschel, August. Sagen, Sitten und Gebraüche aus Thüringen. Vienna: Braumüller, 1878.

Woodbridge, Linda. "Black and White and Red All Over: The Sonnet Mistress amongst the Ndembu." Renaissance Quarterly 40 (1987): 247–97.

——. "'Fire in Your Heart and Brimstone in Your Liver': Towards an Unsaturnalian Twelfth Night." Southern Review 17 (1984): 270–91.

——. "A Strange Eventful History: Notes on Feminism, Historicism, and Literary Study." Exemplaria 2 (1990): 692–96.

———. *Women and the English Renaissance: Literature and the Nature of Womankind, 1540–1620*. Urbana: University of Illinois Press; Brighton: Harvester, 1984.

Wright, A. R. *English Folklore*. London: Benn, 1928.

PART I

RITES OF PASSAGE

1

"Feasts Put Down Funerals":
Death and Ritual in Renaissance Comedy

MICHAEL NEILL

"There is no death," she said. "No, my dear lady,
but there are funerals."
Peter de Vries, *Comfort Me
with Apples*

Hey, ho, 'tis nought but mirth
That keeps the body from the earth.
Francis Beaumont, *The Knight
of the Burning Pestle*

Comedy is essentially a carrying away of death,
a triumph over mortality.
Wylie Sypher

"Men have died from time to time, and worms have eaten them, but
not for love," mocks Rosalind in *As You Like It* (IV.i.96–98).[1] Behind her
lighthearted dismissal of the tragic loves of Troilus, Leander, and all the
other infatuated heroes of the six-thousand-year-old world, lies a very clear
notion of genre: like Francis Bacon, she knows well that "love is ever
matter of comedies."[2] Her own play may begin with talk of a "beginning
that is dead and buried" (I.ii.109), but it ends with a new beginning: "Let
us do those ends / That here were well begun. . . . We'll begin these rites /
As we do trust they'll end, in true delights" (V.iv.167–68, 194–95). Orlando's
melancholy verses may allude to the fatal ends of Cleopatra and Lucretia,
but, within the world of romance that they construct, the "end" of every
sentence is to be the living name of "Rosalinda" (III.ii.131–44). Yet Rosalind's
generic security is less secure than she supposes: even in the green world
of Arden it is impossible altogether to suppress the grim resonance of
"worms." There may be "no clock in the forest" (III.ii.292–3), but *As You*

Like It is aware with Touchstone that "as all is mortal in nature, so is all nature in love mortal in folly" (II.iv.50~51); and his punning talk of mortal folly links the comic stage on which he stands to the "woeful pageants" of Jacques' "wide and universal theatre," where the folly of "second childishness" announces the "last Scene of all" (II.vii.138~67)—a scene immediately hinted at in the entry of Orlando, bearing the "venerable burden" of Adam in his arms. Folly and mortality in this world are never far apart—as Morocco and Arragon reveal in *The Merchant of Venice*, when they open their caskets to discover not the signs of requited love but the impartial mockery of "a carrion Death" and "the portrait of a blinking idiot." Comedy may belong to a golden world, but *"Gilded tombs,"* the death's head announces, *"do worms infold"* (II.vii.63, 69; viii.54); and if Death in tragedy frequently adopts an antic guise, the antics of comedy are often the remembrancers of Death. "I will never die" claims Sir Toby Belch, the figure of Misrule for whom the rule of time is something to be juggled away with words. Feste, however, is there to refute him: "Sir Toby, there you lie" (*TN* II.iii.106~7), and it is as though for a moment the jester had let fall his festival mask to reveal the grin of antic death.[3] Even Falstaff, that "true and perfect image of life" will hear in Doll Tearsheet's poignantly comic endearments the cracked accents of Mors: "Peace, good Doll, do not speak like a death's head, do not bid me remember mine end" (*2H4* II.iv.231~32).

Such delicate subversions of the laws of kind are so characteristic of Shakespearean comedy that Marjorie Garber has concluded, with only a hint of paradox, that "[it] is really about death and dying."[4] Nor is this sort of generic play by any means confined to Shakespeare's work. Indeed the drama of this period typically takes pleasure in confusing "matter of comedies" with the "matter of tragedies." In a notorious passage from the *Apology for Poetry*, censuring the defects of contemporary playwrights, Sir Philip Sidney complained of the carelessness about tragic decorum that led them to thrust in clowns "by the head and shoulders to play a part in majestical matters," mingling the "hornpipes" of comedy with the "funerals" of tragedy, and threatening to reduce all drama to the condition of "mongrel tragicomedy."[5] Although he had in mind the popular dramatists of the 1570s and 1580s, the generic license he so disliked is characteristic of Elizabethan and early Stuart tragedy: in it Kings are tutored by fools, and Princes learn to play the antic, striving to move the wildest laughter in the throat of Death; while the Grim Summoner himself, in the guise of gravedigger or rustic, may often assume the Clown's part.[6]

Where the intrusion of comic characters and episodes into tragedy used to be explained away as a concession to crude popular taste, or justified by appeal to the nebulous doctrine of "comic relief," the work of critics like Susan Snyder has alerted criticism to the sophisticated generic play made possible in tragic structures founded upon a "comic matrix."[7] Often such play is foregrounded by a metatheatrical self-consciousness that allows the characters themselves to delight in the oxymoronic confusions by which "Griefs lift up joys, feasts put down funerals" (*Revenger's Tragedy* V.i.158).[8] Claudius's smooth chiasmus "dirge in marriage and . . . mirth in funeral" (*Ham.* I.ii.12) is an elegant variation on this theme, illustrating the particular sardonic pleasure that Machiavellian villains are liable to take in parading their murderous excesses as comic triumphs: "Here's a sweet comedy," crows Tourneur's D'Amville over his brother's corpse, "'T begins with O / *Dolentis* and concludes with ha, ha, he" (*Atheist's Tragedy* II.iv.84).

Of course the tragic incorporation of the comic extends well beyond such local grotesquerie, the felt presence of a "comic matrix" serving, as Snyder has shown, to force constant ironic adjustments in the audience's response, sometimes to intensify the cruelty of the action, often to mount an implicit challenge to its dominant heroic ethos. What results is a dialectic of kinds that operates most powerfully at the structural level—as for example in the way *King Lear* pits its desolate conclusion against the comic expectations aroused by its use of romance motifs and by the audience's awareness of the comic resolution of the old play of *King Leir*;[9] or in the way *Romeo and Juliet* grafts a tragic catastrophe onto a stock romantic comedy, complicating even its denouement with the standard comic routine of a mock death and resurrection. What results is a system of structural oxymoron that mirrors (and is mirrored in) the play's typically oxymoronic rhetoric:

> All things that we ordained festival
> Turn from their office to black funeral.
> Our instruments to melancholy bells;
> Our wedding cheer to a sad burial feast;
> Our solemn hymns to sullen dirges change;
> Our bridal flowers serve for a buried corse;
> And all things change them to their contrary.
> (IV.v.84–90)

In its patterns of ingenious reversal, climaxing in a double suicide that is also the consummation of marriage, *Romeo and Juliet* resembles an elaborately dramatized exercise in *antimetabole* or *commutatio*, the figure that Puttenham called "The Counterchange," whose inherent reversibility, makes it especially fitted to the flexible regime of comedy.[10]

II

The more one looks at this drama, then, the more striking its fascination with generic interplay becomes, to the point where its opposing kinds, like the ancient masks that traditionally represent them, appear locked in a symmetry so tight that each seems to travesty the other—or perhaps merely to conceal a face that is the other's double. In fact, as this essay will try to show, there is some reason to suppose that Renaissance dramatists tended to envisage the two genres in rather this way, as if caught in a struggle of peculiar intimacy—one fought out repeatedly within the limits of individual plays.[11]

The most explicit expression of this dialectical idea of dramatic form is to be found in the remarkable debate, made up of Induction and Epilogue, which frames the anonymous romance play, *Mucedorus* (ca. 1590).[12] Here the performance is ushered in by the carnivalesque figure of Comedy who enters "joyfully, with a garland of bays on her head," declaring that "the day and place is ours" and promising the audience music, mirth and merriment (Induction 1–7). Her dance of celebration is halted, however, by the appearance of Envy, "his arms naked, besmeared with blood," who threatens to "interrupt your tale / And mix your music with a tragic end." From offstage there sounds the triumph music of tragedy ("*drums within and cry, 'Stab! Stab!'*") while Envy crows over his rival: "In this brave music Envy takes delight, / Where I may see them wallow in their blood.... / And hear the cries of many thousand slain" (30–33). Scornful of Comedy's pleas, he swears to "make thee mourn where most thou joyest, / Turning thy mirth into a deadly dole, / Whirling thy pleasures with a plea of death" (56–58). Comedy responds in an equally militant mood, inviting the audience to see the ensuing drama as an expression of the eternal struggle between the tragic and comic muses:

> Then, ugly monster, do thy worst....
> ... I scorn what thou canst do;
> I'll grace it so thyself shall it confess
> From tragic stuff to be a pleasant comedy.
> (64–70)

This rivalry between generic opposites is worked out in the fluctuating fortunes of a romance plot, whose happy ending enables Comedy to return in triumph, proclaiming the subjection of the play's tragicomic mixture to her own decorum.

In its stiffly allegorical way this generic debate proposes an idea of the relationship between tragedy and comedy not unlike that developed by Northrop Frye. The antithetical intimacy of the two genres, he has argued, reflects their origin in the same ancient seasonal rites of death and renewal; and since "the ritual pattern behind the catharsis of comedy is the resurrection that follows the death, the epiphany or manifestation of the risen hero," tragedy is really nothing more than "implicit or uncompleted comedy"; and comedy, by the same token, always "contains a potential tragedy within itself."[13] In *Mucedorus*, however, as in much Renaissance comedy, the material of potential tragedy tends to be treated with an iconoclastic vigor that is not easily accommodated to Frye's transcendental vision of the comic triumph. The implicit affront to ritual piety is, however, quite consistent with Marjorie Garber's anthropology: for her, comedy is a theatrical rite concerned with "removing the experience of death from a sacred to a neutral zone—a desacralization, a normalization, a refusal to privilege death. . . . a ritual of the lifting of mourning"[14]—a stage counterpart, in fact, of the exuberant rituals of release that succeed funeral in most traditional societies.

The force of Garber's suggestions can be brought home by considering the function of the "jig" in Elizabethan theaters. "Now adayes" wrote one disapproving contemporary, "they put at the end of euerie Tragedie (as poyson into meat) a comedie or jigge."[15] Carelessly examined, the habit (to our eyes so strange) of crowning the performance of a tragedy with one of these lighthearted interludes might almost seem calculated to demonstrate the truth of Frye's paradoxes, asserting the power of the comic order to transcend catastrophe. In the theater, however, where jigs became "a byword for their coarseness and obscenity,"[16] the actual effect of this wild eruption of music, dance, and farce can hardly have been as soothing as Frye's invocation of Dantean mysteries would suggest. Less like ritual consolation than graffiti violently scrawled across some funerary monument, the jig asserted a spirit of pagan defiance closer to the grotesque irreverence of carnival than to the sublime vision of *The Divine Comedy*. Perhaps the best sense of the eldritch mood it might have created is given by the graveyard scene in *Hamlet*, whose Clown seems to derive from the knavish Sexton, a popular character in farces and jigs,[17] with an ancestry that can be traced to the gravedigging Death of the danses macabres.

By aiming to do what Berowne thought impossible, "to move wild laughter in the throat of death," confronting the wildness of Death with a wildness of its own, the jig amounted to a mocking rite of exorcism against the chthonic powers. By lifting, as it were, the *tapu* attendant upon the tragic spectacle of massacre, it released the tensions built up in the audience by the catastrophic action. In this way the form provided a theatrical equivalent for those rowdy and sexually suggestive games such as "Hot Cookies" played at English funerals, whose function, according to Clare Gittings, was to counter, in a ritual of cathartic release, the threat posed to society by the anarchic forces of death.[18] With its significant propensity for "mimicke venerean action,"[19] the jig performed precisely this desacralizing role.

For Northrop Frye, comedy is the master kind, since its providentialist vision embraces and overrides the desolation of tragedy. But the relationship between the genres implied by the jig is dialectical and unending: it exemplifies that system of generic doubles that Mikhail Bakhtin traced to the Roman and Greek roots of European culture.[20] Prominent amongst Bakhtin's "comic doubles" are the satyr plays attached to the Greek tetralogies, together with the "Atellan farces" and parodic mimes that rounded off the performance of Roman tragedies.[21] If these last provide a particularly striking functional parallel for the jig, in Bakhtin's analysis the single most significant influence on the practice of comic doubling in Renaissance literary forms is to be found in the paradigmatic relationship between the medieval traditions of carnival and "official feast" — the latter including most kinds of spectacular public ceremony: triumphs, entries, funerals, religious festivals, and so on. The "official feast" celebrated "all that was stable, unchanging, perennial," and sought above all to instate amongst such eternal verities the values of the existing hierarchy.[22] Carnival, by contrast, in its mockery of official ideology, poured scorn on all that purported to be monumental, unchanging, and complete: it was "the true feast of time, the feast of becoming, change and renewal."[23] Where the official feast, sanctioning existing order, was oriented toward the past, the carnival feast of the marketplace "looked into the future and laughed, attending the funeral of past and present."[24] Where every official feast was "a consecration of inequality," carnival's "world inside out" notoriously assaulted, inverted, or suspended all traditional hierarchies, celebrating, however fleetingly, "the victory of laughter" over all forms of authority and the fear that protects them.[25]

Like carnival, comedy too faces toward the future: performed under the aegis of Hymen who "peoples every town," the endings of romantic comedy especially recall Frye's "old ritual pattern of the victory of summer over winter." The pattern is consciously echoed in the jig-like performance of Holofernes and his companions at the end of *Love's Labour's Lost* — a musical dialogue between Winter and Spring in which, if Winter has the last word, he is allowed it only because his bird, the ill-omened owl, has learned to sing the "merry note" of Spring. For Frye, however, this rite of death and revival is to be discerned only as an underlying structural form, "elusive but still perceptible." Although "the original nature myth . . . is openly established" in the restored heroines of the romances, he suggests that "in the Hero of *Much Ado About Nothing* and the Helena of *All's Well that Ends Well*, this theme . . . comes as close to a death and revival as Elizabethan conventions will allow."[26] For all the brilliance of his approach, Frye oddly underestimates the visibility of death and resurrection motifs in Renaissance comedy. He does so perhaps because his concern with tracing the survival of ancient religious mysteries leads him to ignore humbler and more immediate influences. Arguably, the patterns of mortality and resurrection in Renaissance comedy can best be understood as enactments of an essentially generic contest that translated the popular agon of carnival into a sophisticated literary form. For all its sophistication, however, it was a contest that remained rooted in the social realities of early modern culture, specifically in its ways of attempting to neutralize the anarchic menace of mortality. Nowhere is this more evident than in the treatment of the opposing rituals of funeral and wedding.

Better than any other form, perhaps, great funerals illustrated the characteristic orientation of the official feast towards the past. These elaborately hierarchical processions, spectacularly displaying the immemorial symbols of the deceased's heraldic history, sought not merely to monumentalize the dead but to proclaim the irrefragable power and persistence of the social order in the face of the depredations of death. In the process, the very idea of ending itself was bound to the service of authority by its incorporation as the climax of that solemn progress to the graveside. If the funeral procession, with its panoply of hierarchic order, became the distinctive sign of tragic closure, that was largely because, ideally considered, tragedy was the genre whose function most closely corresponded to that of Bakhtin's "official feast" — not merely in the moral lessons it offered to enforce, but more crucially in the monumentalizing gestures with which it responded to death and the threat of apocalyptic disorder.[27] Comedy, by contrast, confronted death with a defiant celebration of biological continuity, adopting the wedding feast as its conventional signature of ending—one that announced every end as a new beginning. At the same time, it proclaimed its role as the carnivalesque double of tragedy by engaging in extensive burlesque of the pious rituals of death. Mock funerals (and the parodic resurrections often associated with them) figured significantly among the motifs by which carnival proclaimed its orientation to the future;[28] and not surprisingly, they were also a pronounced feature of stage comedy,[29] where their presence directly reflected comedy's dialectical relationship with tragedy. In much the same way, tragedy might incorporate in its spectacles of death and funeral, ironic reminders of wedding revels. At its most bitterly satiric, this propensity is apparent in the murderous entertainments that traditionally produce the denouements of revenge tragedy; but it is equally present in tragedies whose language and action conspicuously eroticize the experience of death.

As Clare Gittings's suggestive study of death and burial practices indicates, the eroticization of the language of death, like the theater's habitual yoking of "mirth in funeral and dirge in marriage," directly echoes the strategies adopted by an emergent individualist culture to cope with the blank undifferentiation of death. When Old Capulet reflects on how with Juliet's death "all things turn them to their contrary," "wedding cheer" becoming "burial feast" and "bridal flowers" converting to funeral wreaths, his conceits depend on the striking resemblances between wedding and funeral rites (especially pronounced in the burial of virgins, bachelors, or women who died in childbirth), which comedy was also able to exploit.[30] In addition to the ceremonial use of flowers, with their symbolism of renewal, funerals shared with weddings the custom of distributing gloves, points, ribbons, bridelaces and (later) rings to the young, as a way of ritually "circumventing the annihilating powers of death."[31] Ophelia's "virgin crants and maiden strewments" inevitably remind Gertrude of the bridal rites she has sentimentally imagined. Even more strikingly, as Lynda Boose notices, "the stage image of [Hamlet and Laertes] competing for possession of Ophelia's shrouded body [recalls] the wedding custom . . . of sewing up the bride in a white sheet before laying her on the flower-strewn bed to await the groom's entrance."[32] The same visual pun, combined with the usual practice of using sheets as shrouds, must have encouraged an early seventeenth-century fashion for turning wedding sheets to winding sheets, in a kind of solemn reversal of the familiar erotic quibble on "dying."[33] In this context the linking of wedding sheets to shrouds will seem a much less extravagantly private conceit than it otherwise might in *Othello,* and take on deeper resonances in the burlesque world of Middleton's *A Chaste Maid in Cheapside,* or even in the misogynist satire of Chapman's *The Widow's Tears;* while the recurrent motif of comic resurrection can be seen to grant a kind of joyous fantasy realization to the symbolism of renewal so conspicuously and touchingly displayed in the rites of late Renaissance funeral.

Among the more elaborate early uses of mock funeral in Elizabethan comedy is that in Nashe's *Summer's Last Will and Testament* (1592), an entertainment whose seesawing moods provide a particularly good example of the dialectical form suggested by the induction to *Mucedorus.* Here comedy appears to snatch the victory from her rival in the very last minutes of the action. The play begins by locating itself in a time of ending, the plague-ridden "latter end of summer" (83), the dog days that Autumn calls "death's messengers" (675); Will Summers's Prologue ushers in the figure of Summer himself, who comes to present his testament, speaking in the language of epitaph: "What pleasure alway lasts? No joy endures: / Summer I was; I am not as I was" (126-27). The action alternates the gay songs and catches of Harvest, Bacchus, and their companions with the strain of memento mori that culminates in Summer's plangent dirge, "Adieu; farewell earth's bliss" (1601-42). But just as it seems about to conclude on a mournfully funereal note, with Satyrs and Woodnymphs carrying out the corpse of Summer to the music of a second dirge (1903-16) that evokes the grim realities of disease-ridden London ("From winter, plague and pestilence, good Lord deliver us"), the Boy-Epilogue and Will Summers intervene to insist upon the insouciant moral that "Light toys chase great cares": "pay for this sport with a *plaudite,* and the next time the wind blows from this corner, we will make you ten times as merry" (1976, 1983-85).

The self-conscious imitation of folk forms in Nashe's piece is a reminder that mock funerals and comic resurrections seem to have been a widespread convention of folk drama. They occur as a standard *burla* in the *commedia del l'arte* with its strong carnival links, as well as playing a significant part in the jig convention;[34] and these origins are apparent in the rough humor characteristic of some earlier and simpler examples of the device. George Peele's *The Old Wives Tale* (ca. 1590), for example—a good part of whose action concerns the attempts of his friends to secure a decent burial for the hero, Jack—turns the death and resurrection routine from the mummers' plays to shamelessly farcical effect in the miraculous resurrection of Huanebango, brought about when Zantippa inadvertently spills water from the well of life over his corpse; and the device is extended in the return from the dead of Jack himself to slay the evil magician, Sacrapant.[35] The same farcical spirit informs the mock resurrections of Marlowe's *The Jew of Malta* and Shakespeare's *1 Henry IV*. In *The Jew*, Barabas's career as parodic anti-Christ reaches its fitting climax in act V, scene i, where his apparently poisoned corpse is treated to a degrading anti-funeral—only for him to bounce to his feet and plan fresh atrocities against the Christians. Falstaff similarly rises from the dead after the slaughter of Shrewsbury, becoming "the true and perfect image of life indeed" (*1H4* V.iv.119), while subjecting Hotspur's corpse—the very form of honorable death—to comic indignity as if in defiance of its "grinning honour."[36]

Perhaps the first playwright fully to explore the potential of the mock funeral was John Marston in his quasi-burlesque tragicomedy, *Antonio and Mellida* (ca. 1599). Amid the revelry of the final act, the usurping Piero confesses his wish to "shut up night with an old comedy" (V.ii.63–64); the exaggeratedly romantic incidents that ensue, by carnivalizing his official feast, successfully convert his tragic design to a comic end, so granting his wish an ironic kind of fulfillment. First Piero's rival, Andrugio, appears in disguise to claim the price on his own head, in what amounts to a species of punning resurrection as he lifts his visor to reveal "Andrugio's head / Royally casqued in a helm of steel" (181–82).[37] Then *"The still flutes sound a mournful sennet"* and Lucio enters with a funeral cortege; seeking an explanation for this "tragic spectacle," Piero enquires "Whose body bear you in that mournful hearse?" (209–10); he is informed that it contains the corpse of the hero, Antonio. Since Marston has been careful to leave the audience no better informed than his characters, it may even seem, amid the general chorus of lamentation, that his curiously unstable play has at last tipped toward a tragic conclusion—until Antonio, with theatrical relish, rises from his coffin pat on the cue supplied by Piero's incautious expression of regret:

> *Piero.*   O that my life, her love, my dearest blood
> Would but redeem one minute of his breath!
>
> *Antonio.*   I seize that breath. Stand not amazed, great states:
> I rise from death that never lived till now.

Piero, keep thy vow, and I enjoy
More unexpressed height of happiness
Than power of thought can reach; if not, lo, here
There stands my tomb, and here a pleasing stage,
Most wished spectators of my tragedy.[38]

(V.ii.243–52)

Marston's hint of a suspended tragic peripety is reinforced by a closing couplet which, as it wryly looks forward to his bloody sequel, *Antonio's Revenge,* suggests the tenuousness of Comedy's triumph over her sombre adversary: "Here ends the *comic* crosses of true love; / O may the *passage* most successful prove" (V.ii.304–5; my emphases).

The comic effectiveness of Marston's scene can be judged from the imitations it produced – like the elaborate mock funeral that opens Dekker's *1 Honest Whore* (1604),[39] or the splendidly farcical business at the end of *The Knight of the Burning Pestle* (ca. 1606). Beaumont's comedy shows the lovelorn Jasper delivered to his mistress in a coffin; the small funeral procession enters just as Luce, already convinced that her lover is dead, has launched upon a Juliet-like lament: "Come, come, O death; bring me to thy peace; / How happy had I been, if, being born, / My grave had been my cradle" (IV.231–38). In keeping with the burlesque spirit of the play, her soliloquy is doubly deflated – both by the patness of the coffin's entry and by the pedestrian verse in which the servant announces its arrival. The boy who precedes the coffin, however, continues at Luce's lofty pitch, craving "a tear / From those fair eyes . . . / To deck his funeral" (247–49), and she responds with proper romantic excess: "First will I sing thy dirge, / Then kiss thy pale lips, and die myself, / And fill one coffin and one grave together" (269–71). The dirge over, she prepares to complete her liebestod, lifting the black cloth draped over the bier – "Thou sable cloth, sad cover of my joys, / . . . thus I meet with death" (286–87) – only to find Jasper rearing out of the coffin to claim his bride: "And thus you meet the living" (288). As a final flourish Beaumont outrageously extends the joke by having Luce bundled back into the casket and smuggled out of her father's house so that the trick can be performed a second time on Old Merrythought.

It is altogether fitting that the sequence of mock resurrections should conclude in Merrythought's house since, as his name suggests, he is this play's presiding genius, "an almost free-floating embodiment of comedy's festive spirit," in Lee Bliss's words.[40] Throughout the play he confronts the vicissitudes of fortune (like his wife's calls to bourgeois duty) with assertions of the miraculous power of laughter to heal all ills. Mirth, he declares, is nothing less than the elixir itself: "this is it that keeps life and soul together. . . . this is the philosopher's stone that they write so much on, that keeps a man forever young" (IV.350–52). Equipped with the sovereign preservatives of laughter and song, the old man remains equally unfazed by the announcement of his son's death and by his appearance as a ghost, "his face mealed"; and when this ghostly Jasper lifts the lid of his coffin — to reveal not his own cadaver, but the lively body of his intended bride — Merrythought imperturbably welcomes a comic resurrection that is, after all, nothing more than a beautifully timed demonstration of the restorative magic of laughter.

In Merrythought's kingdom mortality comes no closer than the grossly theatrical contrivance by which the thespian-apprentice Rafe enters "with a forked arrow through his head" (V.302,SD) to describe his Moorfields combat with "grim cruel Death" (V.342). Rafe's demise has been insisted upon by the stage-audience, George and Nell, whose firm, if somewhat rudimentary, sense of an ending will not otherwise be satisfied, despite The Boy player's desperate appeal to the laws of comic kind: "Take you no care of that . . . is not his part at an end, think you, when he's dead?" (298–301). In a sense George is right, not merely because the decorum of this comedy has already proved infinitely accommodating, but because Ralph's death is enclosed within a frame that insists on its status as part of a "pretty fiction" in which all endings are merely provisional and subject to the miraculous restorative of laughter. His part ended, Rafe himself can rise and "do [his] obeisance to the gentlemen" (V.355–56).

He takes his cue from Merrythought's defiant song in act II, affirming comedy's resistance to death, "'Tis mirth that fills the veins with blood" (II.481ff.). Outraged though she is by the old man's disdain for bourgeois moral verities, Nell is utterly seduced by his ditty, and at the close she finds herself drawn with the rest of the company into another hymn on the same theme, the last of Merrythought's songs. What he produces is a rite of communal celebration, an extravagant version of those banquet-endings in which James Calderwood discovers "a form of social communion [asserting the triumphant resistance of] a collective social body too large for death to attempt."[41] Merrythought's lyric proclaims once again (and in the face of the play's own no-longer-to-be-postponed ending) the carnivalesque power of comedy to resist time, disease, and mortal ends:

Better music ne'er was known
Than a choir of hearts in one,
Let each other, that hath been
Troubled with the gall or spleen,
Learn of us to keep his brow
Smooth and plain as ours are now.
Sing, though before the hour of dying;
He shall rise, and then be crying,
Hey, ho, 'tis nought but mirth
That keeps the body from the earth.
(V.361–70)

It is by no means fortuitous, however, that the last word of this fine litany of defiance should be "earth," and the rhyme with "mirth" serves to point up an ambivalence that tinges almost every comic ending. For even in its moments of most exuberant pretense, comedy seems fated to remind its audience of what it would deny – that its happiest endings amount only to "a kind of arbitrary arrest. . . . [in which] an ephemeral moment of happiness may pose as a permanent state."[42]

Through its complicated arrangement of intersecting metatheatrical jokes, Beaumont's comedy establishes affinities both with the carnivalesque literary tradition represented by the Don Quixote-like travesty from which it takes its name, and with the folk-festival tradition recalled in Rafe's surprising incarnation as a May Lord (IV.404ff.); above all, in Old Merrythought, with his triumphant defiance of tragic ending, it provides the spirit of carnival with its most distinctive voice in the comedy of the period.[43] There is, however, something about the hypersophisticated ingenuity of Beaumont's writing, his way of layering ambivalencies, that may leave even Merrythought (and the audience with him) vulnerable to what the publisher called the author's "privy mark of irony." Thomas Middleton's *A Chaste Maid in Cheapside* (1613), by contrast, performed in the same year that saw the publication of *The Knight of the Burning Pestle*, and evidently indebted to it, is quite unambiguous in its incorporation of carnival motifs. Set "in this strict time of Lent" when "Flesh dare not peep abroad" (II.i.109–10), the play pits the barely suppressed impulses of festival against a Lenten insistence on puritanic restraint. For all that Middleton satirizes the corruption and sensual excess represented by the Allwits, Touchwood Senior, and Sir Walter Whorehound, his comedy ultimately endorses the festive claims of the body; and mock funeral and resurrection are the devices through which its triumph over the grave world is asserted. In its satire of Lenten solemnity and celebration of the immortal flesh, it offers a profane version of *Risus Paschalis,* the Easter Laughter with which the medieval church answered the grimness of Lent.[44]

The Lenten note is established early in the play by the sour presence of the Promoters, officials charged with enforcing its strict rules of fast. Under their hypocritically censorious gaze, flesh—which the dramatist's characteristic system of bawdy puns identifies with sexual vitality and fertility—is reduced to so much dead meat, a brutal emblem of mortality; while to Allwit's imagination the Promoters become the shameless disrupters of a funeral rite,

> planted there
> To arrest the dead corpse of poor calves and sheep,
> Like ravenous creditors that will not suffer
> The bodies of their poor departed debtors
> To go to the grave, but e'en in death to vex
> And stay the corpse with bills of Middlesex.
>
> (II.iii.64–70)

The Promoters, however, are soon to be humbled by the importunity of fleshly appetite and the irrepressible liveliness of the flesh. Confiscating a basket of meat from the Country Wench, they grope hungrily under its loin of mutton for the expected quarter of lamb: "Here's a lamb's head; / I feel it plainly" (II.ii.175–76); to their consternation what they discover, in fine burlesque of a nativity play, is not a joint but a baby, a mocking reminder of the Paschal Lamb.[45] The scheme of religious parody initiated here is completed in the last act with a form of Easter resurrection. Here the heroine at last manages to escape from her tyrannic parents by successfully feigning death—seemingly succumbing to a broken heart on the news of her lover's demise. The debt to Beaumont is transparent; but Middleton also looks back to the feigned death and burial of Juliet, especially in the funeral oration (V.iv.1–20) which crowns one of the most elaborately detailed funeral pageants in Jacobean theater—a tragical spectacle that invites laughter by its monstrously solemn indecorum:

> *Recorders dolefully playing. Enter at one door the coffin of the Gentleman, solemnly decked, his sword upon it, attended by many in black, his brother being the chief mourner. At the other door, the coffin of the virgin, with epitaphs pinned on't. Then set them down one right over against the other,*

*while all the company seem to weep and mourn; there is a sad song in the
music room.*

(V.iv.1)

"Never could death boast of a richer prize," boasts Touchwood Senior;
and the whole company join in a chorus of lamentation, declaring with
Allwit that the marriage of the dead couple "would have made a thousand
joyful hearts." This echo of Merrythought's "choir of joyful hearts" is the
cue for Touchwood Senior to summon Moll and Touchwood Junior from
their coffins: "Up then, apace and take your fortunes; / Make these joyful
hearts" (28–29). The disruption of hierarchic ritual by the spirit of communal festivity announces a gleeful celebration of comedy's triumph over
death, in which the lovers' shrouds become the bed linen for their bridal:
"Here be your wedding sheets you brought along with you; and may you
both go to bed when you please to" (46–48).

Touchwood Senior's indulgence announces comedy's readiness to accommodate the ordinary demands of humankind, the democratic shrug with
which it throws off the tyrannous extremes of tragedy; and his appropriation of shrouds for wedding sheets (wittily inverting the morbid conceits
of *Romeo and Juliet* and *Othello*) is Middleton's irreverent equivalent for
the eroticized death scenes so popular in tragedy of the time. His emphasis,
like Beaumont's, is upon carnival celebration of the flesh, and mirth's
power to preserve it from the grave. But in other comedies the funeral
burlesque, as in *Antonio and Mellida*, is directed mainly toward mockery
of the emotional extravagancies and monumentalizing pretensions of the
tragic world. This is so, for example, in Fletcher's, *The Mad Lover* (1616),
with its absurdly reduplicated mock funerals—the "Souldiers funerall"
accorded to what is supposed to be the mad lover's heart in the middle of
the play, and the equally fake obsequies of his fraternal rival in the last
scene, which predictably usher in resurrection and marriage festivity.

Similarly, in *The Widow's Tears* (1605) Chapman turns Petronius's
misogynist satire on the hypocrisy of female grief into a sardonic universal
demonstration of the claim that "weeping is in truth but laughter under a
mask" (I.136). The last act of the play, set in a graveyard, becomes a kind
of carnival in black, where the miracle of resurrection is reduced to "a
body borne away piecemeal by devout ladies of Venus' order" to be used
by huntsmen "to feed their dogs withal" (V.i.542–50); and where the
restoration of a dead husband leads only to the uncomfortable cobbling
up of his destroyed marriage against the eloquent background of an

outrageously violated family monument. It is a satiric catastrophe whose full effect is very much dependent on its scenic recollection of tragic dramas, like *Titus Andronicus*, *Romeo and Juliet*, and *Antony and Cleopatra*, where tombs and monuments are deployed as symbols of lineage and the heroic transcendence of mortality.

Among several plays owing a debt to Chapman's, Davenant's lively Caroline comedy, *The Wits* (1634), with its fifth act also set "amongst sepulchres and melancholy bones" (V.ii.),[46] was perhaps the last to exploit the full comic potential of the mock funeral. By turning it into a humiliating rite of passage to be undergone by the rakish Elder Palatine before he is considered worthy of marriage to Lady Ample, Davenant was able to give a new twist to the device; but his ending no longer aims for the inclusiveness of carnival celebration: the genteel Palatine may be granted the joys of comic resurrection, but the graveyard setting also provides the occasion for an act of caste revenge on the grasping arriviste, Sir Tyrant Thrift, who is consigned (even more explicitly than his kinsman, Sir Giles Overreach) to a kind of symbolic death. For all its inventiveness there is something a touch exploitative about the use of comic convention in *The Wits*: the funeral motifs in particular have been largely severed from their ritual base and are in danger of turning into freely manipulable clichés of comic plotting—which is exactly what mock funerals and resurrections seem, in their scattered Restoration appearances, to become.[47]

III

Shakespeare shared his contemporaries' fondness for disconcerting disruptions of audience expectation: from *The Comedy of Errors*, that farce so disconcertingly played out against the threat of an innocent old man's execution, to *All's Well that Ends Well*, with its opening scene dressed in the funeral blacks of tragedy, and on to late romances like *The Winter's Tale*, where real deaths are balanced against miraculous restorations, Shakespeare's comic arcadia is never quite free from the shadow of mortal ending. One of the earliest of the comedies, *Love's Labour's Lost*, opens with a meditation upon "brazen tombs" and "the disgrace of death"; while one of the latest, *Measure for Measure*, announces the crisis of its plot with Shakespeare's most powerful meditation on the horror of ending. *Love's Labour's Lost*, in its abrupt refusal to "end like an old play" (V.ii.875), actually grants mortality a partial triumph as the entrance of Marcade, that black-clad messenger from the Dance of Death, suddenly arrests the anticipated wedding revels.[48] Marcade's is an unusually brutal affront to the decorum of comedy; but even in something as playful as *A Midsummer Night's Dream* the mechanicals' botched performance of "Pyramus and Thisby" slyly alludes to the plot's potential for a very different resolution. The tomb where its action concludes serves as a covert reminder of how "quick bright things come to confusion" (I.i.149);[49] and the comedy's curious three part epilogue conjoins a fairy epithalamium for its united couples, with what might almost pass for a pastiche of Hamlet's most ferocious rant, " 'Tis now the very witching time of night" (*Ham.* III.ii.388ff.):

> Now the wasted brands do glow,
> While the screech-owl, screeching loud,
> Puts the wretch that lies in woe
> In remembrance of a shroud.
> Now it is the time of night
> That the graves, all gaping wide,
> Every one lets forth his sprite
> In the church-way paths to glide.
>
> (V.i.375–82)

There is about the "tragical mirth" at Theseus's wedding revels a just sufficient hint of "dirge in marriage" to suggest the ultimate ineffectuality of the king's opening wish to purge his world of grief and "turn melancholy forth to funerals" (I.i.14).

What is different about Shakespeare's way of fracturing the comic surface is that the intimations of mortality often seem more unsettling and profound, tingeing the comic action with a melancholy that the wit of his contemporaries keeps under a tighter control. One reason for this may be that, with the exception of Falstaff's resurrection at Shrewsbury, his use of funeral motifs is less dependent on the traditions of folk-play, jig, and carnival, looking back instead to the strange blend of comic and tragic matter in Euripides' haunting play, *Alcestis*. In this drama of death and resurrection the Renaissance love of generic mixture had, for all Sidney's neoclassic disdain, an excellent classical precedent.

Alcestis begins with a contest between Apollo and Death for the soul of the heroine, who has volunteered to die in place of her husband Admetus; at the end of the contest Death is left in possession of the stage: "Yes, you have words enough," he taunts the departing Apollo, "words win you nothing. / Now she shall come down to the dead."[50] The expected catastrophe is seemingly accomplished at the midpoint of the action, with the performance of Alcestis's funeral rites; but the suggestion of tragic closure is immediately undercut by the entry of Heracles, speaking in the unmistakable accents of comedy: "cheer up! Have a drink! Say to yourself, 'To-day my life's my own; to-morrow it belongs to Fortune.' Put a garland on your head . . . join me in a cup of wine. That's the very medicine to cure your gloomy thoughts and scowling brow." Heracles vows to wrestle with Death and to return Alcestis from the palace of Persephone, while Admetus, unconvinced, continues to lament the fate that has turned "wedding-songs to mourning for the dead." But even as the King plans for his Queen a monument "like a god's," the comic hero returns triumphant, followed by a mysteriously veiled woman whom an initially reluctant Admetus is persuaded to take as his second bride; as they join hands Heracles lifts her veil to reveal the restored Alcestis. "I saw her die: is this truly my wife?" Admetus exclaims, anticipating Claudio and Leontes. "She was under Death's authority," Heracles replies, "I fought with Death." The play concludes with Admetus's proclamation of "dance and festival"—announcing in effect the traditional *komos* of comic closure, while the Chorus reflects on the "surprising ends" to which the gods bring human affairs: "The things we thought would happen do not happen; / Things unexpected God makes possible."

It is the dramatist's sly reflection on the way in which his play has seemed to subvert its own conventions; and it might almost have been in the mind of John Webster when he made his Capuchin reflect on the astonishing "resurrection" of Contarino that averts the tragic catastrophe of *The Devil's Law Case* (1617): "to see how heaven / Can invert man's firmest purpose" (V.v.13-14).[51] But *Alcestis*'s most decisive influence was on the plotting of *Much Ado About Nothing* (1598) and *The Winter's Tale* (1610), with their climactic resurrection scenes.

In *Much Ado About Nothing* the effect is delicately poised between the emotionalism of Euripedes and the burlesque spirit of the *commedia del l'arte*. The feigned death of Hero leads to an elaborate ceremony of mourning that is ultimately exposed as a sober-faced travesty of the funereal endings of tragedy. The Friar urges Leonato to "Maintain a mourning ostentation, / And on your family's old monument / Hang mournful epitaphs, and do all rites / That appertain unto a burial" (IV.i.205-8); and Leonato in turn commands Claudio and his companions to take up the ritual: "Hang her an epitaph upon her tomb, / And sing it to her bones, sing it tonight" (V.i.284-85). Claudio duly attaches his memorial verses to the hearse ("Death, in guerdon of her wrongs, / Gives her fame which never dies") while Balthasar chants his "solemn hymn" of lament:

> Midnight assist our moan,
> Help us to sigh and groan,
>   Heavily, heavily.
> Graves yawn, and yield your dead,
> Till death be uttered,
>   Heavily, heavily.
>
>   (V.iii.16~21)

Although the speech with which Don Pedro ends the scene is made to anticipate a comic peripety, it is by no means accidental that this spectacle of grieving should immediately follow Benedick's Hamlet-like jesting on tombs and "Don Worm" (V.ii.77~86)—for this is the structural equivalent of the graveyard scene, where the funeral of a wronged heroine again ushers in the ending of the play. But the stylized quality of the episode, together with the lyrical formality of its rhymed verse (in this largely prose play), helps to preserve the comic distance necessary to a scene which the extravagant unmasking of the play's end will place in a properly ridiculous perspective. In terms of affect this scene is more than half way to the irreverent carnivalesque mock-resurrections so characteristic of Stuart comedy; yet technically at least its real successors are the restoration scenes of *All's Well*, *Pericles*, and above all *The Winter's Tale*.

The tragicomic designs of these latter plays exemplify the *Mucedorus* dialectic with peculiar clarity. In *All's Well* and *Measure for Measure*, a comic denouement encloses and effectually neutralizes a tragic catastrophe; while late romances like *Pericles*, *Cymbeline*, and *The Winter's Tale*, inverting the practice of *Romeo and Juliet*, make use of an hourglass pattern, in which a tragical pseudocatastrophe in the middle of the play is immediately followed (rather as Time "turns his glass") by a comic countermovement that climaxes in scenes of miraculous restoration and resurrection. In each case the resolution is achieved by the most shameless manipulation of conventional comic strategems, as though to point up the generic clash between the opposed halves of the play.[52] In *Cymbeline* the "death" and funeral of Imogen/Fidele is immediately followed by a surprise "resurrection" that prefigures the elaborate restorations of the final scene. Similarly in *Pericles*, the tragical direction announced in the opening scene by the impaled heads on Antiochus's palace wall, is apparently confirmed by the sea burial of Thaisa that concludes the first half of the play—only however to usher in the counterturn of her recovery by Cerimon from the jaws of the sea.

The parallels between the plotting of *Pericles* and *The Winter's Tale*, with its more elaborate emphasis on beginnings-in-endings, is signaled in Perdita's greeting of her mother's statue — "Dear Queen, that ended when I but began" (*WT* V.iii.45) — which exactly echoes Marina's "my mother, who did end / The minute I began" (V.i.211–12). Perdita, like Marina, is a "poor maid, / Born in a tempest when my mother died" (*Per.* IV.i. 17–18) — and the tempest that tosses Thaisa's coffin upon the strand at Ephesus is echoed in the storm that rages over the deserted foundling on the Bohemian shore, where the shepherds meet with "things dying . . . [and] things new born" in mysterious tragicomic conjunction (*WT* III.iii.113–14). But the oxymoron finds its fullest expression in a final scene powerfully reminiscent of the catastrophe of *Alcestis*. It is organized around a symbolic tomb opening that provides an exact and ceremonious reversal of the funereal endings of tragedy. It begins with a solemn procession to a funeral monument whose stone image recalls the transcendent aspiration of those tragic endings where mortal flesh strives to become perdurable marble. But here the comic power of love performs an opposite metamorphosis: "'Tis time; descend; be stone no more" (V.iii.99). Leontes has seen his wife "As I thought, dead; and have in vain said many / A prayer upon her grave" (139–40); but now (as though the film of their lives were being run backward) Paulina will "fill [her] grave up" (101); and as "dear life redeems" the Queen, Death is left to inherit only the signs of death: "Bequeath to death thy numbness" (100–103).

In the mood of its final scene *The Winter's Tale* is closer to *Alcestis* than any other play of the period. Conspicuously missing from its contest with death, however, is the wild saturnalian note introduced by Heracles — though the clowns share some of his irreverence for death, and Autolycus his festive carelessness. It was this note however that had already become the dominant one in comic representations of death on the early Stuart stage. Like Shakespeare's choric Time, Heracles comes to "o'erthrow law . . . and o'erwhelm custom" (*WT* IV.i.8–9), but he does so with an iconoclastic gusto that has more in common with Old Merrythought. The somber mood that shadows the restorations of *The Winter's Tale*, anticipating Prospero's melancholy contemplation of mortality, shows how far Shakespeare's interest in the comic treatment of death, funeral, and resurrection had moved from the Jacobean norm.

When he returned to these motifs for the last time it was to collaborate with John Fletcher on a plot whose elegant tragicomic symmetries are almost wholly dependent on an ingenious dialectic of mirth and funeral, wedding and lament. *The Two Noble Kinsmen* (1613) is built around twin heroes so barely distinguishable that each might almost pass for the other's double, perfect vehicles of the play's own generic doubling. Shakespeare begins with a wedding rite brutally cut short by the claims of funeral, and ends with a funeral overlaid with wedding festival. But even here the characteristically Jacobean wit of the design is inflected with a peculiar melancholy.

Starting where *A Midsummer Night's Dream* left off, with celebration of Theseus's wedding, *The Two Noble Kinsmen* opens with a scene exemplifying the futility of the Duke's earlier desire to banish melancholy from his revels. An unusually elaborate stage direction details a carefully arranged marriage procession *all'antica*. As the wedding party crosses the stage, a boy sings an epithalamium, strewing flowers before them as he conjures away birds of ill-omen from the bridal chamber. His catalog of floral tributes includes the disturbingly juxtaposed "Oxlips in their cradles growing, / Marigolds on death-beds blowing" (I.i.10–11), their contradictory symbolism foreshadowing the fundamental oppositions of the story. Hardly has the boy's song finished, however, than the wedding pageant is interrupted by "*three* QUEENS *in black, with veils stain'd*" (1.24,SD) begging the right of interment for their husbands: "give us the bones / Of our dead kings, that we may chapel them" (49–50). It is like the intrusion of Death at the Feast, driving the bridegroom to agitated reflection on mortality: "O grief and time, / Fearful consumers, you will all devour!" (69–70); and in her appeal to Hippolyta, the Second Queen constructs a memento mori of peculiar grimness: "Tell him, if he i'th'blood-siz'd field lay swoll'n, / Showing the sun his teeth, grinning at the moon, / What you would do" (I.i.99–101).

In the fourth and fifth scenes, the act that began with wedding winds up in funeral. Theseus returns from his battle with Creon "*victor, [with his* LORDS]". What this stage direction envisages is a formal antique triumph, but one (like Titus's in the first scene of *Titus Andronicus*) oddly touched with morbidity: for the procession also includes a "HERALD *with* ATTENDANTS *bearing* PALAMON *and* ARCITE *on two hearses*"; and once again the celebratory procession is brought up short by the appearance of the mourning Queens. In scene v, which crowns this elaborate processional sequence, the obsequies of the dead kings are shown: "*Music. Enter the* QUEENS *with the hearses of their Knights, in a funeral solemnity, etc.*" The visual echo of the earlier entry with Palamon and Arcite similarly stretched upon their hearses is inescapable; but the procession is accompanied by a song that suggests a more disturbing parallel with the wedding pageant of scene i. Taken together the three pageant entries of the first act anticipate the curious double ending of the play. The melancholy parting of the Queens, its tone fitted to the tragic spectacle they enact, contains intimations of reunion, but a reunion achieved in the shadow of death.

The funeral motif begun by the black spectacle of the Queens is echoed repeatedly in the figurative language and theatrical imagery of *The Two Noble Kinsmen* — most strikingly in the last act, whose tragicomic oppositions are realized in the contrast between Emilia's bridal white (V.i.137,SD) and the black associated with the doomed Arcite.[53] The whole elaborate system of oxymoronic contrasts finds its culmination in the carefully balanced antitheses of Theseus's peroration, which celebrates the play's artful yoking of comic and tragic elements:

> Never fortune
> Did play a subtler game. The conquer'd triumphs,
> The victor has the loss. . . .
> Let us look sadly, and give grace unto
> The funeral of Arcite, in whose end
> The visages of bridegrooms we'll put on
> And smile with Palamon; for whom an hour,
> But one hour since, I was as dearly sorry
> As glad of Arcite; and am now as glad
> As for him sorry.
>
> (V.iv.112–30)

The processional exit that follows, with its combination of wedding and funeral rites, neatly replicates the startling oppositions of the first act, resolving them however within a single ritual frame: dirge finds its place in Palamon's marriage, mirth in Arcite's funeral — his body placed this time not upon a bier, but with a fitting suggestion of regal triumph "in a chair" (86,SD). Now indeed, in a sense that Emilia can hardly have anticipated, "Palamon's sadness is a kind of mirth, / So mingled as if mirth did make him sad, / And sadness merry" (V.iii.51–53). In its artful conflation of ritual and generic opposites *The Two Noble Kinsmen* emerges as a set of tragicomic variations on Hamlet's bitter theme of "dirge in marriage and . . . mirth in funeral," contrived in urbane defiance of the neoclassical rules of decorum. But even as it calls its lovers "from the stage of death"

(123) to the altar of marriage, it asks us to recall the Third Queen's motto from the close of act I, a grim paraphrase of Feste's "Journeys end in lovers meeting" (*TN* II.iii.43) that promises a very different sort of reunion: "This world's a city full of straying streets, / And death's the market-place, where each one meets" (I.v.15~16).

NOTES

1. Unless otherwise indicated, citations from Shakespeare are to G. Blakemore Evans, ed., *The Riverside Shakespeare* (Boston: Houghton Mifflin, 1974).

2. Francis Bacon, "Of Love," *Essays* (London: Dent, 1962) 29.

3. For an account of the play that sees Malvolio as a black-costumed avatar of "the deathly spirit," and Feste as "not a bringer of death, but . . . a constant reminder of it," see Marjorie Garber, " 'Remember Me': *Memento Mori* Figures in Shakespeare's Plays," *Renaissance Drama* n.s. 12 (1981): 3~25 (22~24).

4. Marjorie Garber, " 'Wild Laughter in the Throat of Death': Darker Purposes in Shakespearean Comedy," *New York Literary Forum* 5-6 (1980): 121~26 (121). The point is reinforced in Garber's *Coming of Age in Shakespeare* (London: Methuen, 1981), chapter 7, "Death and Dying." See also James L. Calderwood, *Shakespeare and the Denial of Death* (Amherst: University of Massachusetts Press, 1987): Part 3 "Immortality and Art"; and Michael D. Bristol, *Carnival and Theatre: Plebeian Culture and the Structure of Authority in Renaissance England* (London: Methuen, 1985): chapters 10~11. Bristol notes that "tragical mirth is a dominant character of Carnivalesque mimesis" (177).

5. Sir Philip Sidney, "An Apology for Poetry," in Edmund D. Jones, ed., *English Critical Essays* (*Sixteenth, Seventeenth and Eighteenth Centuries*) (London: Oxford University Press, 1947) 46.

6. For a more elaborate treatment of such comic and satiric uses of memento mori motifs, see Phoebe S. Spinrad, *The Summons of Death on the Medieval and Renaissance English Stage* (Columbus: Ohio State University Press, 1987): chapter 10, "Memento Mockery," *passim*. The element of carnivalesque subversion involved in grotesque episodes of this sort is discussed by Robert Weimann, *Shakespeare and the Popular Tradition* (237~46), and Bristol, *Carnival and Theatre*, chapter 11.

7. Susan Snyder, *The Comic Matrix of Shakespeare's Tragedies* (Princeton, N.J.: Princeton University Press, 1979).

8. See also Vindice's "In midst of all their joys they shall sigh blood!" (V.ii.21). Except where otherwise indicated, all citations from non-Shakespearean drama are to Russell A. Fraser and Norman Rabkin, eds., *Drama of the English Renaissance*, 2 vols. (New York: Macmillan, 1976).

9. *Lear*'s frustration of generic expectation and its cruel game with endings is

well discussed by Stephen Booth in '*King Lear*', '*Macbeth*', *Indefinition and Tragedy* (New Haven: Yale University Press, 1983) 5–20.

10. See, for example, the miraculously orchestrated ending of *Cymbeline*, where "the counterchange / Is severally in all" (V.v.395–98). Patricia Parker's *Literary Fat Ladies: Rhetoric, Gender, Property* (London: Methuen, 1987) 89–93, contains a brilliant analysis of *antimetabole* as the rhetorical counterpart of the comic *mundus inversus* trope.

11. Stephen Orgel, "Shakespeare and the Kinds of Drama," *Critical Inquiry* 6 (1979): 107–23, puts it that for the Renaissance "comedy . . . is not merely an alternative to tragedy, since their operations are fully complementary. . . . The dramatic dichotomy in the Renaissance . . . expressed . . . a real and fruitful inter-relationship between the genres" (118–19).

12. The debate closely resembles the dialogue between Love, Death, and Fortune that frames Thomas Kyd's *Soliman and Perseda*, written at about the same time; though the generic contest is less explicit in Kyd's play, the Triumph of Death over Love precisely signals the victory of Tragedy over Comedy: "Packe *Loue* and *Fortune*, play in Commedies, / For powerfull Death best fitteth Tragedies" (1599 Quarto).

13. Northrop Frye, "The Argument of Comedy," reprinted in Laurence Lerner, ed., *Shakespeare's Comedies: An Anthology of Modern Criticism* (Harmondsworth: Penguin, 1967) 319–20.

14. Garber, "Wild Laughter," 121.

15. R. Knolles, *Six Bookes of a Commonweal* (1606), cited in E. K. Chambers, *The Elizabethan Stage*, 4 vols. (Oxford: Clarendon Press, 1923) II, 551. The fullest account of this curious genre is in Charles Read Baskervill, *The Elizabethan Jig* (Chicago: University of Chicago Press, 1929), which also prints the few surviving examples.

16. Baskervill, *Elizabethan Jig*, 38.

17. Ibid., 226.

18. Clare Gittings, *Death, Burial and the Individual in Early Modern England* (London: Croom Helm, 1984) 105–6.

19. See Baskervill, *Elizabethan Jig*, 112.

20. Mikhail Bakhtin, *The Dialogic Imagination*, ed. Michael Holquist, trans. Carolyn Emerson and Michael Holquist (Austin: University of Texas Press, 1981): 41–83. See also Orgel, "Shakespeare and the Kinds of Drama," who suggests that jigs served "to mitigate the tragic catastrophe" by reminding the audience that "comedy is the end of tragedy" (118, 120).

21. *Dialogic Imagination*, 56; see also Robert Weimann, *Shakespeare and the Popular Theatre: Studies in the Social Dimension of Dramatic Form and Function*, ed. Robert Schwartz (Baltimore: Johns Hopkins University Press, 1978) 5–10.

22. Mikhail Bakhtin, *Rabelais and His World*, trans. Helene Iswolsky (Cambridge, Mass.: M.I.T. Press, 1968) 9.

23. Bakhtin, *Rabelais*, 10.

24. Ibid., 81.

25. Ibid., 10–11. My use of Bakhtin's paradigm does not imply acceptance of his simplified notion of the political function of carnival. Emmanuel Le Roy Ladurie's classic, *Carnival: A People's Uprising at Romans, 1579–80* (London: Scolar Press, 1979) in particular, has shown how carnival's parade of transgression typically functioned in the interests of authority, though it could always be captured for genuinely subversive purposes. See also the useful critique and modification of Bakhtin's arguments in the Introduction to Peter Stallybrass and Allon White, *The Politics and Poetics of Transgression* (London: Methuen, 1986) 1–26. Leah S. Marcus's *The Politics of Mirth* (Chicago: University of Chicago Press) is particularly successful in showing the profound ambivalence of festival activity in early Stuart England, where "festival freedom" was deliberately fostered as an agency of social control, and often interpreted "as a sign of submission to royal power" (7–8).

26. Frye, "The Argument of Comedy," 322–23.

27. See my "'Exeunt with a Dead March': Funeral Pageantry on the Shakespearean Stage," in David Bergeron, ed., *Pageantry in the Shakespearean Theatre* (Athens: University of Georgia Press, 1985) 154–93; see also Nigel Llewellyn, *The Art of Death: Visual Culture in the English Death Rituals* (London: Reaktion Books, 1991), 60–72, 101–8.

28. See for example Bakhtin, *Rabelais*, 61,n.5.

29. For some discussion of the mock-death motif in folk drama see C. L. Barber, *Shakespeare's Festive Comedy: A Study of Dramatic Form and its Relation to Social Custom* (Princeton, N.J.: Princeton University Press, 1959) 36–57; Weimann, *Shakespeare and the Popular Tradition*, 16, 253–54; Bakhtin, *Rabelais*, 354.

30. See Gittings, *Death*, 69, 118.

31. Ibid., 111, 160–61. For further discussion of the dramatic eroticization of death and the concomitant exploitation of the parallels between wedding and obsequy, see Spinrad, *The Summons of Death*, 268–76.

32. Lynda E. Boose, "The Father and the Bride in Shakespeare," *PHLA* 97 (1982): 325–47 (331); Boose's discussion of inverted wedding ritual in the final scene of *Romeo and Juliet* (329) is also pertinent.

33. See Gittings, *Death*, 111–12, 193.

34. See K. M. Lea, *Italian Popular Comedy*, 2 vols. (New York: Russell and Russell, 1962) I, 184ff., and Baskervill, *The English Jig*, 220–23.

35. For comment on the folk origins of the play, see Patricia Binnie's introduction to her revels edition of *The Old Wives Tale* (Manchester and Baltimore: Manchester and Johns Hopkins University Presses, 1980).

36. C. L. Barber identifies Falstaff's revival as a mock resurrection of Mardi Gras, recalling the comic resurrection of St. George in the mummers' plays (*Shakespeare's Festive Comedy*, 205–12). The reappearance of Bottom in *A Midsummer Night's Dream*, identified by Barkan as "a resurrection (even transfiguration)

scene" (*The Gods Made Flesh*, 264), may be seen as another ingenious sophistication of this primitive type.

37. Marston must have thought the coup sufficiently effective to repeat it in *The Malcontent*, where, to the confusion of his enemies, the supposedly dead Malevole unmasks himself at the conclusion of the dance in act V, scene ii, and reassumes his Dukedom. His mock death in scene iii, where he starts up to explain to the astonished Celso that he has been "poisoned with an empty box!" (V.iii.79–80) also owes something to *The Jew of Malta*. Webster (who had been employed to adapt *The Malcontent* for performance at the Globe) also made use of *Antonio and Mellida* in shaping the denouement of *The Devil's Law-Case*, where the disguised Contarino reveals himself to his supposed murderer, Romelio, in the midst of their trial by combat. Webster dispenses with Contarino's funeral, and includes in its place the "dumb pageant" in which Leonora presents Romelio with the monitory spectacle of "two coffins borne by her servants, and two winding sheets stuck with flowers" (V.iv.109,*SD*) – producing from her son a strangely sober-faced burlesque of Bosola's dirge in *The Duchess of Malfi*.

38. In the implication that Antonio's fate may depend simply on the whim of the audience there is a playful anticipation of Suckling's reversible tragedy *Aglaura* (1637/38). The alternative comic ending was purportedly written to relieve the distressed courtly sensibilities of its first audience; but its author took a special witty pleasure in the ingenious generic transformation:

> Tis strange perchance (you'll thinke) that shee, that di'de
> At Christmas, should at Easter be a Bride:
> But 'tis a privilege the Poets have,
> To take the long-since dead out of the grave:
>
> . . . .
>
> They give fresh life, reverse and alter Fate,
> And yet more bold, Almightie-like create.
>   ("Prologue to the Court," 1638, 1–10)

Cited from A. H. Thompson, ed., *The Works of Sir John Suckling* (London: Routlege, 1910).

39. For a discussion of mock funeral in this play see Spinrad, *The Summons of Death*, 223–26.

40. Lee Bliss, " 'Plot Mee No Plots': The Life of Drama and the Drama of Life in *The Knight of the Burning Pestle*," *Modern Language Quarterly* 45 (1984): 3–21 (17). See also Jackson I. Cope, *The Theater and the Dream; form Metaphor to Form in Renaissance Drama* (Baltimore: Johns Hopkins University Press, 1973) 196–210.

41. Calderwood, *Shakespeare and the Denial of Death*, 29.

42. Anne Barton, "*As You Like It* and *Twelfth Night*: Shakespeare's Sense of an Ending," in Malcolm Bradbury and David Palmer, eds., *Shakespearean Comedy*, Stratford-upon-Avon Studies 14 (London: Arnold, 1972), 167–68. See also Harry

Morris's account of the *et in Arcadia ego* motif in *As You Like It*, *Last Things in Shakespeare* (Tallahassee: Florida State University Presses, 1985) 290–94.

43. The elements of folk ritual in the play are given particular stress by Jackson Cope, who sees them as finally overwhelming its coterie satire and self-referential show of formal sophistication (*The Theater and the Dream*, 200)

44. See Bakhtin, *Rabelais*, 78–79.

45. The episode seems to invert such stock routines as that involving Mak the Sheepstealer in *The Second Shepherds' Play*, where, in a travesty of the Christ-child as Lamb of God, a stolen lamb is disguised as a baby. Baskervill in *The Elizabethan Jig* describes a satiric mumming against Bishop Bonner conducted by some Cambridge students in 1562, which partially anticipated Middleton's religious parody: it showed the Bishop " 'carrying a lamb in his hands as if he were eating it as he walked along . . . [together with] the figure of a dog with the Host in his mouth' " (51). The Country Wench's trick with the baby hidden in the basket itself appears in a late jig printed in Baskervill, Thomas Jordan's *The Cheaters Cheated* (1664). Stallybrass and White cite a similar routine from a modern French circus involving a pig (*Transgression*, 59). In Middleton's comedy the episode is linked to the sexual depravity of the major plots via its play on the familiar cant sense of mutton (= prostitute).

46. Cited from A. S. Knowland, ed., *Six Caroline Plays* (London: Oxford University Press, 1962).

47. Notable survivals include Etherege's *The Comical Revenge; Or, Love in a Tub* (1664), where the hero pursues his courtship of the wealthy widow, Mrs. Rich, via a mock funeral and comic resurrection; Buckingham's *The Rehearsal* (1671), which uses the device to illustrate the absurdly old-fashioned dramaturgy of Mr. Bayes; and Richard Steele's underrated comedy, *The Funeral: Or, Grief a-la-Mode* (1701), which in addition to its brilliant satire of the newly established trade of undertaker, includes sentimental resurrections for the heroine, Lady Sharlott, and her benevolent father-in-law, Lord Brumpton.

48. For discussion of Marcade's connection with the *danse macabre*, see René Graziani, "M. Marcadé and the Dance of Death," *Review of English Studies* 37 (1986): 392–95; Graziani cites René du Fail's *Contes D'Eutrapel* (Rennes, 1585), in which the famous Paris Danse Macabre (or "Macchabré") is referred to as "la dance Marcade" after its supposed originator, a "Poète Parisien" called Marcade (394). The play's preoccupation with the idea of ending is suggestively analyzed by Stephen Booth in *'King Lear', 'Macbeth', Indefinition and Tragedy*. Booth remarks that "*Love's Labour's Lost* is so *Lear*-like in its variations on the theme of conclusion that it could . . . be described as a sustained two-hour pun on the word end" (73).

49. Amongst the numerous critics who have noted this function of the play-within-the-play is Leonard Barkan, who relates interestingly to the play's whole use of the motif of metamorphosis (*The Gods Made Flesh: Metamorphosis and the Pursuit of Paganism* [New Haven: Yale University Press, 1986] 270). See also James

Calderwood, who describes the main plot in terms of "a comic movement toward loss of identity in the forests of death" (*Shakespeare and the Denial of Death*, 66); William C. Carroll, *The Metamorphoses of Shakespearean Comedy* (Princeton: Princeton University Press, 1985) 159–66; and Harry Morris, *Last Things in Shakespeare*, 251–52, who relates it to the memento mori motif "[underpropping] the time themes in *A Midsummer Night's Dream*" (248). Morris's study of eschatological motifs in Shakespeare, while predictably concentrating on the tragedies, devotes chapters to *Henry IV* and *As You Like It*, as well as *A Midsummer Night's Dream*.

50. Quoted from Euripedes, *Alcestis and Other Plays*, trans. Philip Vellacott (Harmondsworth: Penguin, 1953) 124; all citations from *Alcestis* are to this edition.

51. Quoted from Elizabeth M. Brennan, ed., *The Devil's Law-Case* (London: Ernest Benn, 1975).

52. For an account of the ending of *All's Well* that stresses its elegiac quality and its incorporation of such standard tragic devices as the *finis coronat opus* formula, see R. S. White, *Let Wonder Seem Familiar: Endings in Shakespeare's Romances* (New Jersey: Humanities Press, 1985) 80ff.

53. Fletcher transfers to Arcite's party the sinisterly dark warrior whom Chaucer had assigned to Palamon: "His hair hangs long behind him, black and shining / Like raven's wings" (IV.ii.83–84)—as though to match the black steed ("owing / Not a hair worth of white" [V.iv.50–51]), ironically a present from Emilia herself, which brings about his death. The same color symbolism controls the violent chiaroscuro of the language in which Theseus and Emilia envisage the combat of the rival friends (V.iii.19–28).

2

Charivari and the Comedy
of Abjection in *Othello*

MICHAEL D. BRISTOL

The abusive language, the noisy clamor under Brabantio's window, and the menace of violence of the opening scene of *Othello* link the improvisations of Iago with the codes of a carnivalesque disturbance or charivari organized in protest over the marriage of the play's central characters. Charivari does not figure as an isolated episode here, however, nor has it been completed when the initial on-stage commotion ends.[1] Despite the sympathy that Othello and Desdemona seem intended to arouse in the audience, the play as a whole is organized around the abjection and violent punishment of its central figures. If certain history plays can be read as rites of "uncrowning" then this play might be read as a rite of "un-marrying."[2] In staging the play as a ceremony of broken nuptials, Iago assumes the function of a popular festive ringleader whose task is the unmaking of a transgressive marriage.[3]

As the action of *Othello* unfolds, the audience is constrained to witness a protracted and diabolical parody of courtship leading to a final, grotesquely distorted consummation in the marriage bed. To stage this action as the carnivalesque thrashing of the play's central characters is, of course, a risky choice for a director to make, since it can easily transform the complex equilibrium of the play from tragedy to *opera buffo*. Although the play is grouped with the tragedies in The First Folio and has always been viewed as properly belonging to this genre, commentators have for a long time recognized the precarious balance of this play at the very boundaries of farce.[4] *Othello* is a text that evidently lends itself very well to parody, burlesque, and caricature.[5] Alteration of the play's formal characteristics, however, would not be the most serious problem encountered in contemplating a carnivalized performance. Since the basis for the charivari is an interracial marriage, many of the strongest effects of this ritual practice would be realized here through use of derisory and stereotypical images of "The Moor."

It is important to remember that Othello does not have to be a black African for this story to work itself out. Racial difference is not absolutely required to motivate any of the fundamental plot moves here. The feelings expressed by the various characters that prompt each of the turns in the action could just as well be tied to some other difference between the two romantic protagonists, and in fact in the concrete unfolding of the story the difference in age seems as important if not more important than the fact of Othello's blackness.[6] The image of racial otherness is thus supplementary to the primary narrative interest here. At the time of the play's earliest performances, the supplementary character of Othello's blackness would be apparent in the white actor's use of black-face makeup to represent the conventionalized form of "The Moor." In the initial context of its reception, it seems unlikely that the play's appeal to invidious stereotypes would have troubled the conscience of anyone in the audience. Since what we now call racial prejudice did not fall outside prevailing social norms in Shakespeare's society, no one in the early audience would have felt sympathy for Othello simply on grounds that he was the victim of a racist society.[7] It is far more probable that "The Moor" would have been seen as comically monstrous. Under these conditions the aspects of charivari and of the comical abjection of the protagonists would have been entirely visible to an audience for whom a racist sensibility was entirely normal.[8]

At the end of the sixteenth century racism was not yet organized as a large-scale system of oppressive social and economic arrangements, but it certainly existed in the form of a distinctive and widely shared *affekt-complex*. Racism in this early, prototypical, form entails a specific physical repugnance for the skin color and other typical features of black Africans. This sensibility is not yet generalized into an abstract or pseudoscientific doctrine of racial inferiority, and for this reason it is relatively difficult to conceive of a principled objection to this "common-sensical" attitude. The physical aversion of the English toward the racial other was rationalized through an elaborate mythology, supported in part by scriptural authority and reinforced by a body of popular narrative.[9] Within this context, the image of the racial other is immediately available as a way of encoding deformity or the monstrous.

For Shakespeare and for his audience the sensibilities of racial difference were for all practical purposes abstract and virtually disembodied,
since the mythology of African racial inferiority was not yet a fully
implemented social practice within the social landscape of early modern
Europe. Even at this early stage, however, it had already occurred to some
people that the racial other was providentially foreordained for the role of
the slave, an idea that was to be fully achieved in the eighteenth- and
nineteenth-century institutions of plantation slavery and in such successor
institutions as segregation and apartheid. The large-scale forms of institutional racism that continue to be a chronic and intractable problem in
modern societies are, of course, already latent within the abstract racial
mythologies of the sixteenth century, since these mythologies enter into
the construction of the social and sexual imaginary both of the dominant
and of the popular culture. In more recent contexts of reception the
farcical and carnivalesque potentiality of the play is usually not allowed to
manifest itself openly. To foreground the elements of charivari and comic
abjection would disclose in threatening and unacceptable ways the text's
ominous relationship to the historical formation of racism as a massive
social fact in contemporary Europe, and in the successor cultures of North
and South America as well as in parts of the African homeland itself.
Against this background the text of *Othello* has to be construed as a highly
significant document in the historical constitution both of racist sensibility
and of racist political ideology.

Othello is a text that severely tests the willingness of an audience to
suspend its disbelief, although the problem is not necessarily that the
situation can degenerate into farce. For many commentators it is not
the potentially ludicrous character of the action, but the exacerbated
pathos of the ending that has provoked discomfort amounting to revulsion with this play. Horace Howard Furness found the play horrible, and
wished Shakespeare had never written it.[10] A more direct form of protest
is described in an anecdote recounted by Stendhal: "L'année dernière
(août 1822), le soldat qui était en faction dans l'intérieur du théâtre de
Baltimore, voyant Othello qui, au cinquième acte de la tragédie de ce
nom, allait tuer Desdemona, s'écria: 'Il ne sera jamais dit qu'en ma prés-
ence un maudit nègre aura tué une femme blanche.' Au même moment le
soldat tire son coup de fusil, et casse un bras a l'acteur qui faisait Othello.
Il ne se passe pas d'années san que les journaux ne rapportent des faits
semblables."[11]

The moral that Stendhal wants to draw from the story of the soldier in

Baltimore is that only someone who is extremely ignorant or stupid—that is, an American—fails to distinguish an actual murder from a dramatic representation of one. In the perhaps more definitive variant of the anecdote, the performance takes place in a barn, and the unlucky actor playing Othello is not merely wounded but killed outright. In this version the soldier's behavior is less a matter of the "perfect illusion" described by Stendhal, but rather a militant defense of white women, notwithstanding the fictional status of Desdemona's "murder." Although the tale about the misguided soldier and the luckless actor in Baltimore may in all likelihood be itself a fiction, the *fantasy* of rescuing Desdemona from the clutches of a murderous black man has probably occurred more than once to various spectators in the history of the play's many performances.[12] Such a wish to prevent the catastrophe, to rewrite the play by disrupting its performance, has its basis in the equivocal ontological and social status of theater as an institutionalized form of representation. The tension and uneasiness provoked by the ambiguous "reality" of every theatrical performance is, however, greatly heightened in the case of *Othello*.[13]

In his ruminations on the ontological status of the representations that confront an audience across the proscenium, Stanley Cavell identifies *Othello* as the exemplary instance of acute theatrical discomfort, amounting to an outright refusal of the mise-en-scène: "What is the state of mind in which we find the events in a theater neither credible nor incredible? The usual joke is about the Southern yokel who rushes to the stage to save Desdemona from the black man. What is the joke?"[14] Cavell's willingness to take this joke seriously suggests that the impulse to rescue Desdemona is not some sort of fantastical aberration, but is in fact a response common to a great many [male?] viewers. Something real is at stake for the audience of *Othello*, even though the actual performance of the play depends on universal acceptance of its status as a fiction:

> At the opening of the play it is fully true that I neither believe nor disbelieve. But I am something, perplexed, anxious. . . . Much later, the warrior asks his wife if she has said her prayers. Do I believe he will go through with it? I know he will; it is a certainty fixed forever; but I hope against hope he will come to his senses; I appeal to him, in silent shouts. Then he puts his hands on her throat. The question is: What, if anything, do I do? I do nothing; that is a certainty fixed forever. And it has its consequences. *Why* do I do nothing? Because they are only pretending? . . . Othello is not pretending.[15]

Does Cavell want to suggest that the Southern yokel is somehow doing the right thing, and that performances of *Othello* should henceforth be disrupted? Such disruption is not actually recommended here, but Cavell is willing to take such a possibility seriously in order to point out that such a violation of theatrical etiquette has substantive moral content. But if this is true, then behaving properly in a theater also has a moral content vis-à-vis the action represented. Cavell does not push the argument to the point of suggesting that suspension of disbelief and acquiescence in the social conventions of performance amounts to complicity in a murder. To the contrary, the disruption of the mise-en-scène would really be a trivial gesture, since the murder will take place no matter what anyone does at any given theatrical performance. For, as Cavell puts it, "Quiet the house, pick up the thread again, and Othello will reappear, as near and as deaf to us as ever. The transcendental and the empirical crossing; possibilities shudder from it."[16] Cavell wants to make himself and his readers accountable for their response as moral agents to what the play discloses, and therefore he must insist on the element of consent and affirmation theater demands from the members of an audience.

Given the painful nature of the story, the history of both the interpretation and the performance of *Othello* have been characterized by a search for anaesthetic explanations that allow the show to go on. These consoling interpretations, and the institutional suspension of disbelief that is the condition of the possibility of any performance, usually work to prevent disruptions of the play in performance. Nevertheless, the history of anguished responses to this play signals a chronic unwillingness amounting at times to outright refusal to participate in the performance of a play as the ritual or quasi-ritual affirmation of certain social practices. *Othello* occupies a problematic situation at the boundary between ritually sanctioned reality and theatrically consensual fiction. Does the play simply depict an inverted ritual of courtship and marriage, or does its performance before an audience that accepts its status as a fiction also invite complicity in a social ritual of comic abjection, humiliation, and victimization? What does it mean, to borrow a usage from French, to "assist" at a performance of this text? At a time when the large-scale social consequences of racist sensibilities had not yet become visible it may well have been easy to accept the formal codes of charivari as the expression of legitimate social norms. In later contexts of reception it is not so easy to accept *Othello* in the form of a derisory ritual of racial persecution, because the social experience of racial difference has become such a massive scandal.

Ritual and theater have a long history of strained and sometimes openly hostile relations. This conflict between authentic hieratic ceremonies and the meretricious performances of actors is, however, deeply equivocal. The manifest antagonism between the liturgical forms of religion and the dramatic spectacles of the theater are continually haunted by the trace of a hidden complicity. The integrity of religious practice depends to a considerable extent, therefore, on the control of access to redemptive media and to places of sanctity within a given community. Such integrity is, of course, of decisive importance for maintaining the collective life of the believers.

For Emile Durkheim, every rite, both in its aspect of ceremonial formality and in the conventional transgression that accompanies it, is a process by which a community reproduces modes of consciousness and social interaction that maintain its solidarity over time.[17] Durkheim argues that ritual depends on a fundamental misrecognition. A community reaffirms its own well-established social hierarchies, experienced by the believers as a manifestation of the sacred. The divine presences evoked in ritual may in fact be nonexistent, but contact with the sacred is not, for that reason, some kind of delusionary fantasy, since the communal life so richly experienced in ritual has a concrete and sensuous actuality that does support and sustain the members of the community.[18] Ritual misrecognition always has some element of objective cogency, no matter how fantastical its overt manifestations may be and no matter how fallacious the interpretations of the participants. Moreover, the "anomie" that appears at the time of the festival is a functional undifferentiation that strengthens the resolution and closure that concludes the rite. Misrecognition is not, therefore, some sort of mistake, but the absolutely necessary condition for the possibility of social continuity. Those responsible for the management of liturgical practice must always ensure that ritual, despite its spectacular accoutrements, is never linked openly to theater. The ontological claims on which ritual depends are not always easy to sustain, for the very good reason that the practical exigencies of any liturgy are not very different from those of a theatrical performance. The distinction between a priest's vestments and an actor's costume is never an easy one to maintain, and this is especially so in a historical setting like Elizabethan and Jacobean England, where some theatrical costumes were in fact expropriated vestments transferred from the altar to the stage.

Contamination of religious authority by illicit contact with theater was a condition that occasioned chronic anxiety during the early modern period, and this anxiety has been examined in a number of recent studies.[19] Stephen Greenblatt's important essay on "Shakespeare and the Exorcists," for example, shows that the scandal of exorcism is precisely its character as a theater that dissembles its own theatricality.[20] The evacuation of religious significance from exorcism, the chastisement of its practitioners, and the instruction of the public in the correct allocation of charismatic and juridical authority are all accomplished by means of a thoroughgoing theatricalization of exorcism. This is done in part by the exposure of various theatrical techniques and special effects used by the exorcists on an unsuspecting audience, and in part by the restaging of the exorcists' performances in a juridical setting. As Greenblatt shows, however, the use of theater as the primary instrument for this evacuation of a vitiated or inauthentic ritual is extremely dangerous. By asserting openly its capacity for dissimulation, theater addresses the element of misrecognition necessary to any liturgical enactment of the sacred. Theater thus has the capacity to theorize all redemptive media and even to make visible the links between ritual, repression, and social contradiction. The strategy of evacuation through the use of a theatrical pedagogy, though carefully focused on specific inauthentic practices, is paradoxically self-condemnatory in the way it foregrounds the element of collective misrecognition on which charismatic and juridical authority depends.

Despite its capacity to theorize ritual practices, theater is not simply the logical "opposite" of liturgy. There are important isomorphisms between these two symbolic protocols. Ritual and theater are based on formalities, on conventional social etiquette, and on the use of selected artifacts or symbols within a well-defined spatial frame.[21] In addition, theater resembles ritual in that it requires its own particular form of "misrecognition" in the form of a temporary and contractual suspension of disbelief. This is, however, a knowledgeable misrecognition that contrasts radically with the unselfconscious and unreflective misrecognition necessary for ritual.[22] Knowledgeable misrecognition is, however, a paradoxical condition, one that can inspire precisely those feelings of acute discomfort experienced, for example, at performances of *Othello*.

The apparent dilemma between a classic sociology of religion that interprets ritual as a necessary though wholly unselfconscious misrecognition and a classic sociology of theatrical reception that interprets performance in light of a contractual misrecognition may be resolved in part by an appeal to Mikhail Bakhtin's category of the carnivalesque. Carnival is an ensemble of practices that seems to be both "full" of positive social content, like a ritual, and "empty" of any substantive social meaning, like a theatrical performance. This theory can help to make sense of the apparently paradoxical notion of a knowledgeable misrecognition that seems to be the condition of the possibility of a theatrical performance. One of the salient features of carnival is its capacity to open up an alternative space for social action.[23] Within the spatio-temporal boundaries of a carnivalesque event, the individual subject is authorized to renegotiate identity and to redefine social position vis-à-vis others. In Bakhtin's reading of Carnival, the social effervescence and the energy generated by a radical popular will to otherness is not simply recaptured for the purposes of the official culture. In its capacity for excess and derangement, carnival empowers the popular element to voice its opposition to the imperatives of official culture.

The theory of Carnival distinguishes between the affirmative character of ritual consciousness as such, and the negative and corrosive force of popular festive form. This distinction corresponds to the distinction between "official culture" — the legitimated stories and interpretations of social hierarchy reproduced in the ideological apparatus — and "popular culture" — the alternative values and interpretations of the social life-world sedimented in the symbolic practices of various excluded or partially excluded groups. Carnival analyzes and dismantles the official order of things, not in a spirit of pure negation, but rather as the expression of an alternative understanding of the social world as an ensemble of material practices.[24] To be sure, this alternative understanding may be profoundly conservative in its thematic content and in its evaluation of various social practices. However, such a conservatism by no means implies a blanket endorsement of all decisions taken by individuals and groups with access to mechanisms of political power, or an indiscriminate willingness to submit to authority. In fact, the knowledge sedimented in the artifacts and the symbolic vocabularies of carnival is a reaffirmation of practical consciousness that may be significantly at odds with the ideologies officially sanctioned by ruling elites.[25] This practical consciousness is best thought of as the outlook of social agents sufficiently knowledgeable to "get on" within the constraints of economic and institutional reality.[26] Such knowledgeability is not always equivalent to the self-understanding of a particular social agent, but is instead sedimented within certain institutional practices, including but not limited to the conventions of theater and of theatergoing.

Bakhtin's view of Carnival is in some sense a development of what appears to be the contrasting position articulated in Durkheim's sociology of religion. It is important to realize, however, that Bakhtin's anthropology preserves the central insight of Durkheim's sociology of religion and of the view that both official ritual and its popular cognates, as moments of greatly intensified social life, tend powerfully toward the reaffirmation of a deeply felt way-of-being-together-in-the-world.[27] The notion of the carnivalesque, however, adds to the sociology of religion an element that helps to account for the possibility of social change, and for the presence of differentiated interests that have to participate in the negotiation of that change. The carnivalesque then would be a mode of authentic cognition, a kind of para-scientific and pre-theoretical understanding of social forms that would disclose whatever is hidden by ritual misrecognition.

The following analysis sketches out a hypothesis that would interpret *Othello* as a carnivalesque text in the Bakhtinian sense. Carnival is operative here as something considerably more than a novel decor for the mise-en-scène, or an alternative thematics for interpretation. The play is read here as the carnivalesque derangement of marriage as a social institution and of the contradictory role of heterosexual desire within that institution. As a serio-comic or carnivalesque masquerade, the play makes visible the normative horizons against which sexual partners must be selected, and the latent social violence that marriage attempts to prevent, often unsuccessfully, from becoming manifest. More specifically, I want to draw attention to the play as an adaptation of the social custom, common throughout early modern Europe, of charivari.[28] This was a practice of noisy festive abuse in which a community enacted its objection to inappropriate marriages and more generally exercised a communal surveillance of sexuality. As Natalie Davis has pointed out, this "community" actually consists of young men, typically unmarried, who represent a social principle of male solidarity that is in some respects deeply hostile to precisely that form of institutionally sanctioned sexuality whose standards they are empowered to oversee.[29]

The relationship of marriage is established through forms of collective representation, ceremonial and public enactments that articulate the private ethos of conjugal existence and mark out the communal responsibilities of the couple to implement and sustain socially approved "relations of reproduction." In the early modern period the ceremonial forms of marriage were accompanied (and opposed) by parodic doubling of the wedding feast in the forms of charivari.[30] This parodic doubling was organized by a carnivalesque wardrobe corresponding to a triad of dramatic agents—

the clown (representing the bridegroom), the transvestite (representing the bride) and the "scourge of marriage," often assigned a suit of black (representing the community of unattached males or "young men").[31] Iago is neither unattached nor young, but part of his success with his various dupes is his ability to present himself as "one of the boys." Iago's misogyny is expressed as the married man's *ressentiment* against marriage, against wives in general, and against his own wife in particular. But this *ressentiment* is only one form of the more diffuse and pervasive mysogyny typically expressed in the charivari. And of course Iago's more sinister function is his ability to encourage a kind of complicity within the audience. In a performance, he makes his perspective the perspective of the text and thus solicits from the audience a participatory endorsement of the action.

The three primary "characters" in charivari each have a normative function in the allocation of marriage partners and in the regulation of sexual behavior. These three figures parody the three persons of the wedding ceremony – groom, bride, and priest. It is the last of these three figures who confers both social and sacred authority on the marriage. The ensemble as a whole, however, is a travesty of the wedding ceremony itself. The counter-festive vocabulary of charivari provides the community with a system of critical resources through which marriage as a social arrangement and as a private form of sexuality may be either negated or reaffirmed.

Charivari features the three primary figures mentioned above, that is a bride, a groom, and a ringleader who may in some instances assist the partners in outwitting parental opposition, but who may also function as a nemesis of erotic desire itself and attempt to disrupt and to destroy the intended bond. In the actual practice of charivari, the married couple themselves are forced to submit to public ridicule and sometimes to violent punishment.[32] In its milder forms, a charivari allows the husband and wife to be represented by parodic doubles who are then symbolically thrashed by the ringleader and his followers. This triad of social agents is common to many of Shakespeare's tragedies of erotic life, and it even appears in the comedies. Hamlet stages "The Murder of Gonzago" partly as a public rebuke to the unseemly marriage of Claudius and Gertrude.[33] This is later escalated to a fantasy of the general abolition of the institution of monogamy, "I say we will have no more marriages." Hamlet's situation expresses the powerful ambivalence of the unattached male toward marriage as the institutional format in which heterosexual desire and its satisfaction are legitimated. His objection to the aberrant and offensive union of mother and uncle is predicated on the idealization of marriage, and in this case on the specific marriage of mother and father. This idealization is, however, accompanied by the fantasy of a general dissolution of the institution of monogamy back into a dispensation of erotic promiscuity and the free circulation of sexual partners. A similar agenda, motivated by a similar ambivalence, is pursued by Don John, in *Much Ado About Nothing,* and by Iachimo, in *Cymbeline.*

The argument I hope to sketch out here requires that readers or viewers of *Othello* efface their response to the existence of Othello, Desdemona, and Iago as individual subjects endowed with personalities and with some mode of autonomous interiorized life. The reason for such selective or willful ignorance of some of the most compelling features of this text is to make visible the determinate theatrical surfaces. To the extent that the surface coding of this play is openly manifested, the analysis presented here will do violence to the existence of the characters in depth. Instead of striving to understand the grandeur and the sublime dignity of the play's hero and heroine, this argument seeks to "stop at the surface" in order to focus attention on the carnivalesque scenario or charivari that governs the dramatic action.

In order to grasp the primary characters of *Othello* at this level of representation it is necessary to withdraw from the position of empathy for the characters as subjects constituted in the way we are constituted, and to seek out an appropriate mode of counter-identification. I believe that the withdrawal of empathy and of identification from the play's main characters is difficult, not least because the experience of individual subjectivity as we have come to know it *is* objectively operative in the text. It has been suggested, in fact, that the pathos of individual subjectivity was actually invented by Shakespeare, or that this experience appears for the first time in the history of Western representation in his plays. A variant of this position would be the view suggested by Brecht and elaborated by Catharine Belsey that a specific array of subject positions characteristic of bourgeois culture was created and elaborated in that great sociocultural laboratory known as Elizabethan Drama.[34] Whether this view is accurate or not, however, there is the more immediate difficulty that we desire, as readers and viewers, to reflect on and to identify with the complex pathos of individual subjectivity as it is represented in Shakespeare's oeuvre. This is especially so, perhaps, for professional readers and viewers, who are likely to have strong interests in the experience of the speaking/writing subject and in the problematic of autonomy and expressive unity. The constella-

tion of interests and goal-values most characteristic of the institutional
processing of literary texts has given rise to an extremely rich critical
discourse on the question of the subject; it is precisely the power and the
vitality of this discourse that makes the withdrawal of empathy from the
characters so difficult. Nevertheless, for these characters to exist as Othello,
Desdemona, and Iago, they have to use the carnivalesque "wardrobe" that
is inscribed within this text, and this wardrobe assigns them the roles of
clown, transvestite, and "scourge of marriage" in a charivari.

The clown is a type of public figure who embodies the "right to be
other," as Bakhtin would have it, since the clown always and everywhere
rejects the categories made available in routine institutional life.[35] The
clown is therefore both criminal and monster, although such alien and
malevolent aspects are more often than not disguised. Etymologically
"clown" is related to "colonus"—a farmer or settler, someone not from
Rome but from the agricultural hinterland. As a rustic or hayseed the
clown's relationship to social reality is best expressed through such contemporary idioms as "He's out of it!," or "He doesn't know where it's at!" In the
drama of the early modern period a clown is often by convention a kind of
country bumpkin, but he is also a "professional outsider" of extremely
flexible social provenance. Bakhtin has stressed the emancipatory capacity
of the clown function, arguing that the clown mask embodies the "right to
be other" or *refus d'identité*. However, there is a pathos of clowning as well,
and the clown mask may represent everything that is socially and sexually
maladroit, credulous, easily victimized. And just as there is a certain
satisfaction in observing an assertive clown get the better of his superiors,
so is there also satisfaction in seeing an inept clown abused and stripped of
his dignity. This abuse or "thrashing" of the doltish outsider provides the
audience with a comedy of abjection, a social genre in which the experience of exclusion and impotence can be displaced onto an even more
helpless caste within society.

To think of Othello as a kind of blackface clown is perhaps distasteful,
although the role must have been written not for a black actor, but with
the idea of black makeup or a false-face of some kind. Othello is a Moor,
but only in quotation marks, and his blackness is not even skin deep but
rather a transitory and superficial theatrical integument. Othello's Moorish
origins are the mark of his exclusion; as a cultural stranger he is, of course,
"out of it" in the most compelling and literal sense. As a foreigner he is
unable to grasp and to make effective use of other Venetian codes of social

and sexual conduct. He is thus a grotesque embodiment of the bridegroom — an exotic, monstrous, and funny substitute who transgresses the norms associated with the idea of a husband.

To link Othello to the theatrical function of a clown is not necessarily to be committed to an interpretation of his character as a fool. Othello's folly, like Othello's nobility and personal grandeur, are specific interpretations of the character's motivation and of his competence to actualize those motives. The argument here, however, is that the role of Othello is already formatted in terms of the abject-clown function and that any interpretation of the character's "nature" therefore has to be achieved within that format. The eloquence of Othello's language and the magnanimity of his character may in fact intensify the grotesque element here. His poetic self-articulation is not so much the *expression* of a self-possessed subject but is instead a form of discursive indecorum that strains against the social meanings objectified in Othello's counter-festive *persona*. Stephen Greenblatt identifies the joke here as one of the "master plots of comedy," in which a beautiful young woman outwits an "old and outlandish" husband.[36] Greenblatt reminds us here that Othello is functionally equivalent to the gull or butt of an abusive comic action, but he passes over the most salient feature of Othello's outlandishness, which is actualized in the blackface makeup essential to the depiction of this character. To present Othello in blackface, as opposed to presenting him just as a black man, would confront the audience with a comic spectacle of abjection rather than with the grand opera of misdirected passion. Such a comedy of abjection has not found much welcome in the history of the play's reception.

The original audience of this play in Jacobean England may have had relatively little inhibition in its expression of invidious racial sentiments, and so might have seen the derisory implications of the situation more easily. During the nineteenth century, when institutional racism was naturalized by recourse to a "scientific" discourse on racial difference, the problem of Othello's outlandishness and the unsympathetic laughter it might evoke is "solved" by making him a Caucasoid Moor, instead of a "Veritable Negro."[37] Without such a fine discrimination, a performance of *Othello* would have been not so much tragic as simply unbearable, part farce and part lynch mob. In the present social climate, when racism, though still very widespread, has been officially anathematized, the possibility of a blackface Othello would still be an embarrassment and a scandal, though presumably for a different set of reasons. Either way, the element of burlesque inscribed in this text is clearly too destabilizing to escape repression.

If Othello can be recognized as an abject clown in a charivari, then the scenario of such a charivari would require a transvestite to play the part of the wife. In the context of popular culture in the early modern period, female disguise and female impersonation were common to charivari and to a variety of other festive observances.[38] This practice was, among other things, the expression of a widespread "fear" of women as both the embodiment of and the provocation to social transgression. Within the pervasive misogyny of the early modern period, women and their desires seemed to project the threat of a radical social undifferentiation.[39] The young men and boys who appeared in female dress at the time of Carnival seem to have been engaged in "putting women in their place" through an exaggerated pantomime of everything feminine. And yet this very practice required the emphatic foregrounding of the artifice required for any stable coding of gender difference. Was this festive transvestism legitimated by means of a general misrecognition of the social constitution of gender? Or did the participants understand at some level that the association of social badness with women was nothing more than a patriarchal social fiction that could only be sustained in and through continuous ritual affirmation?

Female impersonation is, of course, one of the distinctive and extremely salient features of Elizabethan and Jacobean dramaturgy, and yet surprisingly little is known of how this mode of representation actually worked.[40] The practice of using boy actors to play the parts of women is a derivative of the more diffuse social practice of female impersonation in the popular festive milieu. Were the boy actors in Shakespeare's company engaging in a conventional form of ridicule of the feminine? Or were they engaged in a general parody of the artifice of gender coding itself? A transvestite presents the category of woman in quotation marks, and reveals that both "man" and "woman" are socially produced categories. In the drama of Shakespeare and his contemporaries, gender is at times an extremely mobile and shifting phenomenon without any solid anchor in sexual identity. To a considerable degree gender is a "flag of convenience" prompted by contingent social circumstances, and at times gender identity is negotiated with considerable grace and dexterity. The convention of the actor "boying" the woman's part is thus doubly parodic, a campy put down of femininity and, at another level, a way to theorize the social misrecognition on which all gender allocations depend.

Desdemona's "femininity" is bracketed by the theatrical "boying" of her/his part. This renders her/his sexuality as a kind of sustained gestural equivocation and this corresponds to the exaggerated and equivocal rhetorical aspect of Desdemona's self-presentation. As Desdemona puts it, "I saw Othello's visage in his mind"; in other words, her initial attraction to him was not provoked by his physical appearance. The play thus stipulates that Desdemona herself accepts the social prohibition against miscegenation as the normative horizon within which she must act. On the face of it she cannot be physically attracted to Othello, and critics have usually celebrated this as the sign of her ability to transcend the limited horizons of her acculturation. These interpretations thus accept the premise of Othello as physically undesirable and insinuate that Desdemona's faith is predicated on her blindness to the highly visible "monstrosity" of her "husband." In other words, her love is a misrecognition of her husband's manifestly undesirable qualities. Or is it a misrecognition of her own socially prohibited desire? Stanley Cavell interprets her lines as meaning that she saw his appearance in the way that he saw it, that she is able to enter into and to share Othello's self-acceptance and self-possession.[41] On this view Desdemona is a kind of idealization of the social category of "wife," who can adopt the husband's own narrative fiction of self as her own imaginary object. Desdemona is thus both a fantasy of a sexually desirable woman and a fantasy of absolute sexual compliance. This figure of unconditional erotic submission is the obverse of the rebellious woman, or shrew, but, as the play shows us, this is also a socially prohibited *metier* for a woman. In fact, as Stephen Greenblatt has shown in his very influential essay, the idea that Desdemona might feel an ardent sexual desire for him makes Othello perceive Iago's insinuations of infidelity as plausible and even probable.[42] The masculine fantasy projected in the figure of Desdemona cannot recognize itself as the object of another's desire.

Like all of Shakespeare's woman characters, Desdemona is an impossible sexual object, a female artifact created by a male imagination and objectified in a boy actor's body. This is, in its own way, just as artificial and as grotesque a theatrical manifestation as the blackface Othello who stands in for the category of the husband. What is distinctive about Desdemona is the way she embodies the category of an "ideal wife" in its full contradictoriness. She has been described as chaste or even as still a virgin and also as sexually aggressive, even though very little unambiguous textual support for either of these readings actually exists.[43] Her elopement, with a Moor no less, signals more unequivocally than a properly arranged

marriage ever could that the biblical injunction to leave mother and father
has been fulfilled. It is probably even harder to accept the idea of
Desdemona as part of a comedy of abjection than it is to accept Othello in
such a context. It is, however, only in such a theatrical context that the
hyperbolic and exacerbated misrecognition on which marriage is founded
can be theorized.

At the level of surface representation then, the play enacts a marriage
between two complementary symbols of the erotic grotesque. This is a
marriage between what is conventionally thought to be hideous and
repellent with what is most beautiful and desirable. The incongruity of
this match is objectified in the theatrical hyper-embodiment of the primary categories of man and woman or husband and wife. It is not known
to what extent Elizabethan and Jacobean theater practice deliberately
foregrounded its own artifice. However, the symbolic practice of grotesque
hyper-embodiment was well known in popular festive forms such as
charivari. The theatrical coding of gender in the early modern period is
thus still contaminated by the residue of these forms of social representation.

The marriage of grotesque opposites is no more a private affair or erotic
dyad than a real marriage. Marriage in the early modern period, among
many important social classes, was primarily a dynastic or economic alliance negotiated by a third party who represented the complex of social
sanctions in which the heterosexual couple was inscribed.[44] The elopement of Desdemona and Othello, as well as their reliance on Cassio as a
broker or clandestine go-between, already signals their deliberate intention to evade and thwart the will of family. To the extent that readers or
viewers are conditioned by the normative horizons that interpret heterosexual love as mutual sexual initiative and the transcendence of all social
obstacles, this elopement will be read as a romantic confirmation of the
spiritual and disinterested character of their love.[45] However, it can also be
construed as a flagrant sexual and social blunder. Private heterosexual
felicity of the kind sought by Othello and Desdemona attracts the evil eye
of erotic nemesis.[46]

The figure of erotic nemesis and the necessary third party to this union
is Othello's faithful lieutenant, Iago. It is Iago's task to show both his
Captain and his audience just how defenseless the heterosexual couple is
against the resources of sexual surveillance. The romantic lovers, represented
here through a series of grotesque distortions, do not enjoy an erotic
autonomy, though such erotic autonomy is a misrecognition of the socially
inscribed character of "private" sexuality. Iago's abusive and derisory

characterizations of the couple, together with his debasement of their sexuality are a type of social commentary on the nature of erotic romance. The notion of mutual and autonomous self-selection of partners is impugned as a kind of mutual delusion that can only appear under the sign of monstrosity. In other words the romantic couple can only "know" that their union is based on mutual love *and on nothing else* when they have "transcended" or violated the social codes and prohibitions that determine the allocation of sexual partners.

Iago is a Bakhtinian "agelast," that is, one who does not laugh. He is, of course, very witty, but his aim is always to provoke a degrading laughter at the follies of others rather than to enjoy the social experience of laughter *with* others. He is a demythologizer whose function is to reduce all expressivity to the minimalism of the quid pro quo. The process represented here is the reduction of quality to quantity, a radical undifferentiation of persons, predicated on a strictly mechanistic, universalized calculus of desire. Characters identified with this persona appear throughout Shakespeare's oeuvre, usually in the guise of a nemesis of hypocrisy and dissimulation. Hamlet's "I know not seems" and Don John's "it cannot be denied I am a plain dealing villain" are important variants of a social/ cognitive process that proclaims itself to be a critique of equivocation and the will to deception. It is ironic, of course, that these claims of honesty and plain dealing are so often made in the interests of malicious dissimulation. What appears to be consistent, however, in all the variants of this character-type, is the disavowal of erotic attachment and the contemptuous manipulation of the erotic imagination.

The supposedly "unmotivated" malice enacted by this figure is puzzling, I believe, only when read individualistically. Is Iago envious of the pleasure Othello enjoys with Desdemona, or is he jealous of Othello's sexual enjoyment of Emilia? Of course, both of these ideas are purely conjectural hypotheses that have no apparent bearing on Iago's actions. In any case, there is no sustained commitment to either of these ideas, as numerous commentators have pointed out. Nevertheless, there is an important clue to understanding Iago as a social agent in these transitory ruminations. Iago seems to understand that the complex of envy and jealousy is not an aberration within the socially distributed erotic economy, but is rather the fundamental precondition of desire itself. Erotic desire is not founded in a qualitative economy or in a rational market, but rather in a mimetic and histrionic dispensation that Iago projects as the envy-jealousy system.[47] In this system men are the social agents, and women the objects of exchange.

Iago's actions are thus socially motivated by a diffuse and pervasive misogyny that slides between fantasies of the complete abjection of all women and fantasies of an exclusively masculine world.

Iago's success in achieving these fantasies is made manifest in the unbearably hideous tableau of the play's final scene. If the play as a whole is to be read as a ritual of unmarrying, then this ending is the monstrous equivalent of a sexual consummation. What makes the play unendurable would be the suspicion that this climax expresses all too accurately an element present in the structure of every marriage. This is an exemplary action in which the ideal of companionate marriage as a socially sanctioned erotic union is dissolved back into the chronic violence of the envy-jealousy system. Iago theorizes erotic desire, and thus marriage, primarily by a technique of emptying out Othello's character, so that nothing is left at the end except the pathetic theatrical integument, the madly deluded and murderous blackface clown. Desdemona, the perfect wife, remains perfectly submissive to the end. And Iago, with his theoretical or pedagogical tasks completed, accepts in silence his allocation to the function of sacrificial victim and is sent off to face unnamed "brave punishments."

Finita la commedia. What does it mean to accept the mise-en-scène of this play? And what does it mean to *know* that we wish it could be otherwise? To the extent that we want to see a man and a woman defying social conventions in order to fulfill mutual erotic initiatives, the play will appear as a thwarted comedy and our response will be dominated by its pathos. But the play also shows us what such mutual erotic initiatives look like from the outside, as a comedy of abjection or charivari. The best commentators on this play have recognized the degree to which it prompts a desire to prevent the impending debacle and the sense in which it is itself a kind of theatrical punishment for the observers.[48] This helpless and agonized refusal of the mise-en-scène here should suggest something about the corrosive effect on socially inscribed rituals of a radical or "cruel" theatricality.

The idea of theatrical cruelty is linked to the radical aesthetics of Antonin Artaud. However, the English term "cruelty" fails to capture an important inflection that runs through all of Artaud's discussions of theater. The concept is derived from words that mean "raw" or "un-processed." In French "cruauté" expresses with even greater candor this relationship with "le cru" and its opposition to "le cuit." Cruelty here has the sense of something uncooked, or something prior to the process of a conventional social transformation or adoption into the category of the meaningful.[49]

Othello, perhaps more than any other Shakespeare play, raises fundamental questions about the institutional position and the aesthetic character of Shakespearean dramaturgy. Is Shakespeare raw—or is he cooked? Is it possible that our present institutional protocol for interpreting his work is a way of "cooking" the "raw" material to make it more palatable, more fit for consumption?

The history of the reception of *Othello* is the history of attempts to articulate ideologically correct, that is, palatable interpretations. By screening off the comedy of abjection it is possible to engage more affirmatively with the play's romantic liebestod. Within these strategies, critics may find an abundance of meanings for the tragic dimension of the play. In this orientation the semantic fullness of the text is suggested as a kind of aesthetic compensation for the cruelty of its final scenes. Rosalie Colie, for example, summarizes her interpretation with an account of the play's edifying power: "In criticizing the artificiality he at the same time exploits in his play, Shakespeare manages in *Othello* to reassess and to reanimate the moral system and the psychological truths at the core of the literary love-tradition, to reveal its problematics and to reaffirm in a fresh and momentous context the beauty of its impossible ideals."[50] This is recognizably the language of the ritual misrecognition of what the play as a comedy of abjection is capable of theorizing. The fullness of the play, of course, is what makes it possible for viewers and readers to participate, however unwillingly, in the charivari, or ritual victimization of the imaginary heterosexual couple here represented. Such consensual participation is morally disquieting in the way it appears to solicit at least passive consent to violence against women and against outsiders, but at least we are not howling with unsympathetic laughter at their suffering and humiliation.

Colie's description of the play's semantic fullness is based in part on her concept of "un-metaphoring"—that is, the literalization of a metaphorical relationship or conventional figuration. This is a moderate version of the notion of theatrical cruelty or the unmaking of convention that does not radically threaten existing social norms. In other words, the fate of Desdemona and Othello, or Romeo and Juliet, is a cautionary fable about what happens if a system of conventional figurations of desire is taken literally. But the more powerful "un-metaphoring" of this play is related not to its fullness as a tragedy, but to its emptiness as a comedy of abjection. The violent interposing of the charivari here would indeed make visible the *political* choice between an aestheticized ritual affirmation and a genuine refusal of the sexual mise-en-scène or relations of reproduction in which this text is inscribed.

NOTES

1. Francois Laroque, "An Archaeology of the Dramatic Text: *Othello* and Popular Traditions," *Cahiers élisabéthains* 32 (1987), 13–35. See also T. G. A. Nelson and Charles Haines, "Othello's Unconsummated Marriage," *Essays in Criticism* 33 (1981), 5–7.

2. Carol Neely, *Broken Nuptials in Shakespeare's Plays* (New Haven: Yale University Press, 1985).

3. Michael Neill, "Unproper Beds: Race, Adultery and the Hideous in *Othello,*" *Shakespeare Quarterly* 40 (1989), 383–413.

4. Thomas Rymer, *A Short View of Tragedy,* in *Shakespeare: The Critical Heritage,* 6 vols., ed. Brian Vickers (London: Routledge and Kegan Paul, 1974), 2, 27. See also Susan Snyder, *The Comic Matrix of Shakespeare's Tragedies* (Princeton: Princeton University Press, 1979), 70–74.

5. Lawrence Levine, *Highbrow/Lowbrow* (Cambridge: Harvard University Press, 1988), 14–20; Neill, "Unproper Beds," 391–93.

6. Janet Stavropoulos, "Love and Age in *Othello,*" *Shakespeare Studies* 19 (1987), 125–41.

7. G. K. Hunter, "Elizabethans and Foreigners," *Shakespeare Survey* 17 (1964), 37–52; and "*Othello* and Colour Prejudice," *Proceedings of the British Academy* 53 (1967), 139–63. See also Eldred Jones, *Othello's Countrymen: The African in English Renaissance Drama* (Oxford: Oxford University Press, 1965); Martin Orkin, "*Othello* and the Plain Face of Racism," *Shakespeare Quarterly* 38 (1987), 166–88.

8. Karen Newman, "'And Wash the Ethiop white': Femininity and the Monstrous in *Othello,*" in *Shakespeare Reproduced: The Text in History and Ideology,* ed. Jean Howard and Marion O'Connor (London: Methuen, 1987), 143–61.

9. Winthrop Jordan, *White Over Black* (Chapel Hill: University of North Carolina Press, 1968); Elliot H. Tokson, *The Popular Image of the Black Man in English Drama 1550–1688* (Boston: G. K. Hall, 1982).

10. *The Letters of Horace Howard Furness,* ed. Horace Howard Furness Jayne, 2 vols. (Boston: Houghton Mifflin, 1922), 2:149, 156.

11. Stendhal, *Racine et Shakespeare,* ed. Pierre Martino, *Oeuvres Completes,* 37 vols. 18 (Paris: Edouard Champion, 1925): "Last year (August of 1822), the soldier standing guard at the interior of the theatre in Baltimore, seeing Othello who, in the fifth act of the tragedy of that name, was going to kill Desdemona, cried out 'It will never be said that in my presence a damned black would kill a white woman.' At that moment the soldier fired his gun, and broke the arm of the actor who played Othello." [Author's translation.]

12. A concrete example of the enactment of such a fantasy might be the rescue

of Elsie Stoneman by the Ku Klux Klan in D. W. Griffith's *Birth of a Nation*. See Michael Rogin, "The Sword became a Flashing Vision," *Representations* 9 (1985), 161ff.

13. Stephen Greenblatt, "Martial Law in the Land of Cokaigne," in *Shakespearean Negotiations: The Circulation of Social Energy in Renaissance England* (Berkeley: University of California Press, 1988), 133–34.

14. Stanley Cavell, *Disowning Knowledge in Six Plays of Shakespeare* (Cambridge, Mass.: Cambridge University Press, 1987), 98ff.

15. Cavell, *Disowning Knowledge*, 100.

16. Ibid., 101.

17. Emile Durkheim, *The Elementary Forms of Religious Life*, trans. J. Swain (New York: The Free Press, 1967), 39, 57; 463–74.

18. Anthony Giddens, *The Constitution of Society: Outline of the Theory of Structuration* (Cambridge, Mass.: The Polity Press, 1986), 169–74. See also Giddens, *Durkheim* (London: Fontana Press, 1978), and Dominick La Capra, *Emile Durkheim: Sociologist and Philosopher* (Chicago: University of Chicago Press, 1985).

19. Jonas Barish, *The Antitheatrical Prejudice* (Berkeley: University of California Press, 1981); O. B. Hardison, *Christian Rite and Christian Drama in the Middle Ages: Essays in the Origin and Early History of Modern Drama* (Baltimore: Johns Hopkins University Press, 1965); Stephen Mullaney, *The Place of the Stage: License, Play and Power in Renaissance England* (Chicago: University of Chicago Press, 1988); Richard Schechner, *Performance Theory* [revised and expanded edition] (New York: Routledge, 1988); Victor Turner, *From Ritual to Theatre: The Human Seriousness of Play* (New York: Performing Arts Journal Publications, 1982).

20. Stephen Greenblatt, "Shakespeare and the Exorcists," in *Shakespearean Negotiations: The Circulation of Social Energy in Renaissance England* (Berkeley: University of California Press, 1988), 94–128.

21. Erving Goffman, *Frame Analysis: An Essay on the Organization of Experience* (Cambridge: Harvard University Press, 1974).

22. Greenblatt, "Exorcists," 106.

23. Mikhail Bakhtin, *Rabelais and his World*, trans. Hélène Iswolsky (Cambridge: MIT Press, 1968), 145–96, *passim*; see also his *The Dialogic Imagination*, trans. Caryl Emerson and Michael Holquist (Austin: University of Texas Press, 1983), 167–224; and Claude Gaignebet, *Le Carnaval: Essais de mythologie populaire* (Paris: Payot, 1974).

24. See the discussion of "The Texts of Carnival" in my *Carnival and Theatre: Plebeian Culture and the Structure of Authority in Renaissance England* (London: Methuen, 1985), 59–111.

25. See for example Emmanuel Le Roy Ladurie, *Carnival in Romans*, trans. Mary Feeney (New York: G. Braziller, 1979).

26. Giddens, *The Constitution of Society*, 3–4, *passim*.

27. Bristol, *Carnival and Theater*, 26–59.

28. Jacques Le Goff and Jean-Claude Schmitt, eds., *Le Charivari: Actes de la table ronde organisee a Paris 925–27 avril 1977 par l'Ecole des Hautes Etudes en Sciences Sociales et le Centre National de la Recherche Scientifique* (Paris: Mouton, 1977); E. P. Thompson, "Rough Music: Le Charivari Anglais," *Annales: Economies, Sociétes, Civilizations* 27 (1972), 285–312; Henri Rey-Flaud, *Le Charivari: Les rituels fondamentaux de la sexualite* (Paris: Payot, 1985); David Underdowne, *Revel, Riot, and Rebellion: Popular Politics and Culture in England 1603–1660* (Oxford: Clarendon Press, 1985), 99–103.

29. Natalie Davis, "The Reasons of Misrule: Youth Groups and Charivaris in Sixteenth Century France," *Past and Present* 50 (1981), 49–75. On the topic of "male solidarity" see Eve Kosofsky Sedgewick, *Between Men: English Literature and Homosocial Desire* (New York: Columbia University Press, 1985).

30. See Violet Alford, "Rough Music or Charivari," *Folklore* 70 (1959), 505–18; Nicole Belmont, "Fonction de la derision et symbolisme du bruit dans le charivari"; Natalie Z. Davis, "Charivari, honneur et communaute a Lyon et a Geneve au XVIIe siecle"; Martine Grinberg, "Charivaris au Moyen age et a la Renaissance. Condamnation des remariages ou rites d'inversion du temps?," all in LeGoff and Schmitt, *op cit.* See also Michael D. Bristol, "Wedding Feast and Charivari," in *Carnival and Theater*, 162–79.

31. For the importance of "youth groups" and of unmarried men see Davis, "The Reasons of Misrule."

32. Martin Ingram, "Le Charivari dans l'Angleterre du XVIe et du VXIIe siecle. Apercu historique"; Robert Muchembled, "Des conduites de bruit au spectacle des processions. Mutations mentales et declin des fetes populaires dans le Nord de la France," both in LeGoff and Schmitt, *op. cit.*

33. Davis, "The Reasons of Misrule," 75.

34. Catherine Belsey, *The Subject of Tragedy* (London: Methuen, 1985); Bertolt Brecht, *The Messingkauf Dialogues*, trans. John Willett (London: Eyre Methuen 1965).

35. Bakhtin, *Dialogic Imagination*, 158–67.

36. Stephen Greenblatt, *Renaissance Self-Fashioning: From More to Shakespeare* (Chicago: University of Chicago Press, 1981), 234.

37. Newman, "'And Wash the Ethiop white'," 144.

38. Natalie Z. Davis, "'Women on Top': Symbolic Sexual Inversion and Political Disorder in Early Modern Europe," in *The Reversible World: Symbolic Inversion in Art and Society*, ed. Barbara Babcock (Ithaca: Cornell University Press), 147–90.

39. Linda Woodbridge, *Women and the English Renaissance: Literature and the Nature of Womankind, 1540–1620.* (Urbana: University of Illinois Press, 1984).

40. Phyllis Rackin, "Androgyny, Mimesis, and the Marriage of the Boy Heroine on the English Renaissance Stage," *PMLA* 102 (1987), 29–42.

41. Cavell, *Disowning Knowledge*, 129ff.

42. Greenblatt, *Renaissance Self-Fashioning*, 237–52.

43. Arguments for a chaste or virginal Desdemona are found in Nelson and

Haines, "Othello's Unconsummated Marriage," 1–18, as well as in Pierre Janton, "Othello's Weak Function," *Cahiers élisabéthains* 34 (1988), 79–82. The idea of a sexually aggressive Desdemona is to be found in Greenblatt, *Renaissance Self-Fashioning*, 237ff., and in Stephen Booth, "The Best *Othello* I ever saw," *Shakespeare Quarterly* 40 (1989), 332–36.

44. On the "triangular" character of erotic desire see René Girard, *Deceit, Desire, and the Novel*, trans. Yvonne Freccero (Baltimore: Johns Hopkins University Press, 1965), 1–52.

45. Niklas Luhmann, *Love as Passion: The Codification of Intimacy*, trans. Jeremy L. Gaines and Doris Jones (Cambridge: Harvard University Press, 1986).

46. Paul Dumouchel and Jean Pierre Dupuy, *L'Enfer des choses: René Girard et la logique de l'économie* (Paris: Editions de Seuil, 1979). See Also Tobin Siebers, *The Mirror of Medusa* (Berkeley: University of California Press, 1983).

47. Jean-Christophe Agnew, *Worlds Apart: The Market and the Theater in Anglo-American Thought, 1550–1750* (Cambridge: Cambridge University Press, 1986), 6–7, *passim*.

48. In addition to Cavell and Greenblatt, see, for example, Kenneth Burke, "Othello: An Essay to Illustrate a Method," *The Hudson Review* 4 (1951), 165–203; Carol Thomas Neely, "Women and Men in *Othello*: 'What should such a fool / Do with so Good a Woman?' " in *The Woman's Part: Feminist Criticism of Shakespeare*, ed. Carolyn S. Lenz, Gayle Greene, and Carol Thomas Neely (Urbana: University of Illinois Press, 1980), 211–39; Patricia Parker, "Shakespeare and rhetoric: 'dilation' and 'delation' in *Othello*," in *Shakespeare and the Question of Theory*, ed. Patricia Parker and Geoffrey Hartman (London: Methuen, 1985); Edward Snow, "Sexual Anxiety and the Male Order of Things in *Othello*," *English Literary Renaissance* 10 (1980), 384–412; 48. Peter Stallybrass, "Patriarchal Territories: The Body Enclosed," in *Rewriting the Renaissance: The Discourses of Sexual Difference in Early Modern Europe*, ed. Margaret W. Ferguson, Maureen Quilligan, and Nancy Vickers (Chicago: University of Chicago Press, 1986).

49. Antonin Artaud, *The Theater and its Double*, trans. by Mary Caroline Richards (New York: Grove Press, 1958), 42, *passim*.

50. Rosalie Colie, *Shakespeare's Living Art* (Princeton: Princeton University Press, 1974), 167. For other recuperative readings within quite different normative horizons see, for example, Karen Newman, " 'And Wash the Ethiop white,' " 143–61; C. L. Barber, and Richard P. Wheeler, *The Whole Journey: Shakespeare's Power of Development* (Berkeley, University of California Press, 1986), 272–81; Robert Heilman, *Magic in the Web* (Lexington: University of Kentucky Press, 1956); Norman Holland, *The Shakespearean Imagination: A Critical Introduction* (Bloomington: University of Indiana Press, 1964), 197–216; Arthur Kirsch, *Shakespeare and the Experience of Love* (Cambridge: Cambridge University Press, 1981), 10–39.

3

Riddling as Ritual Remedy in *Measure for Measure*

PHYLLIS GORFAIN

The possible ritual significance of an exchange between Pompey and Abhorson in act IV, scene ii of *Measure for Measure* has become obscured over time through a loss of cultural understanding and concomitant editorial intervention.[1] Edward Capell first changed the Folio text in his 1767 edition of Shakespeare's complete works, and, until the very recent Oxford Press Complete Works, all modern editors have unswervingly followed his lead in revising what has become a very difficult passage between the hangman and the bawd.[2] Here is the situation in the Folio: Pompey has just been brought to the prison and offered a bargain by the Provost. His sentence will be mediated and he can escape whipping when he is released if he will aid the hangman. Pompey replies he will "bee glad to receive some instruction from my fellow partner," and the Provost calls in Abhorson, who immediately objects that the bawd "will discredit our mysterie."[3] The Provost refuses to acknowledge much difference between a bawd and a hangman and then leaves the two men alone to work out their contract and Pompey's "instruction." Designated as a clown by the speech prefixes in the Folio, Pompey expresses comic confusion about the hangman's trade as a "Misterie":

> *Clo.* Painting Sir, I have heard say, is a Misterie; and your Whores sir, being members of my occupation, using painting, do prove my Occupation, a Misterie: but what Misterie should be in hanging, if I should be hang'd, I cannot imagine.
>
> *Abh.* Sir, it is a Misterie.

Clo.   Proofe.

Abh.   Everie true mans apparreil fits your Theefe.

Clo.   If it be too little for your theefe, your true man thinkes
it bigge enough. If it bee too bigge for your Theefe, your
Theefe thinkes it little enough: So everie true mans appar-
rell fits your Theefe.

Pro.   Are you agreed?

Clo.   Sir, I will serve him. . . .

(Folio Facsimile, PTL 1889–1902)

The crux arises when Pompey demands "proofe" that the hangman's
occupation is an esoteric craft, and Abhorson, in a stunning non sequitur,
simply claims that a true man's apparel fits a thief. Then, even more
illogically, Pompey explicates the statement only to have the Provost
return and ask if they are agreed, which Pompey – the applicant – informs
him they are, and Abhorson no longer objects.

To make sense of this seemingly nonsensical exchange, Capell elimi-
nated it as an exchange; he removed Pompey's explication and transformed
the dialogue into a monologue by Abhorson. For over two hundred years,
editors have therefore presented us with this passage:

Abhor.   Sir, it is a mystery.

Pom.   Proof?[4]

Abhor.   Every true man's apparel fits your thief. It if be too
little for your thief, your true man thinks it big enough.
If it be too big for your thief, your thief thinks it little
enough. So every true man's apparel fits your thief.

(IV.ii.34–45)[5]

The problem is that such rewriting does not solve the problem. The
passage still makes no dramatic sense. Even if editors make the shared
discussion into a logical monologue, Abhorson's rejoinder remains irrelevant to the issue at hand. So editors, in addition to the revision of
speakers, may add a footnote to explain that hangmen customarily confis-
cated the clothing of the executed.[6] But this historical information does
not account for the *action;* what is Abhorson doing in making this sudden
claim? To make logical sense of the speech act, editors simply make
Pompey's lines, which seem to explicate Abhorson's claim, into a continua-

tion of Abhorson's speech rather than a separate utterance. In trying to explain editorial practice, a contemporary distinguished editor of Shakespeare suggested to me that Capell may have noticed that the last sentence of Pompey's speech begins with a logical conjunction, "So," and it reiterates Abhorson's initial statement; this rhetorical conclusion indicates the speech is a unified syllogism and that a mistake has occurred in the Folio speech attribution.[7] By awarding Pompey's entire speech to Abhorson, editors give Abhorson, who is otherwise characteristically laconic, a mini-lecture while they silence the more characteristically witty trickster Pompey. The editorial working assumption has been, however, more technical than theatrical, more bibliographic than experimental. The editors propose their changes on the assumption that the passage is a muddle and that the Folio must be in error through a mistake in "transmission." Editors believe they are obliged to straighten out—by rewriting the Folio text—what they take as an apparent bungle in the printing process.[8]

But Gary Taylor has pointed out how unlikely a transmission error is when given this kind of speech prefix context. His research and that of other bibliographers has shown that it is far more likely that a speech-heading will be deleted than interpolated in the transmission process, and that the source of most misattributions—a vocative in the text being read as a speech heading by a printer—seems impossible in this passage.[9] Restoring the Folio passage then resists the inertia of accepted editorial practice and its justifications; as a result we can investigate the Folio passage and question the contribution it makes to the larger structure of the play. Such a strategy enables critics and acting companies to discover a meaningful stage action in this confusing passage. While editors defend making the dialogue into a single speech for several reasons—they find a similarity of subject matter in the two utterances and, conversely, they find no obvious motivation for Pompey's explanation—they place a higher value on creating a logical single speech than on the dramatic value of asking what possible action could be taking place which might make sense in terms of theme, plot, and characters. In this essay, I want to explore such questions, which can be opened up by provisionally accepting the Folio text.

Thinking in dramatic terms, we now can approach the restored passage with questions about the characters and their more typical styles. We inquire into motives and consequences. Given the passage as rewritten by the editors, we must ask what would motivate the laconic Abhorson to lecture Pompey about apparel in order to satisfy the tapster's challenge. We can ask of the Folio, why does the trickster Pompey supply a paradoxical exegesis for this puzzling statement made by the cryptic Abhorson? More to the point, what happens as a result? The Provost returns and asks if the two are agreed, and Pompey, ever impudent and quick to reply, provides the affirmative. Why would the little sermon created for Abhorson by the editors lead to that reply? In the Folio, this reply might make sense because the passage is not a monologue, but an exchange. When an exchange results in an agreement, it would seem to be a symbolic action. That is, a coordinated dialogue by both Abhorson and Pompey leads to a conclusion that they are "agreed," as if their collaboration in executing a syllogism through dialogue were an analogic, magical, performative speech act; their behavior serves as a model insuring their future collaboration in executing malefactors. Suddenly we see that the passage, retained as a dialogue, might be taken as an action, as a particular genre: a riddling dialogue that functions as an initiation rite. The seeming irrelevance of the subject matter now can be performed as meaningful when the entire interchange performs a switch into a different key, into another framework of reference.

Folkloristic analysis can, moreover, help us recover the cultural practices in which we can understand the exchange as a riddling dialogue. This leads to a theatrical solution in which the puzzling dialogue will be performed as a deliberate puzzle; the riddle becomes a device within a parodic ritual of initiation into a specialized craft. Indeed, such initiations were conducted for apprentices by guilds and other "mysteries," and in universities and schools for entering students by older cohorts. Such initiatory rites were also travestied by thieves and rogues, as represented in popular prose literature on the Elizabethan world of crime.[10] Returning to the Folio enables contemporary acting companies to search for clear stage actions that will bring this Elizabethan underworld situation to life on stage. Using the modern editions leads directors to invent distracting stage business to mask the nonsensical passage, but once a director and actors realize that the Folio lines can be performed as a riddling exchange, they do not have to cover up the puzzling passage. Instead they can find exciting ways to stage a mock rite of passage and then also discover how this genre of action will clarify other incidents of riddling and initiation in the play.

Recognizing Pompey and Abhorson's Exchange
as a Riddling Event

Riddle questions need not be posed as grammatical interrogatives, but can be stated as propositions which elicit a riddle answer. Riddling events then consist in a dialogue of two utterances, an interrogative proposition and answer, shared by two speakers, or "voices," using a notion of voice as the articulation of an identifiable formal position. In a riddling event, the two fictive voices are structurally defined.[11] Riddling then represents a dialogue between challenge and solution that comprises an agonistic exchange of understanding and power within a performed genre. A signal that Pompey and Abhorson's exchange functions as an initiation may be found in the manner of the Provost's exit and return. The Provost leaves the two men alone to complete their transaction and reenters to ask, "Are you agreed?" Pompey's reply, quoted above, suggests that a reciprocal agreement has been reached. This response makes little sense if Abhorson has just done all the talking. But if the passage is performed not only as a dialogue but also as a riddling test, then the dialogue promotes the bawd to executioner's assistant, and the Provost's actions acknowledge that instruction has been accomplished and a contract struck.

Recognizing this exchange as a riddle creates a generic event and opens up powerful generic meanings. Genres matter. We recognize genres because of conventional arrangements of terms; as a result, genres both depend on and reproduce expectations about relationships in social space and time. As they organize our interpretations of the world and constitute our relationships, genres exert social and epistemological consequences.[12] If, therefore, editors decide for us that Abhorson delivers the explanation as a syllogism, the play loses the possibility of an initiation achieved through riddling, a genre which formalizes the acquisition of understanding through confusion.

The Provost earlier refused to acknowledge much difference between the bawd and the executioner: "Go to," he rebukes Abhorson, "you weigh equally: a feather will turn the scale" (IV.ii.28). His metaphors echo against the play's title while also highlighting the equivalent value of the two occupations and their transferability. The theme of exchange and substitution not only aligns this incident with many others in the play, it introduces the possibility of an exchange of position through a riddling initiation. Moreover, the very structure of exchange is central to the social exchange in a riddling dialogue that enables the riddlee to attain the answer that he or she can later use to become the riddler in a new exchange. Furthermore, the riddle itself trades answers for questions; the riddling answer supplies a new term, which resolves a lack, for the problematic term, which produces confusion. Just as Pompey's supplying an answer — an answer that links thieves and true men — solves the problem of how hanging is a mystery, the supply of the answer makes of the illegal bawd Pompey a legal, "true man," who may now legitimately steal life and clothing. Pompey has assured the Provost he could switch from having been "an unlawful bawd time out of mind" to becoming, for the nonce, "a lawful hangman" (IV.ii.14–15). Pompey's puns and distorted logic further link his bawdry to execution, underscoring how the passage from one occupation to the other will be an exchange, one to be accomplished through the formal exchange of a riddling dialogue:

> *Prov.*   Come hither, sirrah. Can you cut off a man's head?
>
> *Pom.*   If the man be a bachelor, sir, I can; but if he be a married man, he's his wife's head; and I can never cut off a woman's head.
>
> (IV.ii.1–4)

This humorous contrast implies an ironic equation between the two occupations, while the wordplay additionally strengthens the appropriateness of the verbal exchange as a symbolic role exchange.[13]

Identity between the two "trades" could be intensified in performance. In Shakespearean double-casting, the same actor could have played both Mistress Overdone and Abhorson (his name, which might be freely translated as "son of a whore," also alludes to his own genealogical derivation from Pompey's work).[14] As Pompey then swaps one superior for another, their differences become only apparent. The parodic elevation of Pompey from bawd to hangman would then underscore this pattern of ironic equivalence between the two "trades," dramatize the theme of substitution, and correspond to other incidents of problematic interchangeability in the play.[15]

The parodic quality of this ritual would have been more evident to an Elizabethan audience aware of the transgressive ceremonies of initiation performed by the many societies of vagabonds and rogues who symbolically represented to Elizabethans not so much the forces of utter disorder as a kind of inverted social order of travestied hierarchy and ritual. Popular prose literature detailed their practices, tricks, and ruses and included accounts of their initiatory practices. A later dramatic work, *Beggar's Bush*, by Beaumont and Fletcher, depicted one of these beggars' initiations on stage. Like the passage in *Measure*, the initiation involves a riddling question that associates a willingness to mistreat words by punning with a willingness to mistreat women:

> *Clause:*   . . . welcom him, all.
>
> *Higgen:*   Stand off, stand off: I'll do it,
> We bid ye welcom three ways; first for your person,
> Which is a promising person, next for your quality,
> Which is a decent, and gentle quality,
> Last for the frequent means you have to feed us,
> You can steal 'tis to be presumed.
>
> *Hubert:*   Yes, venison, and if you want—
>
> *Higgen:*   'Tis well: you understand right,
> And shall practise daily: you can drink too?
>
> *Hubert:*   Soundly.
>
> *Higgen:*   And ye dare know a woman from a weathercock?
>
> *Hubert:*   If I handle her.
>
> *Gerard:*   Now swear him.
>
> *Higgen:*   I crown thy nab with a gage of ben bouse . . .
>
> . . . .
>
> I pour on thy pate a pot of good ale.
> And by the Rogues [oth] a Rogue thee instal:
> To beg on the way, to rob all thou meets;
> To steal from the hedge, both the shirt and the sheets:
>
> And lye with thy wench in the straw till she twang.[16]

The rogues' initiation includes a question about knowing the difference between a woman and a weathercock, and the punning reply by the initiand results in his successful entry into the vagabond's association. Handling a woman allows him to "know" the difference between her parts and those of a "weathercock." Such carnal knowledge and entry proves he has the knowledge to enter the male association, where his success is imaged in terms of playing a woman like a musical instrument. Beaumont and Fletcher's dramatic picture of a rogues' initiation helps make imaginative sense of the Provost's question about Pompey's willingness to cut off a woman's head as a test of his hardness as a future executioner. Pompey's punning reply bawdily anticipates his later riddling initiation. Both dramas represent parodic initiations and test the initiand's mastery of disorder by using imagery of theft; the theme of controlling women in sexual knowledge matches up with the later seizure of language and knowledge in punning.

Wordplay throughout the *Measure for Measure* passage, perhaps less evident to us than to Elizabethans, then frames the passage as a form of serious play. Further quibbling on proverbial sayings, literalizing dead metaphors, and triple punning may well introduce the kind of linguistic reordering typical in riddling. Some of the wordplay is really genre-play. For example, Pompey seizes a proverbial saying such as "a hanging look," to hint that Abhorson looks like one who does hanging rather than to signify that he appears downcast, the normal meaning. At the same time, the trickster tapster puns on "favour," confusing social courtesy with physiognomy:

> *Pom.*   Pray, sir, by your good favour—for surely, sir, a good favour you have, but that you have a hanging look—do you call, sir, your occupation a mystery?
>
> (IV.ii.30–32)

That pun materializes the abstract into the anatomical; and a similar process occurs when Pompey repeats the term, "hanging," almost punning on a "dead" metaphor, to refer to his own hanging, literally and sexually. Again he literalizes a folk expression, "I'll be hanged": "Painting, sir, I have heard say, is a mystery; and your whores, sir, being members of my occupation, using painting, do prove my occupation a mystery. But what mystery there should be in hanging, if I should be hanged, I cannot imagine." (IV.ii.34–38)

This repeated recasting of folk expressions exposes the multiplicity of lexical references as well as the plurality in social language as a set of speech strategies. Speaking requires more than grammatical competence; we also need competence in the rules of the speech community: customs for politeness, conventions about how and when to speak, decorum governing appropriate topics, and the like. So Pompey's speech play undermines and refreshes speech practices as he swiftly mocks not only our semantic reliance on singular referentiality but also our social reliance on speech conventions. Moreover, his flaunting of genres revives the serious sense of death hidden in our careless expressions. The contradiction about the true man's apparel fitting a thief, which Pompey's reply resolves, is not an affront to the laws of physics: why shouldn't a thief be the same size as a true man? The claim contradicts social conventions, governed by Elizabethan sumptuary laws, that clothing should serve as a moral and social marker. Thus the dialogue capsizes neither logic nor natural law, but social expectations. If Abhorson's enigmatic assertion and Pompey's reply are performed as a riddling ritual that releases Pompey from the threat of whipping, Pompey's explanation manipulates not only wit but also folk genres and social conventions. All Pompey's deconstructive strategies awaken our everyday sleepiness of expression, our verbal numbness to the body and its mortality. Pompey strips away these protections in his carnivalesque speech throughout the play.

Puns also work as a powerful device in riddling. In their tiny warfares of meanings and epistemologies, puns transmute expected syntactic arrangements to release hidden ideas and values. Such wordplay lays bare the inherent ambiguity in the linguistic system. Like the laws of Vienna, the laws of language prove inadequate to the complexities of their applications. The punning on "mystery" and "proof," in particular, encapsulates the many interchanges of subject and object throughout the play. Repeatedly, characters project themselves onto others or serve as substitutes for them, sometimes with disastrous and finally with reformative results. This kind of commutation of terms occurs here at the verbal level as words refer to themselves and each other. More specifically, "mystery" referred to an initiation rite, to a riddle or enigma, and to a craft, profession, or trade. All three senses operate simultaneously when the hangman poses a "mystery" (riddle) as a "mystery" (ritual) into a "mystery" (trade). When Pompey recognizes the riddling "mystery," and provides an answer to it, he implicitly proves that hanging is a mystery: a craft requiring initiation. He then solves a mystery at three levels; as he solves the riddle, he passes an initiation and enters the craft. The puns on "mystery" mean that the "proof" Pompey asks for is one he cites.

The puns on "proof" also express a reciprocity of actor, action, and agency. A proof could be a validation or evidence, a person who gives evidence, the process of proving, the instrument for testing, and (as a verb) to test. So Pompey and Abhorson develop a circular proof that unites prover, proven, and proof. Abhorson presents a proof (test of Pompey) by posing a proof (the instrument of testing, the riddle). Abhorson thereby proves (furnishes adequate evidence) that his occupation is a mystery; moreover, by proving the proof (answering the riddle), Pompey, himself a proof (a witness) demonstratively proves (establishes the fact) that hanging is a mystery. Proofs prove proofs. The bawd trades places with the hangman, and vice versa. So the true man's apparel and that of the thief will become equally fitting. The triple puns on proof and mystery help establish this exchange as a playful event and serve as another instance of the substitutions of terms which the play explores at other levels.

Performing the Exchange

Even when we recognize the incident is a riddling event, the sense of the words requires clarification through performance, in gesture and prop. Indeed, once directors begin to explore the performance implications of the passage as a dialogue, they will find revealing actions to perform. For example, in a student production at the University of California, Santa Barbara, director Homer Swander had Abhorson enter with a hangman's rope tied in a noose.[17] Pompey then snatched the noose to illustrate his point: "If it be too little for your thief, your true man thinks it big enough." Pompey placed the noose around his wrist and, with his fist clenched, tightened the noose as if the "thief" were, indeed, being hanged. Obviously such a punitive fit would seem acceptable to the true man. Then Pompey loosened the "apparel," to demonstrate the next clause: "if it be too big for your thief, your thief thinks it little enough." Now the noose hung loosely around his wrist, and he swiftly removed his fist; so the "thief" escaped. Clearly the bigger noose was quite small enough to please the thief, who would hardly wish a snugger fit.

If the performance choice of using the noose as "apparel" had been performed on Shakespeare's stage, older language usage would have made the prop even more evidently a visual pun. In the OED, "apparel" denotes not only clothing made to measure, made to fit, but also the equipment or apparatus needed for a specialized occupation or task; in another technical usage, "apparel" also referred to the rigging of a ship. Thus, the Globe audience might have found the hangman's rope very fitting as "apparel." Riddling on "fit" also exploits its diverse definitions, as given in the OED, including a "mortal crisis," which could "betoken death." Indeed, in the action Swander found to gloss the riddle, the noose does place the thief into a kind of "fit," in more than one sense.

Just as Pompey, having seized the hangman's rope, can adjust the noose, he can make every true man's apparel fit; thus he solves the mystery and enters it. Pompey, like a thief with words, refashions language to make the answer fit. In most riddling exchanges, the answer creates a semantic fit by extending language through metaphors, puns, or another cognitive transformation.[18] Just as the noose may be a metaphoric "true man's apparel," adjusting the rope matches the cognitive process of approximating meanings. Our brave verbal apparel tries to conceal the loose fit between signifiers and signifieds, a link that we hope our semblances of truth will tighten. But linguistic playfulness always liberates the play in the system. Moreover, performance choices, here the use of prop and gesture, are essential to understand Pompey's lines as the answer to Abhorson's proposition; the words alone do not complete the action any more than the letter of law is sufficient to know what measures are fit.

The stage actions also reveal that "fit" means one thing to the true man (when the "apparel" is too little for the thief, the true man is pleased) and means the opposite to the thief (when the "apparel" is too big, allowing escape, the thief thinks it little enough). Yet the riddle tricks us into thinking that fit is universal. Instead, when the true man is pleased with the fit, the thief is not, and vice versa. Only if we take both points of view and separate them in time, can we achieve unequivocal fit. Positions in time and space qualify measures, which must be registered against circumstances and interpreters. Perspectives change measures. So subjects and objects may differ in how they evaluate a given situation. Therefore, while the riddle playfully asserts the seeming interchangeability of some positions, the obvious partiality of the solution warns us that simple substitutions do not work as well as the trickiness of wordplay makes them appear to do.

Even if one does not use the hangman's noose, or treat the passage as a riddle, the terms "apparel" and "fit" reverberate with other language in the script. We hear characters repeatedly question when or how one is fit for death or for life; what measures fit what crimes; and how well we fit into the offices and clothing from which we claim authority. But if actors perform the exchange between Pompey and Abhorson as a riddle, and if the riddle uses a hangman's noose as the apparel made to fit in a specialized way, more complex meanings become manifest on stage.

The Folio creates the possibility of an ironic exchange of power, rather than a comical torture. In the Folio, a riddling dialogue permits a verbal and symbolic transaction and transfer of power from Abhorson to Pompey, in a parodic ritual exchange. The interrogative proposition in a riddle introduces an asymmetry of knowledge between riddler and riddlee; that imbalance is righted when the riddlee advances the correct answer or the riddler tells the answer to a baffled opponent. The symbolism of balance in a play entitled *Measure for Measure,* and replete with imagery of scales and weights, is damaged when Abhorson is given such unilateral power. A riddling initiation, in contrast, begins with an inequality of power and knowledge and then evens out differences, at many levels, through test and discovery rather than through mutilation. This concise process can serve as a precise model for the pattern we see elsewhere in the play; the play as a whole may spring into shape as a similar game.

Riddling, Masking, Knowledge, and Gender

Only after viewing the Santa Barbara production did I realize that a director could go even further and have the hangman award the rope to Pompey after his explanation; the noose then becomes an emblem of Pompey's initiation through a successful manipulation of words. If he had to "steal" the rope to give his explanation, then he receives the rope as his legitimate tool as he becomes a "lawful hangman." He could then hold up the rope as a proof of his accomplishment when the Provost returns to ask if they are agreed. Using a rope as both Pompey's prop and his reward also resonates with Pompey's several jokes about hanging and with an Elizabethan expression that linked rope-tricks with inflated rhetoric, bawdy wordplay, and sexual acts that could "deserve hanging."[19]

On the other hand, the hangman could bestow on Pompey the executioner's mask to mark his change in office. The image of a hood or veil appears in several other incidents where lowering veils and masks coincide with motifs of gender, speaking, knowledge, revelation of identity, ritual, or riddling. This fascinating pattern, which connects to an elaborate code of behavior for chaste women to be silent, invisible, and fully obedient to patriarchal rules,[20] appears in several of the play's incidents, starting in the nunnery, where the door cannot be opened to Lucio until Isabella learns that a sister of the Order of St. Clare cannot speak to a man unless veiled and in the presence of the Prioress. Claudio had already told Lucio that Isabella's youthful feminine power resides in her "prone and speechless dialect" which can "move men" (I.ii.173–74). The tryst with Angelo—within a walled garden, further enclosed by a vineyard and accessible only through two locked doors—will also take place in silence and darkness. That cultural imagination of muteness, shrouded face, locked doors, and either curtailed or illegitimate sex continues when

Mariana arrives veiled at the public assembly to make her claims. The Duke orders that she not speak until she unveils, but she refuses to do so until her "husband" bids her; when she does remove the veil, she also verbally answers riddles she has constructed about Angelo's carnal knowledge of her bare face (as a synecdoche for her other open parts) and his lack of knowledge of that knowledge. As she restores that knowledge, disclosing her face with the story of his knowledge of her body, her riddling answers restore a larger knowledge of identity and resolve contradictions about her own ambiguous sexual status.

When Lucio plucks Friar Lodowick's hood away from the Duke's face, Mariana's revelations are confirmed and a new round of restored identities begins. Those revivals culminate when Claudio is unmuffled by the Provost. His climactic unveiling, depending on the stage interpretation, can catalyze the processes of resurrection that may ensure fertile, legitimate, and responsible reproductive sexuality in Vienna.

The hangman's handing over his mask, in a kind of metatheatrical joke, could thus be an appropriate stage image as the award to Pompey for uncloaking truth in this riddle. A director needs to consider what symbolic award could signal the ritual elevation of Pompey to executioner and how the riddling award accords with other images in the script associated with riddling and revelation.

Cultural Meanings in Pompey's Test

During the last two decades, most folkloristic studies of riddling have analyzed riddle structure either to define the genre, to classify and compare riddles, or to understand the function of riddling in culture.[21] Poststructuralists suspect that unequivocal coherence cannot be found in isomorphic likenesses between expressive and social formations. Deconstructionists would likely challenge earlier theories that the structural features of riddles furnish reassuring force in social situations. By combining both structuralist analysis and deconstructionist openness to disorder, I would argue that the artificiality and reflexivity of riddles, as games which signal their own constructed and playful status, subvert but do not cancel their potential for constituting order. The very tension between form as triumph and form as imposition calls attention to the differences riddles do straddle.

Characters as well as the audience almost necessarily consider correspondences between repeated situations in a play whose title, *Measure for*

Measure, surely names the central problem of achieving equivalencies and balances. Shakespeare, not structuralists, invented these characters who explicitly try to sort out dilemmas of judgment by making comparisons, sometimes rather detailed ones, with others whom they see as extensions of self. Just as consistently, however, characters attempt to measure a situation either by the absolute measuring stick of a law or religious code, by a self-knowing measure, or by locating equivalent values or substitutable acts and words, only to discover both the necessity and frailty of using structural parallels as a means of achieving justice or order.

As folklorists establish analogic correspondences between elements of riddle form, they often find parallels in structural formations at many levels: in sound, grammar, logic, formal game relations between participants, and in the social relationships and competing values of the larger context. As a result, many social scientists interpret riddles as expressive models of relationships in the larger cultural context. As riddles move from cognitive confusion to clarification, theorists assert, they can symbolically transform external asymmetrical social power into equality through the symbolic exchange of knowledge. Through the same kind of analogic force that operates in homeopathic magic, where like produces like, a riddling event then seems a mimetic model *of* conflict or tension. As it achieves balance through some form of redefinition or reinterpretation, a riddle may also then function as a magical model *for* bringing about transformative resolutions. A character's ability to arrive at the correct riddle conclusion often serves, particularly in literature and myth, as a metaphoric demonstration and assurance of the person's larger problem-solving abilities. So successful riddlers, by virtue of answering a conundrum, frequently earn status elevations such as marriage, ascension to monarchy, or other forms of power.

Other studies of riddling focus more on the rhetorical and semiotic dimensions of riddling. One team of linguistic folklorists explain that the most powerful social function of a riddle performance is not to render the information in the answer, but to display riddling competence.[22] To riddle is to proclaim one's ability in a type of language game that plays with cultural meanings.[23] Thus, when Pompey answers Abhorson's riddle, the two of them communicate their complementary skills in manipulating the many genres of "mystery." This riddle as a mock ritual might then signify Pompey's aptitude for this kind of problem-solving and Abhorson's power to test Pompey.

Kenneth Burke's theories about speech genres as rhetorical strategies for handling situations have guided the theories of another anthropologist, who contends that the operative referent of a riddle is not primarily the semantic content of the words.[24] Instead Crocker emphasizes riddles as performances to achieve novel semantic and cultural relationships through incongruity. Riddles then recast a situation through puns and humor; they achieve new perspectives through paradox; they remoralize a situation demoralized through inaccuracy; and they accomplish this through a high level of performance competence by the participants. Reciting a riddle is not sufficient to make it "work"; only a good performance can elevate understanding and action to higher planes of possibility.[25] If Pompey and Abhorson display onstage their competence as riddlers, they revive the moral complexities in their situation, redefining vexed notions of honesty, sufficiency, fit, and proper dessert.

The Duke's "Riddle"

When the Duke mentions a "riddle" in act III, scene ii (l.223), he does not speak of a formal riddle, as folklorists define it. Rather, the Duke simply voices the word "riddle" to condense figuratively his view of a paradoxical moral world. The incident does not depict a riddling exchange. Nonetheless, if we analyze the significance of the Duke's term, "riddle," we may better understand how his language resonates against both Pompey's riddle in act IV and the riddling testimony of Mariana at the play's denouement.

When the Duke speaks of the world as a "riddle," he has just been subjected to an extended view of widespread social iniquity.[26] This scene takes place, clearly, just outside the prison, and the Duke serves as a subjective center as a series of other characters enter and depart, offering him moral education. The force of this sequence would have been intensified on the Elizabethan stage: in the Folio, all of act III appears as a single scene, and it would have been staged on the unlocalized Elizabethan stage without a break. In the prior incidents, all within the jail, the Duke overhears Claudio and Isabella and then devises the bed trick with the young novice. But after those incidents, the theatrical conventions of place and time would have permitted the Duke to remain on stage, perhaps not even moving, while the audience would understand that the locale had switched from the interior of the prison, from which Isabella exited, to the street, where Elbow leads Pompey to prison. Following the Folio signals about staging, the Santa Barbara production staged this long scene as one continuous action. The Duke remained stationary at the center of the stage as we realized that he had motionlessly traveled from inside the prison to outside its walls. Moreover, the unmoving Duke then seemed to stand at the vortex of society, as it revolves into the prison, which gradually absorbs the populace of Vienna as inmates, visitors, or imprisoning officials. The Duke's centrality defines the exchangeability of these two realms as his perspective defines our own subjectivity. Like Pompey, who will be comically initiated into the "mystery" of execution through solving a mystery about iniquity and truth, the Duke here undergoes a psychological initiation into Viennese society and discovers his own relationship to iniquity, truth, and therefore to his identity.[27]

He stands by as the officers, headed by Elbow, take Pompey off to prison, and he watches the wily Lucio refuse to aid the tapster. He also listens as Lucio maligns him and disparages Angelo. Following Lucio's departure in this long, busy scene, the scandalized Duke has a moment for a formal soliloquy, in couplets, about the inevitability of calumny even for the most virtuous of rulers. The dialogue then resumes in prose as Mistress Overdone is escorted to prison. The Duke watches this procession, and after the Provost and bawd enter the prison, Escalus, the Duke's respected assistant, remains to exchange words with the strange friar.

In striking prose, the Duke paints a damning view of the world as a "riddle" when Escalus queries:

> *Esc.*   What news abroad i'th'world?
>
> *Duke.*   None, but that there is so great a fever on goodness that the dissolution of it must cure it. Novelty is only in request, and it is as dangerous to be aged in any kind of course as it is virtuous to be constant in any undertaking. There is scarce truth enough alive to make societies secure; but security enough to make fellowships accurst. Much upon this riddle runs the wisdom of the world. This news is old enough, yet it is every day's news. . . .

> (III.ii.216–24)

No sooner does the Duke pose this riddling paradox about news which is not new, a society in which novelty, security, fellowship, and truth have problematic relationships, and cures require the extremity of a "fit," than he queries Escalus about his own nature.[28] The close affinity between the Duke's sketch of the world and the issue of time, his language of riddling, his practice of equivocation, and the question of his own identity will—if effectively staged—all come together again in the other riddling incidents of acts IV and V.

In those incidents, formal riddles will be posed. But the "riddle" to which the Duke refers is not such a riddle. Rather, he states a paradox about truth and its sufficiency, and calls that paradox, or perhaps the larger news he relates, a "riddle." Remarkably, the same problem of "enough," which will figure wittily in Pompey's riddle answer, occurs here as the Duke antithetically reports that while scarcely enough truth exists to secure society, enough security exists to curse fellowships. After all, he has just seen one fellow fail to aid another—"security enough to make fellowships accurst"—and he has beheld the foolish Elbow taking the tricky Pompey to jail and has had to listen to Lucio slander the Duke—"scarce truth enough . . . to make societies secure." If such news is an old riddle, the Duke's chiasmus suggests that the latest gospel is a riddle in this loose sense. Such is the playful and novel knowledge into which the play initiates us.

Immediately following his long social commentary, the Duke asks Escalus about himself, for his initiation into the body of society has influenced him to seek self-knowledge. After Escalus renders him a flattering portrait, Vincentio remains alone on stage. There he ends the long scene with a pithy soliloquy in tetrameter couplets. Justifying the bed trick he is about to supervise, he concludes: "Craft against vice I must apply" (III.ii.270). The Duke employs a highly contrived style—aphorism, rhyme, verse, metaphor, and other tropes—to rationalize his use of craft to right a wrong. Because of his stilted effort (and perhaps his forced self-righteousness), editors and critics have questioned the aesthetic value and therefore even the authenticity of these lines. But discomfort with the Duke's technique completely misses his special use of contrivance. Through rhetorical and poetic cunning, he implicitly rationalizes not only the trick, but also this mode of rationalization. Vincentio applies evident verbal craft against the vice of his trick just as he applies the craft of his trick against the vice of Angelo and his city. Furthermore, if he addresses us, joining Vienna to our world, does he suggest that theater is also, then, craft applied against vice? We should indeed ask: to whom does the Duke address this justification? He may speak to himself or directly to the audience. Either way, the rhetorical force of using craft to cure vice will chime against the rhetorical craft of the riddling paradoxes which the Duke fashioned as a moral response to a complex world.

Mariana's Riddle

Riddling again enacts craft against vice at the close of the play and again associates craft with the manipulation of women's bodies as a way to manipulate language and knowledge. Both forms of performed vice use reversals to re-reverse disorder, much as if they were forms of ritual redress.[29] At the close of the play when Mariana poses her formal riddle, her puzzling lines echo the themes of sexuality, gender, knowledge, self-knowledge, and identity:

> Enter MARIANA [veiled].
>
> *Duke.*   Is this the witness, friar?
> First, let her show her face, and after, speak.
>
> *Mar.*   Pardon, my lord; I will not show my face
> Until my husband bid me.
>
> *Duke.*   What, are you married?
>
> *Mar.*   No, my lord.
>
> *Duke.*   Are you a maid?
>
> *Mar.*   No, my lord.
>
> *Duke.*   A widow, then?
>
> *Mar.*   Neither, my lord.
>
> *Duke.*   Why, you are nothing then: neither maid, widow,
> nor wife!
>
> . . . .
>
> *Mar.*   My lord, I do confess I ne'er was married;
> And I confess besides, I am no maid.
> I have known my husband; yet my husband
> Knows not that ever he knew me.
>
> (V.i.169–88)

As the scene continues, Mariana draws out even more elaborate paradoxes on the problem of knowing by punning further on carnal knowledge.

When Mariana does unveil herself, the revelation of her identity requires her to provide a brief narrative to explain her riddling, as is done in neck riddling, a specialized form of riddling common in folktales and some-times performed in actual cultural contexts, such as wakes. In the tales that contain these riddles, prisoners frequently save their necks or reduce their full sentences by posing an insoluble riddle for their judges (in another common variant, a suitor poses an insoluble riddle in a courtship test). Folklorists have dubbed these riddles as "neck riddles" because successful riddling saves the prisoner's neck by baffling the judge.[30] The riddles prove impossible to answer unless the riddlee learns a secret experience of the riddler's; the answer, necessarily provided by the riddlee, is frequently a stylized, verse narrative of the hidden event. Solutions then depend on experience, not word tricks or logic.[31] Mariana's answers depend on her secret liaison with Angelo, a story that she finally relates, in a series of couplets.

In addition, Mariana's account of illegitimate sex which may be taken as legitimate thematically resembles the same motifs in the tales that explain many neck riddles.[32] In these stories, as in Pompey and Mariana's riddles, notions of what is lawful and unlawful are redefined in the redemptive action of the neck riddle, frequently an action performed by a sacrificial female who must undergo some kind of seeming vice to restore order. The theme of remedy and redemption pervades the language of the script, and when Angelo's vice regency generates so much business in Vienna's prison, the Provost offers Pompey the chance to "redeem [him] from [his] gyves" if he will assist the overworked hangman. If Pompey's test then parodies the theme of redeeming assistance, Mariana's riddling more profoundly quibbles on the many levels of legitimate knowledge and sexual remedy which the play explores and which her riddles reflexively mirror. Her subtle riddling dialogue functions like a neck riddle in that Mariana's game helps win Isabella's eventual freedom from prison (although at first, her contradictions keep Isabella confined as a slanderer of Angelo); and when her riddling is resolved, both women and Friar Peter are pardoned. The judging Angelo then faces his own sentence for fornication. Isabella acknowledges her new knowledge of the body and of desire, able to put herself in the place of Angelo emotionally and even morally, as she does in her plea for Angelo's pardon. Until she performs that kind of empathetic substitution, Angelo remains under sentence by the riddling Duke.

Conclusion

In its finale, the script does not show us clearly if Isabella nonverbally accepts the Duke's proposal, denies it, or postpones a definite answer, for she has no further lines after his first offer. The first time the Duke proposes marriage, he breaks off his brief advance in mid-line: "but fitter time for that" (V.i.491). What motivates that obvious self-correction? The actors must find a fit answer. Again, the right fit requires the right time, place, and persons, and this script poses for actors the same kind of problems the characters have been learning to solve. Through imaginative and moral placement of self in another's position, the tests and proofs in this play teach characters how flexible must be the measures by which they measure themselves, measure their measures, and measure their words. So, what scale of character or plot plausibility can tell us how the silent Isabella "answers" the Duke? What measure can we use? When the ending of the play in performance is as ambiguous as is the script, the audience has to imagine themselves in the fictive position of Isabella to find not only an answer, but, more fundamentally, the measure by which to do so.

Like the Duke's "riddle," *Measure for Measure* can become a craft applied against vice. Answers are not made to measure; they are uncertain, relative, virtual, and knowable only through experience. Through playing with knowing in riddles, the play sportfully initiates us into that kind of ludic knowledge which through the experience of art can exchange craft for vice, play for evil, and awareness for mistaking. If we restore the Folio text, and directors stage the dialogue between Pompey and Abhorson as a riddle, Pompey's promotion can become a subtle replica and mockery of the other replacements and initiations in the world of Vienna. Finding the actions of riddling and parodic ritual in the script takes us into the fuller mystery of this play in performance.

NOTES

1. A different version—shorter and with a different emphasis—of this essay has appeared in *Assaph: Studies in the Theater* 5 (1989). I am indebted to Homer Swander for our wide-ranging forms of collaborative work on Shakespeare and performance, through A.C.T.E.R. (Alliance for Creative Theater, Education, and Research). More specifically, this article grows out of a series of exchanges we had about *Measure*, which he initiated when he was directing the play at the University of California, Santa Barbara, in the spring of 1985. The collaborative process which led both to this article and to Professor Swander's production represents the kind of creative exchange between scholars and theater which A.C.T.E.R. supports. I am also grateful to David Bevington, Craig Coletta, Alan Dessen, and David Young for reading and commenting on earlier drafts of this essay; an original and much shorter version was read and discussed at the seminar on Ritual and Elizabe-

than Drama led by Linda Woodbridge at the Shakespeare Association of America Meeting in Seattle, Washington, on 4 April 1987.

2. Capell's edition is entitled Mr. *William Shakespeare, his comedies, histories, and tragedies* . . . (London: Dryden Leach for J. R. Tonson, 1767), vol. 2, p. 65. The new edition of *Measure for Measure* in the Oxford Collected Works, under the general supervision of Stanley Wells and Gary Taylor, has been edited by John Jowett, who returns to the Folio speech assignments in the crucial passages between Pompey and Abhorson (Oxford: Clarendon Press, 1986). The restored passage is reproduced as in the Folio in both the modernized spelling edition (p. 913) and in the original spelling edition (p. 913). Stanley W. Wells, *William Shakespeare: A Textual Companion* (Oxford: Clarendon Press, 1987), has a note on this restoration that refers the reader to a note by Gary Taylor, "*Measure for Measure*, IV. ii. 41-46," *Shakespeare Quarterly* 29:3 (Summer, 1978): 419-21.

3. Charles Hinman, ed. *The Norton Facsimile: The First Folio of Shakespeare* (New York: W. W. Norton, 1968), 93.

4. Modern editors vary the end punctuation for this line; it is a period in the Folio, but making this switch does not change the nature of the action; in either case, Pompey's line has an interrogative function.

5. Here, and elsewhere when I use a modern edition, I quote from Lever's New Arden text.

6. For example, J. W. Lever's note in the New Arden edition (London: Methuen, 1965), 102.

7. David Bevington, personal communication.

8. For example, Lever finds, "One stage in the syllogism, relating the executioner to the thief, is missing, and the faulty distribution may be due to a gap at some stage of transmission" (102).

9. Taylor, "*Measure for Measure*, IV.ii.41-46."

10. See Frank Aydelotte, *Elizabeth Rogues and Vagabonds* (Oxford: Clarendon Press, 1913; rept. London: Frank Cass, 1967), 30-31, for contemporary accounts of beggars' initiations. Keith Thomas, "Age and Authority in Early Modern England," *Proceedings of the British Academy* 62 (1976): 205-48 relates problems of apprenticeships and initiations, and his *Rule and Misrule in the Schools of Early Modern England* (Reading, England: University of Reading Press, 1976) explores the kind of school initiations Phillip Aries discusses in France in his work, *Centuries of Childhood: A Social History of Family Life*, trans. Robert Baldick (New York: Vintage Books, 1962).

11. Bakhtin emphasizes that speech articulates social positions within a specific socio-historical situation and is supported by ideology. Speech says who one is and where one stands in relation to other speakers and languages. Represented speech, in a riddle, which mimes an exchange, then represents two positions, highly stylized and formalized, in the reciprocal and antithetical positions of interrogator and answerer. See discussions of dialogical language and voice throughout Mikhail Bakhtin.

12. John D. Dorst, "Neck-riddle as a Dialogue of Genres: Applying Bakhtin's Genre Theory," *Journal of American Folklore* 96:382 (1983), 415, explains that genres are conventionalized ways of seeing; genre rules do not preclude genre flexibility, however; quite the contrary, as a means by which we organize our experience, "genres are constitutive of human consciousness," and since, as Bakhtin suggests, consciousness itself arises in the process of social exchange (communication) under particular historical conditions, particular genres change and become borderline, hybrid, and parodic to enact different types of cognition and relationships. See also Mikhail Bakhtin, *The Dialogic Imagination: Four Essays by M. M. Bakhtin,* ed. Michael Holquist, trans. Caryl Emerson (Austin: University of Texas Press, 1981).

13. Earlier, Isabella sets up a similar verbal antithesis, defending her refusal to save her brother's head by giving up her maidenhead: "I had rather my brother die by the law, than my son should be unlawfully born" (III.i.188–90). Isabella contrasts two subjects: brother/son; two actions: die/be born; and two adverbial situations: lawfully/unlawfully. This three-way contrast, voiced with such aphoristic force, provides a serious parallel to the comic contrast Pompey articulates to the Provost, perhaps from the very same position in the prison, on stage.

14. Joseph Kramer made this suggestion in a Shakespeare course I attended in spring 1967 at the University of California, Berkeley.

15. A number of fine articles address various aspects of the pattern of substitution, conversion, and balance in the play. Among recent discussions are: Nancy Leonard, "Substitution in Shakespeare's Problem Comedies," *ELR* 9 (1979), 281–301; Jan Kott, "Head for Maidenhead, Maidenhead for Head: The Structure of Exchange in *Measure for Measure," En torno a Shakespeare: Homenane a T. B. Spencer,* ed. Manuel Conejero (Valencia: University de Valenica Inst. Shakespeare, 1980), 93–113; J. S. Lawry, "Imitations and Creation in *Measure for Measure," Shakespeare and the Arts,* ed. Cecile Cary and Henry Limouge (Washington, D.C.: University Press of America, 1982), 217–29; Richard A. Levin, "Duke Vincentio and Angelo: Would 'A Feather Turn the Scale'?" *Studies in English Literature, 1500–1900,* 22:2 (1982), 257–70.

16. Beaumont and Fletcher, *Beggars Bush,* act III, scene 3, quoted in Aydelotte, 30.

17. The play was performed at the University 9–10 June 1985, and I served as an informal dramaturge for this production, having pointed out to the director that the Folio passage, which he believed could make sense in a stage action, could make sense as a riddling initiation.

18. Some helpful riddle studies in this regard are: Roger Abrahams, "Introductory Remarks to a Rhetorical Theory of Folklore," *Journal of American Folklore* 81 (1968), 143–58; Robert A. Georges and Alan Dundas, "Toward a Structural Definition of the Riddle," *Journal of American Folklore* 76 (1963), 111–18; Thomas A. Green and W. J. Pepicello, "The Folk Riddle: A Redefinition of Terms," *Western*

Folklore 38 (1979), 3–20; Green and Pepicello, "Wit in Riddling: A Linguistic Perspective," *Genre* 11 (1978), 1–13; Charles T. Scott, "On Defining the Riddle: The Problem of a Structual Unit," *Genre* 2 (1969), 129–42.

19. Moreover, if Pompey has engaged in a "rope trick" on stage (as he did under Swander's direction), there might have been another visual pun, since scholars have shown that "rope" was probably a bawdy term for the penis, and that "roperipe," "ropery," and "rope tricks" probably punned in some way on rhetoric, bawdy talk, and over-done uses of language. See Joel Fineman, "The Turn of the Shrew," *Shakespeare and the Question of Theory,* ed. Patricia Parker and Geoffrey Hartman (New York: Methuen, 1985), 142–44; Richard Levin, "Grumio's 'Rope Tricks' and the Nurse's 'Ropery,'" *Shakespeare Quarterly* 21 (1971), 82–86; Anne C. Lancashire, "Lyly and Shakespeare on the Ropes," *JEGP* 68 (1969), 237–44; and the note by editor Brian Morris, the New Arden edition of *The Taming of the Shrew* (New York: Methuen, 1981), 189–90. An association between "rope tricks" on the part of the persons trying to sound more learned than they are could also possibly be linked to the term "neck verse," referring to the Latin verses scholars could recite to escape hanging. See note 29, below.

20. Excellent secondary studies of this literature include: Suzanne W. Hull, *Chaste, Silent, and Obedient: English Books for Women, 1475–1640* (San Marino: Huntington Library Press, 1982); Ruth Kelso, *Doctrine for the Lady of the Renaissance* (Urbana: University of Illinois Press, 1956); Linda Woodbridge, *Women and the English Renaissance: Literature and the Nature of Womanhood, 1540–1620* (Urbana: University of Illinois Press, 1984); Peter Stallybrass, "Patriarchal Territories: The Body Enclosed," *Rewriting the Renaissance,* ed. Margaret Ferguson, Maureen Quilligan and Nancy J. Vickers (Chicago: University of Chicago Press, 1986), 123–42.

21. In addition to studies mentioned in note 18, one could also note Roger D. Abrahams and Alan Dundes, "Riddles," *Folklore and Folklife,* ed. Richard Dorson (Chicago: University of Chicago Press, 1971), 129–43; Alan Dundes, "Summoning Deity through Ritual Fasting," *American Imago* 20 (1963), 213–20; Phyllis Gorfain and Jack Glazier, "Ambiguity and Exchange: The Double Dimension of Mbeere Riddles," *Journal of American Folklore* 89 (1976), 189–238; Ian Hamnett, "Ambiguity, Classification, and Change: The Function of Riddles," *Man* 2 (1967), 379–92; John Roberts and Michael R. Foreman, "Riddles: Expressive Models of Interrogation," *Directions in Sociolinguisitics: The Enthnography of Communication,* ed. John J. Gumperz and Dell Hymes (New York: Holt, Rinehart, and Winston, 1972), 180–210.

22. William J. Pepicello and Thomas A. Green, *The Language of Riddles: New Perspectives* (Columbus: Ohio State University Press, 1984), 216.

23. Pepicello and Green, *The Language of Riddles,* 128.

24. J. Christopher Crocker, "The Social Functions of Rhetorical Forms," *The Social Use of Metaphor,* ed. J. David Sapir and J. Christopher Crocker (Philadelphia: University of Pennsylvania Press, 1977), 33–66.

25. Crocker, "Social Functions," 40–45.

26. The OED points out that a biblical passage translated as "mystery of iniquity" frequently occurred as a proverbial expression in this period; thus iniquity and riddling were conceptually linked.

27. Many anthropological theorists of play compare secular plays with ritual processes; the comparison must not be careless, for significant points of intersection and difference reveal the distinctions between the obligatory and sacred transformations enacted by ritual and the optative and experimental innovations represented in ludic forms. See Roger Abrahams, "Toward an Enactment-Centered Theory of Folklore," *Frontiers of Folklore*, ed. William R. Bascom (Boulder, Colo.: Westview, Inc., 1978), 79–120; Don Handelman, "Play and Ritual: Complementary Frames of Metacommunication," *It's a Funny Thing, Humor*, ed. A. J. Chapman and H. C. Foot (Oxford: Pergamon Press, 1977), 185–92; Victor Turner, *From Ritual to Theater: The Human Seriousness of Play* (New York: Performing Arts Journal Publications, 1982).

28. The Duke's phrase, "a fever on goodness" so great that only "the dissolution of it must cure it" could remind one of a "fit," in the sixteenth-century sense of a "moral crisis, a bodily state . . . that betokens death," or, "a paroxysm . . . of a periodic or constitutional ailment," see OED. The sense of a mortal crisis as a fever, a narrow straight through which a resurrection occurs, is a famous conceit, of course, in Donne's "Hymn to God My God, In My Sickness" (published 1633). The narrow "fit" of Pompey's riddle can play on this paradox of a cure attained through extremity and homeopathic likeness.

29. Victor Turner explains such uses of ritual inversion to re-reverse disorder; see especially his collected essays in *From Ritual to Theater* (see note 27).

30. See studies of the neck riddle in John D. Dorst's article cited in note 11; Roger Abrahams, *Between the Living and the Dead* (Helsinki: Folklore Suomalainen Tiedeakatemia, 1980), FFC no. 225; and F. J. Norton, "The Prisoner Who Saved His Neck with a Riddle," *Folk-lore* 53 (1942), 27–57. In previous articles I have compared the riddling in five Shakespeare plays with this tradition: see "Puzzle and Artifice: The Riddle as Metapoetry in *Pericles*," *Shakepseare Survey* 29 (1976), 11–20; "Riddles and Reconciliation: Formal Unity in *All's Well that Ends Well*," *Journal of the Folklore Institute* 13 (1976), 266–81; "Contest, Riddle, and Prophecy: Reflexivity through Folklore in Structure in *Macbeth*," *Mississippi Folklore Register* (1977), 143–57, and "Toward a Folkloristic Approach to Literature: Riddles in Shakespearean Drama," *Southern Folklore Quarterly* 40 (1977), 143–57. Neck riddles and neck verse bear a similar folk logic; neck verse, a passage in Latin from the scriptures, printed in black letter, usually quoting the beginning of the fifty-first psalm, could be read to prove one deserved "benefit of clergy" in order to gain a pardon from hanging. The tales containing neck riddles manifest the same underlying folk belief: a demonstration of a special competence with language and arcane knowledge can "magically," in a kind of metaphoric exchange, confer impunity in a particular moment of liability.

31. Elli Köngäs Maranda, "The Logic of Riddles," *Structural Analysis of Oral Tradition*, ed. Pierre Maranda and Elli Köngäs Maranda (Philadelphia: University of Pennsylvania Press, 1971), 189–234, analyzes how riddle structures guide discovery of the hidden terms which constitute the riddle answer in true riddles; the structure of the neck riddles distinctly differs from this process although this subgenre of the riddle employs many of the same techniques of synechdoche and stylistic features; Roger Abrahams, "Between the Living and the Dead," 10, also explains that neck riddles, instead of using semantic contradictions to confuse, use the cultural contradictions of self-sacrifice.

32. Some folklorists have argued that all neck riddles, which bear a similarity of theme (involving, most often life out of death, and "self-sacrifice by a female loved one as a means of defeating . . . death"), derive from a common ancestor; see Abrahams, "Between the Living and the Dead," 10. Often the hidden event concerns problematic sexual or family relationships, unusual births or compounding deaths; frequently the theme of life out of death (a posthumous birth, a Caesarean section, animals born in the skull of another dead creature, a daughter nursing an imprisoned father) involves making a seemingly unnatural sexual or familial relationship into an innocent or redeeming one. Thus the lifesaving function of the neck riddle in the larger story is matched by the story of redemption within it.

4

Shakespeare's Maimed Birth Rites

JEANNE ADDISON ROBERTS

The standard modern interpretations of Shakespeare's romantic comedies accept Northrop Frye's analysis of them as celebrations of sexual
consummation and the establishment of new generations supplanting the
old (Frye 163–64). Certainly young couples abound in these comedies. I
have counted thirty-four in the first twelve comedies. And yet, curiously,
what ought to be the next stage in the recurring rituals—the generating of
yet another generation—is almost universally suppressed, disrupted, or
deformed in Shakespeare's works.

There are, of course, references to the promise of propagation in the
comedies. As Benedick decides in *Much Ado About Nothing* to entertain
the idea of matrimony, he announces portentously that "the world must
be peopled" (II.iii.242). Rosalind dreams of her child's father (I.iii.11) in
As You Like It; and Hymen who "peoples every town" (V.iv.143) presides
over the eight lovers coming like animals to the ark at the play's end.
Oberon specifically blesses the bride beds and the expected issue of the
"couples three" at the end of *A Midsummer Night's Dream,* but his catalog
of such possible "blots of Nature's hand" as moles, hare-lip, scar, and
prodigious marks cannot but cast a shadow over his benison (V.i.403–12).
A different sort of abnormal birth is celebrated by the Abbess/Mother
who appears miraculously at the end of *The Comedy of Errors* and declares
at the family reunion that she has "gone in travail" for thirty-three years,
finally delivering herself of her burden after this monstrously prolonged
"pregnancy." She even speaks of going to a gossips' (i.e., godparents') feast
to celebrate nativity after "so long grief" (V.i.401–7). The King at the end
of *Cymbeline* imagines an even more bizarre birth, envisioning himself as
miraculously "A mother to the birth of three" (V.v.369).[1] Images of births

may thus be distorted even in happy moments or in comedy which celebrates the preliminary pairing. But outside the generic confines of comedy, births in Shakespeare are almost uniformly grim; the customary ritual processes are never completely accomplished; and, on occasion men, like the King in *Cymbeline*, seem to assume sole responsibility for the birth.

A study focused on these maimed rites is perhaps in danger of perpetuating the simplistic assumptions which seem to lie behind the problems. Women, long accustomed to having their world views shaped by images of male-produced literature and by the ideas of male teachers and leaders, obviously have internalized some of their values. One of the most important projects of feminist criticism is to bring to consciousness a realization of the reductionist views of women which permeate earlier art and to begin to discard assumptions which cannot be reconciled with each other or with reality. Births continue to be traumatic, and this continues to be a major problem for women and for men.[2] The causes are no doubt complex, but one of them is certainly the limited number of categories into which men have historically relegated women. Even so subtle and sensitive a writer as Shakespeare, who actually depicts the relatively "infinite variety" of a Cleopatra, does not altogether avoid derogating her as "whore" because of her sexuality or, conversely, of elevating Hermione because of her presumably sixteen years of enforced chastity. As in *The Winter's Tale*, the birth trauma crystalizes a crisis of seemingly irreconcilable opposites in the male perception of women, and both male and female audiences need to see this in order to combat it.

I will suggest that the maimed birth rites which occur in patriarchal creations reflect the fears and tensions of the father when faced with birth—the moment which confronts him with undeniable evidence of female sexuality and arouses anxiety over both frightening female powers and his own paternity. Pregnancy forces the recognition of an unsettling metamorphosis of the female body, of the reality of blood and physical stress, and, as mere sexual intercourse does not, of manifestly irreversible consequences. Female traditions make possible the acceptance of these effects. Indeed in prepatriarchal societies they seem to have been reverenced. Countless surviving prehistoric figures of the Great Goddess, usually apparently pregnant, and often with exaggerated genitalia or multiple breasts, eloquently attest to an era which venerated women for their creative powers (Neumann plates 1–53). But for patriarchal males these mysterious realities are suspect and fraught with danger. Sigmund Freud argues that birth is "the first of all dangers to life and the prototype of all the later ones that cause us to feel anxiety" (11:173). He is, of course, referring to the trauma of the child; but the trauma to the father seems no less significant. I hypothesize that such tensions and anxieties would not have occurred in this form in archaic matrilinear societies and that they are, at least in part, the result of the reductionist definition of women in terms of their usefulness to men,[3] and of the separation of functions and aspects which were once more variously and harmoniously integrated in the concept of the Great Goddess. The Goddess herself, although multifarious in her aspects, perhaps because of her association with the three phases of the moon, was often defined as triple. Her association with the moon connected birth naturally with the stages of waxing, waning, and fullness, thus linking it with growth, maturity, and death. Under the control of the Great Goddess, frequently imagined as the "Triple Hecate," birth was awe-inspiring, perhaps frightening, but not divorced from other natural phenomena.

There is widespread agreement on the existence of a prehistoric society in ancient Europe that was matrilinear and nonpatriarchal if not actually matriarchal.[4] Remnants survive in the form of religious icons apparently celebrating female fertility and in many ancient myths and legends. Because of her potency and variety, the Triple Goddess was able to assimilate what later seem contradictory functions. As Moon Goddess she could be patron of virgins, benign mother, and angel of death. Foreshadower of Diana, Venus, Cybele/Demeter, and Proserpina, she ruled over sky, earth, and underworld. Gerda Lerner, in her recent landmark work, *The Creation of Patriarchy*, meticulously weighs the evidence for early European Goddess worship and concludes that, at least from the fourth millennium forward, the evidence for the primacy of the Great Goddess is abundant and convincing (148).

Historians disagree on the causes of the shift from this early culture focused on the female to the patriarchy of historical record. The change has been attributed to the discovery of the male role in conception, to the invention of the plow, to the development of agriculture, to the incursions of Indo-European culture into Europe, and to the influence of the Judeo-Christian tradition. Lerner attributes the change to multiple causes, but concludes that "in the course of the agricultural revolution the exploitation of human labor and the sexual exploitation of women become inextricably linked" (52).

Whatever the cause of the shift, it is clear that memories of Goddess worship survived it—perhaps because the first actual experience of most human beings is of a link with a great and seemingly all-powerful mother. It has been argued that the later cult of the Virgin Mary was promoted as a way of incorporating the Goddess into Christianity, and it is conceivable that the very idea of the Christian Trinity was an appropriation of the memory of the Triple Goddess to patriarchal uses. We know that such appropriations were commonplace, and that Augustine and other church fathers countenanced the idea that early religions foreshadowed Christianity. Edgar Wind describes a sculpture of the Triple Goddess on the tomb of Pope Sixtus IV and suggests that "As pagan goddess of the moon she foreshadows the triple glory of the Christian sun" (241–58). George Wither in his emblem book of 1635 provides another interesting example. Reprinting an old emblem of three interlocking crescent moons, an image similar to early Hecate symbols and certainly evocative of the Goddess, he adds as commentary,

> What in this *Emblem*, that mans meanings were,
> Who made it first, I neither know nor care;
> For, whatsoere, he purposed, or thought,
> To serve my *purpose*, now it shall be taught;
> Who many times, before this Taske is ended,
> Must picke out *Moralls*, where was none intended.
>   This knot of *Moones* (or *Crescents*) crowned thus,
> Illustrate may a Mystery to us,
> Of pious use (and, peradventure, such
> As from old *Hieroglyphicks*, erres not much)
> *Old-times*, upon the *Moone*, three *names*
> bestow'd;
> Because, three diverse wayes, her selfe she show'd
> And, in the *sacred-bookes*, it may be showne,
> That *holy-Church*, was figur'd by the *Moone*.
>   (111)

Ernst Curtius suggests that "In messianically and apocalyptically excited periods, faded symbolic figures can be filled with new life, like shades which have drunk blood" (104). There is ample evidence that the Renaissance was such a period. And whether or not Shakespeare was consciously aware of conflict between the traditions of patriarchal Christianity and memories of the Goddess, remnants of the struggle can be found embedded in his works.[5] Shakespeare's tendency to employ the simplistic division of female characters into the three categories of Virgin, "Whore" (i.e., sexu-ally active woman), and Crone might in itself be seen as a perverted memory of the Goddess.[6] Vincenzo Cartari, in his 1587 collection of lore on the ancient gods, a work certainly known to Robert Burton, and possibly to Shakespeare, prints an image of three forms of the Triple Goddess—the virginal Diana, the sexual/maternal Luna, and a veiled Hecate/Perserpina. All three are figures of power. The first two are active and perhaps frightening: Diana is winged, wearing a quiver of arrows, and with a minature lion in each hand; Luna carries a flaming torch in one hand and serpents in the other, and wears a crescent moon on her head; the motionless Perserpina, is completely veiled and mysterious.[7] In Shake-speare the figure of Hecate, repeatedly invoked by name, most interestingly in *Macbeth* and *A Midsummer Night's Dream*, illustrates the force of the dual traditions extremely well, with the destructive power of the witches in the one and the magical resonance of the Triple Hecate in the other.

The first known Heqit seems to have been one of the oldest goddesses of predynastic Egypt, with a name derived from the Egyptian word for "intelligence" or "tribal ruler" (Budge 159; Walker 50). She first appears in Greek literature in Hesiod's *Theogony*, which describes her as a pre-Olympian Titan who shared rule later with Zeus, offering aid particularly in war, athletics, and hunting (109–13). Very early she is referred to as tri-form, three-faced, the "Triple Hecate" who surfaces in Puck's reference in *A Midsummer Night's Dream* (V.i.384). The goddess of the meeting place of roads, she was sometimes called Trivia—Tri-Via. The trivializa-tion of the word is a mark of the trivialization of the Goddess.[8] As moon goddess, Hecate personified aspects which reflected its phases: waxing, full, and waning. In Archaic Greece her cyclical image was also revealed in her roles as Creator/Preserver/Destroyer. She ruled heaven, earth, and the underworld, and later acquired many names in each manifestation—Luna, Cynthia, Semele, Diana, Venus, Lucina, Ceres, Juno, Perserpina, and many others.[9] Indeed, she seems to have been a manifestation of that Great Goddess who predated patriarchy. In Apuleius's *The Golden Ass*, which may have been a source of *A Midsummer Night's Dream*, the Goddess appears to Lucius in his final vision, saying that she is called Ceres, Mother of Gods, Minerva, Venus, Diana, Perserpina, Juno, Bellona, and Hecate, but that her true name is Isis (547). As the original trinity, the Goddess, whatever her name, is later linked with both the three fates and the three furies, and finally domesticated into the Eumenides. Again the degeneration of her images is clear. My point is that in the matrilinear tradition Hecate was an extremely powerful deity, primarily benign, even as she guided her followers from birth toward inevitable death (although her underworld was not a place of punishment but a return to the mother). Only in later history and especially in the Christian era was she demoted to the status of goddess of witchcraft. Her decline paralleled the suppression of Goddess worship, the rise of patriarchy, and the general devaluation of women. The disintegration and displacement of her powers in turn problematized the rituals of birth.

As the aspects of the Triple Goddess shrank into commonplace clichés about women, patriarchal society easily assimilated the young virgin, who became an instrument and guardian of paternal power. The mother/wife was effectively desexualized and incorporated in the faint echo of Goddess worship which survived in the form of veneration of the Virgin Mary. And the Crone was essentially reduced to a menacing reminder of death. When faced with the fact of birth, the male's great difficulty seems to be in harmonizing Virgin and "Whore," and the result in literature is the depiction of births as clouded, ominous, divisive, or catastrophic. I will focus on the Virgin/"Whore" dichotomy as it underlies and disrupts the transition from wife to mother.

Birth rituals seem to be marked by certain recurring patterns from earliest history and perhaps prehistory. They feature blessing of the marriage bed, rites and charms to insure fertility, birth, washing, parental acknowledgment, naming, gift giving, welcoming into family and community, and later the "purification" or "thanksgiving" of the mother.[10] Shakespearean births are notably deficient in the fulfillment of these stages. Actual births in *Titus Andronicus*, *The Winter's Tale*, *Pericles*, and *Henry VIII* are all conspicuously clouded, and the rituals, except in *Henry VIII*, are truncated or aborted.

In *Titus Andronicus* the mother rejects the child; it receives no name; its own brothers vie for the right to kill it; only the surprisingly fervent determination of Aaron the Moor to claim his child (a claim strongly supported by the child's color) and to preserve it fulfills ritual expectations (IV.ii.65–110). But Aaron's paternal instincts terminate with his death. No community welcomes the child, although the hard-won concession that Aaron wrings from Lucius that he will save, nourish, and raise the boy (V.i.84–86) may qualify as Lucius's grudging, and quite possibly unreliable, acceptance of a kind of paternal responsibility.

Paulina brings the newborn daughter to her father in *The Winter's Tale*, she says, because of the need to confer about godparents (II.iii.39–40);

but, in spite of her detailed assurance that the babe is the copy of the father, Leontes refuses to acknowledge the child and casts her out of the community, condemning her to probable death. She is named Perdita by a misleading "ghost" of her supposedly dead mother, who appears to Antigonus in a dream; and there are no godparents or witnesses. Only belatedly is she welcomed into the all-male shepherd's family. Similarly in *Pericles* Marina is born to a "dying" mother, who seems to have no clear memory of the event or her miraculous recovery (III.iv.6~8). The child is acknowledged by her father and perfunctorily named, apparently without formal witnesses, but then very rapidly consigned to a foster family.

Only in *Henry VIII* are the birth rites properly observed, and even here they are somewhat shadowed. The wished-for son turns out to be a daughter. The bearer to the King of the news of the birth feels poorly recompensed by the mere 100 pounds she receives for her messenger role, even though she, like Paulina, has taken the trouble to assure the father that the child is as like to him as cherry to cherry (V.i.163~76). However, Henry duly goes to greet the stranger and her mother, implicitly acknowledging paternity. He personally arranges for three godparents (in conformance with the new Anglican practice)[11] and presides at a sumptuous christening where munificent gifts clearly signal the welcome of the community. Indeed the press of the crowd is such that the porter complains that there is such a "fry of fornication" that "this one christening will beget a thousand" more (V.ii.36~37). Duly named, Elizabeth is celebrated in Cranmer's prophecy in terms so laudatory that Henry concludes (with hyperbole and selective memory): "Thou has made me now a man! Never, before / This happy child, did I get any thing" (V.iii.64~65).[12] Elizabeth will bring peace and prosperity but not fertility. Shakespeare is bound by history to concede that her heir will spring not from her body but phoenix-like from her ashes. She will die aged and virginal, like a "most unspotted lily" (V.iii.56~61). Even at this triumphant moment, female fertility and virginity cannot be reconciled. The male yearning to have it both ways cannot be satisfied.[13] Only as an afterthought to this resounding scene does Henry lead the assembly to visit the Queen. And in spite of the happiness of the moment, no one in Shakespeare's audience could have been oblivious to the next chapters of the real Anne Boleyn's story—her delivery of a still-born son a few months later and her own subsequent trial and execution.

Actual birth rituals in Shakespeare are thus never completely satisfying. Even references to pregnancy and childbirth tend to be grim. Richard III's birth is recalled in the most appropriately ominous terms by King Henry just before his murder:

> The owl shriek'd at thy birth, an evil sign;
> The night-crow cried, aboding luckless time;
> Dogs howl'd, and hideous tempest shook down trees;
> The raven rook'd her on the chimney's top,
> And chatt'ring pies in dismal discords sung;
> The mother felt more than a mother's pain,
> And yet brought forth less than a mother's hope,
> To wit, an indigested and deformed lump.
>   (3H6 V.vi.44–54)

Queen Margaret manages to implicate Richard's mother in her violent and justified condemnation of the son, saying to her

> From forth the kennel of thy womb hath crept
> A hell-hound that doth hunt us all to death;
> That dog, that had his teeth before his eyes . . .
> Thy womb let loose to chase us to our graves.
>   (R3 IV.iv.47–54)

His mother merely describes his birth as "a grievous burthen" (IV.iv.168). Macduff and Posthumus are "untimely ripped" from their mothers' wombs, and the latter's birth follows immediately upon the death of his father and two brothers. As we have seen, Tamora in *Titus Andronicus* condemns her newborn baby to immediate death, and Julietta in *Measure for Measure* declares her repentance for her premature pregnancy, acknowledging it as an evil (II.ii.19, 35). Death or apparent death of the newly delivered mother follows on the heels of birth in the case of Titania's pregnant votaress in *A Midsummer Night's Dream*, Thaisa in *Pericles*, and Hermione in *The Winter's Tale*.

Obviously these events in the plays are shaped by history, narrative necessity, and genre; and doubtless happy, ritualistically correct births present less potential for drama than traumatic ones. But the volume and tone of the evidence is impressive. The dramatic emphasis on the danger of the moment of birth is both historically and psychologically sound. Women and children did die in great numbers, and the great danger of childbirth justifies the service of thanksgiving for safe delivery in the post-1549 Anglican Book of Common Prayer.[14] But the less obvious perils to the father and to the community go beyond the risk of loss of life.

Babies are prototypical exemplars of liminality, as described by Victor Turner (94–96, 106). They are associated with death, the womb, passivity, silence, near-nakedness, anonymity, absence of kinship rights, and, after the initial gender identification, with a minimization of sexuality (94–106). As such liminal creatures they disturb social organizations in ways which endanger both themselves and society and therefore offer rich dramatic opportunities. Births also force a confrontation with social problems which have been previously suppressed or ignored, and I believe it is possible to see Shakespeare's treatment of pregnancy and birth as an almost paradigmatic representation of a male problem created by patriarchal society — the reductionist fragmentation of the female and the extreme difficulty of reconciling the image of the "whore" or sexually active woman with those of wife and mother.

Clearly these categories are defined in terms of sexual relationship to males. In Shakespeare, virgins are overwhelmingly the predominant category of female. I have counted thirty-five examples of the type. A few are dubious, and there may be more. Their virginity causes relatively few problems. Property of their fathers, at least in theory, they will become property of their spouses. But the necessary transition from sexual abstinence to fertility is fraught with dangers, attested to repeatedly in Shakespeare, of incorporating "whore," chaste wife, and mother into one female figure.

Shakespeare follows the trend of desexualizing motherhood in his portraits of presumably chaste wives such as Brutus's Portia, Calphurnia, and Mistress Page. The great majority of these women are either barren or childless (some are mothers only of daughters, a kind of barrenness in many minds), and sexuality is an important aspect only of those whose virtue is doubted. Although Shakespeare's texts suggest an amazing variety of sexually active women, from prostitutes and madams (Doll Tearsheet and Mistress Overdone) to women who may be in fact serially monogamous (Regan, Gertrude, Cleopatra), all of those whose sexuality is emphasized or questioned are shadowed by the implication of "whorishness." And yet, strikingly, the "whorish" women are the fertile ones. They are pregnant (Jacquenetta, Hermione, the Juliet of *Measure for Measure*) and mothers of sons (Gertrude, Cleopatra, Queen Margaret, Tamora, Cymbeline's queen, Sycorax). For all practical purposes, mature, potentially sexually active women on Shakespeare's stage are perceived as either virgins or whores; and it is the "whores" who shape the future. This dilemma obviously works to create the crisis for men of the birth trauma and helps to explain the scarcity of mothers in the plays.

There are, of course, some mature women who are specifically characterized and seen as mothers (the Abbess of *The Comedy of Errors*, Lady
Capulet, Gertrude, the Countess of Rossillion, Vergilia); but they are rare,
and they often fade out of their plays for long periods even when they
exist. The major exception is Volumnia, mother of Coriolanus, and she is
so thoroughly the product of patriarchal Roman society that she has
almost none of the expected maternal characteristics. A widowed mother
and grandmother, she seems in fact a type of crone.

Patriarchy has had the most trouble with the middle term of the female
trinity. The confusion of names bestowed on her suggests the ambivalence
about her. The object of desire was both Diana, the chaste huntress who
turned Actaeon into a stag when he viewed her naked beauty in the
forest, and Venus, the lascivious goddess of love and beauty whom Prospero
excluded from his nuptial masque for Ferdinand and Miranda (IV.i.87–101).
Female sexuality, obviously essential for human preservation, was sought
after, but also feared, and repressed. Minerva, goddess of wisdom and
knowledge, was confused with Bellona, Roman goddess of war (whose
bridegroom Macbeth was said to be), who was in turn merged with an
Asian moon goddess linked with fertility (Linche Sii verso).

In Shakespeare the vacillation between Venus and Diana is a regularly
occurring theme, and it helps to explain, I think, why the inescapable
realities of pregnancy and birth confront the males with almost irresolv-
able dilemmas. Men demand and cherish the "purity" of their wives and
daughters yet require fertility to achieve progeny. "Purity" and "chastity"
become almost inseparable from celibacy, and the necessary sexuality
seems inevitably contaminated. Whereas prehistoric man would have
found these qualities inseparable aspects of one Goddess, patriarchal
society has created a climate which drastically limits such possibilities.

Shakespeare's depiction of Joan La Pucelle may be read as illustrating
the confusion of responses to women in general. Although history,
Holinshed, and political alignments determined the outlines of her portrait,
Shakespeare shaped the material and supplied the ambiguous details. As
Leslie Fiedler points out, her very appellation is a pun—Pucelle is virgin in
French but puzzel or whore in English (52). A matrilinear heritage emerges
in her description of her inspiration. Joan claims special revelation from
"God's mother" and inspiration from St. Katherine, Christian patron of
childbirth (I.ii.78, 100). Fiedler hypothesizes that Shakespeare "sensed"
that Joan was an adherent of the cult of the Great Goddess, adding that
court records show that she had been inducted into the ancient rites of the

mother, that she hung wreaths on the *Arbre des Dames,* and consorted with fairies—that she was, in fact, a "witch" in the sense of follower of the Goddess (62–63). Shakespeare does evoke this "memory" in the scene where, faced with defeat, Joan calls up familiar spirits, fiends whom she has nursed with her blood; but in Shakespeare they are helpers and agents of "the lordly Monarch of the North," presumably the devil, rather than Goddess servers (V.iii).

Although linked obliquely with motherhood by her dependence on God's mother and St. Katherine, and by the image of nursing devils, Joan's name is a constant reminder of her virginity; and the insistence on her virginity and saintliness and her identification as "Astrea's daughter" resonate through the first part of the play. However, her escalating association with sexuality begins to turn the tables. Charles calls her "Bright star of Venus" and compares her to Helen, mother of Constantine, herself an ambiguous figure (I.ii.143–45).[15] Joan's promises, he says, are like Adonis's garden—prime icon of fertility. He later links her with Rhodope, a renowned courtesan memorialized with a great pyramid by an Egyptian pharoah (I.vi.21–22). After that, reduced to a "giglot wench" (IV.vii.41), she merges with Circe, becoming an ugly witch, a "Fell banning hag," and enchantress (V.iii.34–42), and a drab. The last epithet comes from her rejected father, who claims her as "the first fruit of [his] bach'lorship" and finally wishes that she had been nursed fatally with ratsbane or devoured by a ravenous wolf (V.iv.13–32).

Joan still manages to maintain some dignity and respect, however, maintaining that she is virtuous and holy, inspired from above by celestial grace, that she never consorted with evil spirits, and concluding,

> Joan of Aire hath been
> A virgin from her tender infancy,
> Chaste and immaculate in very thought
> Whose maiden blood, thus rigorously effus'd
> Will cry for vengeance at the gates of heaven.
> (V.iv.49–53)

It is only when she claims to be with child by Alanson or Reignier that all respect crumbles and York concludes persuasively that the strumpet has known so many that she knows not whom to accuse (V.iv.80–81). Although Holinshed records that Joan's execution was delayed for nine months in case she was in fact pregnant, Shakespeare never makes clear whether she was or not. Her pleading her belly may betray weakness or hypocrisy; she may or may not have been a disciple of the Goddess. But Shakespeare's scene creates the indelible impression that her death sentence is vindicated by her pregnancy—real or pretended. York's last words to her departing figure, "Break thou in pieces and consume to ashes, / Thou foul accursed minister of hell!" (V.iv.92–93) leave at least the suspicion that he is actually cursing her for being a woman who has hopelessly confused the categories of Virgin, Whore, and Mother.[16] Birth has not evoked any stages of ritual, but the underlying perils are apparent.

Premarital pregnancies are in fact rare in Shakespeare. Jacquenetta's in *Love's Labour's Lost* seems to be redeemed by her low class status, and Don Armado's vow to "hold the plough" for her for three years even after he has learned that she is two months "gone" with child (we have only Costard's word that Armado and not Costard himself is the father), and by apparent social acceptance. Julietta's pregnancy in *Measure for Measure*, dubiously sanctified by a prenuptial contract, precipitates near tragedy as the visible sign of the "corruption" of Vienna but is in the end tacitly accepted (she neither speaks nor is spoken to in the final scene) by the social group. In *The Taming of the Shrew* and *Hamlet* Shakespeare has suppressed the premarital pregnancies or possibility thereof which characterize his sources.[17] Whether the motive behind this is middle class morality or distaste for the subject or both, we cannot say.

The importance of both premarital and postmarital chastity for women is stressed throughout the canon. Sexual activity and fertility, although desirable within limits, are severely restricted. The opposition of Diana and Venus is ubiquitous. The wife in *The Comedy of Errors* is caught between her virtuously virginal sister and the courtesan. She seems to opt rather discontentedly for chastity, although there is time for her to have had sex with the wrong brother when she mistakenly entertains him at dinner. The problem of the problem comedies is to reconcile virginity and fertility—Isabella with Julietta in *Measure for Measure*, and Helen (legendary protegé of Venus) with Diana in *All's Well That Ends Well*. In each case the odds for successful union, though hopeful, are uncertain. Bertram agrees to accept Helen if her offspring can be proven to be his, and Isabella remains silent in response to the Duke's marriage proposal. Hamlet wants Gertrude to be both virginal and maternal. *The Tempest* struggles to bless Miranda's marriage with "Earth's increase, [and] foison plenty" (IV.i.110) but, although Juno and Ceres (mothers and patrons of motherhood) are welcome, Venus (sexuality) is bafflingly excluded. As late as *Two Noble Kinsmen* the struggle between Diana, Venus, and Mars, patrons respectively of Emilia, Palamon, and Arcite, continues unabated. It is resolved by the union of Diana and Venus only by default, as a fluke accident eliminates Arcite, the champion of Mars.

Historically, as we have seen, patriarchy co-opted, diminished, and perverted the powers of the prehistoric Goddess. Men assumed control of fertility, once apparently the sole province of women. In ancient Athens the annual Thesmophoria, festival of Demeter, which had as its purpose securing the fertility of the fields, was held at harvest time and was open only to women (Harvey 177). However, in Rome, locus classicus of patriarchy, the Lupercalia, the purpose of which was similarly to secure fertility, was presided over by males and began in the cave of Romulus and Remus, who were suckled not by a woman but by a wolf. Significantly, the festival was held in February, Roman month of purification, a fact which seems to suggest some possibility of pollution as cause or perhaps inevitable concomitant of infertility (ibid., 250–51). Caesar, in hoping to cure Calphurnia's barrenness, looks not to a goddess, although at least two, Juno and Lucina, were available, but to Mark Antony, who, as Lupercus, might touch her with fertilizing power.

The association of birth and pollution was strong in the ancient Hebraic tradition. Mosaic law, set forth in Leviticus 12, stipulates that a woman is unclean for seven days ("like as she is uncleane when she is put a parte for her disease") and must remain "in the blood of purification" for thirty-three days. For a maid-child the time was doubled. During that time she must "touche no halowed thing, nor come in to the sanctuarie." After forty or eighty days the mother was to bring a lamb and a young pigeon to the synagogue as a sacrifice "for sin." Even the Virgin Mary performed this rite (Luke 2.21–24), and February 2 became in the seventh century The Feast of the Purification of the Blessed Virgin Mary, later known as Candlemas. At least one commentator has suggested that this feast was instituted by Pope Gelasius to curb the excesses of the Roman Lupercalia.[18] In any case, both feasts suggest that the power and the glory of fertility had shifted emphatically to the male and that whatever complicity was allowed to the female was contaminating.

The 1549 edition of the Anglican Book of Common Prayer preserved the service of The Purification of Women. But Protestant objections and misunderstandings were immediately forthcoming, and in the 1552 Book the title was changed to The Thanksgiving of Women after Child-birth, Commonly Called the Churching of Women.[19] The locus of the ceremony was also gradually moved from the church door to the Holy Table, and finally in 1662 to "some convenient place." Remnants of the purification rite remain in the English tradition that the woman should be veiled and should bring "accustomed offerings." By contrast, as late as 1951 the Roman rite is still described as beginning at the porch or door of the church and moving inside after the woman has been sprinkled with lustral water. The priest's violet stole, worn outside the church, is changed to white inside, again suggesting a remnant of purification rite (Fortescue 252, 397).

Shakespeare may have shared Protestant uneasiness at the idea of the need to purify women after childbirth; I find no clear traces of this rite in his work. Because of the traditional requirement, medical or liturgical, of an interval between the birth and the mother's attendance at church, and because baptism was to be done speedily, baptisms frequently preceded churching and were therefore performed in the absence of the mother. This practice had the effect of deemphasizing the centrality of the woman. Godparents replaced parents, but the father was regularly in evidence. The custom of rapid christening may help to account for the absence of Queen Anne from her daughter's baptism in *Henry VIII*, but the need for time for recuperation seems more likely to lie behind Hermione's complaint in *The Winter's Tale* that she has been denied the usual child-bed privilege. In *Titus Andronicus, The Winter's Tale, Pericles,* and *Henry VIII* we do not see the newly delivered mothers after the births, and in the first three there is a hiatus, in two a substantial hiatus, before the mothers reappear. Anne, of course, never does reappear. Like the Goddess herself, the mothers go into eclipse.

Goddesses are invoked in Shakespeare, but typically by men who control or attempt to control them, and their prayers are typically not for fertility. There are some interesting permutations. Diana in Shakespeare is usually referred to as chaste and virginal, but it is notable that both the mothers in *The Comedy of Errors* and in *Pericles* retire to temples in Ephesus on being separated from their families; and, as the famous multi-breasted statue of the Diana of Ephesus attests, the ancient deity of that city was a fertility figure. Thaisa rather incongruously prays to Diana on recovering from the trials of childbirth and her ordeal at sea, and she retires specifically to Diana's temple. Pericles calls on Lucina, apparently unavailingly, to aid his wife in her difficult childbirth. Both Edmund and Lear call on Nature as fertility goddess—Edmund to celebrate his own illegitimate conception and Lear to curse his recalcitrant daughter Goneril. His prayer shockingly demands the cancellation of his own posterity:

> Hear Nature, hear, dear goddess, hear!
> Suspend thy purpose, if thou didst intend
> To make this creature fruitful.
> Into her womb convey sterility,
> Dry up in her the organs of increase,
> And from her derogate body never spring
> A babe to honor her.
>
> (I.iv.275–81)

Richard II speaks in a proprietory tone to the Earth on his return to England; but in a curious reversal of roles, he sees himself initially as the mother:

> Dear earth, I do salute thee with my hand . . .
> As a long parted mother with her child
> Plays fondly with her tears and smiles in meeting,
> So weeping, smiling, greet I thee, my earth,
> And do thee favors with my royal hands.
>
> (III.ii.6–11)

But subsequently he rather asks favors, as if of a mother, begging her not to feed his enemies and to trouble them with spiders, toads, nettles, and death-dealing adders (III.ii.12–22). Timon of Athens similarly invokes the Spirit of the Earth as a "common mother" whose "womb unmeasurable and infinite breast / Teems and feeds all." He remembers that she is also engenderer of the "black toad and adder blue, / The gilded newt and eyeless venom'd worm" and of all "abhorred births" and enjoins her to feed him one root and then abandon human fertility in favor of beasts: "Ensear thy fertile and conceptious womb / Let it no more bring out ingrateful man! (IV.iii.177–88)

Shades of an archaic Goddess and memories of her rituals are perhaps evoked by these references to her disparate aspects. She emerges more clearly in the fertile Egypt of Cleopatra. Herself identified with Isis, the Egyptian Queen tantalizes us with the question of whether she can be both "whore" and "wife." We see teeming Egypt subdued by sterile Rome, but the play's end intriguingly suggests an apotheosis of woman/goddess which defeats the best laid plans of Octavius.

The Triple Hecate is evoked most clearly and specifically, however, in *A Midsummer Night's Dream* and *Macbeth*, both plays centrally concerned with fertility and progeny. *Macbeth* seems a play calculated to eradicate female fertility altogether and therefore, ironically, fatally to doom Macbeth's project of founding a royal line.[20] Motherhood is explicitly, even gratuitously, renounced in Lady Macbeth's unsexing of herself, in the murder of Lady Macduff, and in the denial even of female participation in Macduff's birth. The Weird sisters, themselves descendants of the revered Triple Goddess Wyrd of Anglo-Saxon mythology, have diminished into "secret, black, and midnight hags" (IV.i.48). The name of Hecate evokes in Macbeth not the pleasures of natural process but a world where nature seems dead, where witchcraft celebrates "Pale Hecat's off'rings" and murder stalks ghostlike toward its innocent prey (II.i.49-56). Macbeth propels himself relentlessly toward a world in which the exclusion of all but one aspect of the Great Goddess insures sterility.

Hecate certainly connotes witchcraft and fatality to Shakespeare, but her name also occasionally calls up the memory of the more positive and powerful Triple Hecate of the matrilinear tradition. King Lear parallels "the sacred radiance of the sun" with the "mysteries of Hecate and the night" (I.i.110).[21] The love-sick Orlando in As You Like It invokes the aid of the "thrice-crowned queen of night" with her "chaste eye," "pale sphere," and "huntress' name" (III.ii.2-5). And A Midsummer Night's Dream presents an extended celebration of the realm of the Queen of the Night in the moon-drenched, magical landscape where fairies run with the dragon-drawn chariot of the Triple Hecate (V.i.384). Titania's very name recalls the connection of the Goddess with the pre-Olympian Titans overthrown by the patriarchal Zeus. All three phases of the moon are suggested in the play—the waning old moon which postpones the marriage of Theseus and Hippolyta, the new moon which Hippolyta imagines like a silver bow new bent in heaven, and the full moon of fertility, floods, and erotic dalliance. Even the multiplication of romantic couples in the nighttime forest suggests the possibility (here suppressed except perhaps in the case of Titania and Bottom) of the mass coupling of fertility rituals.

The whole play might be viewed as a contest between matriarchy and patriarchy. Hippolyta suggests both the appeal of the virgin and the threat of the Amazon warrior, a woman wooed only by the sword and won by injuries. Hermia and Lysander set forth from Athens in revolt against the patriarchal decree of her father and Theseus. They intend to seek a matriarchal refuge with his wealthy aunt beyond the forest. But the forest, magnified and mystified, and erotically charged, becomes the focus of the play. Titania, the Faerie Queen, is a powerful and appealing force—almost equal to Oberon; and all the faeries except Puck serve the Faerie Queene.

Both the pregnant votaress of Titania, who has given birth to the change-ling boy, and the chaste vestal, "imperial vot'ress of Diana," are luminous presences even in their absence, suggesting respectively the presence of both Venus and Diana.[22] But the Diana figure remains serenely untouched by sexuality, while the Venus figure dies in childbirth. Ceres, the powerful and perennially fertile mother grieving for her lost Proserpina, is recalled in the disarray of nature caused by the quarrel of Oberon and Titania. The overwhelming pressure towards the fertility and consummation appropri-ate to Midsummer's Eve (said to have been a day for Goddess celebration in Celtic prehistory) overcomes such temporary blocking forces as the resistance of Egeus and Theseus, the confusion of sex objects, and pre-sumably even the propriety of the city-bred Hermia herself, who insists, when preparing to sleep in the forest, that her lover "lie farther off" (II.ii.44). Oberon promotes consummation for mortals and even unleashes temporarily the extramarital lusts of his wife. Peter Brook, in his landmark production of the play, made the union of Bottom and Titania an orgiastic fertility rite; and Frank Kermode wrote in 1961 that Bottom had known the love of the triple goddess in a vision (219). Ambiguous as it may be, the Athenian forest displays and tolerates female eroticism.

But all is not sweetness and light. Women in this play are made the objects of a considerable amount of Old Boy humor. We laugh at the fight between Hermia and Helena because it confirms clichés about what is thought of as "feminine" behavior. Oberon gets the boy. Hermia is recon-ciled with her father and still gets her man, but in the farcical subplot Thisby dies as the result of her rebellion. The female power embodied in Titania holds out temporarily against the demands of her husband; but the frightening prospect of female insurrection and the naked revelation of female lust are safely curbed in Oberon's final victory. Magic is a metaphor for male power in this play. It serves to veil unpleasant realities. Titania's display of lust, a game licensed by male magic, is at first fun, but it becomes a nightmarish memory after the restorative second application of magic juice. Oberon sees the fresh and fragrant flowers Titania has used as a coronet for Bottom's hairy temples as weeping at their own "disgrace." He taunts her at his pleasure, and under the magic spell she begs his patience and quickly yields up the changeling boy (IV.i.51–61). The male has achieved his progeny without bothering to beget it; and, although no ritual accompanies this male "adoption," the consigning of the child to "proper" parentage restores order and presumably fertility. The threat to patriarchy is quelled even in the permissive world of the forest. Primordial memories of the Faerie Queene as Great Mother and of the mysteries of Midsummer's Eve are evoked and suppressed. The forest trope allows the idea of matriarchy to surface but ends, like *Macbeth*, by denying it. And, as we have seen, although new births are anticipated in the final scene, the prospect calls for Oberon's potent patriarchal magic to ward off disastrous "blots of [female] Nature."

I do not mean to propose that Shakespeare's treatment of fertility and birth represents a personal bias, but rather that it epitomizes social and cultural biases preserved in narrative and generic forms. His plays may achieve some of their modern resonance from the fact that males, and therefore females, still struggle with the problems of reconciling Venus and Diana into a woman who can be daughter, wife, mother, and mistress, if not whore. The ineluctable fact of birth propels the dilemma into consciousness in a way that cannot be ignored. Birth rituals probably end badly more often in literature than in life, but maimed rites engender powerful drama. Shakespeare involves us in such rites in ways which attest to both the intensity and the persistence of the conflicting feelings surrounding the processes of birth. In his plays the magic of birth rituals succeeds neither in controlling the future nor in erasing the past.

NOTES

For permission to reprint small portions of this chapter, the author thanks the Augustinian Historical Institute, publisher of *Proceedings of the PMR Conference*; and the Southeastern Renaissance Conference, publisher of *Renaissance Papers 1990*.

1. Marilyn Williamson sees this appropriation of the language of female procreation as a manifestation of the miraculous new order (164–65).

2. A *New York Times* article ("Suspicions") reported, in connection with the murder of Charles Stuart's pregnant wife, that "up to 45 percent of women who are battered are assaulted while pregnant." The implication is that the assaulters are the fathers.

3. Sigmund Freud defines "three inevitable relations that a man has with a woman—the woman who bears him, the woman who is his mate, and the woman who destroys him" ("Caskets" 12:301). Other reductionist categories include the virginal maiden/daughter, curiously omitted by Freud. Such systems may combine or confuse the sexually active categories of wife/mother/whore. Freud argues that for married men birth creates a triangle reminiscent of that which caused him anxiety as an Oedipal child and threatens him with deprivation of his wife's "maternal affection" (11:173).

4. For detailed descriptions of the Goddess, see Robert Graves, Erich Neumann, and, more recently, Gerda Lerner. All three posit an ancient prepatriarchal culture that revered a goddess of many names.

5. The recollections and perversions of the Goddess are discussed in my "Shades of the Triple Hecate" and *The Shakespearean Wild*.

6. The categories Virgin/Whore/Crone derive from images of women in art. Elizabethan drama portrays the divisions as maid/wife/widow. In Shakespeare chaste wife becomes almost indistinguishable from Virgin, and Whore merges with unchaste wife or sexually threatening woman. "Purity" becomes for reproductively capable women an ultimate virtue. The Crone is feared, demeaned, and vilified. Having lost her potential for fertility, she is no longer useful to men. Widows may be feared for their freedom from male control, and old women in general are associated with death both because they function as preparers of corpses for burial and because they are seen as reminders and harbingers of dissolution. This third member of the trinity is not central to my argument.

7. Burton refers to images from this work and advises his readers to "see more in Carterius and Verdurius" (3, 408). Antoine Du Verdier's translation of an early edition of Cartari into French appeared in 1581. See also Linche, especially Hiii verso-Hiv verso, and Mii for descriptions of Diana and the Gran Madre. (This translation is a modified version of Cartari.)

8. The Medieval curriculum includes, as the Trivium, the study of grammar, logic, and rhetoric, thought of as the lower group of the liberal arts. This term, already trivialized, also seems to derive from the ancient association with crossroads.

9. These stages in various cultures are discussed by Ann Warren Turner (*passim*) and by Arnold van Gennep in his discussion of pregnancy and childbirth (41–46). Edward Berry has a slightly different formulation, including the "naked immersion of the infant," a step for which I find no provision in the post-Reformation descriptions of either Roman or Anglican baptism rites. Berry describes the ritual as a rite of passage for infant and mother. There is no mention of father (25). (In private correspondence Berry points out a passage in the Church of England *Constitutions and Cannons Ecclesiasticall*, London, 1604, G2ᵛ, which refers to either dipping the infant in water or laying water on the face.) Van Gennep describes some rites that include the father.

10. Van Gennep explains why birthing mother and new child are viewed as "strangers" disturbing the established order (41, 50).

11. The Roman rite specifies one godparent, or at most two. It also excludes priests from this role unless they have been granted special permission (Fortescue 378–79). The Anglican custom is to have two godparents of the same sex as the child and one of the opposite sex. Henry VIII observes this expectation. The 1559 Book of Common Prayer simply mentions godmothers and godfathers (270).

12. Coppélia Kahn explains that daughters may "function as mothers to their fathers by 'delivering' them to new identities as fathers." She suggests further that

they unite chastity and fertility in this birth (221). At least this speech is an interest-ing variation on the stereotype of females being "made women" by motherhood.

13. Freud identifies the difficulty as that of combining the male's affectionate and sensual feelings. He concludes that "anyone [obviously male] who is to be really free and happy in love must have surmounted his respect for women and have come to terms with the idea of incest with his mother and sister" ("Debasement" 11:186). The respect for women is associated with the affectionate and connects easily with the Virgin, while the sensual is tainted by the memory of forbidden incestuous desires for family members.

14. See discussion of the rite below.

15. Geoffrey of Monmouth called Helena a Queen and identified her as the daughter of King Coel of Britain and wife of Constantius, father of Constantine. Other historians claimed that she was a public courtesan and that Constantine was born of a union consummated without benefit of clergy (Davis 232–33).

16. Mary Douglas identifies Joan of Arc as a prototypical example of the intruder who threatens socially established categories and therefore, like the witch, evokes fear and revulsion. Douglas points out Joan's anomalous presence as "a peasant at court, a woman in armour, an outsider in the councils of war" (103).

17. In George Gascoigne's *Supposes*, Shakespeare's source for *The Taming of the Shrew*, the Bianca figure is pregnant by her lover (*Riverside* 107–8). Ophelia's predecessor in Saxo-Grammaticus is a courtesan, and in Belleforest she is Hamlet's mistress (*Riverside* 1136–37).

18. *The Catholic Encyclopedia*, "Candlemas" (3, 245) attributes this view to Jacques-Paul Migne but denies its validity.

19. For a discussion of the history of this rite, see Shepherd 305–8. The most recent revision of the American Book of Common Prayer (1977) changes the title to "A Thanksgiving for the Birth or Adoption of a Child," and provides for participation by the father.

20. See Adelman for a splendid elaboration of this idea.

21. There is an interesting textual crux here: Q1-2 read "mistresse"; F1 reads "miseries"; and F2 emends, probably correctly to "mysteries."

22. Montrose's excellent article relates the ambiguity of *A Midsummer Night's Dream* to the ambiguity of feelings about Queen Elizabeth, whose image is evoked by the love-proof votaress of Diana.

WORKS CITED

Adelman, Janet. " 'Born of Woman': Fantasies of Maternal Power in *Macbeth*," in *Cannibals, Witches, and Divorce: Estranging the Renaissance*. Ed. Marjorie Garber. Baltimore: Johns Hopkins University Press, 1987, 90–121.

Apuleius. *The Golden Ass*. Trans. W. Adlington (1566). Ed. S. Gaslee. London: Heinemann, 1925.

Berry, Edward. *Shakespeare's Comic Rites*. Cambridge: Cambridge University Press, 1984.

The Book of Common Prayer, 1559: The Elizabethan Prayer Book. Ed. John E. Booty. Charlottesville: University Press of Virginia, 1976.

Budge, E. A. Wallis. *The Dwellers on the Nile*. London: The Religious Tract Society, 1926.

Burton, Robert. *The Anatomy of Melancholy*. 3 vols. Ed. A. R. Shillets. Intro. A. H. Bullen. London: Bell, 1893. (Edited from the second edition, 1651, with author's corrections.)

Cartari, Vincenzo. *Le Imagini De i Dei de gli Antichi*. Venice: 1587.

Curtius, Ernst Robert. *European Literature and the Latin Middle Ages*. Trans. Willard R. Trask. Princeton: Princeton University Press, 1953. Reprinted 1973.

Davis, Elizabeth Gould. *The First Sex*. New York: Putnam's, 1971.

Douglas, Mary. *Purity and Danger: An Analysis of Concepts of Pollution and Taboo*. London: Routledge and Kegan Paul, 1966. Reprinted 1976.

Fiedler, Leslie. *The Stranger in Shakespeare*. New York: Stein and Day, 1972.

Fortescue, Adrian. *The Ceremonies of the Roman Rite Described*. London: Burns Oates and Washbourne, 1951.

Freud, Sigmund. "On the Universal Tendency to Debasement in the Sphere of Love," "A Special Type of Choice of Object Made by Men," and "The Theme of the Three Caskets," in *The Standard Edition of the Complete Psychological Works*. Ed. and trans. James Strachey. 24 vols. London: Hogarth, 1953–74. 11:179–90; 11:165–75; 12:291–301.

Frye, Northrop. *Anatomy of Criticism*. Princeton: Princeton University Press, 1957. Reprinted 1973.

The Geneva Bible: A Facsimile of the 1560 Edition. Intro. Lloyd E. Berry. Madison: University of Wisconsin Press, 1969.

Gennep, Arnold van. *The Rites of Passage*. Trans. Monika B. Vizedon and Gabrielle Caffee. Chicago: University of Chicago Press, 1960. Reprinted 1972.

Graves, Robert. *The White Goddess*. International Authors N.V., 1948. Amended and enlarged, New York: Farrar, Straus, and Giroux, 1966.

Harvey, Paul. *The Oxford Companion to Classical Literature*. Oxford: Clarendon, 1937, revised 1946.

Hesiod. *Homeric Hymns and Homerica*. Trans. Hugh G. Evelyn-White. London: Heinemann, 1914.

Kahn, Coppélia. *Man's Estate: Masculine Identity in Shakespeare*. Berkeley: University of California Press, 1980.

Kermode, Frank. "The Mature Comedies," *Early Shakespeare*. Ed. John Russell Brown and Bernard Harris. London: Arnold, 1961.

Lerner, Gerda. *The Creation of Patriarchy*. New York: Oxford University Press, 1986.

Linche, Richard, trans. *The Fountaine of Ancient Fiction*. London, 1599. (This is a modified version of Cartari in English.)

Montrose, Louis Adrian. " 'Shaping Fantasies': Figurations of Gender and Power in Elizabethan Culture," *Representations* 2 (1983), 61–94.

Neumann, Erich. *The Great Mother: An Analysis of the Archetype.* 2d ed. Princeton: Princeton University Press, 1955. Reprinted 1974.

Roberts, Jeanne Addison. "Birth Traumas in Shakespeare," *Renaissance Papers* (1990): 55–65.

———. "Shades of the Triple Hecate in Shakespeare," *Proceedings of the PMR Conference* 12/13 (1987–88): 47–66.

———. *The Shakespearean Wild: Geography, Genus, and Gender.* Lincoln: University of Nebraska Press, 1991.

Shakespeare, William. *The Riverside Shakespeare.* Ed. G. Blakemore Evans, et al. Boston: Houghton Mifflin, 1974.

Shepherd, Massey Hamilton. *The Oxford American Prayer Book Commentary.* New York: Oxford University Press, 1963.

"Suspicions Came Too Late in Boston," *New York Times,* 21 January 1990:25.

Turner, Ann Warren. *Rituals of Birth from Prehistory to the Present.* New York: McKay, 1978.

Turner, Victor. *The Ritual Process: Structure and Anti-Structure.* New York: Aldine, 1969. Reprinted Ithaca: Cornell University Press, 1977.

Walker, Barbara G. *The Crone: Women of Age, Wisdom, and Power.* New York: Harper and Row, 1985. Reprinted 1988.

Williamson, Marilyn. *The Patriarchy of Shakespeare's Comedies.* Detroit: Wayne State University Press, 1986.

Wind, Edgar. *Pagan Mysteries in the Renaissance.* London: Faber and Faber, 1958. Revised 1968.

Wither, George. *A Collection of Emblems.* London, 1635.

PART II

RITES OF RULE:
AUTHORITY AND GRACE

5

The Monarch and the Sacred: Shakespeare and the Ceremony for the Healing of the King's Evil

DEBORAH WILLIS

Recent historical criticism has been preoccupied with questions of subversion and orthodoxy in Renaissance drama; this essay is a contribution to that discussion. In their rush to construct a model of the "dominant ideology" of Shakespeare's culture, however, some critics have too glibly assumed that Renaissance Christianity always and necessarily served state power.[1] I focus instead on a religious ceremony and several plays of Shakespeare—all of which invoke a sacred magic on behalf of the monarchy—in order to explore what might be called the subversiveness of the sacred. These cultural artifacts dramatize some of the ways that supporters of the monarchy, in seeking to advance its claims by making use of religious forms, also subjected the monarchy to the unsettling implications those forms could carry with them.

II

William Clowes, one of Queen Elizabeth's surgeons and later Serjeant Surgeon to James I, included in his 1602 treatise on scrofula—known then as the "King's Evil"—an account of his own attempt to cure a patient afflicted by the disease. After Clowes had treated him unsuccessfully for over a year, the patient had gone his way. But by chance Clowes ran into him again in London, much changed: in fact, his patient's "Colour and complexion was so greatly altered and amended" and his person in such "comely manner attired, otherwise than before I had seen him" that

Clowes did not immediately recognize the man. The former patient had in the meantime been presented "unto our most Sacred and Renowned Prince the Queen's most excellent Majesty, for the cure of the said Evill: which through the gift and power of Almightie God, by her Grace's only meanes, laying of her blessed and happie hands upon him, she cured him safely within the space of five months." The patient told Clowes, "I thank God and the Queen of England, I am by her Majesty perfectly cured and healed: and after Her Grace had touched me, I never applyed any medicine at all, but kept it cleane, with sweete and fresh cleane cloathes, and now and then washed the sore with white Wine; and thus all my griefes did consume and waste cleane away." He showed Clowes the "Angell of Gold"—that is, the coin placed round his neck by the Queen at the ceremony—as further confirmation of his story. Clowes, impressed by the encounter, declares in his account that he now "confidently" affirms and "steadfastly" believes "that (for the certaine cure of this most miserable Malady) when all Arts and Sciences doe faile, Her Highness is the only Daystarre, peerless and without companion." He concludes with an extended prayer for Elizabeth's safety, happiness, and long life.[2]

Although some of Clowes's enthusiasm is undoubtedly due to his desire for continued preferment within the Queen's corps of surgeons, we need not be too surprised by his report of her Majesty's success in curing a disease that sometimes healed itself or went into remission and that may sometimes have been hysterical in origin. What seems more surprising is that the Supreme Head of the Protestant church in England would employ a practice so "papist" in nature. The practice of touching for the King's Evil had its roots in medieval tradition, and according to legend originated with Edward the Confessor, that "superstitious prince, who was sainted for his ungodly chastity," as one Puritan described him.[3] Like many practices associated with the medieval church, it was magical in character, and implied belief in a compelling supernatural power that was the property of a specially designated person and operated more or less mechanically. Such practices were routinely condemned by Protestant reformers as "superstition" or "conjuration"; seemingly "miraculous" powers must be either diabolic in origin or nonexistent, they argued, and the presumption that man could command God's power by means of objects, words, or the attributes of his person, was blasphemous. Touching for the King's Evil also resembled the magical healing techniques that orthodox authorities in the reign of Elizabeth and James I were busy trying to eradicate. Their targets were not only the Catholic church, but also the "cunning men," wizards, and white witches who populated the countryside and who—independent of any religious institution—dispensed a variety of magical cures. Authorities hoped to shepherd the clients of such men and women into the hands of the medical profession and the orthodox clergy.[4]

Indeed, Queen Elizabeth and especially James I appear to have had qualms about the power imputed to them. At the time of his coronation, James pronounced that "neither he nor any other King can in truth have power to heal the disease called the Evil, the age of miracles being past."[5] But soon enough James came under pressure from his English counselors and began touching for the Evil; within a few years Shakespeare deemed it appropriate to allude to the practice in *Macbeth*. Far from dying out as the Reformation gathered strength, the practice flourished throughout the seventeenth century and into the eighteenth.

It is not difficult to guess why James's counselors would have been anxious to preserve the practice. Touching for the King's Evil gave the monarch an opportunity to display the sacredness of the king and to take advantage of a centuries-old belief in the supernatural nature of kingship, a belief which appears to have been felt most intensely by those at a distance from the world of the court. Popular belief provided the material for a ceremony the Crown could shape to its own ends, giving rise, in France as well as in England, to an elaborate spectacle performed before an audience.[6] Such a ceremony was highly useful as propaganda, especially when the legitimacy of a king was in question. Elizabeth's cures were valuable confirmations of the legitimacy of a Protestant monarch after the Papal Bull of Excommunication. For Charles I and the civil war period, the royal touch testified to the righteousness of the principle of monarchy itself and to the sacrilege of killing the king.

Yet how were Protestant monarchs—and, for that matter, the subjects responsive to the ceremony—able to reconcile their belief in the royal touch with Protestant principle? Court authorities attempted to recast the practice by making it part of a religious ceremony and by providing it with a theoretical frame that would distance the practice from the superstitions it resembled. They stressed that God's was the miracle, not man's, that He bestowed it only as He saw fit, and that the monarch used only prayer (as distinct from magic spells) in his cures. William Tooker, author of a panegyric to Queen Elizabeth's healing power, stresses the orthodox line when he reports Elizabeth's words to a Gloucestershire gathering, "would, would that I could give you help and succour: God, God is the best and greatest physician of all: he, he is Jehovah, wise and holy, and he will relieve your sickness: to him you must pray."[7] The orthodox formulation reduces the blasphemous potential of the practice; the cures no longer operate mechanically but only at God's discretion. (Indeed, here the healing power no longer even seems to be a special property of the monarch.) Furthermore, in the official accounts God's "miracle" is at least partially naturalized. The monarch's prayers do not replace the treatments prescribed by physicians, they merely add something extra. To Reginald Scot, for example, the Queen does not offend God because she "onelie useth godlie and divine praier, with some almes," and refers her cures to God and the physicians.[8]

But Protestant scruples led some to a more thoroughgoing naturalism. Because open skepticism about the royal cures could be considered treasonous, it is—ironically—the skepticism of James himself that is most fully documented. James complied outwardly with his English counselors' request that he maintain the practice of touching for the Evil, but state papers show him glancing uneasily over his shoulder at his more rigorously minded Scottish ministers, and worrying out loud that he was committing a superstitious act.[9] On one occasion, he mockingly parodied the practice.[10] His early biographer, Arthur Wilson, asserts that the king knew the practice to be "a device to aggrandize the virtue of kings when miracles were in fashion. But he let the world believe it, though he smiled at it in his own reason, finding the strength of the imagination a more powerful agent in the cure than the plasters his chirurgeons prescribed for the sore."[11] For James, it appears, the royal touch was a theatrical ruse that nevertheless had its own kind of power to cure. Is this ruse a cynical—and perhaps damnable—"device to aggrandize the virtue of kings"? Or is it a benevolent accommodation undertaken for the good of his subjects? James seems to have wavered between the two attitudes, never completely making up his mind.

Thus, at least three ways of interpreting the royal touch were available to the Elizabethan-Jacobean audience. They include:

1. The magical: The monarch's cures are the product of a supernatural power mysteriously inhering in the king's person, which operates mechanically to heal the afflicted person. In this version, the monarch's cures highlight the mystical nature of royal blood and of the royal office. (This is the popular view, especially associated with the common people.)

2. The orthodox: The monarch's cures are the product of a mysterious combination of prayer and natural process. Here, the monarch has a primarily intercessive power, and his cures indicate God's special favor for

the legitimate kings and queens of England. (This is the "official" view of state and church authorities.)

3. The theatrical: The monarch's cures are the product of the power of the human imagination responding to a ruse. Here, the monarch's cures may indicate his skill as a benevolent role-player, or his participation in a "popish" sham. (This is the view of James and possibly of a sophisticated courtly elite; in its darker version, it is the view of Puritan critics.)

Borrowing Stephen Greenblatt's terms, we might see in these latter two versions the Protestant "evacuation" of a medieval belief, in which the magical content of the belief is emptied out, while its form is made available for a new, metaphorical use.[12] Clearly, James's version offers the most thoroughgoing evacuation of the practice; his psychologistic account drains the royal touch not only of its magic but of all trace of supernatural presence. Yet is this evacuation complete? The curative power James ascribes to the human imagination is surprisingly great—greater than that of the medical treatments prescribed by the doctors. The compelling power associated with magical objects and rituals seems to linger on in James's account, linked instead to the imagination.

In the case of the official version of the practice, the evacuation of magic is even less complete. Rather than redefining God's "miracle" as purely figurative, official accounts were ambiguous about its exact nature. Was there some sort of "natural vertue" to the monarch's person that produces them, as Scot suggests by listing the phenomenon under "strange properties and vertues natural"? Or did God answer prayers by some more direct form of intervention? The age of miracles was past in most cases but perhaps not in all. Furthermore, it seems clear that authorities tolerated many beliefs that would, from a strict Protestant point of view, appear heretical. As Keith Thomas has demonstrated, the royal touch was not really purged of its magical character despite its orthodox framework. To some the monarch's power to heal the King's Evil was bound up with the holy oil used to consecrate the monarch at his coronation, to others it was already present at accession; most continued to think of it as a supernatural quality inherent in the monarch's person. The emphasis of the ceremony itself on the monarch's healing hands appealed to such assumptions, and the official proclamations regulating the ceremony link the monarch's cures to his sacred touch and to the invocation of God's name, thereby suggesting both a magic of the body and a magic of the word. The official version of the practice was thus open-ended enough to accommodate a variety of magical beliefs.[13]

We would be wrong, however, to attribute the "impure" character of the practice entirely to a strategy of equivocation undertaken to advance the interests of the Crown. Undoubtedly that is a factor—yet the promiscuous mix of beliefs associated with the practice is also a product of the permeability of the boundaries between magic, religion, and natural science at this time. The orthodox view of illness, for example, was a synthesis of religion and science, in which sick persons were encouraged to consider their spiritual condition as well as the physical causes of their illness; cure was to be sought through prayer and repentance as well as medical treatment. Furthermore, many otherwise orthodox authorities tolerated some types of magical belief, while still others held that such beliefs could ultimately be reconciled with science and religion. Richard Napier, for example, a doctor who was also an Anglican clergyman, made use of astrological and magical healing techniques as well as medical ones. Napier's approach was eclectic and practical; he was willing to use whatever seemed to him to work. And what was true of a sophisticated member of an elite was even more true of the less educated populace away from urban centers.[14]

This heterogeneity of belief was possible in part because, though state and church authorities crusaded against a variety of magical beliefs, they did not have a very explicit or consistent account of divine intervention with which to replace the older one. If illness is a matter for both God and the physicians, what is God's role in the cure? Is it a matter of providential timing, in which God operates primarily through natural means? Or does God somehow intervene more directly? Orthodox believers tended to emphasize the natural, yet they were unwilling to rule out the possibility of more direct forms of intervention. In the absence of a fully articulated account of God's workings, it was easy for older habits of mind to help fill the gaps. What we have in this period, then, is not a single authoritative account of divine intervention but a profusion of beliefs that marked out a number of different locations where "God" or "the supernatural" might be presumed to touch upon the world. Some of these beliefs were in open conflict, but many, even most, coexisted in an uneasy and unsettling alliance.

III

In the ceremony for the healing of the King's Evil, the monarch himself is a primary locus of the sacred. What, more specifically, is the nature of the monarch's sacredness? And what possibilities does the intertwining of magical and orthodox belief open up for the presentation of the royal image?

I will focus on Elizabeth's performance of this ceremony, in part because of its suggestiveness for Shakespearean romance, and in part because of its special power. It is probably no accident that Elizabeth's performance is so well documented; by displaying Elizabeth as a compassionate healer, the ceremony cast her in one of her favorite roles, that of nurturing mother of the realm. The ceremony might especially play on subliminal associations with a specific mother, the Virgin Mary. (The reader may recall Clowes's use of the term "Daystarre" [morning star], one of the traditional symbols of the Virgin, suggesting that Clowes's mind is moving along this line.) In the days of her predecessors, prayers to Mary and the saints were used to begin the ceremony; during Elizabeth's realm they were abandoned, no doubt for theological reasons—yet their abandonment also opened up a space Elizabeth herself could fill. The healing power attributed to the monarch is similar to the powers often attributed to saintly figures by the medieval cult of the saints, and the biblical passages used in the ceremony make explicit the analogy between saint and monarch. By showcasing Elizabeth, the Virgin Queen, interceding with the Father and bringing about a miraculous cure, the ceremony could hardly avoid playing on associations with Mary and the female saints.[15]

Accounts dwell on Elizabeth's devotional appearance and contrast her purity with the unclean sores of the diseased: "How often have I seen her most Serene Majesty prostrate on her knees, body and soul wrapt in prayer, calling upon God and beseeching the Saviour Christ for such as these," wrote William Tooker, the Queen's chaplain who officiated at the ceremony, "how often have I seen her with her exquisite hands, whiter than whitest snow, boldly and without disgust pressing their sores and ulcers and handling them to health, not merely touching them with her fingertips: how often have I seen her worn with fatigue, as when in one single day during the preparation for the last Passover she healed eight and thirty persons."[16] Passages such as this suggest that Elizabeth was careful to present an image of piety and self-sacrifice in keeping with her saintly role. They also highlight the royal spectacle's focus on the meeting of opposites—high and low, clean and unclean, human and divine—a meeting embodied especially in the moment of touch. As we have seen, accounts focus lovingly on Elizabeth's hands: in Clowes's account, her "blessed and happie hands"; in Tooker's, her "exquisite hands, whiter than whitest snow." The rubrics of the ceremony do the same: "her most serene Majesty lays her hands on each side of them that are sick and diseased with the evil, on the jaws, or the throat, or the affected part, and touches the sore places with her bare hands, and forthwith heals them: and after their sores have been touched by her most healing hands the sick persons retire a while."[17] Here the instruction that she touch the sore places with her "bare" hands seems especially designed to emphasize opposition. By bringing the Queen and the afflicted subject so close together, the gesture highlights the difference between them. At the same time, the gesture points in the direction of transformation: the afflicted flesh will become healthy, pure, clean, like the flesh of the Queen herself.

At the beginning of the ceremony, the sick persons are brought to kneel before the Queen, and the Chaplain reads from Mark 16.14–20. In this passage the resurrected Jesus exhorts his disciples to convert "all the world" and lists the "tokens" that will display their faith, among them the power to heal the sick. As the Chaplain repeats "They shall lay their hands on the sick, and they shall recover," the Queen lays her hands on each afflicted person. The Chaplain then reads a second passage, John 1.1–14. The sick persons file past the Queen, who gives them a gold coin—an Angel—on a ribbon. This passage links the Queen to John the Baptist, bearing witness to the light, while the gold coin represents the "true light" itself.

The final part of the ceremony breaks away from the focus on the meeting of opposites—or, at any rate, repositions it. The Queen, who hitherto has represented the divine, the pure, and the healthy, in contrast to the human, the polluted, and the sick, now joins with her subjects in an assertion of common humanity, "meekly kneeling on her knees," according to the rubrics, and leading the congregation in prayer (the kyrie, the Lord's prayer, some versicles and responses, and a special prayer for the "eternal health of all such as put their trust" in God). The Queen, no less than her subjects, is obliged to confess her need for mercy and "help from above."

In the first sections of the ceremony, the Queen is displayed as a sacred person with a vaguely defined but nevertheless compelling supernatural power—as if, in fact, she were almost a divinity herself. These final moments, however, display her submission to God's authority, and stress her likeness to her subjects, their shared experience of sin, their need of spiritual assistance, and so forth. The ceremony thus pulls in two directions, celebrating on the one hand a sacred mystery of the royal blood, and on the other, the sovereignty of God and an exemplary Christian piety.

The Queen, then, is the locus of two quite different kinds of sacredness. As a magical healer, she provides her subjects with access to supernatural help of a sort they can never hope to possess for themselves; they are necessarily confined to the dependent role of a suppliant. But as the possessor of an exemplary piety, she is a model to be imitated, and in this regard, her sacredness can be transferred to her subjects through emulation. In the case of the former, she possesses a unique power that is an unchanging, innate quality of her being. In the case of the latter, she possesses an exemplary faith, but it is essentially no different than that of any other pious Christian. Such a faith can be acquired—and lost—by anyone, regardless of social status. The ceremony makes the queen simultaneously an object of idealization and of identification, a reinforcer of social hierarchy and of Christian egalitarianism.

Some of the discrepancies involved in this combination can be highlighted by a consideration of the different implications of the monarch's healing power and that of the saint or disciple. The ceremony's use of the passage from Mark presents the monarch as the bearer of a faith passed down a long line of holy persons from Christ himself: the image suggestively parallels the long line of royal persons from whom the king has inherited his healing power. Yet the miraculous performance of the disciple or saint was intended to reproduce the faith it displayed, potentially able to turn its audience into believers similarly capable of miracles. The king's power, by contrast, cannot be passed on to anyone else. The royal touch was, in fact, a prerogative jealously guarded by the Crown, which investigated and punished those who claimed to have a similar healing touch. The participants in the ceremony were compelled to remain spectators of the royal power, cut off from acquiring it in turn, and thus the ceremony was a suggestive reminder of their place in the hierarchy of social relations and their dependence on the monarch. Furthermore, the special piety of the monarch cannot logically be a crucial aspect of his ability to heal; the miraculous power is inherited with the office of king, regardless of its possessor's saintly qualities.

To an extent, Elizabeth's version of the ceremony replays a tension evident throughout the history of the royal touch. As Marc Bloch has shown, the practice of touching for the Evil is a hybrid even in its infancy in the twelfth century, the consequence of cross-breeding pagan belief in the divinity of kings and Christian belief in miracle-working saints.[18] Early forms of the practice involve two gestures, the laying on of hands and the making of the sign of the cross while invoking God's name, combining an age-old belief in the magical efficacy of touch with the forms of Christian faith. Even then, the practice seems torn by two competing urges—to celebrate the sovereignty of kings, and to display their submission to the sovereignty of God.

But when we encounter the practice in Elizabeth's day its contrariety seems especially pronounced. Her performance embodies elements of the cult of saints and of the Virgin, but removes them from the dominion of the Roman church; it is in line with Protestant belief in the divine right of kings, but at odds with Protestant distrust of miracle and idolatrous faith; it celebrates the divinity of kings but recalls also their humanity; it is biblical in its sources, but unbiblical in its emphases.

What keeps these tensions from flying apart? For one thing, the figure of the disciple provides the monarch's role with an analogue that similarly yokes together contrary meanings; though Protestants and Catholics battled over the cult of the saints, they shared the biblical notion of the disciple who is both first and last—called to a humble role while acquiring special powers by virtue of his intense faith. In addition, Elizabeth employed the ceremony at a time before Protestant orthodoxy had consolidated itself and before the tensions between magical, religious, and scientific beliefs had hardened into contradiction. Mistress of ambiguity and double meanings, by temperament or policy disinclined to pursue religious questions very deeply, and dedicated to iconic forms of self-presentation, Elizabeth was perhaps uniquely suited to take advantage of this historical moment.

In any event, Elizabeth's performance of the ceremony seems to have been an especially powerful one. As Virgin, saint, Queen, sacred object, and human sinner, Elizabeth was the focus of a spectacle that appealed by visual and rhetorical means to an audience steeped in magical belief as well as to those of more orthodox faith. By displaying the Queen as an object both strange and familiar, divine and human, the spectacle could work to strengthen the bonds between the monarch and her subjects, arousing in them loyalty, gratitude, and awe.

Yet even Elizabeth's rich performance was not able to contain all the tensions involved in the ceremony, as the controversy surrounding its use suggests. Elizabeth's use of the ceremony allows her to tap into the energies of both popular and orthodox religious forms, and put them at the disposal of the secular interests of the Crown. Yet in so doing she also makes herself subject to the implications those belief-systems carried with them. The Protestant restatement of the practice goes farther in emphasizing the monarch's submission to God and puts pressure on him to present himself in terms of Christian piety and devotion; he must be, or at least seem to be, a Protestant saint. Furthermore, in stressing the ambiguity of the monarch's healing power it also dilutes the monarch's sacred mystique, raising questions about the uniqueness of the royal blood and the idea of an inherited sacred power. In so doing, the ceremony registers the much larger forces at work that were making the monarch look more and more like everyone else.

IV

Shakespeare's only direct reference to the royal touch occurs, as mentioned earlier, in *Macbeth*. In Malcolm's description of the healing power of the English King (who is, in Holinshed, Edward the Confessor, though the play leaves him unnamed) we can see all the marks of the orthodox account of the practice:

> *Malcolm.*   Comes the King forth, I pray you?
>
> *Doctor.*   Aye, Sir; there are a crew of wretched souls,
> That stay his cure: their malady convinces
> The great assay of art; but at his touch,
> Such sanctity hath Heaven given his hand,
> They presently amend.
>
> *Malcolm.*   I thank you, Doctor.
>
> *Macduff.*   What's the disease he means?
>
> *Malcolm.*   'Tis call'd the Evil:
> A most miraculous work in this good King,
> Which often, since my here-remain in England,
> I have seen him do. How he solicits Heaven,
> Himself best knows; but strangely-visited people,
> All swoln and ulcerous, pitiful to the eye,
> The mere despair of surgery, he cures;
> Hanging a golden stamp about their necks,
> Put on with holy prayers: and 'tis spoken,
> To the succeeding royalty he leaves
> The healing benediction. With this strange virtue,
> He hath a heavenly gift of prophecy;

And sundry blessings hang about his throne,
That speak him full of grace.

                                        (IV.iii.140–59)[19]

As in the orthodox accounts, here the king's power comes with the imprimatur of a medical doctor, who is unable to cure the "wretched souls" himself. The precise nature of the king's power is explicitly left ambiguous: "How he solicits Heaven, / Himself best knows." His performance of the cure is accompanied by "holy prayer," and both the Doctor and Malcolm insist the power must ultimately be attributed to "Heaven." The cures, taken with the other "blessings" that surround his throne, are outward signs of virtue and divine favor: they "speak" the king full of "grace." At the same time, the king's power retains a magical aspect in being focused on his hands. The power appears to be innate and inheritable, yet we may detect a little uneasiness here: it is "spoken" that the king will leave a healing "benediction." The king may be leaving only a set of prayers to his successors. Shakespeare registers even the moments of uneasiness in the orthodox version of the practice.

How does this moment function in the play? The English King's sacred power to heal contrasts with the demonic power of the witches to poison and destroy; it also contrasts with the magic the witches seduce Macbeth into believing he has—a magic of equivocation that comments ironically on Macbeth's lack of a true king's power. But the audience is distanced from the sacred magic of the true king; the healing touch belongs only to the English King, who never appears on stage, and Malcolm has no parallel power. In fact, Malcolm describes the English King's healing touch just after he has performed his peculiar test of Macduff's virtue, a test that may reassure us about Macduff but leaves us—and Macduff—a little doubtful about Malcolm himself. In this play, there is a magic that lures men into transgression (associated with the witches' powers of divination and their suggestive wordplay); there is another sort of magic that punishes or warns of punishment after transgression has occurred (associated with the birds that shriek, the horses that eat each other, the forest that moves); but there is no magic to make the king himself a compelling or charismatic figure who could discourage transgression before it begins. Malcolm's description of the English King's healing touch registers a yearning for a magic of kingship that he does not himself possess. Moreover, the play links Malcolm to the language of healing in ways that may intensify our awareness of his lack of a power equivalent to that of the English king. In the scenes immediately preceding and following Malcolm's description of the royal touch, we hear increasingly of infection and disease — of the "infected air" the witches ride upon, the diseased mind of Lady Macbeth, the "distemper'd cause" of Macbeth, the "sickly weal" of Scotland itself. The "medicine" Malcolm offers, while tantalizing us with the hope of a genuine cure for Scotland's ills, ultimately seems inadequate to the task. Malcolm's attempt to minister to Macduff's grief, for example, is a peculiarly ambivalent one. "Give sorrow words; the grief, that does not speak, / Whispers the o'erfraught heart, and bids it break" (IV.iii.209–10), he first instructs Macduff when they hear of the death of Macduff's wife and children. But before Macduff has had a chance to do so, Malcolm cuts him off: "Be comforted: Let's make us med'cines of our great revenge, / To cure this deadly grief" (213–15). As Macduff proceeds to give voice to his grief, Malcolm becomes more insistent: "Dispute it like a man" (220). Malcolm applies his "medicine" unevenly. It is as if he is made anxious by the expression of sorrow he has himself recommended, and rushes prematurely to make Macduff's "grief / Convert to anger" (228–29).

The conversion of grief into an anger that takes military form really is, of course, in one sense a "cure" for the disease Macbeth has brought to Scotland. Malcolm may not possess a magical healing touch but he does manage to summon a powerful army. The Scottish nobles who join Malcolm in V.ii. use language that again links him to a military "medicine":

> Well; march we on,
> To give obedience where 'tis truly ow'd:
> Meet we the med'cine of the sickly weal;
> And with him pour we, in our country's purge,
> Each drop of us.
>
> (V.ii.25–29)

Yet Malcolm's use of military force, though it purges the land of Macbeth, does not necessarily purge the land of the problem of rebellion. Such a "medicine" recalls the inadequacy of military force at the beginning of the play; Malcolm may prove no more effective than his father, Duncan, in generating a loyalty that will prevent rebellion before it starts.

The play represents both Duncan and Malcolm as legitimate kings who possess a measure of sacredness and virtue. (To this extent they are presented in terms consistent with the royal healing ceremony, which stressed the monarch's piety and submission to God.) Yet neither are able to produce ties of loyalty strong enough to end Scotland's cycle of rebellions permanently. They are not altogether incapable of producing loyalty, of course; their ability to do so is derived especially from the rewards they are able to give their subjects for their loyal service. Both use the imagery of gardening to present themselves as a source of nurturance for their kingdom, nurturance which takes the form of the honors they bestow on loyal subjects (see, for example, I.iv.28–29, 32–33; V.ix.28–31). Shakespeare focuses, however, on the inadequacies of the system of preferment. The honors Duncan gives out generate as much envy and resentment as they do allegiance: for every Banquo, there is a Macbeth. Duncan himself stresses his inability to reward his thanes adequately: "would thou hadst less deserv'd," he says to Macbeth, "That the proportion both of thanks and payment / Might have been mine! only I have left to say, / More is thy due than more than all can pay" (I.iv.18–21). In other contexts, the king's distribution of honors can be presented as a display of generosity that links the "grace" of the king to divine grace; here, an explicitly religious vocabulary comes into play only to register the failure of the system of preferment to produce a wholly satisfying display of the king's sacredness. Duncan feels he has committed a "sin" of ingratitude until he is able to reward Macbeth's service (I.iv.15–16); and because he cannot reward Macbeth fully, the sense of sin lingers on even as he attempts to dispel it.

The reassertion of the political order that occurs in the final scene seems disturbingly precarious in part because Shakespeare does not solve this problem; that is, he does not imagine an alternative to the system of preferment that might generate loyalty more efficiently. Nor does Malcolm's virtue provide an effective means for doing so; his youth and self-righteousness make him a rather unsatisfying king, and Macduff's loyalty seems to proceed from his horror at Macbeth's deeds rather than from a deeply felt tie to Malcolm.

Also disturbing is the fact that the witches are still at large. Conventional Christianity held that evil was God's "rod," to be used to correct sinners, then cast in the fire when no longer needed; yet there is little sense in the play that the witches are marked out for destruction. Indeed, by the end of the play they are so closely allied with the providential order as to be almost indistinguishable from it: their malice blurs into divine justice. The providential order tolerates the witches' devices of entrapment and implicitly authorizes a system of preferment that arouses envy as well as loyalty; in so doing, it seems to be encouraging the production of traitors as well as exacting justice upon them. By incorporating only a demonic magic into the play's orthodox framework, Shakespeare makes the providential order seem skewed: it undermines the king's power almost as much as works on his behalf. Without a sacred magic or some equivalent to counteract the demonic magic that tempts and punishes, the monarchy is left in an enfeebled condition, threatened by the possibility of repeated rebellion, its victory temporary at best.

By contrast, in the romances Shakespeare does imagine a sacred magic that can operate on behalf of the monarchy. Though these plays do not explicitly refer to the royal touch, they conceive of the sacred in terms similar to those used by the royal healing ceremony and its defenders, pushing inherited forms in orthodox directions while retaining some elements of magical belief. Like the ceremony, several of the romances draw upon a tradition associated with miracle-working saints and employ a vocabulary of faith, healing, and magic. Also like it, they associate an innate, quasi-magical power with royal blood, and make use of their religious materials in ways that help legitimize and extend the monarch's power.

Nevertheless, in these plays a sacred magic is not focused on the monarch himself, but on other members of the royal family – generally wives and daughters. In fact, the royal husbands and fathers who are the plays' protagonists do not possess much sacredness at all; their relation to the sacred is worked out by means of providential passages through affliction, passages that "new create" the king by producing conversion-like changes of heart. In this regard, Shakespeare elaborates on that aspect of the healing ceremony that legitimizes the king by displaying his submission to divine authority and the traits he shares with the common Christian. Kings in these plays are not primarily objects of idealization but of identification. In fact, in undergoing a process that is presented in terms of both healing and conversion, they play a role that more closely approximates that of the afflicted subject in the royal ceremony than that of the monarch. The roles of royal wives and children, on the other hand, more closely resemble that of the monarch; they are made into idealized objects, and it is largely their sacred magic that enables the kings' regeneration.

In order to explore in more detail the implications of this formulation of the monarch's relation to sacredness, I would like to focus on *Pericles*.[20] Though I believe the pattern I am sketching here to a large extent also shapes *Cymbeline, The Winter's Tale*, and some aspects of *The Tempest*, this play provides, in the person of Marina, the most vivid example of a royal family member who possesses a sacred magic. Marina, in fact, especially recalls Elizabeth's performance of the healing ceremony; she too appears as mother, Virgin, saint, and sacred physician. Pericles, on the other hand, is afflicted with melancholy, set in motion by his discovery of an incestuous relationship between Antiochus and his daughter. Only Marina's "sacred physic" (V.i.74)[21] is able fully to cure Pericles and to contain the anxieties about kings, sacredness, and female sexuality that the play has released in its early scenes.

Like the power of the Lord Cerimon who brings Thaisa back from the brink of death — and like that of the monarch in the royal healing ceremony — Marina's power hovers ambiguously between the orthodox and the magical. Cerimon's cure is presented in terms largely consistent with a providentially grounded medical model: the "heavens" work through "Nature." At the same time his wonder-working skill has a magical aspect: his knowledge of "blest infusions / That dwell in vegetives, in metals, stones" enables him to release the innately curative powers of these elements (see III.ii.31–39, 94–99); moreover, his "physic" is a "secret art" (32) and his use of music has a ritual quality (90–93). Does he use fire merely to warm Thaisa or to arouse "the fire of life" (85) by means of a sympathetic magic? Do his mysterious "boxes" (83) contain medicines or magic potions? The audience does not know.

In a similar manner, the play presents Marina primarily in terms consistent with an orthodox naturalism, emphasizing her virtuous actions, skills, and use of "holy words" (IV.vi.133). Yet, in contrast to her father, whose virtuous character must be brought to completion by his passage through "necessity," Marina's virtues seem to be innate qualities of her being. Pericles, we are made to feel, lacks a patience and a willingness to submit to the will of the gods that Marina has from the beginning; though she shares with her father an elegiac sense of loss, she refuses to reproach the gods in situations that have caused Pericles to do so and she perserveres where Pericles becomes paralyzed. The play calls attention to Marina's noble education and excellence in the arts, yet this focus on nurture does little to diminish our sense that Marina's virtues are innate; "absolute Marina" is, for example, contrasted with Philoten, the daughter of Dionyza, who has received the same education but whom Marina greatly overshadows (IV.Chorus.17–33).

The play especially stresses Marina's rhetorical skill, which she uses to talk her way out of bad situations and to produce conversions. She "preaches divinity" to the customers of the bawdy-house, converting them to chastity: "Fie, fie upon her!" the Bawd protests, "she's able to freeze the god Priapus, and undo a whole generation. We must either get her ravish'd or be rid of her. When she should do for clients her fitment and do me the kindness of our profession, she has me her quirks, her reasons, her master-reasons, her prayers, her knees; that she would make a puritan of the devil, if he would cheapen a kiss of her" (IV.vi.3–10). Yet despite the Bawd's emphasis on Marina's "reasons" and "master-reasons," Marina's conversions seem to emanate automatically from her person rather than from a divinity beyond who works through holy words; the gentlemanly brothel-goers have merely to come into her presence and to hear her voice—as distinct from what she says—in order to be turned to the path of virtue. "She conjures: away with her!" says the Bawd later (IV.vi.147), comically taking Marina's prayers for witchcraft, yet in so doing she also seems to be responding to the quasi-magical aspects of Marina's effect on others. In the brothel scenes, such a magic is especially associated with Marina's absolute commitment to chastity and with her class origins. Like the fire that seems to kindle the "fire of life" in Thaisa, Marina's chastity reproduces itself in her audience as if by sympathetic magic, and the Bawd is persuaded that her ability to produce conversions would be destroyed only if they were able to "crack the glass of her virginity" (IV.vi.142).

Marina's cure of her father's melancholy—her "sacred physic"—similarly seems to derive from properties of her person that operate almost irresistibly to produce a sudden transformation. Lysimachus, commenting on her "goodly presence" immediately before presenting her to her "kingly patient," hints at least faintly at the notion of a sacred magic emanating from the royal presence (V.i.65, 71). As Marina recounts her history to her (as yet unrecognized) father, hints of magical and miraculous possibility come into play; she describes how she "hath been gaz'd on like a comet" (V.i.86), and alludes to the improbabilities of her history. Her account of her birth has a riddling, miraculous sound: she was not born "of any shores; / Yet . . . was mortally brought forth" (103–4). Pericles, at first disbelieving, wonders in turn if Marina is sent "by some incensed god" to mock him; if she is "a fairy motion," and finally, just before accepting her story as true, if she is the "rarest dream that e'er dull'd sleep / Did mock sad fools withal" (143, 153–54, 161–62).

Such supernatural possibilities are raised only to be set aside; we know Marina's history is explainable in naturalistic terms. Yet her recital of her past produces for Pericles an epiphany that may, or may not, be a genuine miracle—that is, when he hears the "music of the spheres" (V.i.225–31). The "rare dream" that Pericles momentarily imagines Marina to be also points toward the supernaturally inspired dream-vision of the goddess

Diana he will have during the "slumber" induced by his hearing of the "heavenly music." Later, in the final scene, Pericles will refer to Cerimon's healing-resurrection of Thaisa as a "great miracle." As is the case with the monarch's "miracle" in the royal healing ceremony, Marina's and Cerimon's cures hover between the literally and the figuratively miraculous.

Shakespeare, in linking Marina's "sacred physic" to the indirectly perceived intervention of benevolent gods who work through chance arrangements, nature, and human skill, brings her power into line with an orthodox providentialism that could tolerate an ambiguously defined notion of the miraculous, but not an explicit magic. Marina, strictly speaking, has no autonomous supernatural (therefore no magical) healing power of her own with which she can cure her father. Nevertheless, a quasi-magical aura lingers about Marina in a way that might make the rigorously minded Puritan in the audience suspect idolatry, a magic associated with her position as Pericles' daughter, as well as with her innate virtues, her "goodly presence," and her seemingly inexorable power to cure and convert those around her. She possesses the very virtues that Pericles needs: patience, courage, and chastity. As their reunion progresses, Pericles turns her into a rich moral emblem, rather like a figure in a Morality play. "Falseness" cannot come from Marina (V.i.120), we are told; she is "Modest as Justice" (121); she seems "a palace / For the crown'd Truth to dwell in" (121–22); she looks like the figure of "Patience gazing on kings' graves" (138). And as Pericles addresses Marina as "my most kind virgin" (140), the audience is invited to recall Marina's chastity and the way this father-daughter pair contrast with the pairing of Antiochus and his daughter. Marina's insistent chastity helps to transform the anxieties associated with female sexuality and incest aroused at the beginning of the play, as if the very strength of her commitment could help her father ward off forbidden impulses. But more explicitly, Pericles' description of Marina as a "palace / For the crown'd Truth to dwell in" is suggestive of the importance of chastity in a royal heir: as a pure vessel, she contains an unpolluted inheritance from Pericles and can pass it on to succeeding generations.

In turning her into an emblematic figure, Pericles reinforces the audience's sense that Marina's virtues are innate qualities of her being. And as an embodiment of an ideal patience and fortitude, Marina seems magically to complete Pericles' identity in the areas we have perceived him to be lacking; his sense of having found "another life" (207) through Marina may especially derive from his perception of her as an idealized extension of himself. He is, moreover, able to associate his whole family line, past and future, with an ideal set of virtues.

In investing sacred presence especially in Marina and in keeping Pericles' attention almost idolatrously focused on her, Shakespeare imagines Marina's role in terms that strongly recall that of the monarch in the royal healing ceremony. The play presents Marina as an instrument of higher powers, yet also suggests she has a semiautonomous, sacred power of her own. Her sacred power derives from her position as daughter and her seemingly innate virtues of chastity, patience, and fortitude, and these virtues play a role much like that of the monarch's ability to heal scrofula: they reveal the providential benevolence of the gods; they show that those gods have blessed and providentially guided the monarch; and they further legitimize the monarch's rule by displaying a (presumably inheritable) set of virtues associated with the royal line and beneficial to the kingdom as a whole.

In conferring upon Marina these significances, Shakespeare helps to create a context in which the foregrounding of the royal child's virtues can be used for purposes similar to those served by the royal healing ceremony. Indeed, in some ways Shakespeare's play suggests a strategy that could work on behalf of the monarchy even more effectively than that of the ceremony. Shakespeare's play arouses anxiety about the monarch's relation to sacredness and about the apparent cruelty of the gods, then transforms it into trust; the ceremony does not address such anxieties at all. The play places at the disposal of the monarchy emotions associated with parental pride, inviting its audience to share the monarch's pleasure in his child's virtues and the sense of renewal he finds through them; in conferring these on a marriageable daughter, the play also holds out the promise of the extension of that pride through subsequent generations, fusing the hopes of heads of households with national hopes for stable succession and the peaceful expansion of kingdoms. The ceremony, on the other hand, lacks a familial dimension, presenting the monarch instead as a solitary figure—a Virgin Queen, a saintly physician.

Moreover, given the skepticism of James and his Scottish counselors about the monarch's sacred healing power, it is possible that for those in and around James's court it was easier to sustain certain kinds of belief within the context of romance than within the context of orthodox religion. Romance could provide rough equivalents for beliefs that would not hold up under scrutiny elsewhere, and keep alive a sense of semiautonomous supernatural forces, of miraculous happenings, and of a sacred magic inhering in royalty. In locating a quasi-magical power in the innate virtues of a royal daughter, Shakespeare's strategy might have a special ability to withstand the pressures of Calvinist doctrine.

Nevertheless, Shakespeare's formulation of a sacred magic that can operate on behalf of the monarchy has its own kind of precariousness. If, in rendering the nature of the monarch's cures more ambiguous, the royal ceremony also diluted the idea of the monarch's possession of a unique sacred power, Shakespeare's play moves even farther in this direction: Marina's virtues are impressive, but not unique possessions of royalty. Furthermore, while in *Pericles* and the other romances, royal children and wives are invested with an innate sacredness, the monarchs themselves are curiously lacking in such qualities. They stand apart from the sacred loci imagined in these plays, acquiring their legitimacy instead through a change of heart—a conversion—that displays their submission to a divine will but does not identify them with it. By making the monarch undergo "heaven-directed" changes of heart, Shakespeare suggests a divine sanction for the monarch's rule, yet at the same time emphasizes his dependence on others and the unfinished nature of his character. In recovering a sacred magic for the monarchy, Shakespeare also contributes to a discourse in which the monarch's legitimacy derives from his submission to a sacredness most visible in persons less powerful than himself.

NOTES

1. See, for example, Jonathan Dollimore's argument in *Radical Tragedy: Religion, Ideology and Power in the Drama of Shakespeare and His Contemporaries* (Chicago: University of Chicago Press, 1984). Dollimore's provocative discussion of "radical tragedy" is inscribed within a flawed historical argument. Dollimore's account of the "dominant ideology" of Shakespeare's period misleadingly suggests that Christian providentialist belief was inevitably tied to Tudor political ideology. Radical tragedy, he argues, contributed to skepticism about providentialist belief; this skepticism, in turn, contributed to the crisis of the English Civil War. Dollimore conveys the impression that in the early seventeenth century the subversion of religious beliefs always went hand in hand with the subversion of the political order. Such an argument fails to acknowledge the important role played by the intensification of Christian providentialism among those groups most active in initiating the civil war; challenges to (as well as defenses of) the monarchy almost always appealed to providentialist assumptions.

2. William Clowes, *A right frutefull and approved treatise for the artificiall cure of that malady called in Latin, Struma, and in English, the Evill, cured by Kynges and Queenes of England* (London, 1602). A biographical sketch of Clowes and a short

selection from this work are included in *The Selected Writings of William Clowes, 1544–1604,* ed. F. N. L. Poynter (London: Harvey & Blythe, 1948). There is a surprising amount of historical literature on the practice of touching for the King's Evil. For a fine introduction to the practice in sixteenth- and seventeenth-century England, see Keith Thomas, *Religion and the Decline of Magic* (New York: Scribner's, 1971), 192–211. For a summary of the practice and the ceremonies that accompanied it in England from medieval times to its demise in the eighteenth century, see Raymond Crawfurd, *The King's Evil* (1911; reprinted Oxford: Clarendon Press, 1977). Useful as Crawfurd's book is, its citations are maddeningly inadequate. For a critical study of the practice in its historical context in both England and France, see Marc Bloch, *The Royal Touch: Sacred Monarchy and Scrofula in England and France,* trans. J. E. Anderson (London: Routledge & Kegan Paul, 1973). Bloch offers an excellent bibliography. Other helpful, though less comprehensive, studies include: Charles W. Gusmer, *The Ministry of Healing in the Church of England: An Ecumenical-Liturgical Study* (Great Watering: Mayhew-McCrimmon, 1974), 86–90; and Thomas Joseph Pettigrew, *On Superstitions Connected with the History and Practice of Medicine and Surgery* (Philadelphia: Barrington and Haswell, 1844).

3. Lucy Hutchinson, quoted in Thomas, *Religion,* 197.

4. For an overview of the Protestant attack on "superstition" and the campaigns against popular magical healing practices, see Thomas, *Religion,* 51–77, 253–79.

5. G. B. Harrison, *A Jacobean Journal* (London: Routledge and Sons, 1941), 31. James's qualms are well documented; Elizabeth's are a matter of speculation. See Crawfurd, *King's Evil,* 75–76, 82–85.

6. Bloch, *Royal Touch,* 28–48.

7. William Tooker, *Charisma sive donum sanationis seu explicatio totius quaestionis de mirabilium sanitatum gratia . . .* (London, 1597); the translation is taken from Crawfurd, *King's Evil,* 75.

8. Reginald Scot, *The Discoverie of Witchcraft* (1584; reprinted Carbondale: Southern Illinois University Press, 1964), XIII.ix.

9. Crawfurd, *King's Evil,* 82–83.

10. An observer reports that the king "laughed heartily" when a Turkish ambassador's afflicted son was brought before him and brusquely ran his hands over him, "marry without Pistle or Gospell." Quoted in Crawfurd, *King's Evil,* 85.

11. Arthur Wilson, *The History of Great Britain, being the Life and Reign of King James the First* (London, 1653), 289.

12. See Stephen Greenblatt, "Shakespeare and the Exorcists," in *Shakespeare and the Question of Theory,* ed. Patricia Parker and Geoffrey Hartman (New York: Methuen, 1985), 182.

13. Thomas, *Religion,* 195–97.

14. For a brief summary of the orthodox view of illness, see Thomas, *Religion,* 85–89. For a discussion of the blurring of magic and medicine and of orthodox attitudes toward magical healing, see Thomas, *Religion,* 189–92, 253–63, 267–79.

Thomas shows not only that doctors sometimes resorted to magical techniques (and that "natural" and "magical" cures were often confused in the minds of their patients) but that the attitude of church and state authorities toward "white" magic was sometimes ambivalent. Magical healing was condemned in theory but often tolerated in practice (see especially 257–58). For a detailed account of Richard Napier's medical practice, see Michael MacDonald, *Mystical Bedlam: Madness, Anxiety, and Healing in Seventeenth-Century England* (Cambridge, Mass.: Cambridge University Press, 1981).

15. For some other studies of Elizabeth's presentation of herself as a sacred object, see Roy Strong, *The Cult of Elizabeth* (Wallop, Hampshire: Thomas and Hudson, 1977); and Clifford Geertz, "Centers, Kings, and Charisma: Reflections on the Symbolics of Power," in *Local Knowledge: Further Essays in Interpretive Anthropology* (New York: Basic Books, 1983), 121–46.

16. Tooker, *Charisma*; translated in Crawfurd, *King's Evil*, 74.

17. Tooker prints the ceremony in Latin, but most scholars agree that the service was probably given in English; this passage and subsequent passages from the ceremony are taken from the translation in Crawfurd, *King's Evil*, 72–74. (See also Bloch, *Royal Touch*, 386, n.73.)

18. Bloch, *Royal Touch*, 51–55.

19. All quotations from *Macbeth* are taken from the Arden Edition, ed. Kenneth Muir (London: Methuen, 1977).

20. Despite the problems of authorship raised by the first two acts of *Pericles*, I have followed many others in assuming the shape of the play as a whole to be consistent with Shakespeare's aims. The last three acts extend the play by building on the imagery of acts I and II, and if Shakespeare wrote only the latter parts of the play, he did so in such a way as to convey a sense of the play's unity of purpose. Furthermore, my main focus of concern is Marina, who appears only in the sections all agree were authored by Shakespeare.

21. All quotations from *Pericles* are from the Arden Edition, ed. F. D. Hoeniger (London: Methuen, 1963).

6

Ritual as an Instrument of Grace: Parental Blessings in *Richard III, All's Well That Ends Well,* and *The Winter's Tale*

BRUCE W. YOUNG

Grace — the word, the concept — is a key element in the texture and structure of a good many of Shakespeare's plays, and in several it is connected with ritual. Nowhere is the connection closer than in the case of the ritual blessing given by parents to their children. This ritual, which held a significant place in Renaissance daily life, appears or is referred to in about half of Shakespeare's plays, where it has many functions, ranging from the comic to the awe-inspiring. One of its most important functions is to convey grace. This close alliance between the parental blessing and grace is worth exploring, for it has implications for everything from our understanding of Shakespeare's stagecraft to our interpretation of his characters.

The word *grace* has a wide range of theological and nontheological senses in Shakespeare's plays. Meaning "beauty," "virtue," or "any quality that pleases," grace is a standard against which some characters are judged ("O graceless men"); it is a measure of other characters' goodness ("as tender as infancy and grace").[1] In a somewhat different sense — an influence from heaven that blesses, regenerates, and saves — grace may serve to transform characters and affect the unfolding of plots.[2] Grace in yet another sense — "good will," "generosity," "graciousness," "bounty" — may perform a similarly dynamic and transforming function, but this time as a power exercised by human beings. Grace in any or all of these senses is present in many plays as one of two opposing forces, the other being any of the malign or destructive forces associated with what Friar Lawrence calls "rude will":

> Two such opposed kings encamp them still
> In man as well as herbs, grace and rude will;
> And where the worser is predominant,
> Full soon the canker death eats up that plant.
> (*Rom.* II.iii.27–30)

Two such forces coexist in plays as well as human hearts and, as they enter into conflict, help outline the plays' structures and imbue them with dramatic tension and power.

Though the concept of grace is found throughout the Shakespearean canon, I will look here at three plays in which grace is connected with ritual – specifically with the parental blessing ritual. The plays are *Richard III*, *All's Well That Ends Well*, and *The Winter's Tale*. In *Richard III*, where *grace* would not seem on first impression to be the keynote, the word and its relatives (*gracious*, etc.) appear more often than in any other Shakespearean play. These words occur much less often in *All's Well That Ends Well*, where, nevertheless, important aspects of the play are informed by the concepts of grace and gracelessness. *Grace* has been recognized as a key word in *The Winter's Tale* (e.g., by Mahood and Tinkler), and there, as clearly as anywhere, the concept is related to the ritual blessing given by a parent to a child.

The parental blessing was one of the most important and pervasive rituals of Renaissance England.[3] Indeed, it seems to have been peculiar to England during the Renaissance.[4] It goes back at least to the fourteenth century, and probably much earlier; and it appears to have been practiced by Catholics and Protestants, Puritans and non-Puritans, with little variation in form or meaning into the early seventeenth century.[5] In "well-ordered" households the ritual took place daily, morning and evening, with each child kneeling before its parents, both father and mother, and saying (to quote William Perkins), "Father I pray you bless me, Mother I pray you bless me" (469), or words to that effect.[6] Each parent would respond to the request by calling on God to bless the child and using one or both hands to signify the conferring of the blessing.

Renaissance writers describe several different forms of the blessing, suggesting that the precise gesture used may have varied from person to person or from time to time. Richard Hooker, the great Anglican theologian, refers to the *"imposition of handes"* (2:321). This would mean the placing of one or both hands on the head of the child who is kneeling before the parent. The same gestures are described by an eighteenth-century traveler visiting England, with the added information that children may kiss the hands that have blessed them (César de Saussure, *A foreign view of England in the Reigns of George I. and George II.* [1902], quoted in Legg 168). Another possible form of blessing, supported by pictorial and literary evidence, is the holding of one or both hands *above* the head of the recipient, not actually on it (see Whitforde, sig. D4ᵛ).

The child's kneeling to receive the blessing was in part a recognition of the parent's superior authority and maturity and an expression of respect for the parent's age, status, and (in some cases) virtue and wisdom. By kneeling, children—and this apparently included the adult children of aging parents—also acknowledged the parent as one of the sources of their own being and identity.[7] The ritual thus symbolized and affirmed the intimate connection, physical, spiritual, and emotional, between parent and child and brought to mind the duties of both: the parent's duty to educate, nourish, love, and discipline the child; the child's duty to love, honor, obey, and (when necessary) care for the parents. Though subordination— that is, location at a lower point in a hierarchical system—was certainly one of the notions conveyed by the child's kneeling, this subordination did not necessarily imply unconditional submission to a parent's wishes; it certainly did not mean that the child's agency and identity were entirely subsumed within those of the parent.[8]

Besides its symbolic, social, and emotional functions, kneeling served the practical function of enabling the parent to conveniently place hands on the child's head. The child's kneeling also effectively stationed the parent between the child and the heavens as a kind of quasi-priestly intermediary ready to bestow heavenly influence on the child. That is how Richard Hooker depicts the parent's role in giving a blessing, which he compares both with blessings described in the Bible and with blessings given in his own time by ministers. In these various blessings, someone with a special "callinge" and "dutie" to act for the good of others is able, through prayer, to *"blesse"*—that is, "to obteine the graces which God doth bestowe" (2:321). Besides viewing the parental blessing as a sacred act, involving heavenly grace, Hooker also sees it as a sign of the parent's feeling of responsibility and love for the child and of the connection between them. The *"imposition of handes,"* he says, betokens "our *restrayned desires* to the partie, whome wee present unto God by prayer" (2:321). The hands serve as an instrument for conveying heavenly power that will bless the child, but they also allow physical contact between parent and child and thus enable the blessing to serve as an expression of parental affection. Affection is also expressed by the child's kissing the parent's hands, an action that is sometimes made explicit in Shakespeare's depiction of the ritual.[9]

The sense of Hooker's phrase "restrayned desires" is probably that in the blessing ritual the parent's affection for the child, though strong and deep, is restrained within formal bounds, directed in a controlled, ceremonial way. The blessing is thus an example of what Shakespeare calls "ceremonious affection" (*Lr.* I.iv.59): it expresses deep feeling, but gives that feeling shape and social, even mythic, significance, so that it fits meaningfully into the order of human society and the cosmos. For, besides symbolizing the bond of love and identity between parent and child, the parental blessing was viewed as a sacred act linking a particular family and its life with the order of the universe and the powers of heaven. Further, the ritual seems to have been seen as a way of linking a child with the family in the larger sense of lineage and even with the whole human lineage going back to the beginning of time.[10] Though a familiar daily practice, the ritual was connected in the Renaissance mind with customs of great antiquity, highly charged with religious associations. In particular, the blessing ritual was viewed as parallel to and in some sense a continuation of the blessings given by the biblical patriarchs, and like these ancient blessings, the ritual was thought to be an instrument of supernatural influence and prophetic insight.[11]

Because the blessing ritual was seen as possessing such power, it was certainly used at times as an instrument of social control. In particular, parents who wished to affect their children's behavior might threaten to withhold their blessing until the children obeyed. Yet we seriously distort the meaning and function of the blessing ritual if we treat it—as some historians and critics have done—exclusively or primarily as a means of domination. As much as anyone, historian Lawrence Stone has been responsible for distortion of this kind. In books that have strongly influenced recent Shakespearean studies, Stone calls the blessing ritual "a symbolic gesture of submission," and he uses it to support his thesis that in England of the sixteenth century, more than at any other time, "the husband and father lorded it over his wife and children with the quasi-absolute authority of a despot" (*Family* 171; *Crisis* 591).[12] Following Stone's lead, Coppélia Kahn lists parental blessings among several customs of Shakespeare's England that she sees as "routine, visible reminders of patriarchal power" (16).[13]

In my view, Stone (along with those dependent on him) is essentially wrong in his understanding of the parental blessing. To connect the ritual primarily with "tyranny" or "despotism," as Stone has done, is to level significant differences—differences the Renaissance was careful to maintain, at least in theory—between parental authority used appropriately and lovingly and parental authority abused with destructive or coercive effect. Moreover, the parental blessing was not exclusively or primarily an expression of "patriarchal power," at least if that phrase is understood as referring only to men. Mothers and fathers both gave blessings. Both had what Houlbrooke calls "quasi-sacerdotal" authority (145). Nowhere have I found evidence that blessings by fathers were deliberately privileged over those given by mothers. In Shakespeare's plays, mothers' blessings occur almost as often as fathers', and the blessings performed by women are at least as potent, both in the theater and in the plays' imagined worlds, as those performed by men.[14]

I am not arguing that the ritual had no association, in the minds of Shakespeare's contemporaries, with parental authority or filial duty. But other elements were at least as important: in particular, the ritual was viewed as signaling, even reinforcing, the intimate and loving bond that ideally existed between parent and child. It was seen as a means by which parents conveyed to their children divine influence—"blessing"—intended to enhance the children's happiness and prosperity. Though parents offered their good wishes and influence *by virtue* of their authority as parents, they did not normally perform the ritual *in order* to assert their authority and use it to dominate or coerce the child. The blessing could be, and sometimes was, used as an instrument of domination, but it was more commonly used and understood as an instrument of grace: that is, of love, generosity, good will, and divine power intended to bless the child.

Shakespeare sometimes uses parental blessings to underscore a parent's role as an authority figure.[15] This is especially true of those blessings joined with advice and coinciding with a child's "taking leave" of a parent.[16] But even in these cases, the blessing ritual itself is used, not to control the child's behavior or even, strictly speaking, to give permission, but rather to offer love, advice, and empowering influence that will aid the child once permission has been granted. Sometimes, in fact, the ritual paradoxically involves parents' humbling themselves before their children or receiving life from children to whom they had earlier given life.[17]

Apart from a few parodic uses suggesting familial and even cosmic disorder (*Lr.* II.iv.153–58, III.ii.11–12; *Cor.* V.iii.22–62, 169–89; *Sir Thomas More* Addition III, lines 8–12), Shakespeare's treatment of the blessing ritual is almost always positive.[18] The only clearly negative uses of the motif involve a parent's withholding blessing or cursing a child.[19] These, indeed, show parents' tyranny or lack of grace. But they do so precisely because a *blessing* is positive, suggestive of harmony and mutual love. In *Lear,* the cursing of Cordelia leads to disaster; and the withholding of a blessing in *The Winter's Tale* helps set in motion a series of terrible, tragic events. But it should be noted that it is the failure to bless that is disastrous. The critical failure is a failure of generosity and love, a cutting off or denial of the living connection between parent and child symbolized by the blessing ritual. Even its negative uses, then, effectively emphasize the link between the parental blessing and grace, for it is the ritual's distortion or absence that signals or produces disaster.

The blessing ritual is mentioned three times in *Richard III* and appears mainly for ironic effect, to emphasize the distance between Richard and grace in any of its senses. The first reference, near the beginning of the play, is made by Clarence as he attempts to convince his murderers that Richard loves him:

> Tell him, when that our princely father York
> Blest his three sons with his victorious arm,
> And charg'd us from his soul to love each other,
> He little thought of this divided friendship.
> Bid Gloucester think of this, and he will weep.
> (I.iv.235–39)

The irony is not only that Richard has arranged for Clarence's death, but also that he would be insensible to the kind of appeal—dependent on reverence for the blessing ritual—that his brother is making.

The two remaining references to the blessing ritual are nicely balanced, one occurring about a third of the way into the play while Richard is on the rise, the other near the end of the play, just before Richard's defeat and death. In the first, Richard, already responsible for the death of his brother Clarence and soon to be responsible for the deaths of others, kneels before his mother with the pretense of seeking her grace (i.e., her favor, her beneficent influence). He says, "Humbly on my knee / I crave your blessing"; and she responds: "God bless thee, and put meekness in

thy breast, / Love, charity, obedience, and true duty!" Richard's reply is
"Amen!" But he adds in an aside—"and make me die a good old man! /
That is the butt-end of a mother's blessing. / I marvel that her Grace did
leave it out" (II.ii.105–11). In the last line quoted, "Grace" is a "courtesy-
title" (OED, s.v. 'grace,' II.16b). But in context, the title suggests other
meanings of *grace*: "virtue," "kindness," "mercy," "beneficent influence of
heaven" (Schmidt, s.v. 'grace'). The implication is that Richard's mother is
a person of virtue and a source of heavenly influence. We know from his
words and behavior here and elsewhere that Richard summons such images
of heaven and virtue only to mock them. The thought of dying a pious death
strikes him as laughable, for, as he takes pleasure in asserting, his nature is
not pious—not "gracious." Such virtues as "meekness," "love, charity,
obedience, and true duty," are, as he sees it, not only contrary to his
nature, but contrary to his aim: namely, self-serving power, which requires
an efficient ruthlessness quite opposed to the generous, merciful disposition implied by the word *grace*. Richard's appearance, too, distances him
from grace. "Rudely stamp'd," "Deform'd, unfinish'd," as he himself says
(I.i.16, 20), Richard lacks grace in the sense of "beauty, attraction, charm"
(Schmidt, s.v. 'grace'). Indeed, the play presents his deformed body as
symbolic—even as a manifestation—of his moral deformity.

Far from being merely horrifying, though, Richard's mocking of his
mother's blessing allows him to forge a curiously intimate bond with his
audience. It is hard to avoid laughing when he says, "I marvel that her
Grace did leave it out"; it is hard to avoid admiring the wit and energy of
the whole aside. And the fact that it is an aside means that we are offered
the special privilege of overhearing what most on the stage do not hear. In
more than one sense, we are "taken in."

But it is more than the speaker's wit and the special conditions of the
aside that allow Richard's seductive appeal to work its spell on us in this
scene. It is easy for us, like Richard, to be put off by ceremony and by calls
to "meekness" and "obedience"; it is easy, too, for us to resist expressions
of love, especially when these are joined with an implied challenge to our
moral standing. There is something appealing, in other words, in the very
qualities that make Richard a villain, especially his resistance to pious
conformity and the rational, pragmatic spirit that he has turned entirely to
self-advancement. Richard is certainly no victim of what Nietzsche would
later call "slave morality." He expresses no reverence for tradition or
ceremony and, in fact, seems to find in these nothing more than empty
forms that he can use for his own ends.

For a time, other characters share his attitude, especially Buckingham, who counters the Cardinal's objection to violating sanctuary with "You are . . . / Too ceremonious and traditional" (III.i.44-45). The play treats this antagonism toward ritual and tradition with a curious detachment. Explicit commentary and judgment are kept at a minimum (in the case I have just referred to, the Cardinal simply gives in), with the effect that we find few obstacles to fellow feeling with the villains of the play, at least on this matter of "tradition." By the end of the play we have reason enough to see Richard's attitude as deficient; in particular, his mockery of the blessing ritual—one expression of his scorn for the past and for the complex social and cosmic connections that hold the world together—helps explain his incapacity for normal or happy human relationships. But because in the course of the play we have become Richard's accomplices in some measure, the shock of understanding what his attitudes mean strikes us with even greater force.

The blessing ritual is referred to again near the end of *Richard III*; this blessing is given to Richmond "by attorney"—that is, through his stepfather—"from [his] mother" (V.iii.83). One effect of this blessing, with its prophetic wish "for Richmond's good" (line 84), is to prepare us for Richmond's victory. While the play's earlier references to the blessing ritual came when Richard was on the rise, this last one comes shortly before his fall and signals Richmond's replacing him as the play's dominant force. Because Richmond, unlike Richard, does not reject or mock his mother's blessing, the blessing serves to notify us of the normality of his relationship with his mother and to set him, as Richard's main antagonist, more sharply in contrast to the title character, whose familial relationships are anything but normal.

The entire play establishes a similar contrast by its frequent use of *grace, graces, grac'd,* and *gracious,* words which, as a group, appear more often here than in any other of Shakespeare's plays. Though often used merely as titles ("her Grace"), these words, whatever their overt meanings, carry implications of courtesy, gracefulness, good will, mercy, and virtue, and so stand in stark contrast to what happens in the play—especially the murder of kindred and children that forms part of Richard's project of deceptive and ruthless self-advancement. It is as if the words associated with grace, normally positive in their connotations, help create a backdrop against which Richard and his dark deeds appear all the more distinctly.

Indeed, Richard himself sometimes puts on an affectation of grace—

appearing publicly, for instance, in religious meditation between two "reverend fathers." The irony of the scene is underlined when Buckingham calls him "most gracious prince," "your gracious self," and responds to Richard's pretended scruples with "My lord, this argues conscience in your Grace" (III.vii.61–62, 100, 131, 174). The phrase "your Grace" or "his Grace," often referring to Richard, is sometimes used with unintentional irony, as when Hastings, about to be accused of treason, says, "I thank his Grace, I know he loves me well; / But for his purpose . . . , / I have not sounded him, nor he deliver'd / His gracious pleasure" (III.iv.14–17). Some characters, on the other hand, make it plain that they find Richard ungracious. His mother, in response to a proverb that would indicate "he should be gracious," says, "I hope he is, but yet let mothers doubt" (II.iv.20, 22). Queen Elizabeth identifies him as one who has "avoided grace" and wishes "grace had blest [him] with a fairer life" (IV.iv.219, 221). Richard's distance from grace is thus defined both by actions and by words, actions and words that, ironic or not, have the consistent effect of setting Richard and grace in opposition.

It is worth noting that grace, at least when we are to understand it as genuinely present, is most often associated with women. While the men of the play are almost all deceived or exploited by Richard, most of the women oppose him, and even those who yield to him (Lady Anne and perhaps Queen Elizabeth) see his true nature. The blessing ritual, too, is associated mainly with women. Perhaps because the authority to perform it derives from natural powers and relationships—and perhaps, too, because blessing, like cursing, is viewed as possessing supernatural power—the blessing ritual indicates women's access to a power independent of and in some ways superior to that found in the political structures within which the play's men operate. For, though women are not the main political powers in the play—unlike the men, that is, they do not violently compete for positions of prestige and domination—they wield power of other kinds.

One evidence of these women's power is that most of them seem beyond Richard's control. Rather than dominating them in the same way he dominates men, he berates or mocks them or seeks through marriage to obtain access to their power. At various points, he appears to be afraid of women and of the truth-revealing and prophetic power of their words (see I.iii.42–318 and IV.iv.136–98). By mocking his mother's blessing early in the play, Richard has given indirect expression to the discomfort he feels when confronted by her power, even when it is exercised with benevolent intent. By the end of the play, his mother's power helps to bring about his downfall. Convinced that her son is beyond the reach of grace, she reverses her blessing and says, "Take with thee my most grievous curse" (IV.iv.188), a curse she joins explicitly with a wish for his defeat in battle.

Like Richard, Bertram, in *All's Well That Ends Well,* is at odds with grace. But here the opposition is more complex and subtle, as might be expected, given the ambiguities of Bertram's character. Bertram is drawn in two directions: in one direction, by Parolles and by his own immaturity and unrestrained desires; in the other, by several "gracious" women—his mother, Helen, and Diana—and by the King. These characters are associated in one degree or another with grace or gracelessness. Parolles is "out" of "grace" in two senses—"favor" and "virtue" (V.ii.47, 50). Diana, on the other hand, is associated with grace (III.v.26, V.iii.133). Bertram's mother, though the word *grace* is not used to describe her, is nevertheless a figure of grace: she is virtuous, and she exercises good will toward Helen. Of course, it is hard not to see her as a dominating figure, too, especially toward her son. This is even more true of the King, who, eager to impose his will and vindicate his honor, forces Bertram to receive the gift of a gracious wife. Though explicitly associated with grace (II.iii.167, V.i.31, V.iii.87, 128), the King at times seems impelled more by "rude will," a force Shakespeare elsewhere contrasts with grace. Perhaps the King's exercise of his power, and even the Countess's exercise of hers, are analogous to the theological concept of "irresistible grace": power that the recipient cannot refuse. Yet there is something conceptually dissonant in a grace—a generosity—that makes no allowances for the freedom and integrity of the receiver, that gives freely but insists on being received.[20]

We may feel similar discomfort with Helen herself, the gift who wants to be given, the giver who has to circumvent the projected receiver's resistance. Yet she, more than anyone else in the play, is identified with grace, both as a word (I.iii.220, II.i.160)—she is even called an "herb of grace" (IV.v.17)—and as a concept. She is virtuous as well as generous—gracious, that is, both as gift and as giver. And she is also associated with grace in the sense of divine, regenerative power. Her cure of the King is in several senses an act of grace: it is a virtuous act, performed by a "blessed spirit" (II.i.175); it is an act of good will; and it is a deed accomplished with heavenly help—"a showing of a heavenly effect in an earthly actor" (II.iii.23-24). In her cure of the King, as well as in her eagerness to marry, we may see what Carol Thomas Neely has described as "her blend of virtuous modesty and sexual energy" (68). But far from depriving her of grace, Helen's association with sexuality helps expand the notion of grace to include life-giving powers of all kinds, natural and supernatural.

Bertram is the hardest character in this play to locate in relation to grace. Though he has his virtues and is sometimes well spoken of (e.g., III.iii.1–3), he has such glaring faults that his mother wonders "What angel shall / Bless this unworthy husband" (III.iv.25–26). Yet his case is not quite hopeless: Helen has asked Bertram's mother to "bless him at home in peace," and his mother, though worried that "he cannot thrive," thinks so highly of Helen's prayers, "whom heaven delights to hear / And loves to grant," that she has some hope for her son's redemption (III.iv.10, 26–27). Bertram uses the word *grace* ironically when he tells Parolles he will "grace" – that is, honor – the "worthy exploit" intended to result in Parolles's exposure (III.vi.68). Besides Bertram's conscious irony, the word *grace* here may carry irony in another sense as well, one Bertram does not intend; for this "exploit" leads to his break with Parolles and prepares for his return to "grace." With this possible exception, however, Bertram is not strongly associated with the words *grace* or *gracious*.

But here again, words alone do not tell the whole story. Helen's request that the Countess of Rossillion "bless" her son "at home" indicates that she sees the Countess as a source of blessing, and thus of grace in its several senses. Yet how can the Countess bless a son who resists her counsel and runs from what she thinks he should welcome? Perhaps we can find an answer in the one instance in the play in which Bertram willingly receives blessing from his mother, for here she is not so much a counselor or maker of plans as she is the performer of a ritual.

The ritual she performs is a mother's blessing, given very early in the play – near the beginning of the first scene – just before Bertram takes his leave. The original text does not specify Bertram's or the Countess's actions, and most editors of the play have failed to notice – or at least to tell readers – that something unusual is taking place.[21] But close attention to the language should make it clear to those who know of the custom that the Countess is giving a parental blessing. The ritual begins when Bertram says, "Madam, I desire your holy wishes" (I.i.59): he is asking for his mother's blessing, and he should be kneeling at this point, ready to receive it. "Holy wishes" may be a Shakespearean variation on the usual wording of such a request, but the phrase is apt for several reasons. As Richard Hooker pointed out, the laying on of hands signifies the parent's "desires" toward the child – in other words, what the parent wishes. And Bertram sees his mother, or at least her wishes, as holy not only because mother-hood itself is sacred, but also because in giving him a blessing she is performing a sacred ritual and calling upon the heavens.

As the Countess begins her reply – saying, "Be thou blest, Bertram, and succeed thy father / In manners as in shape!" – she should place one or both of her hands on or above Bertram's head. (This is assuming, of course, that she follows the usual form.) She will keep her hands in position, and Bertram will continue kneeling, while she gives six lines of motherly counsel reminiscent of Polonius's advice to Laertes, which also accompanies a ritual blessing and is also given at the time of a child's departure (*Ham.* I.iii.52–82).[22] That she is giving a mother's blessing, involving the usual gestures, is confirmed by the words she uses near the end of the ritual: "What heaven more will, / That thee may furnish, and my prayers pluck down, / Fall on thy head!" (I.i.61–70).[23]

This blessing, if it is acted out ritually on the stage, will inevitably affect how viewers experience and interpret the play. The ritual emphasizes a crucial moment of interaction between mother and son. It sounds a theme at the opening of the play – the theme of grace versus gracelessness – that will stay longer in an audience's memory if it is seen as well as heard. For those aware of the historical background, the ritual will also bring to mind the attitudes and ideas associated with the parental blessing in Renaissance England. Its being acted out and seen is essential to its full effect, for the gestures themselves are expressive. Kneeling suggests humility and reverence. The parent's hands, extended toward or placed on the child, suggest the bond of affection and responsibility between the two, a bond that includes the parent's role in conveying God's blessing or grace to the child and the child's acknowledgment of connection with the parent.

Besides increasing the scene's dramatic effectiveness, the blessing ritual in this first scene also complicates – which is to say, enriches – an audience's interpretation of Bertram and of the play. As with Richard in *Richard III*, Bertram's receiving a parental blessing may be set in ironic contrast with his subsequent gracelessness. Yet Bertram, unlike Richard, gives no hint when the blessing takes place of being insincere in the humility and reverence he expresses toward his mother. Bertram says very little, and perhaps his restraint can be taken as evidence that he feels ambivalent as a son. By tone of voice or facial expression, he could even show himself irritated or impatient. But the scene certainly does not exclude the possibil-ity of his being at least passively "gracious" – willing to receive blessing and instruction, respectful of tradition and familial bonds. His request for a blessing can thus be taken as a sign of his essential, though undeveloped and untested, goodness.

However the scene is interpreted, the giving of a blessing serves as a prototype for events that come later in the play. The blessing is one instance, the first, of a gracious woman appealing to heaven to bless Bertram. In this and later appeals, the Countess and Helen may be taken as exercising the "prophetic power" commonly ascribed to parental blessings. Yet they are also doing more. Most clearly in Helen's healing of the King and in the Countess's blessing of her son, the play associates these women with natural and divine powers and shows them exercising these powers to bless another person. Given the women's role as wielders of supernatural power, both the Countess's blessing of Bertram and Helen's healing of the King may be taken as prefiguring yet another miracle: Bertram's spiritual regeneration, his entry – or his partial entry, or perhaps his efforts at entering – into a state of grace.[24] If his protestations of repentance and love in the last scene are genuine, it is possible he has attained such a state.

Perhaps the concept of grace, understood in its broadest sense, can help us resolve some of the play's difficulties, including the conflict between the women's generosity and their apparent coercion or manipulation of Bertram. It is true that Helen schemes. And it is true that in the final scene, Helen – along with the King, the Widow, Diana, and (unwittingly) Bertram himself – helps drive Bertram into a corner, deprive him of defenses, and bring him to see what he is and what he has done. Yet far from being truly coercive or brazenly manipulative, Helen at several crucial points shows her willingness to let Bertram accept or reject her.[25] Even at the end, when she has fulfilled his seemingly impossible conditions, she asks, "Will you be mine now you are doubly won?," leaving it to him to make her a wife in more than name (V.iii.306–14). In contrast to the King – the play's most extreme example of a "grace" that ignores the will of the receiver – Helen, even in the bed trick, uses something much closer to the "sweet and gracious perswasions" (Oliver Whitbie, *London's Returne* [1637/8], quoted in Tyacke 218) that were opposed in Renaissance thought to "irresistible grace." She wants to do more than trick Bertram into accepting her. She wants to change his heart. And apparently – though again the play is capable of multiple readings – his heart changes. I am thinking especially of Bertram's saying, "Both, both. O, pardon!" – simple and revealing words that constitute his first, undoubtedly shocked response at seeing Helen again and hearing her say, " 'Tis but the shadow of a wife you see, / The name, and not the thing" (V.iii.307–8).

On one level, we may see his change of heart as the result of the divine power of regeneration, conveyed to him through Helen's prayers and his mother's blessing and also prefigured by the healing of the King. But on a more restrictedly human level, what can have effected the change? Maybe surprise, maybe the collapse of his pretensions to male superiority as he sees himself so thoroughly exposed. But maybe it is grace, this time in the sense of love, persistent and generous. Certainly Bertram has shown himself capable of responding to love (Helen says, "I found you wondrous kind" [V.iii.310]). Grace, as embodied in Helen, is tenacious, resourceful, even demanding, yet it leaves to the possible receiver of grace the freedom to ignore or respond to its demands. Bertram's response is not entirely clear, but there is some evidence that his resistance to grace has softened, some evidence even that he is capable of offering grace in return.

Still the mystery of a changed heart remains. How can power from outside affect that intimate center of the individual person, that place not simply governed by the will, but from which the will arises? Perhaps what makes this a "problem play" is not so much its skeptical view of human nature as it is its presentation of problems before which the rational intellect must confess itself inadequate. Among these problems is the mystery of grace, whether the word is taken in its divine or its purely human sense.

In *The Winter's Tale*, a parental blessing takes place in the climactic scene — perhaps the most prominent appearance of the ritual in the Shakespearean canon — and its function is emphatically to convey grace. *Grace*, as a host of critics have perceived, is a crucial word and a crucial concept in *The Winter's Tale*. F. C. Tinkler, for instance, asserts that "Grace and Graciousness" are the "keynote of the play" (345). The concept, though not the word, occurs in the play's short first scene. When Archidamus, one of Polixenes' courtiers, laments that Bohemia can never adequately repay the hospitality he and his fellow courtiers have received in Sicily, Camillo responds, "You pay a great deal too dear for what's given freely" (I.i.17–18). The idea is repeated in the last scene, when Paulina tells Leontes that his visit to her "poor house" is "a surplus of [his] grace, which never / [Her] life may last to answer" (V.iii.6–8). *Grace* here means "bounty," "generosity"; it refers to giving that expects no repayment, that is motivated solely by a desire for another's good. Such "grace" is an expression of good will, of a desire to bless, of the value placed on others for their own sake, not for what they can give in return.

Perhaps the most memorable occurrences of the word *grace* are in act I, scene ii, where the word is repeated three times within twenty-five lines. The word takes on a different sense with each appearance, but the effect of the scene is to associate and even mingle these several senses. In its first appearance, when Hermione exclaims, "Grace to boot!," it means heavenly influence. In context—Polixenes has just suggested that he and Leontes have fallen from their childhood innocence—the word brings to mind the divine influence needed to regenerate sinful hearts and redeem humankind from their fallen state. Nineteen lines later, playfully asking Leontes to tell her on what previous occasion she spoke well, Hermione uses the word *grace* as a personal name, with the meaning of "virtue," applied to this earlier good deed ("O, would her name were Grace!"). When he identifies the deed—her offer of herself to him as wife—she says, " 'Tis Grace indeed." *Grace* here means graciousness and generosity, as well as virtue, all these meanings being implied by the words Leontes quotes her as having said years before: "I am yours for ever" (I.ii.80, 99, 100, 105).

We shortly learn that Leontes doubts Hermione's gracious offer at the very moment he remembers it. Yet Hermione soon makes it clear, if it has not been clear before, that she is the play's most powerful figure of grace. Even when she defends herself most vigorously, she retains the abundant good will that marked her first responses to false accusation: "you, my lord, / Do but mistake"; "How will this grieve you, / When you shall come to clearer knowledge"; "I never wish'd to see you sorry, now / I trust I shall" (II.i.80–81, 96–97, 123–24). Generous, virtuous, associated with "great creating Nature" and with the divinely endowed power to give life, Hermione (like the women of *All's Well That Ends Well*) has the power to bless and redeem.[26] She is so close to ideal, in fact, that we may find it hard to accept her as a real human being. Yet what helps make her believable and appealing is that, though associated with sanctity and grace, she is vulnerable and human as well. She is capable of playful joking and camaraderie and can talk openly, though chastely, of sexual matters. Throughout the play she is associated with the concrete processes of life—pregnancy, childbirth, and her own warm, bodily presence. She is physically affectionate, so much so that her physicality threatens Leontes and arouses his suspicions. And though she may sometimes seem close to perfect, she, like other humans, requires grace—that is, blessing from a source outside herself. Having fallen out of "grace"—that is, out of favor—with her husband (III.ii.47), she trusts in "pow'rs divine" and holds that the unjust treatment she is receiving will be for her "better grace" (III.ii.28, II.i.122). She thus acknowledges not only her less than perfect humanity, but her dependence on other human beings and on the favor and providential care of heaven.

Grace is responsible in several senses for the restoration of happiness in the final scene. Leontes has undergone a fundamental change of heart and has, according to Cleomines, been forgiven by the heavens (V.i.1–6). Divine grace has also been at work in the restoration of Perdita and her betrothal to Florizel (V.i.35–36, V.iii.150–51). Paulina's whole project, culminating in this scene, may be viewed as a work of grace, even in its harsher aspect of confronting Leontes with his misdeeds and provoking his repentance. Though the heavens do not literally restore Hermione to physical life, they aid in restoring her to life within her family. The "grace" with which the play ends is thus not a state of purely isolated personal virtue, but a condition that requires the blessing of the gods and that depends on generous, trusting relationships with other human beings. Hermione is now restored to her husband's favor (i.e., "grace")—as he, having undergone a far more radical change, is to hers. Though she does not yet speak to him, she "hangs about his neck" and has apparently offered her hand before he gives his. She gives every evidence of being now, as Leontes remembers her, "as tender / As infancy and grace" (V.iii.105–12, 26–27).

The word *grace* is also associated with Perdita. She is "grown in grace / Equal with wond'ring" ("grace" here suggesting "beauty," "virtue," "graciousness," and "gracefulness") (IV.i.24). She and Florizel are a "gracious couple," "gracious" (as Leontes's words make clear) suggesting qualities that beget "wonder" and even approach divinity (V.i.131–34). Perdita, product, we are told, of "good goddess Nature," is the most radiant example of the sanctity and divinity infused from heaven into the human world (II.iii.104). But Perdita is more than merely "radiant": she is passionate, plain-spoken, even stubborn. She is associated with fertility and the forces of nature. Indeed, the "grace" with which she is endowed includes these forces and has come to her by natural means. Grace in its various senses has come to her especially from her mother, acting in cooperation with "great creating Nature" (IV.iv.88), an entity which in turn is the "instrument" or "handmaid" of the gods.[27]

Another instrument of grace, also associated closely with Hermione and Perdita and combining the human with the divine, is the parental blessing. Unlike *Richard III* and *All's Well That Ends Well*, where the blessing ritual is most prominent near the beginning, *The Winter's Tale* does not actually present the ritual until the climactic closing scene.

Indeed, the preceding action may be viewed from one angle as a series of failed blessings, lost or incomplete opportunities that find their fulfillment at the end of the play. The first such opportunity is offered in act II, scene iii, when Paulina presents a newborn daughter to Leontes and "commends it to [his] blessing" (line 67). Instead of taking the child in his arms and praying for divine protection—as Henry VIII does in giving the newborn Elizabeth her first father's blessing (H8 V.iv.10–11)—Leontes refuses to acknowledge the child as his, and even threatens its life. His horror of being linked with "another's issue" leads him to imagine seeing Perdita grow up to "kneel / And call [him] father," as if requesting a blessing (WT II.iii.155–56). In other words, he imagines—and again rejects—another opportunity to bless his child.

After sixteen years of separation from her, Leontes is again given the opportunity to bless his daughter. He blesses her unwittingly in act V, scene i, when he welcomes her and calls her "goddess" (lines 130–31); and a formal blessing doubtless takes place as part of the reunion described in act V, scene ii.[28] But the fulfillment of these allusions to the blessing ritual is reserved for the last scene, and there the ritual is performed by Perdita's mother, not by her father.

The first hint of the blessing comes early in the scene when Perdita kneels before what appears to be a statue of her mother and says:

> And give me leave,
> And do not say 'tis superstition, that
> I kneel, and then implore her blessing. Lady,
> Dear queen, that ended when I but began,
> Give me that hand of yours to kiss.
>
> (V.iii.42–46)

The reference to superstition, especially joined as it is here with kneeling before a "statue," may reflect the anxiety felt by some during the seventeenth century as to whether kneeling for a parental blessing might be among the "reliques of Popish . . . superstition" (Ames 94).[29] But surely the primary associations Perdita's words and gestures should evoke are the filial love and reverence of a daughter for her mother as she kneels for a mother's blessing. Besides the kneeling, the idea of kissing a parent's hand would also suggest love and reverence to an audience familiar with the ritual, which often included such a gesture.

Later in the scene, as the statue apparently comes to life and it becomes clear that this is the living Hermione, Paulina tells Perdita, "kneel / And pray your mother's blessing," and then says to the mother: "Turn, good lady, / Our Perdita is found." Hermione's words indicate that she is now giving a parent's blessing: "You gods, look down / And from your sacred vials pour your graces / Upon my daughter's head!" (V.iii.119–23). The power of this blessing comes partly from the words used: the rhythms, the imagery, the word "grace" with all the meanings it has accumulated through the course of the play—beauty, gracefulness, virtue, favor, graciousness, generosity, forgiveness, and unconditional love. The blessing's power comes also from the gestures used: the kneeling of Perdita, Hermione's lifting of her hands to appeal for heaven's graces (a gesture not specified by the text or by editors, but surely appropriate), and her placing of her hands at the same time on or above her daughter's head to symbolize the bestowal of those graces on her and to affirm the bond newly created between her daughter and herself.

Besides the gestures, the words of the blessing would also have been familiar and resonant to an early audience. Despite the pagan context, Hermione's appeal to the heavens to bestow graces on her daughter closely resembles the words some Renaissance parents used in blessing their children. According to Peter Erondell, a parent might say, "I pray the strong Almightie God to increase his graces in you, and to blesse you," or "I pray God to blesse you all my Children, and to increase his graces in you" (sig. E7ᵛ, P5ᵛ)—words close to Hermione's "pour your graces / Upon my daughter's head!" The emotions associated with the blessing ritual are heightened in *The Winter's Tale* by the long separation between mother and daughter that is now ending. But even here Shakespeare is drawing on a concept familiar to his contemporaries. Besides its daily practice with children living at home, the blessing ritual also served to mark a child's reunion with a parent after separation. Hugh Rhodes, writing in the sixteenth century, advised:

> When that thy parents come in syght,
>   doe to them reverence:
> Aske them blessing if they have
>   bene long out of presence.
>   (73)

"Long out of presence" is a weak understatement if we are thinking of the separation of Perdita and Hermione. Yet the very flatness of Rhodes's verses reveals, by contrast, how *The Winter's Tale* lifts to mythic height what would have been a common experience for many of the play's first viewers.

We can guess at the experience of these first viewers by remembering that this ritual, taking place on stage at a moment of thematic and emotional climax, was one most of them had taken part in daily as children and still performed daily as parents. Such viewers must have seen in this parental blessing a striking combination of the wonderful and the ordinary. The blessing ritual would thus have helped give the scene the effect suggested by the Friar's words in *Much Ado About Nothing*: "Let wonder seem familiar" (V.iv.70).

Despite its familiar features, though, this blessing at the end of *The Winter's Tale* is not entirely ordinary. For one thing, the role of the child is emphasized more strongly here than in many other occurrences in Shakespeare and, undoubtedly, in contemporary life. As a result, in this play the offering of grace, the conveying of divine power, does not go in one direction only, from parent to child. Just as, during the "wide gap of time," Paulina and Leontes reversed the usual sovereign-subject relationship, so the younger generation prove in some ways to be the teachers and healers of their parents. Mamillius "makes old hearts fresh" (I.i.39); young Florizel, Polixenes tells us, "with his varying childness cures in me / Thoughts that would thick my blood" (I.ii.170–71). Perdita especially is associated with divine, regenerative power and is even described as a life-giving goddess of the spring (IV.iv.1–3; V.i.131, 151–52). With these allusions to children's restorative power in the background, it is difficult not to see in the ritual blessing of the last scene a reciprocal act: Hermione calls for heavenly grace to descend upon her daughter, yet Perdita conveys grace—love, regenerative power—in return. It is as if Perdita, especially now that Hermione can see and touch her, brings the resurrection of her mother to completion, giving birth to the woman who bore her.[30]

Another feature of the blessing in *The Winter's Tale* that, at least to a degree, reverses expectations is the fact that it is given by Perdita's mother, not her father. It is not that fathers' blessings were privileged over mothers'; the evidence suggests strongly that they were not. Yet, with both parents alive and especially given Leontes's failure to bless Perdita as an infant, we might expect to see both a mother's and a father's blessing—as indeed we do in *Pericles*.[31] The foregrounding of the mother's blessing in *The Winter's Tale* is doubtless in part a matter of dramatic construction: the second of two climactic blessings might seem anticlimactic. Yet it is likely that this foregrounding has thematic significance as well. The presence of a mother's blessing in the last scene probably has something to do with the association of both the ritual and women with grace. Indeed, all three of the plays emphasized here present women as possessing special kinds of creative or transforming power. All three also offer a picture of women's solidarity with each other and of their contrast with "graceless" men. Especially in *The Winter's Tale*, the parental blessing functions as a means one woman has of expressing her solidarity with another. And in the other plays it serves as an instrument women use to instruct and influence men.[32]

These plays thus join with other historical evidence in calling into question one of Lawrence Stone's central assertions: that parental blessings functioned mainly to reinforce patriarchal power, whether this is taken to mean a parent's power over a child or a man's power over a woman. Though Shakespeare probably emphasizes the role of children and women more than many of his contemporaries would have done, he is nevertheless drawing on common features of the blessing ritual: their performance by both women and men and their use to express love as well as—even much more than—difference in status. Stone's connection of the blessing with "the utter subordination of the child" (*Family* 171) and Coppélia Kahn's description of it as an "extreme" expression of patriarchal power (16) hardly seem accurate reflections of Shakespeare's use—or his contemporaries' experience and understanding—of the custom.

Indeed, a careful review of Shakespeare's plays and of other evidence from the period makes it clear that, for almost everyone, the parental blessing was an unusually positive act. Associated with ancient biblical precedents, it was believed to convey heavenly influence that could regenerate and sanctify. The parental blessing was also an affirmation of the bond linking parent and child and of the generosity and good will that ideally characterized this bond. Because parents are conduits through which heavenly influence is made available, and because for Shakespeare children too may serve as conveyers of such influence, the blessing links heaven and earth. Specifically, in *The Winter's Tale* the parental blessing serves as an image of what has happened through the whole course of the play, what happens most clearly as the play closes: from their sacred vials, the gods are pouring "grace" in all its senses into the world of human life.

This is not, of course, quite how the blessing is used in *Richard III* or *All's Well That Ends Well*. The blessing Bertram receives, though it perhaps prefigures his eventual redemption, also serves ironically to point up his disgrace. Richard asks for a blessing only to mock it. But in both plays, the ironic effect of the blessing depends on the positive qualities associated with it. The values associated with the parental blessing—sanctity, virtue, generosity, and love—are the values in opposition to which Richard and Bertram (through much of his play) define themselves.

It is certainly not by chance that Richard III, one of Shakespeare's most thoroughgoing individualists, makes light of the parental blessing ritual. The ritual is an affirmation of connectedness, of belonging, on the social and cosmic levels, as well as on the level of the family. The ritual was especially valued during a time when belonging was the norm and when identity was defined largely in terms of one's social relationships.[33] But the association with social connectedness also helps explain the decline of the custom, a decline that was noticed during the seventeenth century and that continued into the eighteenth. In a period when views of the cosmos and of the social order were changing, when individual conscience and egalitarian ideals were increasingly emphasized, a ritual that involved one person's kneeling to another apparently began to seem out of place, even offensive.

Another cause for the custom's decline may have been the growth of scientific rationalism and the increasing split between the sacred and the secular that resulted. In contrast to a view that would either dismiss the sacred or relegate it to a transcendent realm separate from ordinary experience, the view on which the parental blessing relies sees the sacred and secular as overlapping, even perhaps (like all binary oppositions) implying and depending on each other. In the parental blessing, the arbitrariness of the sacred/secular opposition is especially clear and the distinction between the two breaks down. Though clearly a sacred ritual, the parental blessing does not set itself within boundaries intended to keep out the world of everyday experience. In contrast to rituals performed in a special, sacred space by an ordained minister—rituals designed, that is, to avoid as much as possible any association with the profane and the natural—the parental blessing is given either at home (in a kind of natural sacred space) or at any other location where parent and child meet, and it is given by persons who acquire their authority through participation in the natural processes of conception and birth. The parental blessing thus serves to affirm the sacredness of this world, this time and place of ordinary experience.

Shakespeare was apparently aware of the movement in his culture toward separating the sacred and secular, but he tends either to ignore or blur the distinction. In All's Well, for instance, Helen describes her medicine as being "sanctified / By th' luckiest stars in heaven" (I.iii.245–46), and she herself is viewed as an earthly being through whom the heavens act. In *The Winter's Tale*, the sacred expresses itself largely through "nature" and in the processes of life: Nature is called a goddess (II.iii.104: "good goddess Nature"; cf. II.ii.58: "law and process of great Nature," and IV.iv.88: "great creating Nature"); the oracle and the isle of Delphos are associated with fertility and natural beauty (III.i); the gods act through a storm and a bear, and the Shepherd and his son, seeing a newborn child, "bless" themselves (III.iii); Perdita is associated with "grace" and called a "goddess," and she and Florizel are said to beget "wonder" (IV.i.24; V.i.131–34); Hermione is called "sacred" throughout, and her living, breathing presence is associated in the last scene with magic, majesty, and sanctity (V.iii).

Some have argued that in such portrayals of the divine within nature Shakespeare is secularizing the sacred, that—belonging to a culture that increasingly ignores or eliminates the sacred—he is reappropriating "the sacred" as a metaphorical rather than a literal category. I would argue that, instead, Shakespeare's characteristic move is to resist the narrowing and attenuation of the sacred and to take the broad (and traditional) view that makes the domain of the sacred very large and that makes fluid the boundaries between the sacred and the secular. This view is nicely summed up in *All's Well* in Lafew's response to Helen's healing of the King, a response that acknowledges the interpenetration of the divine and the natural and that criticizes attempts to narrow or eliminate the sacred: "They say miracles are past, and we have our philosophical persons, to make modern and familiar, things supernatural and causeless. Hence is it that we make trifles of terrors, ensconcing ourselves into seeming knowledge" (II.iii.1–5).[34] Since the blessing ritual was an element of daily life in which the link between the divine and the natural was still felt to be real, Shakespeare's frequent use of the ritual suggests that his own view is something close to Lafew's.

Though the blessing ritual had been practiced and praised for decades by both Catholics and Protestants and by both Puritans and their antagonists, during the early 1600s the ritual came increasingly to be associated with other ceremonies that Puritans found obnoxious. The decline of the blessing ritual was already noticeable by 1657, when Bishop Robert Sanderson, lamenting the neglect of the parental blessing and other practices, offered as one cause the association commonly made between such ceremonies and "popish" practices: "These last *two seven* years [that is, since 1643] the having of *God-fathers* at Baptism, *Churching* of Women, *Prayers* at the burial of the dead, Children asking their Parents *blessing*, &c.,

which whilome were held *innocent;* are now by very many thrown aside, as rags of *Popery"* (73–74). The problem at root seems to have been differing views of grace. Calvinists emphasized the grace of predestination, God's absolute sovereignty in choosing how and to whom he gives grace; some even worried that ritual of any kind might constitute a blasphemous attempt to force the hand of an all-powerful God. By contrast, Arminians (who were accused of affinities with "popery") emphasized the grace made available through the sacraments, and saw in religious ceremonies "the beauty of holiness" rather than the danger of superstition or blasphemy.[35]

The growing split between the sacred and the secular was related to this dispute concerning grace. In a world increasingly viewed as purely secular, grace—if it enters at all—might be expected to operate at a level entirely inapproachable by human will or action. One consequence of this attitude, an attitude that both Calvinists and rationalists might find appealing, was that many came to view ritual as essentially irrational or empty of real power. Also prompting antagonism toward ritual was the increasing emphasis both political and religious liberals placed on individual freedom. Especially among Presbyterians, Puritans, and Quakers, there was widespread feeling against kneeling, which was seen as idolatrous or inconsistent with an individual's God-given dignity and freedom of conscience.[36] The English Civil War, along with other events, led many to seek their own social and religious paths, rather than ones determined by family or tradition. The words Shakespeare gives Richard—"I have no brother, I am like no brother; / . . . / . . . I am myself alone" (*3H6* V.vi.80, 83)—though the words of a villain, have some affinity with the ideal, increasingly attractive since the Renaissance, of unique and autonomous individuality.

There are many reasons to think that Shakespeare had some sympathy with this ideal—I am thinking of Cordelia, for example, and other children with domineering parents. But Shakespeare also saw the potential evils of individualism, especially if unconstrained by other values. I believe that what he proposes in place of either extreme is a fusion of opposing values—individuality and community, freedom and submission, personal integrity and love—brought about by the free offer of oneself to others. Such an offer, though not without its risks, is shown in the climactic scenes of plays like *The Winter's Tale* to result in an expansion and enriching, not a diminishing, of personal identity.

One of Shakespeare's symbols for this offer and the fusion of values it can bring is the parental blessing. Through this ritual of kneeling and blessing, an individual is connected with a family and, since the blessing conveys heavenly grace, with the cosmos. Yet the blessing is focused intimately and concretely on an individual—it is the cosmos and the family that affirm the value of that individual as much as it is the individual who acknowledges being connected with the family and the cosmos. In both directions, the ritual is a way of celebrating the presence of grace—goodness, beauty, heavenly power—in the world and in the individual. In both directions, it is also an expression of grace in the sense of good will, graciousness, generosity.

Understanding the parental blessing ritual can help editors, directors, and actors of Shakespeare's plays do their work more effectively. But more fundamentally, such an understanding can help all of us retrieve ideals that, for many in our century, have seemed unreal or out of date, ideals that, in the words of Vaclav Havel, "have lost their depths and dimension" and have come to seem "long-lost wanderers from faraway times." The ideals Havel wants to retrieve—"love, friendship, mercy, humility . . . forgiveness"—are the very ones that Shakespeare associates with the word *grace* and that he presents, often with great power and penetration, in conjunction with the parental blessing.

Living in an age when ritual is less pervasive and less valued, and after centuries during which even the most enduring words and concepts have undergone tarnishing and transmutation, we may find it difficult to understand Shakespeare's ideals without an effort of historical imagination. Yet we still, most of us, are moved and enlightened by Shakespeare's representations of intimate human associations and of the forms through which these express themselves. One thing an effort of historical imagination can do is to help us see that we are not held inescapably within the constraints of what we take to be our historical situation. Shakespeare's plays break through the closed horizons we imagine as surrounding us to offer visions of human life in which sociality and individuality, human and divine grace, are related and in which love and generosity have concrete meaning. Speaking to us from another time and place and often, as in the blessing ritual, through words and gestures unfamiliar to us, Shakespeare can nevertheless help us to see our own possibilities in the visions he presents and to acknowledge that these possibilities are not beyond our grasp.

NOTES

1. "O graceless men" is from *2 Henry VI* IV.iv.38 (cf. *Shr.* V.ii.160); "as tender as infancy and grace" is from *The Winter's Tale* V.iii.27. All quotations from the plays

are from *The Riverside Shakespeare*. The various definitions of *grace* are para-
phrased from Schmidt and from *The Oxford English Dictionary*, hereafter OED.

2. For theological senses of the word *grace*, see (among Renaissance sources)
Preston, Prime, and Wilson (s.v. 'grace'). For a modern discussion of the Arminian
versus Calvinist controversy concerning grace, see Tyacke.

3. For a fuller discussion of the ritual and its place in Shakespeare and in
Renaissance family life, see my article "Parental Blessings in Shakespeare's Plays,"
and Houlbrooke, 31, 41, 145, 168, 188.

4. Such is the report of contemporary observers from France and Italy. See, for
instance, Erondell, sig. E7ᵛ, E8ᵛ ("I mervaile verie much that French-men . . . doe
not make [children] aske their parentes blessing"), and the Venetian ambassador's
report in *Calendar*, 451 (describing this "admirable custom of [England], well
worthy of imitation"). Note also Fynes Moryson's claim that the custom was practiced "in no other kingdom that I know" (quoted in Scott 53) and John Donne's
question, "Children kneele to aske blessing of Parents in England, but where else?"
(9:59).

5. Fourteenth-century evidence for the custom is found in *The Good Wife*. In
some form, it may have been practiced throughout Europe during the Middle Ages
(see Weiser 139). For examples of non-European and non-Christian versions of the
blessing ritual, see Crawley, 4–6.

6. For other descriptions of the blessing and the words used, see Becon, fol.
519ᵛ, 524ᵛ; Erondell, sig. E7ᵛ, E8ᵛ, P5ᵛ; Stapleton, 12; and Stubbes, sig. C4.

7. See Becon, fol. 524ᵛ ("bow[ing] the knee" to ask for a blessing is one way of
showing "honorable reverence toward [parents], as parsons representing the majestie
of God"); Cleland, 178 ("The bowing of the knee declareth that we submit our
selves to him [before whom we bow], & that we wil not remaine equal, but wil
humble, and make our selves inferiour"); and Shakespeare's Prince Hal in *2 Henry
IV* IV.v.146–48 (kneeling is a "prostrate and exterior bending" that witnesses a
"most inward true and duteous spirit"). It appears that during the sixteenth and
early seventeenth centuries the practice of kneeling before parents was commonly
maintained into adulthood. In the early 1500s Sir Thomas More, on seeing his
father, "would goe to him, and reverently kneelinge downe in sight of all, aske him
blessing" (Ba. 59). In the seventeenth century, the adult Nicholas Ferrar similarly
knelt for his mother's blessing (Wordsworth 201). In 1622 the Venetian ambassador reported seeing Londoners kneel in public places, "no matter what their age,"
to ask a parent's blessing (*Calendar* 451).

8. Even on an issue so crucial as a child's potential marriage partner, the
consistent advice of moralists was that, though a parent's advice and consent
should be sought, the child's wishes must always be respected. The legal requirement was that, "without Consent [i.e., of the bride and groom] there cannot be any
Matrimony" (Swinburne 51). Shakespeare presents the same position in *Romeo
and Juliet* (I.ii.16–19), *The Winter's Tale* (IV.iv.404–10), and elsewhere. Of course,

both in Shakespeare and in Renaissance life outside the theater, parents sometimes exceeded their proper authority. (See my article "Haste, Consent, and Age at Marriage.")

9. For example, *The Winter's Tale* V.iii.118. Note also the kissing of parents in *Two Gentlemen of Verona* II.iii.26, 28; and the parent's kissing a child while blessing her in *Henry VIII* V.iv.9–11.

10. See, for instance, *The Good Wife*, where a blessing is used to convey to a child whatever good can derive from "alle our forme-faderes that were or arn" as well as from all "patriarches and prophetes that evere weren on live" (170).

11. For the associations with the biblical blessings described in Genesis 27, 48, and 49, see Babington, 205, 211; Erondell, sig. E8ᵛ; Hooker, 2:321; Mayer, 260; Richardson, sig. H2ᵛ; *The Good Wife*, 170; and a source used by Shakespeare for *Lear*—*The True Chronicle History of King Leir*—where Leir bestows on Cordella "the blessing, which the God of *Abraham* gave / Unto the trybe of *Juda*" (394). Though some writers emphasized the prophetic power of the blessing (e.g., James I: "the blessing or curse of the Parents, hath almost ever a Propheticke power joyned with it" [76]), Mayer and others distinguish between the truly prophetic blessings of the ancient patriarchs and the "ordinary blessings" of contemporary parents (Mayer 260; Gouge 438).

12. Stone's view has been challenged by other historians of the family, notably Ralph Houlbrooke, who argues that Stone overestimates the degree to which family patterns changed during the Renaissance and later periods, and who notes that "much evidence of love, affection and the bitterness of loss dating from the first half of Stone's period [i.e., 1500–1650] has simply been ignored" (15). It might be added that several facts about the parental blessing—its widespread practice over several hundred years, its pious observance by an early sixteenth-century figure like Sir Thomas More, and the lack of evidence from the late 1500s and early 1600s for any noticeable increase in emphasis placed on the custom—make it difficult to accept Stone's thesis that deference toward parents, including the deference shown through the blessing ritual, grew markedly from 1530 to 1640 (*Family* 171).

13. Kahn, like other Shakespearean critics who have commented recently on the blessing ritual, is dependent on Stone's one-paragraph discussion for her understanding of the custom and its historical context, and shows no evidence of additional research into what the parental blessing would have meant to Shakespeare's contemporaries or how exactly it would have been performed. Kahn cites Stone's "The Rise of the Nuclear Family," which contains a paragraph on the custom (41) virtually identical with a paragraph in *Family* (171). Stone himself and most of the other historians who discuss the parental blessing base their discussion on a handful of sources (Stone cites half a dozen more or less contemporary sources, three or four of which he quotes or discusses) and neglect what I believe is abundant evidence for a different interpretation.

14. Of the blessings actually performed or spoken on stage, eight or nine are given by mothers, twelve by fathers. Of other references to blessings, four to six are to ones given by women; nine to eleven are to ones given by men. The blessings have similar functions and use similar words, whether given by men or women. Compare, for instance, *Henry VIII* IV.ii.133 and *Cymbeline* V.v.350~51; *Winter's Tale* V.iii.121~23 and *Tempest* V.i.201~02; *Richard III* V.iii.84 and *Richard II* I.iii.78; *Titus Andronicus* I.i.167 and *Richard III* II.ii.109; *King John* III.iii.71 and *Hamlet* I.iii.57; *Hamlet* I.iii.57~81 and *All's Well* I.i.64~72; and *Merchant of Venice* II.ii.92~93 ("thou art mine own flesh and blood"), *Pericles* V.i.213 ("th' art my child"), V.iii.48 ("Blest, and mine own!"), and *The Winter's Tale* V.iii.123 ("mine own").

15. In five or six cases, blessings are tied closely to the idea of filial duty or parental authority, but are still generally positive and are certainly not coercive or harshly oppressive. (See *Cor.* V.iii.50~52; *2H4* IV.v.146~48; *Cym.* III.v.30~32; *AYL* I.i.3~4; *R3* I.iv.235~38.) In two other episodes, harder to classify, fathers concerned to protect their sons want to use their blessing to keep the sons from going into battle (see *1H6* IV.v.32~55 and *Cym.* IV.iv.43~50). In both cases, the fathers finally yield to their sons' wishes and send them off with a blessing.

16. See *King John* III.iii.69~71; *Hamlet* I.iii.52~82; *All's Well That Ends Well* I.i.59~70. In the latter two cases, Shakespeare is drawing on the common association made in his time between the parental blessing and the giving of advice. See (among others) William Cecil, Baron Burghley, *Certaine Precepts, or Directions, for the Well Ordering of a Mans Life;* Sir Walter Raleigh, *Instructions to his Sonne;* John Norden, *The Fathers Legacie; with Precepts Morall and Prayers Divine;* Elizabeth Joceline, *The Mothers Legacie, to Her Unborne Childe;* Dorothy Leigh, *The Mothers Blessing, or the Godly Counsaile of a Gentle-woman;* Nicholas Breton, *The Mothers Blessing.*

17. See *Hamlet* III.iv.170~72, and *Lear* IV.vii.46~48, V.iii.10~11. See below for a discussion of the child as life giver in *The Winter's Tale* and other plays.

18. Of his thirty to thirty-five references to the ritual, twenty-two mark a joyful reunion or reconciliation or otherwise represent a positive affirmation of the parent-child bond. (See *Tit.* I.i.161~68; *TGV* II.iii.23~29; *R3* II.ii.104~11, V.iii.83~85; *Jn.* III.iii.69~71; *MV* II.ii.77~95; *Ham.* I.iii.52~82, III.iv.170~72; *AWW* I.i.59~70; *Lr.* IV.7.56~58, V.iii.10~11, V.iii.196; *Cor.* II.i.169~71, V.iii.68~76; *Per.* V.i.204~13, 223, V.iii.44~48; *Cym.* V.v.264~69, 347~56, 368~72; *WT* V.iii.42~46, 118~23; *Tmp.* V.i.178~80; *H8* IV.ii.131~38, V.iv.9~11.) In many cases, the parental blessing is not only willingly, but earnestly sought by a child (e.g., *R2* I.iii.69~77; *Lr.* IV.vii.56~57). The parents normally respond to the request with words that express a generous, even fervent desire for the child's welfare and happiness. (See the instances already cited from *Tit.; R3; Jn.; R2; Ham.* I.iii; *AWW; Cor.* II.i, V.iii.68ff.; *Per.; Cym.* V.v; *WT; Tmp.;* and *H8.)*

19. In addition to the instances of parents cursing their children—*1 Henry VI*

V.iv.25–33; *Richard III* IV.iv.188; possibly in *Winter's Tale* IV.iv.458 (though it is not likely the shepherd means seriously to curse Perdita); allusively in *2 Henry VI* III.ii.155 and *King John* III.i.256–57; and most memorably in *Lear* I.i.204, I.iv.300, II.iv.146, 170—blessings are withheld, sometimes with an implied cursing, in *Winter's Tale* II.iii.67, 154–57; *Romeo and Juliet* III.v; and possibly *Othello* I.iii and *Midsummer Night's Dream* I.i (though in these last two the idea of blessing or cursing is not explicitly introduced).

20. "Irresistible grace" may be defined as power (in a religious sense, "God's power") "overcoming all resistance in the will of man" (Henry Leslie, *A Sermon preached before His Majesty at Windsore* [1625], quoted in Tyacke 169). This Calvinist view may be contrasted with Arminius's assertion that "God does not forcibly convert men but rather moves them 'by mild and sweet persuasion' " (Tyacke 39).

21. *The Riverside Shakespeare,* for instance, gives no stage directions indicating a blessing at this point. After reading an earlier paper on parental blessings, however, G. Blakemore Evans stated that he would add stage directions for kneeling and blessing if he were to edit the play again (see Evans).

22. Among the differences between the two blessings is that the Countess's is shorter and less morally ambiguous than that given by Polonius.

23. This image (associated with the blessing ritual) of grace or blessings falling on one's head also appears in *Cymbeline* V.v.350–51; *Winter's Tale* V.iii.121–23; *Tempest* V.i.178–81, 201–2; and *Henry VIII* IV.ii.131–33.

24. The connection between Helen's roles as healer and giver of grace is illuminated by a passage in which Richard Hooker draws a similar connection between two kinds of blessings ascribed to Jesus Christ (both also associated in Hooker's mind with parental blessings): "Hee which with imposition of handes and prayer did so great workes of mercie for restauration of bodilie health was worthilie judged as able to effect the infusion of heavenlie grace into them whose age was not yeat depraved with that malice which might be supposed a barre to the goodnes of God towardes them" (2:322). It is open to question whether Bertram is still (like the children blessed by Christ) young or innocent enough to yield to grace.

25. Her choice of Bertram, for instance, is put in the form of an offer—"I dare not say I take you, but I give / Me and my service, ever whilst I live, / Into your guiding power" (II.iii.102–4)—and when he rejects her, she tries to drop her suit ("Let the rest go" [line 148]).

26. Besides the insistent association of Hermione with grace (see I.ii.233, 459, II.ii.19, II.iii.29, III.ii.198), note other references to her as a quasi-divine figure: for example, "most sacred lady" (I.ii.76), "spotless / I' th' eyes of heaven" (II.i.131–32), "her sainted spirit" (V.i.57), "There's magic in thy majesty" (V.iii.39).

27. For a discussion of this concept, which goes back to the Middle Ages and beyond, see Tayler, 74.

28. Besides the fact that the blessing ritual accompanies similar father-daughter

reunions in other late plays (*Per.* V.i.213; *Cym.* V.v.264–66), the actions and physical contact described in *The Winter's Tale* suggest at the very least an appropriate setting for a parental blessing (V.ii.13–14: "There was . . . language in their very gesture"; 53–54: "then again worries he his daughter with clipping her").

29. Compare Paulina's later reference to "unlawful business" (line 96).

30. The situation echoes a phrase in *Pericles:* "Thou that beget'st him that did thee beget" (V.i.195). A few lines later Pericles gives a blessing to this daughter who "beget[s] him." These parallels between *The Winter's Tale* and *Pericles* suggest that the reciprocally life-giving relationship between parent and child, symbolized by the blessing ritual, is a deliberate, significant element in both plays. Something very similar takes place in *Lear:* Cordelia asks to be blessed by a father who is kneeling to her; later Lear, on his way to prison, says, "When thou dost ask me blessing, I'll kneel down / And ask of thee forgiveness" (IV.vii.56–58, V.iii.10–11). The motif of the life-giving child also occurs in *Titus Andronicus* I.i.166 (Titus Andronicus calls his daughter "the cordial of mine age") and *The Tempest* V.i.

31. See V.i.204–13, 223, V.iii.44–48. See also *Henry VIII* IV.ii.131–38 and V.iv.9–11. In plays other than *The Winter's Tale* in which only one parent gives a blessing—for example, the mother in *Richard III, King John, All's Well,* and *Coriolanus;* the father in *Titus Andronicus, Lear,* and *Cymbeline* — the lack of symmetry may be explained by the absence (usually through death) of the other parent.

32. Women's solidarity is also expressed in a blessing of sorts the Countess of Rossillion gives Helen (*AWW* I.iii.253–54). Non-Shakespearean representations of women's solidarity, expressed through a mother's blessing, may be found in the fourteenth-century poem *The Good Wife* and the seventeenth-century dialogue *The French Garden* (Erondell sig. E7ᵛ, E8ᵛ). A number of sources also represent mothers instructing their children, including sons (see Joceline; Leigh; Breton).

33. As Peter Laslett notes, only about one percent of England's population in this period "lived as solitaries" (199). The value of belonging is reflected in the words of Henry Smith, a popular London preacher: "*Woe to him which is alone . . .* because he hath none to comfort him" (19). A similar attitude may be seen in Hermione's calling Perdita "mine own" (almost her first words to her daughter) and in Paulina's behavior, described by a "gentleman" in the next to the last scene: "She lifted the Princess from the earth, and so locks her in embracing, as if she would pin her to her heart, that she might no more be in danger of losing" (V.iii.123, V.ii.76–78).

34. Compare Hamlet's similar view: "There are more things in heaven and earth, Horatio, / Than are dreamt of in your philosophy" (I.v.166–67).

35. For a discussion of this dispute, see Tyacke, especially 7, 10, 55.

36. See, for example, Barclay, 515 ("it is not lawful for Christians to kneel, or prostrate themselves to any man, or to bow the body, or to uncover the head to them"); Bradshaw, 9 ("the Idolatrous kneeling of Papistes"); and Ames, 79, 88, "An Addition," 40–41 (requiring kneeling and other ceremonies is a burden to con-

science and a restriction of Christian liberty). Note also Samuel Butler's description of "An Hypocritical Nonconformist," whose "mortal Hatred to Ceremonies" derives from seeing them as "Signs of Submission" (54). Gouge's discussion of the parental blessing (437–39) makes it clear that objections to the practice were being raised as early as the 1620s.

WORKS CITED

Ames, William. *A Fresh Suit Against Human Ceremonies in God's Worship.* 1633.

Ba., Ro. *The Lyfe of Syr Thomas More, Sometymes Lord Chancellor of England.* Ed. Elsie Vaughan Hitchcock and P. E. Hallett. EETS OS 222. London: Oxford University Press, 1950.

Babington, Gervase. *Certaine Plaine, Briefe, and Comfortable Notes, upon Every Chapter of Genesis.* 1596.

Barclay, Robert. *An Apology for the True Christian Divinity.* 1675. 7th ed. London, 1765.

Becon, Thomas. *Works.* 1564.

Bradshaw, William. *A Proposition Concerning Kneeling.* 1605. Amsterdam: Theatrum Orbis Terrarum; Norwood, N.J.: Walter J. Johnson, 1979.

Breton, Nicholas. *The Mothers Blessing.* 1602.

Butler, Samuel. *Characters.* Ed. Charles W. Daves. Cleveland: Press of Case Western Reserve University, 1970.

Calendar of State Papers. Venetian. 1621–1623. Vol. 17. Ed. Allen B. Hinds. London: His Majesty's Stationery Office, 1911.

Cecil, William, Baron Burghley. *Certaine Precepts, or Directions, for the Well Ordering of a Mans Life.* 1617.

Cleland, James. *The Institution of a Young Noble Man.* 1607. New York: Scolars' Facsimiles & Reprints, 1948.

Crawley, Ernest. *Oath, Curse, and Blessing.* Ed. Theodore Besterman. London: Watts, 1934.

Donne, John. *The Sermons of John Donne.* Ed. Evelyn M. Simpson and George R. Potter. 10 vols. Berkeley: University of California Press, 1953–62.

Erondell, Peter. *The French Garden.* 1605. Menston, Eng.: The Scolar Press, 1969.

Evans, G. Blakemore. Letter to author, 20 April 1985.

The Good Wife Taught Her Daughter; The Good Wyfe Wold a Pylgremage; The Thewis of Gud Women. Ed. Tauno F. Mustanoja. Helsinki: Suomalaisen Kirjallisuuden Seura, 1948.

Gouge, William. *Of Domesticall Duties.* 1622.

Havel, Vaclav. "Excerpts from Speech by the Czech President." *New York Times.* 2 January 1990, late ed.: A13.

Hooker, Richard. *Of the Laws of Ecclesiastical Polity.* Vols. 1–3 of *The Works of*

Richard Hooker. Ed. W. Speed Hill, et al. 4 vols. Cambridge, Mass.: Harvard University Press, 1977–82.

Houlbrooke, Ralph A. *The English Family, 1450–1700.* London: Longman, 1984.

James I. *Basilikon Doron.* 1603. (STC 14354.)

Joceline, Elizabeth. *The Mothers Legacie, to Her Unborne Childe.* 1624.

Kahn, Coppélia. *Man's Estate: Masculine Identity in Shakespeare.* Berkeley: University of California Press, 1981.

Laslett, Peter. *Family Life and Illicit Love in Earlier Generations.* Cambridge: Cambridge University Press, 1977.

Legg, J. Wickham. *English Church Life from the Restoration to the Tractarian Movement.* London: Longmans, Green, 1914.

Leigh, Dorothy. *The Mothers Blessing, or the Godly Counsaile of a Gentle-woman.* 1616.

Mahood, M. M. *Shakespeare's Wordplay.* London: Methuen, 1957.

Mayer, John. *A Commentary upon the Whole Old Testament.* London, 1653.

Neely, Carol Thomas. *Broken Nuptials in Shakespeare's Plays.* New Haven: Yale University Press, 1985.

Norden, John. *The Fathers Legacie; with Precepts Morall and Prayers Divine.* 1625.

The Oxford English Dictionary. 13 vols. Oxford: Clarendon, 1933.

Perkins, William. *A Treatise of the Vocations or Callings of Men.* 1603. In *The Works of William Perkins.* Ed. Ian Breward. Appleford, Eng.: Sutton Courtenay, 1970.

Preston, John. *De Gratia Convertentis Irresistibilitate.* 1652.

Prime, John. *A Fruitefull and Briefe Discourse in Two Bookes: The One of Nature, the Other of Grace.* 1583.

Raleigh, Sir Walter. *Instructions to his Sonne.* 3d ed. 1633.

Rhodes, Hugh. *The Boke of Nurture, or Schoole of Good Maners.* 1577. In *Manners and Meals in Olden Time.* Ed. Frederick J. Furnivall. EETS OS 32. 1868. New York: Greenwood, 1969.

Richardson, John. *Choice Observations and Explanations upon the Old Testament.* 1655.

Sanderson, Robert. *36 Sermons.* 1657. 8th ed. Ed. Izaak Walton. London, 1689.

Schmidt, Alexander. *Shakespeare-Lexicon.* 3d ed. 2 vols. Berlin: Georg Reimer, 1902.

Scott, A. F., ed. *Every One a Witness: The Stuart Age.* London: White Lion, 1974.

Shakespeare, William. *The Riverside Shakespeare.* Ed. G. Blakemore Evans, et al. Boston: Houghton Mifflin, 1974.

Smith, Henry. *A Preparative to Mariage.* 1591. (STC 22685.5.)

Stapleton, Thomas. *Tres Thomae.* Douay, 1588.

Stone, Lawrence. *The Crisis of the Aristocracy 1558–1641.* Oxford: Clarendon Press, 1965.

———. *The Family, Sex and Marriage in England, 1500–1800.* New York: Harper and Row, 1977.

———. "The Rise of the Nuclear Family in Early Modern England." In *The Family in History*. Ed. Charles E. Rosenberg. Philadelphia: The University of Pennsylvania Press, 1975.

Stubbes, Philip. *A Perfect Pathway to Felicitie*. 1592.

Swinburne, Henry. *A Treatise of Spousals or Matrimonial Contracts*. 1686.

Tayler, Edward William. *Nature and Art in Renaissance Literature*. New York: Columbia University Press, 1964.

Tinkler, F. C. "The Winter's Tale." *Scrutiny* 5 (1937): 344–64.

The True Chronicle History of King Leir. In *Narrative and Dramatic Sources of Shakespeare*. Ed. Geoffrey Bullough, 7:337–402. London: Routledge and Kegan Paul, 1975.

Tyacke, Nicholas. *Anti-Calvinists: The Rise of English Arminianism c. 1590–1640*. Oxford: Clarendon Press, 1987.

Weiser, Francis X. *Handbook of Christian Feasts and Customs*. New York: Harcourt, Brace, 1958.

Whitforde, Richard. *A Werke for Housholders*. 1533.

Wilson, Thomas. *A Christian Dictionarie*. 1612.

Wordsworth, Charles. *On Shakespeare's Knowledge and Use of the Bible*. 2d ed. London: Smith, Elder, 1864.

Young, Bruce. "Haste, Consent, and Age at Marriage: Some Implications of Social History for *Romeo and Juliet*." *Iowa State Journal of Research* 62 (1987–88): 459–74.

———. "Parental Blessings in Shakespeare's Plays." *Studies in Philology* 89 (1992): 179–210.

PART III

RITES OF RULE:
MONARCHY AND THE
BODY POLITIC

7

"The Form of Law": Ritual and Succession in *Richard III*

WILLIAM C. CARROLL

> Deformed persons are commonly even with nature,
> for as nature hath done ill by them, so do they
> by nature . . . Therefore it is good to consider
> of deformity, not as a sign, . . . but as a cause,
> which seldom faileth of the effect.
> —Bacon, "Of Deformity"

In her study of rites of passage and other ritual actions in Shakespearean drama, Marjorie Garber describes Richard III (along with Macbeth) as unique among tragic characters: "Of all Shakespeare's characters . . . two in particular stand out as examples of a contrary linguistic pattern, a regression rather than a progression—a failure of maturation emblematized by a failure in language."[1] Garber then describes in detail the initial power and eventual failure of Richard's rhetorical powers in the play, until the multiple fragmentations of his nightmare at Bosworth Field. Richard's failure to develop, to progress through rites of passage to some kind of maturity, is a particular instance, as I hope to show, of a much larger general failure of ritual in *Richard III*. This failure of ritual may be seen both in the transgressions of specific cultural rites and in the violation of "form" generally in the world of the play. I will argue, as well, that the play's interrogation of ritual form is not merely formalistic, but also a representation of perhaps the central political problem facing the Tudor dynasty in the 1590s: the issue of succession. After Henry VIII, the course of true succession never ran smoothly. From one perspective, it may appear that *Richard III* perfectly enacts the Tudor myth of succession—underneath all the chaos, violence, and betrayal, the sanctity of succession remains intact as the Tudor reign begins; and yet, as we will see, even that principle, that "form of law," is compromised in the play. I propose, then, another way of understanding the putative conservatism of the play's ending, in the accession of the first Tudor, Henry VII. The way to this understanding is first through an examination of Richard's relentless and, in every sense, fruitless assault on ritual and order.

"Deform'd" (I.i.20)[2] in many ways himself, with no delight except to spy his shadow in the sun "And descant on mine own deformity" (I.i.27), Richard makes music from his own pain; but it becomes evident that however much he derides his own shape, his bitterest hatred is reserved for form itself. His strategy throughout, of course, is to represent himself as a defender of "form," particularly in the "form of law." When the Duke of Buckingham, for example, proclaims of the just-executed Hastings that "the subtle traitor / This day had plotted, in the council-house, / To murder me and my good lord of Gloucester" (III.v.38–39), the Lord Mayor queries "Had he done so?" and is roundly answered by Richard himself in his high ironic vein:

> What, think you we are Turks or infidels?
> Or that we would, against the form of law,
> Proceed thus rashly in the villain's death,
> But that the extreme peril of the case,
> The peace of England, and our persons' safety,
> Enforc'd us to this execution.

To which the Mayor quickly replies, "Now fair befall you! He deserv'd his death" (III.v.40–47). Richard's tender regard for the "form of law" – which he admits has already been set aside – is not surprising given his consistent desire throughout the play to make vice appear in the guise of virtue. Richard's effort to preserve the outward "form of law" reaches quite far, as the next scene shows us. Here a Scrivener enters with paper in hand:

> Here is the indictment of the good Lord Hastings,
> Which in a set hand fairly is engross'd
> That it may be today read o'er in Paul's.
> And mark how well the sequel hangs together:
> Eleven hours I have spent to write it over,
> For yesternight by Catesby was it sent me;
> The precedent was full as long a-doing
> And yet within these five hours Hastings liv'd,
> Untainted, unexamin'd, free, at liberty.
> Here's a good world the while! Who is so gross

That cannot see this palpable device?
Yet who's so bold but says he sees it not?

(III.vi.1-12)

Hastings' "indictment" may be a farce, but no one will say so or question the mere "form" of law; thus it carries all the effectual power of a real indictment.[3] At the beginning of the play, in another instance, Clarence asks the two murderers who threaten him,

Are you drawn forth among a world of men
To slay the innocent? What is my offence?
Where is the evidence that doth accuse me?
What lawful quest have giv'n their verdict up
Unto the frowning judge? Or who pronounc'd
The bitter sentence of poor Clarence' death?
Before I be convict by course of law,
To threaten me with death is most unlawful.

(I.iv.170-77)

This concern for legal niceties is both ironic (considering Clarence's own past history of treachery and betrayal) and naive. It is an instance of the powerful naivete which afflicts virtually everyone in the play, a continuing belief in the forms, rites, and order of social life – of the "law," in particular – which are everywhere, in fact, betrayed. If we find Clarence's naivete amusing early in the play, we can only find Buckingham's – of all characters! – later in the play to be shocking. Even the worst characters, even Richard himself, still place trust in the "course of law" and the very ritual forms they have elsewhere helped to undermine. The play thus enacts a radical division between public manifestations of hieratic form and ritual, and the private appetites which undermine and devour them.

Few if any forms of law in *Richard III* survive unblemished. The grisly circumstances of Richard's own birth suggest the originating transgression in natural law against "form" in general which is, contra Bacon, both "cause" and "sign" in this play. Richard himself tells us how he was

Cheated of feature by dissembling Nature,
Deform'd, unfinish'd, sent before my time
Into this breathing world scarce half made up –
And that so lamely and unfashionable
That dogs bark at me, as I halt by them.

(I.i.19-23)

This disruption heralds the arrival of something quite unnatural in the world, foreshadowing the "deform'd" and "unfinish'd" nature of virtually every rite of passage or social form in the play. Richard's very first victim, his brother Clarence, is done in through a hideous perversion of the sacrament of baptism: Richard tells him—as he is sent to prison—that perhaps the King "hath some intent / That you should be new christen'd in the Tower" (I.i.49–50); Clarence has already of course been "christen'd" as the fulfillment of the prophecy "which says that 'G' / Of Edward's heirs the murderer shall be" (I.i.39–40). Clarence's drowning in the malmsey-butt is not only a horrid joke on the promised christening, but perhaps also, as Antony Hammond suggests, "a grotesque parody of the Eucharist . . . at the behest of the anti-Christ Richard . . . Clarence is 'made a sop of,' a human host soaked in wine, by murderers who call him a 'bloody minister,' debate of theology, and make comparisons of their acts with those of Pilate" (Arden 112).

In resisting the murderers, moreover, Clarence engages them in a high-rhetorical debate about the sacred origins of authority, conducted in the theological-philosophical vocabulary of a belief system in which no one in the play actually seems to believe:

> Cla.   I charge you, as you hope to have redemption,
> By Christ's dear blood, shed for our grievous sins,
> That you depart and lay no hands on me:
> The deed you undertake is damnable.
>
> 1M.   What we will do, we do upon command.
>
> 2M.   And he that hath commanded is our King.
>
> Cla.   Erroneous vassals! The great King of kings
> Hath in the table of His law commanded
> That thou shalt do no murder. Will you then
> Spurn at His edict, and fulfil a man's?
> Take heed! For He holds vengeance in His hand
> To hurl upon their heads that break His law.
>
> (I.iv.178–89)

The "table of His law" has in this world already declined into the "course" and mere "form of law," where man's "edict" holds sway over God's. Redemption by Christ's blood has likewise devolved into another kind of mockery, a mechanical series of formulaic confessions by Richard's victims before their murders. In promising God's vengeance, finally, Clarence sounds eerily like Gaunt in *Richard II,* predicting divine vengeance on Richard for the murder of Woodstock. Clarence's rhetoric fails to move the murderers, in any event, who point out that he himself is "a traitor to the name of God" in his own treachery and betrayal: "How canst thou urge God's dreadful law to us, / When thou hast broke it in such dear degree?" (lines 198–99). The divinity that doth hedge a king is thus everywhere invoked but never observed.

Clarence is accused, in particular, of ripping open "the bowels of thy sovereign's son" (line 196), but in the skill of murdering children, Clarence must necessarily defer to his master in this trade, his brother. Richard's revenge for his own betrayal as a child is harsh, and in kind: his first instincts are to murder children, particularly those to whom nature has not done ill, and those for whom social relation has not been transgressed. "Tetchy and wayward" (IV.iv.169) in his own infancy, his birth "a grievous burden" to his mother, Richard quite naturally settles his hatred on those whose births were natural and noble, whose passage through this stage did not leave them deformed or unfinished. To one of Clarence's children, we learn, Richard wept (this just before they learn their father has been murdered), "And pitied me, and kindly kiss'd my cheek; / Bade me rely on him as on my father, / And he would love me dearly as a child" (II.ii.24–26). Richard follows Buckingham at the end of this scene – "I, as a child, will go by thy direction" (II.ii.153) – to take on the child of his brother Edward, now become Edward V: "So wise so young, they say, do never live long" (III.i.79). Even Richard's metaphors here suggest the "unfinish'd" curtailing of seasonal order and transition: "Short summers lightly have a forward spring" (III.i.94).

In ordering his most infamous assault against children, the Tower murders, Richard exclaims, "I wish the bastards dead" (IV.ii.18), thus justifying his order by denying the legitimacy of their succession. Tyrrel's description of the murdered princes, "this piece of ruthless butchery" (IV.iii.5), on the other hand, turns them back into "gentle babes ... girdling one another / Within their alabaster innocent arms." They seem no less than heavenly cherubs here, as the verse waxes pastoral-poetic: "Their lips were four red roses on a stalk / And in their summer beauty kiss'd each other. / A book of prayers on their pillow lay ... " (IV.iii.9–14). When Richard takes stock of his situation at the end of this scene, his attention focuses almost exclusively on his enemies' children, whose natural maturation and marriage he would disrupt and undermine: "The son of Clarence have I pent up close; / His daughter meanly have I match'd in marriage; /

The sons of Edward sleep in Abraham's bosom" (IV.iii.36–38). Finally, when wooing Queen Elizabeth for her daughter, Richard makes an appeal now ironic and chilling, promising to begin anew the cycle of birth and maturation which he has nearly finished annihilating:

> If I have kill'd the issue of your womb,
> To quicken your increase, I will beget
> Mine issue of your blood upon your daughter.
> A grandam's name is little less in love
> Than is the doting title of a mother.

Richard then notes that grandchildren "are as children but one step below . . . of your very blood; / Of all one pain," with the single exception, he says in one of his greatest sophistries, "save for a night of groans / Endur'd of [the daughter], for whom you bid like sorrow" (IV.iv.296–304). Reducing the experience of birth to "a night of groans," Richard proleptically reveals the future pain of his own victims here. His final appeal to Elizabeth carries this nasty ambiguity to an extreme: "But in your daughter's womb I bury them [her dead children] / Where, in that nest of spicery, they will breed / Selves of themselves, to your recomforture" (IV.iv.423–25). For Richard the womb is always a tomb, the source of his birth but also the source of his imprisonment. His imagery is doubly revealing here, for Elizabeth's dead children will somehow, in her daughter's womb, reproduce incestuously and autonomously ("they will breed / Selves of themselves"). Richard's irony and bitterness run so deep that he can claim not to know "that Englishman alive / With whom my soul is any jot at odds, / More than the infant that is born tonight" (II.i.70–72). His quest to slay the first-born of the kingdom—those most likely to inherit—of course links Richard with another infamously bloody king, Herod—one also identified in tradition, as Scott Colley has demonstrated, as a "crippled, incestuous tyrant."[4]

As with the law, the "form" of marriage is both desired and violated by Richard throughout the play. His wooing and marriage of Lady Anne, most notoriously, suggest the extent of Richard's perversions of the ritual of traditional courtship rites and the orderly process of marriage.[5] Richard's language frequently suggests a particularly perverse transgression against marriage as well—incest:

> I'll marry Warwick's youngest daughter—
> What though I kill'd her husband and her father?

> The readiest way to make the wench amends
> Is to become her husband, and her father:
> The which will I, not all so much for love
> As for another secret close intent,
> By marrying her which I must reach unto.
>   (I.i.153–59)

In wooing Queen Elizabeth, we saw, he promised to "beget / Mine issue of your blood upon your daughter." The suggestion of incest is not only with the mother but with the daughter, for "I must be married to my brother's daughter" (IV.ii.60) in order to solidify his claim to the throne. At the same time he seeks "some mean poor gentleman, / Whom I will marry straight to Clarence' daughter" (IV.ii.53–54), who by the next scene has been "meanly . . . match'd in marriage" (IV.iii.37). In urging Queen Elizabeth to woo her daughter on his behalf, Richard urges "my mother" (IV.iv.325) to acquaint her daughter "with the sweet, silent hours of marriage joys" (IV.iv.330). The poetical alliteration here masks the most outrageous vision of marriage in the play.

Richard will even go so far in his assault on marriage as to "Infer the bastardy of Edward's children" (III.v.74) and, if necessary, allow Buckingham to tell the Mayor and citizens that Edward himself was illegitimate, and thus his own mother had violated the state and form of marriage:

> Tell them, when that my mother went with child
> Of that insatiate Edward, noble York
> My princely father then had wars in France,
> And by true computation of the time
> Found that the issue was not his-begot.
>   (III.v.85–89)

Buckingham complies by reviving the unsavory rumors of Edward's "contract with Lady Lucy, / And his contract by deputy in France" (III.vii.5–6) as well as Edward's "own bastardy" (line 9). This latter issue, Richard instructs Buckingham, is to be gingerly approached "Because, my lord, you know my mother lives" (III.v.93). This tender regard for his mother comes to an abrupt end in IV.iv, when the Duchess of York describes herself to her son as "she that might have intercepted thee – / By strangling thee in her accursed womb" (lines 137–38).

The natural form and order of marriage and birth, then, represent for Richard what he is denied, what he desires, and what he must violate. His actions make a mockery of the power and sanctity of these rites, but no sooner has he emptied them of all cultural force, turned them inside out, than he tries to crawl back inside them himself; even the empty shell of ritual is preferable to his own shape. The restoration of authenticity to these forms comes of course in the royal shape of Richmond. In consulting with Richmond before the battle at Bosworth Field, Stanley invokes the terminology of ritual before a now-receptive audience:

> Farewell; the leisure and the fearful time
> Cuts off the ceremonious vows of love
> And ample interchange of sweet discourse
> Which so long sunder'd friends should dwell upon.
> God give us leisure for these rites of love!
>   (V.iii.98–102)

The "sweet discourse" of these "rites of love" contrasts starkly with the "keen encounter of our wits" (I.ii.119) which Richard, the "jolly thriving wooer" (IV.iii.43), initiates with Lady Anne and Queen Elizabeth. The play's only other reference to the "ceremonious," by contrast with Richmond, is Buckingham's cynical and dismissive rebuke to the Cardinal's defense of the principle of sanctuary:

> You are too senseless-obstinate, my lord,
> Too ceremonious and traditional.
> Weigh it but with the grossness of this age,
> You break not sanctuary in seizing him.
>   (III.i.44–47)

Richmond on the other hand is careful to observe the ceremonious and the traditional, from his planned marriage to Elizabeth through his prayer before the battle, to his oration to his troops. His final speech in the play brings together explicit ritual and the "form of law" generally, now even invoking the highly charged term "sacrament" which accompanies his oath to marry Elizabeth:

> Inter their bodies as become their births.
> Proclaim a pardon to the soldiers fled
> That in submission will return to us;
> And then, as we have ta'en the sacrament,
> We will unite the white rose and the red.
>   (V.v.15–19)

Each line of this speech invokes a different ritual or principle of order: the decorum of funeral rites; the royal pardon; the subject's obedience of hierarchical authority; the ritual of the "sacrament"; and the union of opposites. Richmond says all the right things that could be said.

As with the term "ceremonious," the only other reference in the play to a "sacrament" is sacreligious, the Second Murderer's insistence on Clarence's earlier betrayal of his family: "Thou didst receive the sacrament to fight / In quarrel of the House of Lancaster" (I.iv.192–93). Richmond's taking of the "sacrament," however, leads not to a "fight" but to "this fair conjunction" of the two houses in marriage. The offspring born of this re-sanctified rite will be equally hallowed:

> O now let Richmond and Elizabeth,
> The true succeeders of each royal house,
> By God's fair ordinance conjoin together,
> And let their heirs, God, if Thy will be so,
> Enrich the time to come with smooth-fac'd peace,
> With smiling plenty, and fair prosperous days!
> (V.v.29–34)

The "sacrament," under "God's fair ordinance," to "conjoin together" is an attempt to reinvest the ritual's lost power after the "dire division" (line 28) practiced by Richard. The "heirs" who will result from birth will be the Tudors, whose current avatar must have looked on in pleasure as her grandfather is shown as a representation, indeed virtually a reincarnation, of the power of ritual, of all that is "ceremonious and traditional."

Richmond's command at the end to "Inter their bodies as become their births" reminds us by contrast of still another set of rites of transition that Richard systematically violates throughout the play—those of execution, and of burial. We have already seen how Richard's false piety over the "form of law" is made a mockery in the seizure and executions of both Clarence and Hastings. The initial "order" by Edward for Clarence's death was reversed, "but," as Richard says in one of his bitterest ironies,

> he, poor man, by your first order died,
> And that a winged Mercury did bear;
> Some tardy cripple bore the countermand,
> That came too lag to see him buried.
> (II.i.88–91)

There is no need here to rehearse the myriad ways in which Richard sends his victims off to the executioners: when they are marched off to what Buckingham calls "the block of shame" (V.i.28), none has time to reflect on what has happened, or to enact the established Renaissance conventions of execution.[6] These conventions are truncated everywhere, as indicated in Richard's command to Clarence's murderers:

> But sirs, be sudden in the execution,
> Withal obdurate: do not hear him plead;
> For Clarence is well-spoken, and perhaps
> May move your hearts to pity, if you mark him.
>   (I.iii.346–49)

Richard himself attempts to displace the role of executioner onto others, particularly in his encounter with Lady Anne:

> Is not the causer of the timeless deaths
> Of these Plantagenets, Henry and Edward,
> As blameful as the executioner?
>
> . . . .
>
> Your beauty was the cause of that effect.
>   (I.ii.121–25)

The reversal of cause and effect works splendidly on Anne, for when he offers himself as a potential victim, laying open his breast and giving her a sword while confessing his murders, she lets the sword fall: "Arise, dissembler; though I wish thy death, / I will not be thy executioner" (I.ii.188–89).

Richard's disruptions of conventional burial rites are equally offensive and self-conscious, beginning with his intervention in the funeral cortege of Henry VI in I.ii. Here even the corpse is witness to Richard's crimes— "see, see dead Henry's wounds / Open their congeal'd mouths and bleed afresh." The cause of this unnatural phenomenon, according to Anne, is Richard's "presence that exhales this blood / From cold and empty veins where no blood dwells" (I.ii.55–59). At the end of the scene, Richard promises that the body of Henry will be "solemnly interr'd / At Chertsey Monastery" where he will "wet his grave with my repentant tears" (I.ii.217–19), but then orders the bearers to take the body "to Whitefriars" (line 231) instead. The body of Clarence, in another example, is to be hidden "in some hole / Till that the Duke give order for his burial"

(I.iv.271), while the bodies of the murdered princes were buried by the chaplain of the Tower, according to Tyrrel, "But where, to say the truth, I do not know" (IV.iii.30). The only successful burial rite in the play, it would seem, is what Richard describes as a psychological one: "And all the clouds that lour'd upon our House / In the deep bosom of the ocean buried" (I.i.3-4). Richmond's command at the end, "Inter their bodies as become their births," by contrast would allow even "the bloody dog" Richard (V.v.2) a proper burial.

It would seem, then, that Richard's every effort in the play is to violate what he has been denied, to insure that every principle of social order, form of law, or cultural rite remains "unfinish'd" or "deform'd," as his own birth was. And yet there is one structure of social order which remains absolutely sacred for Richard throughout the play: it is what might be termed the Ur-"form" of passage that is embodied in all the other rites and forms—the principle of succession. By "succession" I mean, most generally, the stated or implied logic of transition from one condition to another: from the womb to life, from life to death, from a single state to marriage; more specifically, "succession" is the logical movement through time of the law (natural or social) from boy to man, from heir to inheritor, and most importantly, from subject to king.

Belief in the power of the ordering form of succession is unchallenged by Richard, indeed his movement toward the crown absolutely depends on it. He never questions the *right* of Clarence to take the crown before him, for example, nor the right of Edward's son; he accepts his place in this hierarchy even as he works to undermine hierarchy in general. His slander that his brother Edward was illegitimate rests in part on the assertion that the proof "well appeared in his lineaments, / Being nothing like the noble Duke, my father" (III.v.90-91), which Buckingham dutifully echoes to the Mayor in a positive restatement of this belief: "I did infer your lineaments— / Being the right idea of your father, / Both in your form and nobleness of mind" (III.vii.12-14). How this deformed hunchback might resemble his father is a question the Mayor and the citizens do not address; the mere assertion of proper "form" once again goes unquestioned. Lineage and lineaments count for everything.

More than the principle of *physical* succession, however, the principle of *legal* succession is most critical for Richard. Buckingham's claim before the Mayor and the citizens—

> we heartily solicit
> Your gracious self to take on you the charge
> And kingly government of this your land,
> Not as Protector, steward, substitute,
> Or lowly factor for another's gain,
> But as successively from blood to blood,
> Your right of birth, your empery, your own.
>   (III.vii.129~35)

—is to be sure hypocritical cant, but it is also in fact the fundamental principle on which Richard has based his own claim, and on which he has acted to remove his brother and nephew—what Buckingham calls "the lineal glory of your royal House" (III.vii.120). When he is momentarily uncertain of the effectual power of his claim, Richard moves to eliminate this dynastic weakness: "I must be married to my brother's daughter, / Or else my kingdom stands on brittle glass" (IV.ii.60~61). What Richard *never* entertains is the possibility of simply seizing power; he desires to inherit it "successively," to reclaim everything that "dissembling Nature" has "cheated" him of.

The psychology of Richard's logic thus mirrors the logic employed by Edmund in *King Lear*. There the principle of lineal succession doubly defeats Edmund, who is both a younger brother and a bastard, and who therefore can appeal only to the "law" of "Nature" (I.ii.1),[7] because his half-brother, "Legitimate Edgar" (I.ii.16)—the epithet is made to seem part of his proper name—is in fact Gloucester's son "by order of law" (I.i.19): "Well then," Edmund concludes, "Legitimate Edgar, I must have your land" (I.ii.15~16). Edmund's boast that "if not by birth," he will "have lands by wit" (I.ii.190) is quickly translated into a scheme by which, as I have argued elsewhere,[8] Edmund seeks to *become* Edgar rather than destroying the social order which denies him; Edmund rather wishes to exchange places with Edgar in the social hierarchy, to take his brother's place. The principle of lineal succession is denounced, desired, and finally achieved by Edmund, when his father offers to modify the law: "Of my land, / Loyal and natural boy, I'll work the means / To make thee capable" (II.i.83~5).

The connection between Richard and Edmund here is that for both characters the principle of "lineal glory," the "form" and "order of law," is both the principle which denies them and so must be annihilated, and the principle which will define them and so is constantly desired.

Yet when both achieve their stated goals, the triumph is bitter and short-lived. R. B. Heilman has noted the pattern in which, at his moment of triumph, Richard suddenly loathes what he has previously desired to achieve.[9] Richard's deepest hatreds, like Edmund's, are always reserved for himself.

Richard believes—and rightly—that he was "born so high" (I.iii.263) and that accordingly he is "the Lord's anointed" (IV.iv.151). When told that Richmond has come "to claim the crown," Richard is genuinely surprised and indignant, and reasserts one last time the principles of legitimacy and succession:

> Is the chair empty? Is the sword unsway'd?
> Is the King dead? The empire unpossess'd?
> What heir of York is there alive but we?
> And who is England's King but great York's heir?
> Then tell me, what makes he upon the seas!
> (IV.iv.468–73)

There are no good answers to these questions—for Richmond ironically seems to be the one seizing power—but only the knowledge that Richmond and Elizabeth can correctly be called "the true succeeders of each royal House" (V.v.30) only *after* Richard has been killed.

Wolfgang Clemen has observed that the final scene of *Richard III* "is an undramatic epilogue in which Richmond, even less individual than in the earlier scenes, once more becomes the mouthpiece of a higher power."[10] As a result, Richmond's self-confidence and the ceremonial tone of his final speech have struck some (but by no means all) readers as unearned, even compromised. Certainly Richmond's language is that of a re-sanctification of the power of ritual and the "form of law," as the very action of the brief scene itself is. Yet how can an audience at this point easily accept the reaffirmations of the principle of lineal succession? Richard's attacks on marriage, birth, and death also undermine and as it were profane the order of succession which lies beneath them. It is easy enough to see, then, that Richard cannot retain the one principle having already annihilated the others. But what he has shown the audience is that these rituals *can* be emptied out and made arbitrary. He has contaminated everything.

Yet one instance of "succession," ironically, will endure, and serve forever to tarnish Richard's name; its power is indicated in the dialogue upon the Tower, which is not present in any of the sources of the play:

> *Prince.* I do not like the Tower, of any place.
> Did Julius Caesar build that place, my lord?
>
> *Buckingham.* He did, my gracious lord, begin that place,
> Which since, succeeding ages have re-edified.
>
> *Prince.* Is it upon record, or else reported
> Successively from age to age, he built it?
>
> *Buckingham.* Upon record, my gracious lord.
>
> *Prince.* But say, my lord, it were not register'd,
> Methinks the truth should live from age to age,
> As 'twere retail'd to all posterity,
> Even to the general all-ending day.
>
> (III.i.68–78)

The record or report of history, handed down "successively from age to age," is invoked just as Richard announces his intention to commit the notorious act which will be linked with him to the general all-ending day:

> *Richard.* [Aside] So wise so young, they say, do never
> live long.
>
> *Prince.* What say you, uncle?
>
> *Richard.* I say, without characters fame lives long.
>
> (III.i.79–81)

Julius Caesar, the Prince concludes, "now he lives in fame, though not in life" (III.i.88); so too will Richard's murder of the princes become the report of "succeeding ages." "Why should calamity be full of words?" the Duchess of York asks after the murder of the princes; because, their mother replies, words are "Windy attorneys to their clients' woes, / Airy succeeders of intestate joys, / Poor breathing orators of miseries." (IV.iv.126–29).[11] Long after Richard's fabled rhetoric fails, after he fails to reproduce his reign "successively" and dies "intestate" himself, the "breathing orators" of language itself—condemning him—will be his only legacy.

An essential distinction between Richard's experience of the nature of ritual and the audience's experience must be made here, for the play as a whole suggests a far more ambivalent attitude than that of the moral lessons drawn in the final scene. A. P. Rossiter was perhaps the first but certainly not the last scholar to suggest that *Richard III* is a qualification of, rather than a celebration of, "the Tudor myth" of history; this historic myth, Rossiter observed, "offered absolutes, certainties" such as Richmond expresses, but Shakespeare, he argued, "always leaves us with relatives, ambiguities, irony, a process thoroughly dialectical."[12] Rossiter arrives at this conclusion via a far different route than the one I have taken here, of course, but I share his skepticism as it relates to a reaffirmation of ritual power in this play. If any value or principle is undermined here, it is surely the logic of ritual, and the logic of "succession" itself. The more strongly Richard depends on it and Richmond reaffirms it, the more doubtful it becomes.

In his ironic conservatism, Richard III stands in contrast to his namesake Richard II, who routinely violates, in the later play, the principle of succession which has made him king. York upbraids Richard for his seizure of Gaunt's estate:

> Did not [Gaunt] deserve to have an heir?
> Is not his heir a well-deserving son?
> Take Herford's rights away, and take from time
> His characters, and his customary rights;
> Let not to-morrow then ensue to-day:
> Be not thyself. For how art thou a king
> But by fair sequence and succession?
>   (II.i.193–99)

There seems a much greater division between *Richard III* and *Richard II* here than the few years which separate their composition, for *Richard II* casually undermines the very logic for which Richard III killed.

Hamlet remarks that in writing satire against the public theater, the writers for the boy actors "do them wrong to make them exclaim against their own succession" (II.ii.348–49). Richard III repeatedly, with evident satisfaction, violates sacraments, rites, and order itself while nevertheless seeking to maintain their outward form; though he never exclaims against succession—indeed, he seeks its encompassing logic—his very actions annihilate his own claim to succession. Soon enough, his chair is empty, the "empire unpossess'd," and a new set of "true succeeders" takes over.

The ironies of Richard III's bloody quest are intensified by the historical situation of the early 1590s. Written and performed during a period of extraordinary urban unrest—what one historian has termed "an epidemic of disorder"[13]—*Richard III* seems in many ways a rejection of disorder and a reaffirmation of law: the soon-to-be Henry VII puts an end to the civil violations of Richard. Yet it is the bloody butcher himself, Richard, who most clearly aligns himself with the ideology of legal and "natural" succession; and it is the re-sacramentalized emblem of "ceremonious" order, Richmond, who intervenes when the "chair" of state is *not* "empty," when the "empire" is *not* "unpossess'd." Richmond's own actions – the killing of Richard – finally bring about the conditions which allow him to be termed not a usurper but *one* of the "true succeeders" to the throne. Richmond's way, through marriage, is thus the inverse of Elizabeth's, herself a true succeeder to the throne through a process that exposed the law of succession as something as much constructed (through Henry VIII's will) as "natural." The issue of succession in *Richard III* is thus put under interrogation, and we find that the monarch who believes in its absolute force is a monster, while the monarch who comes to power by indirections, invoking succession as an attribute which can be acquired, is the ostensible hero, the first Tudor. The last Tudor, if she attended closely to this play, would have noticed a kind of prophetic interpretive slippage in the chief principle underlying her power. Like Richard III, Elizabeth would leave her chair empty with no immediate heir; but long before she was dead, Cecil understood that the new monarch would take power not only through the "form of law," of succession, but through the pragmatic politics of negotiation. *Richard III*, I believe, represents an early temblor of the shocks to come in the English understanding of the monarchy.

NOTES

1. Marjorie Garber, *Coming of Age in Shakespeare* (London: Methuen, 1981), 100. For a general discussion of the concept of "rites of passage" and its usefulness in literary analysis, see Garber's introductory chapter. See also Edward Berry, *Shakespeare's Comic Rites* (Cambridge: Cambridge University Press, 1984), 1–32. Berry does not discuss *Richard III*. I am using the term "ritual" primarily as Garber and Berry do, following Arnold van Gennep's *The Rites of Passage*, trans. Monika B. Vizedom and Gabrielle L. Caffee (Chicago: University of Chicago Press, 1960; original ed. 1908). I also follow to some extent Victor Turner's description of ritual as "formal behavior for occasions not given over to technological routine, having reference to beliefs in mystical beings or powers" in *The Forest of Symbols* (Ithaca: Cornell University Press, 1967), 19.

2. Quotations are from the Arden *Richard III*, ed. Antony Hammond (London: Methuen, 1981). Quotations from other plays are from the relevant Arden editions.

3. In *Shakespeare's Ghost Writers* (New York: Methuen, 1987), Marjorie Garber describes how the Scrivener's speech reflects "the play's preoccupation with

writing and the preemptive – indeed pre*script*ive – nature of its political design" (38).

4. Scott Colley, "Richard III and Herod," *Shakespeare Quarterly* 37 (1986): 451–58.

5. See the summary by Lawrence Stone in *The Family, Sex and Marriage in England 1500–1800* (New York: Harper & Row, 1977), which distinguishes five distinct stages: the written legal contract between the parents; the spousals; the public proclamation of banns in church; the wedding in church; and the sexual consummation (31–37).

6. See the scaffold conventions described by Lacey Baldwin Smith, "English Treason Trials and Confessions in the Sixteenth Century," *Journal of the History of Ideas* 15 (1954): 471–98: "The form of these confessions [on the scaffold] followed a fairly set pattern. Those about to suffer announced that they had come hither to die, and they were careful to point out to the surrounding multitude that they had been judged by the laws of the land and that they were content to accept the penalties which the law required. After granting the legality of their execution, they usually went on to hold themselves up as examples of the frightful fate in store for those who dared to sin against God and their king. Finally, they ended up by requesting their audience to pray on their behalf that God and king would mercifully forgive them their trespasses, and then, in a closing burst of loyalty, they expressed the hope that their gracious sovereign might long and happily reign over the kingdom in peace and tranquillity. Rarely was a word of complaint or bitterness heard at these executions, and usually both the innocent and guilty humbly prostrated themselves before the royal will and confessed the iniquities of their lives" (476).

7. The title page of the 1608 Quarto of *Lear* also identifies Edgar as "sonne and heire to the Earle of Gloster"; in this case, "sonne and heire" is no redundancy.

8. " 'The Base Shall Top Th'Legitimate': The Bedlam Beggar and the Role of Edgar in *King Lear*," *Shakespeare Quarterly* 38 (1987): 426–41.

9. Robert B. Heilman, "Satiety and Conscience: Aspects of *Richard III*," *Antioch Review* 24 (1964): 57–73.

10. Wolfgang Clemen, *A Commentary on Shakespeare's Richard III* (London: Methuen, 1968; original ed. 1957), 235.

11. See the Arden note on this difficult passage, 339–40.

12. A. P. Rossiter, "Angel with Horns: The Unity of *Richard III*," reprinted in *Shakespeare: The Histories*, ed. Eugene M. Waith (Englewood Cliffs, N.J.: Prentice-Hall, 1965), 84.

13. Roger B. Manning, *Village Revolts: Social Protest and Popular Disturbances in England, 1509–1640* (Oxford: Oxford University Press, 1988), 187. See also *The European Crisis of the 1590s*, ed. Peter Clark (London: George Allen & Unwin, 1985).

The Mockery King of Snow:
Richard II and the Sacrifice
of Ritual

NAOMI CONN LIEBLER

When Richard cancels the scheduled joust between Bolingbroke and Mowbray, his action appears to illustrate his inability to rule: "We were not born to sue but to command; / Which . . . we cannot do to make you friends" (I.i.195–96). The joust is (or would have been) one of several ritual events depicted in the play whose close observation mark the normative relationship of king to state but here, in Richard's crisis of kingship, are aborted or evacuated of meaning. Close examination of those rituals, and of the way Richard handles them in his crisis reveals a complex portrait of the king as one who attempts to hold on to certain aspects of a traditional order while violating others. Since that order is itself in the process of change, Richard participates in but does not control the destruction of tradition and, at the same time, of himself. Responsibility for the monarchic disorder that governs this play devolves on other heads besides the king's.

The ritual function of the joust and similar events can be understood in terms offered by Victor Turner. When a "norm-governed social life is interrupted by the breach of a rule controlling one of its salient relationships," a state of crisis results, which splits the community into contending factions. Redress is undertaken by those in authority, ususally in the form of ritualized action, either legal, religious, or military. The aim of such action is to defuse the conflict, and then, if "the situation does not regress to crisis," to reconcile the conflicting parties through the outcome of the ritualized action; failing that, the alternative solution is a "consensual recognition of irremediable breach" and a "spatial separation of the parties." If neither solution works, the state of crisis prevails "until some radical restructuring . . . sometimes by revolutionary means, is undertaken" (*Ritual to Theatre* 92).

Richard's handling of the joust in the play's sources, severely contracted in the way Shakespeare structures it, shows a complicated dynamic in which the king emerges as a participant in the monarchic crisis, not as its instigator. Both historically and in Shakespeare's representation, Richard's reign was a troubled time in which old orders gave way to new. It is frivolous to attribute the toppling of whole social and political structures to one individual, even to a king, let alone to one who is removed or removes himself from the throne. Given the patterned terms Turner uses to describe such crises, the management of ritual in Shakespeare's play gives us access to the social and political complex of meanings in the changes we see.

The play begins, of course, *in medias res*. The initiating breach was the murder of Thomas of Woodstock, Duke of Gloucester, in which Richard may or may not have been implicated, and for which Bolingbroke accuses Mowbray of treason; Mowbray counters with a similar charge. The ritual of trial by combat was prescribed by tradition in such cases; Shakespeare employed it again in the fifth act of *King Lear*, when Albany charges Edmund with treason and Edgar arrives to take up Albany's cause. By the time of Richard's reign, the ritual itself had devolved into a somewhat theatricalized event, and by Shakespeare's time, in England as well as on the continent, it was more often associated with carnival festivities than with judicial decisions.[1] The one-to-one combat of the joust had originated as a substitute for the dangerously chaotic *mêlée* of the tournament, involving whole armies, that had disturbed the reigns of Henry II and Richard I; the latter attempted to regulate his knights' participation by requiring royal licenses for combats. In time the joust, using blunted weapons and forbidding a fight to the death, replaced the tournament and ultimately became mere ceremony (Bucknell 148).

Chaucer's *Knight's Tale*, written during Richard II's reign, gives a detailed account of the preparations for a combat between Palamon and Arcite, which Theseus, whose control is much better than Richard's, cancels swiftly and authoritatively. The Chaucerian version presents in six lines what Shakespeare stretches out over two scenes. Theseus's herald announces:

The lord hath of his heigh discrecioun
Considered that it were destruccion
To gentil blood to fighten in the gyse
Of mortal bataille now in this emprise.
Wherfore, to shapen that they shal nat dye,
He wol his firste purpos modifye.

(lines 2537–42)

The herald then announces in the next nineteen lines the rules and restrictions for the combat, especially stipulating that no lethal weapons be used, and that opponents may only capture each other. The combat has been transformed into a joust, and Theseus's pacific command receives boisterous popular approval (lines 2561–64). Shakespeare's Richard, pleading the same cause, more than doubles the length of the herald's proclamation, and delivers it himself, closing the distance between king and combatants. His decision, however, does not get the same response as Theseus's.

The account of the cancellation in Froissart's *Chronicle* (translated 1523–25) reveals Richard's predicament in terms omitted by Shakespeare. The king's councillors warn him of popular revolt if the combat proceeds: "The Londoners and dyvers other noble men and prelates of the realm say howe ye take the ryght waye to distroye your lygnage and the realme of Englande. Whiche thynge they saye they wyll natte suffre. And if the Londoners rise agaynste you, with suche noble men as wyll take their parte, ye shall be of no puyssaunce to resyst them," (Bullough 3:424–25). Having impressed upon Richard his inability to control his citizens, the councillors remind the king of the people's love for Derby (Bolingbroke) and their hatred for "the erle Marshall" (Mowbray), and to point out that when the quarrel first arose, Richard should have broken it and commanded peace. Furthermore, Richard should have shown Derby some preferential affection in order to maintain the popular good will. Because he did not do that, say the councillors, he is rumored to favor Mowbray. They close with a plea for his attention to their words: "sir, ye had never more nede of good counsayle than ye have nowe" (Bullough 3:425).

Froissart's account shows a Richard whose power depends upon his people's approval, and who takes the advice of his councillors in order to claim that approval. Their advice also included the plan to banish both Mowbray and Bolingbroke. Shakespeare omits the scene of counsel, and has Richard acknowledge it only obliquely in chastizing Gaunt's grieving: "Thy son is banish'd upon good advice, / Whereto thy tongue a party-verdict gave. / Why at our justice seem'st thou then to low'r?" (I.iii.233–35). Gaunt replies that he argued as a judge, not as a father: "A partial slander sought I to avoid, / And in the sentence my own life destroy'd" (241–42), taking upon himself what in Froissart's account was Richard's predicament. There are no councillors in the play to tell the king that he should have commanded peace. Richard tries that on his own initiative and it does not work. It is the first form of post-ritual redress noted in Turner's pattern. The banishment is his second choice (in Turner's terms, the "consensual recognition of irremediable breach . . . followed by the spatial separation of the parties"); it is prompted in part by his councillors' advice but more by the combatants' refusal to obey, which takes up a substantially greater proportion of the scene than does the brief exchange between Richard and Gaunt. The power of the king is compromised as much by the combatants' stubbornness as by his own, and his advisers', vacillation. The disruption of order is present from the start, and resides both within the king's character and outside it.

The universality of the pattern Turner describes indicates that structures of authority sometimes do not prevail over recalcitrant subjects. Such "failures of authority" may indicate a king's unfitness. They may equally well indicate his subjects' violation of their contractual allegiance. Shakespeare's kings never seem to operate in an unreal world of absolute power. When they are shown trying to do that (e.g., Lear, Macbeth, Richard III) they are inevitably punished. In *Richard II* Shakespeare shows a monarch hewing closely to a normative pattern for the resolution of conflicts. His effort is overpowered by Bolingbroke's and Mowbray's immobility. Froissart's document presents a clear image of Richard caught in a kind of "Woodstock-gate," and helpless before the threat of popular uprising. Working toward theatrical rather than historical clarity, Shakespeare gives Richard the opportunity to control, and thereby directs our attention to the centrality of the monarch. This is figured both visually and politically in the opening scene as he stands between the two antagonists; the image prefigures as well his isolation at the center of his circle of supporters in the center of the play (III.ii), when he sits upon the ground and talks of graves. As the first test of his authority in the play, the episode of the combat becomes an emblem of the play's political/ritual crisis.

Roy Strong's history of tournaments further establishes the opening scene's context: "As the middle ages drew to their close . . . [tournaments] were staged more and more often under the auspices of government; and what had been a warlike private pursuit became a festival ritual of homage and service to the crown. The introduction of an element of disguise went back as far as the thirteenth century with the 'Round Table' tournaments, and in the fourteenth century this was developed still further. In 1343 the challengers at a tournament in Smithfield came dressed as the Pope and his cardinals. Forty-three years later Richard II looked on to see knights led in by silver chains held by ladies mounted on palfreys" (13). Thus the situation presented to Richard at the beginning is not only one that discloses a failure of kingly authority but one for which the ritual prescribed to close the rupture in the kingdom had long since become theatricalized and ambiguous. By the fourteenth century, tournaments had been transmuted from serious battle to regulated jousts, and jousts in turn had become forms of entertainment, a part of the ceremonial pageantry. Nevertheless, Froissart's account clearly shows that the activity retained the potential for real danger, not only to the combatants but to the commonwealth as well. And there is no suggestion in Shakespeare's play that the combat between Mowbray and Bolingbroke was meant to be merely ceremonial. Historically speaking, by Richard's time it should have been, and it would have been if Richard had declared it so. The difference between theatricality and actual *mêlée* in the fourteenth century depended upon the ad hoc rules of the game. Richard's own sense of theatricalism in the play has often been cited as evidence of his unfitness to rule, but as Alvin Kernan and, more recently, David Scott Kastan have pointed out, the Lancasters, father and son, are no less thespian in mounting their kingly personae (Kernan 254; Kastan 470). All the characters of the second tetralogy live in theatrical times.

Strong's account indicates that the late fourteenth century had long since ceased to honor the original adjudicating function of ritual combat.[2] He adds, however, that its growing theatricalism "must not be taken as evidence of decline and decadence" but rather of "the ability of the form to respond both to the evolution of the aristocrat as courtier and to the demands of nationalistic chivalries, which focused the loyalty of knights on the ruling dynasty" (12). He justifies the shift as an adaptive strategy, a compromise between the total extinction of old ways and the movement of social progress, apparently under the assumption that such progress is always entirely a positive construction. But social change occurs at some cost, at least in terms of stability and peace. If the ritual of combat did not decline and decay, its function altered radically and politically. Shakespeare's use of it to set the stage of his play reveals his concern for the progress of a civilization at those moments in its history when the rituals and ceremo-

nies that once signified and guaranteed its orderly functioning and integra-
tion had been reduced to outward shows. When such a "crisis of ritual"
occurs in a community, as René Girard writes, "the whole cultural founda-
tion of the society is put in jeopardy. The institutions lose their vitality; the
protective facade of the society gives way; social values are rapidly eroded,
and the whole cultural structure seems on the verge of collapse" (*Violence*
49). Girard's generalization aptly describes the ritual crisis of Richard's
monarchy.

The dilution by Richard's time of the ritualistic force of the joust
prefigures what happened more disastrously, as the play eventually
represents, to the sacred permanence of the king's enthronement: "Not all
the water in the rough rude sea / Can wash the balm off from an anointed
king" (III.ii.54–55). Richard counts on his protected status as God's anointed
deputy on earth. But as we have begun to see, when one traditional action
loses its meaning, the significance of and adherence to others are also
thrown into question. Since rituals are acts of faith, the very act of
questioning is itself dangerous to stability. The play takes up at other
points what happens when traditional understanding of God's rules is
subject to human inquiry. The Duchess of Gloucester's appeal to Gaunt to
support her accusation against Richard merits a whole scene, set between
the two parts of Richard's combat dilemma. Besides inculpating Richard
in Woodstock's death, the scene sets forth the inherent ambiguity in
Richard's England regarding kingly unassailability when the king is involved
in a murder. The Duchess appeals to the older law of retribution for the
murder of a husband and a brother. Gaunt's response advises the widow
to go complain to God. Gaunt's refuge, like Richard's, is in the code of the
king's divine ordination. The Duchess's sympathetic plea, the fact that she
can question the king's immunity, exposes the instability of that code. Like
Richard's command to Mowbray and Bolingbroke, England's belief in the
divine ordination of the king lacks the force of communal agreement. The
historical records, including Holinshed, show that in the matter of Richard's
deposition the code of divine ordination was in fact ignored. The deposition was not Richard's own idea—he is, as we shall continue to see, a
believer in tradition—but was forced upon him by both Henry and Parliament (Bullough 3:406).[3] The conditions for social collapse that Girard
describes are set up in the first act of the play, and all the travesties of
formal order that follow are blazes on the trail toward that end. The
detailed formal preparations for the combat (I.iii.7–45), with its official
formulaic pronouncements by the marshall, and by Bolingbroke and

Mowbray of their names, titles, and charges against each other; Richard's ceremonial decoronation before his followers in III.iii (147–53) and again before Bolingbroke in IV.i (203–15); York's agonized narrations of Henry's *entrée* into London, followed by the deposed and publicly degraded Richard in V.ii (23–36); all of these punctuate the play with instances of rituals aborted, inverted, and finally rejected in favor of a new order, which in turn proved more disordered than Richard's.

The traditional critical response to this series of events is that it was Richard's responsibility, that his was the first rupture in parceling out the kingdom to profiteers, "Like to a tenement or a pelting farm" (II.i.60), and then appropriating Hereford's estate, "tak[ing] from Time / His charters and his customary rights" (II.i.95–96). But as even those who hold this Richard-centered view have noted, "the old world is breaking up" (Kernan 247). Shakespeare creates enough sympathy for Richard at several points — most powerfully in "Of comfort no man speak! / Let's talk of graves, of worms, and epitaphs" (III.ii.144–77) at the center of the play — to suggest more ambivalence than blame in our responses. In other plays, Shakespeare shows what real disregard for order can unleash. At similarly transitional moments, we see Antony in *Julius Caesar* spring the mob to riot and then absolve himself: "Mischief, thou art afoot, / Take thou what course thou wilt" (III.ii.259–60); later, in *Antony and Cleopatra*, he would "Let Rome in Tiber melt, and the wide arch / Of the rang'd empire fall!" (I.i.33–34) for the sake of his tawny queen. At the height of his dereliction, Lear exhorts the heavens to "Strike flat the thick rotundity o'th' world, / Crack nature's molds, all germains spill at once, / That make ingrateful man!" (III.ii.7–9). Unlike these later creations, Richard in crisis cleaves to order, the old order, the order of the generation of York and Gaunt, which he honors even as it passes. There is an interesting and subtle irony in this alignment of Richard and Bolingbroke's father. It reminds us that Richard is not absolute villain and that Henry is not absolute savior. Even though (or perhaps because) it means his death, Richard ensures the legal passage of control to Bolingbroke before he is finished. Doubtless he has no choice, but his gesture lends formality, hence legality, to the inevitable. Whatever else he misconstrues in his troubled government, he retains to the end a clear sense of purpose in honoring the ritual underpinnings of his civilization.

The king realizes his negligence by the middle of the play. He stands far from his London court, with Aumerle, Carlisle, and his soldiers, on the wild Welsh coast. Wales, in this play as in *Henry V*, is home to fierce, primitive, superstitious, mystical, and above all, loyal men like the Welsh captain in II.iv,

and Fluellen in the later play. At the margin of England's map, Wales is the
appropriate locus for Richard's transition, and it is where he stays until he
is brought back to Westminster, "plume-pluck'd," for the formal transfer
of power in IV.i. At the Welsh outpost, Richard becomes liminal; such
figures are "neither here nor there; . . . betwixt and between the positions
assigned and arrayed by law, custom, convention, and ceremonial. . . . Their
behavior is normally passive or humble" (Turner, *Ritual Process* 95):

> I weep for joy
> To stand upon my kingdom once again.
> Dear earth, I do salute thee with my hand,
> Though rebels wound thee with their horses' hoofs.
>
> . . . .
>
> So weeping, smiling, greet I thee, my earth,
> And do thee favors with my royal hands.
>
> . . . .
>
> Mock not my senseless conjuration, lords,
> This earth shall have a feeling. . . .
>   (III.ii.4–24)

Such reverent animation of the land belongs to a ritual-centered king.[4]
With the fatal exception of the leasing out, the synecdoche of the land was
Richard's concern from the start. When he stopped the combat, in the
lines that amplify Chaucer's model, he did so

> For that our kingdom's earth should not be soil'd
> With that dear blood which it hath fostered;
> And for our eyes do hate the dire aspect
> Of civil wounds plough'd up with neighbours' sword.
>   (I.iii.125–28)

Yet it will come. The Bishop of Carlisle, keeper of Christian ritual in this
play by virtue of his office, warns Bolingbroke's followers:

> If you crown him, let me prophesy,
> The blood of English shall manure the ground
> And future ages groan for this foul act; . . .
>
> . . . .
>   . . . And this land be call'd
> The field of Golgotha and dead men's skulls.

O, if you raise this house against this house,
It will the woefullest division prove
That ever fell upon this cursed earth.

(IV.i.136–47)

His office may be Christian, but his diction casts the civil war in terms of pre-Christian ritual: the blood of the *pharmakos,* in this case the English nation, will fertilize the soil; the dead crop of the "cursed earth" is only skulls. Properly conducted in a culture where such rites still have active meaning, a blood libation would insure fertility, but this England-in-transition has sacrificed its rituals under Richard and will continue to do so in the new (dis)order under Bolingbroke.

In his speech, if not in action, Richard often appears as the last true defender of the old faith. From his and the play's opening lines—"Old John of Gaunt, time honoured Lancaster, / . . . according to thy oath and band" (I.i.1–2)—Richard shows himself wrapped for security in tradition and ritual. The ceremonial quality of his language and his reliance on Gaunt's loyalty to the old codes has been well noted (e.g., Berger 215). Much has been made in the critical literature of Richard's neglect of the laws of inheritance, but this neglect is actually brief, confined to Bolingbroke, and committed for political expedience. Richard is certainly not alone in it; at some point in the play, all of the principals neglect the laws of inheritance, most notably in accepting Richard's deposition and Henry's accession. York's admonition, "for how art thou a king / But by fair sequence and succession" (II.i.198–99), is thrown into ironic relief by the sequence and succession of the rest of the play: Bolingbroke's "right" to be king, whatever its retributive justice, is certainly not granted by the code York endorses in that line. Moreover, the principle of "fair sequence and succession" is problematic for all claimants in this play and in the historicity behind the play: Richard succeeded his grandfather Edward III in 1377, not his father Edward who had died the year before, and therefore never inherited the throne. Richard became king by parliamentary action, not by intact dynastic inheritance (Saccio 19). Richard's deposition, in turn, further muddied the question of inheritance: noting the omission of Henry's coronation from the play, Bullough refers to Hall, who "passes lightly over the ceremony to point out that 'who so ever rejoysed at this coronacion, or whosoever delighted at his high promocion,' certainly the rightful heir, Edmund Mortimer, Earl of March was not pleased" (Bullough 3:364). The rule of primogeniture became ambiguous when Edward III died, and remained so down through the generations of Tudors. Thus everyone who moves to Henry's side in the course of the play does so not from principled adherence to ancient law but for political exigency; nearly everyone who does not (except for Aumerle, who comes around eventually) is destroyed. The old ways are past, or passing.

In fact, only Richard clings to ritual. His deposition is widely recognized as an inverted coronation ceremony (e.g., Girard, *Violence* 304). It is usually cited as evidence of Richard's unfitness: he gives up his crown too quickly, too willingly, to his eager cousin. It is, however, also evidence of his care for the proper formalities of his civilization's rites. We should focus as much attention as Richard does, and as Shakespeare does, on *how* he gives it up. There are two decoronation scenes, the first (III.iii.143–75) perhaps a rehearsal for the second (IV.i.201–22). The earlier scene occurs, like his homage to the earth, in Wales, at Flint Castle. Richard appears on the walls, with his supporters, and receives Northumberland as Henry's emissary:

> What must the king do now? Must he submit?
> The King shall do it. Must he be depos'd?
> The King shall be contented. Must he lose
> The name of king? A God's name, let it go!
> I'll give my jewels for a set of beads,
> My gorgeous palace for a hermitage,
> My gay apparel for an almsman's gown,
> My figur'd goblets for a dish of wood,
> My sceptre for a palmer's walking staff,
> My subjects for a pair of carved saints,
> And my large kingdom for a little grave, . . .
>
> . . . .
> What says King Bolingbroke?

The meticulous catalog of what Richard will trade refers to the outward signs of his state, the concrete ways in which medieval/Renaissance England "knew" its monarch from any other man. They are the symbols that most actively occupied Richard's attention as well: the name, jewels, palace, robes, plate, sceptre, subjects, kingdom. Their externality is echoed in the scene's locus—at an outpost, atop the "rude ribs of that ancient castle" (32), in the open air. Although they are outward signs, they are not superficial, but as tangible and fragile as the land itself. We have just heard, although Richard has not, Bolingbroke tell Northumberland the conditions he will offer to King Richard. He will "Even at his feet lay my arms and power, / Provided that my banishment repeal'd / And lands restor'd again be freely granted" (39–41). Conditional allegiance is no allegiance, and Henry intends none; his repetition of the name "King Richard" four times in a speech of thirty-six lines rings with sarcasm (like Richard's "What says King Bolingbroke?"). More interesting, however, is the threat that Henry offers if Richard rejects his conditions. He will "lay the summer's dust with show'rs of blood / Rain'd from the wounds of slaughtered Englishmen. . . . The rage be his, whilst on the earth I rain / My waters—on the earth, and not on him" (43–44, 59–60). Henry's token respect of the king's person is meaningless in the face of his anarchy against the king's other body, the kingdom and its population. Furthermore, he immediately retracts even that token respect when Richard, "the blushing discontented sun," appears just after these lines. Caught up in his blood-rain metaphor, Henry expands it to a cloudburst that will "stain the track / Of his bright passage to the Occident" (65–68), that is, to the west, where the sun sets. York, in attendance, catches his drift immediately and warns against it: "Yet looks he like a king. . . . Alack, alack, for woe, / That any harm should stain so fair a show" (68–71). And Richard apparently intuits Henry's specific threat, as he counterwarns in similar diction: "Yet know, my master, God omnipotent, / Is mustering in his clouds on our behalf" (85–86) an appropriate inheritance of pestilence upon succeeding generations. This blood-rain is what Richard offered to prevent at the start of the play, what Carlisle later warned would issue from Bolingbroke's accession, what Bolingbroke himself now actively and irresponsibly threatens, and what in fact plagues his subsequent rule. It is, arguably, to stave this off as much as to submit to the inevitable that Richard so readily capitulates.

The care with which Richard enumerates his relinquished symbols belongs to all ritual; it is the appropriate preparation for the formal and final rite of the second, "real," deposition scene in IV.i. Now we are at Westminster, in the full court. The procession into the hall is fully ceremonial: "*Enter, as to the Parliament.*" As at the beginning of the play, the scene begins with reciprocal charges of treason, this time by Bagot and Aumerle, with Bolingbroke adjudicating. The wheel is coming full circle. Again there is no resolving combat. Henry says, "These differences shall all rest under gage / 'Till Norfolk be repeal'd" (86–87), but Carlisle informs the court that Norfolk is dead. Thus the prescribed restorative ritual is again aborted. In this ominous and official setting, Richard's full deposition occurs. The process is the precise reverse of the order of investiture:

> Now mark me how I will undo myself.
> I give this heavy weight from off my head
> And this unwieldy sceptre from my hand,
> The pride of kingly sway from out my heart.
> With mine own tears I wash away my balm,
> With mine own hands I give away my crown,
> With mine own tongue deny my sacred state,
> With mine own breath release all duteous oaths.
> All pomp and majesty I do forswear;
> My manors, rents, revenues I forgo;
> My acts, decrees, and statutes I deny.
> God pardon all oaths that are broke to me!
> God keep all vows unbroke are made to thee!
>   . . . .
> God save King Harry, unking'd Richard says. . . .
>   (203–20)

The speech is both pitiable and dangerous. Richard undoes *himself*, as well as his kingship. In denying his acts, decrees, and statutes he erases all record of his existence and occupation of the throne. This is more than the passage of control; it widens the hole in the historical record, the breach in the "fair sequence and succession" of the Plantagenet dynasty that began with the death of Edward III. This is nihilism of the most terrifying order, "mark'd with a blot, damn'd in the book of heaven" (236).

Girard reminds us that the traditional monarchic system is rooted in the function of the king as surrogate sacrificial victim: "The sacred character of the king — that is, his identity with the victim — regains its potency as it is obscured from view and even held up to ridicule. It is in fact then that the king is most threatened" (*Violence* 304). Of the scene here considered he says, "the king acts as his own sacrificer, transforming himself by quasi-religious means into a double of all his enemies and their surrogate victims as well. He is himself a traitor, in no way different from those who do him violence:

> Nay, if I turn mine eyes upon myself,
> I find myself a traitor with the rest;
> For I have given here my soul's consent
> T'undeck the pompous body of a king. . . .
>   (247–50)   (*Violence* 304)

Richard's identification with his enemies is more than histrionic. From the aspect of ritual it is also accurate. Shakespeare is at all points in this play assiduous in emphasizing the factor of kinship, especially that of Richard and Bolingbroke. The play insistently refers not only to the tragedy of state but of family as well, in the manner of Sophocles. Among the several scenes that illustrate this insistence, two in particular do so with great force.

Just after Richard imaginatively turns his eyes upon himself in the lines quoted above, he calls for a mirror in order to see himself literally (274–92). In the mirror he sees "the very book indeed / Where all my sins are writ, and that's myself." The replication of his face in the mirror enables him, in Girard's terms, "to polarize, to literally draw to himself, all the infectious strains in the community and transform them.... The principle of this metamorphosis has its source in the sacrifice of the monarch and ... pervades his entire existence" (*Violence* 107). When Richard shatters the glass and says to Bolingbroke, "Mark, silent king ... / How soon my sorrow hath destroy'd my face," Bolingbroke equivocates, "The shadow of your sorrow hath destroy'd / The shadow of your face" (291–94). And well he might; it is urgent for him to distinguish rigorously between the substance and its replicated image. Besides the face reflected in the glass, so easily "crack'd in an hundred shivers," the other double of Richard is Bolingbroke himself. Shakespeare unmistakably presents this relationship to us earlier in the same scene, just before the formal deposition:

> ... Here, cousin, seize the crown.
> Here, cousin.
> On this side my hand, and on that side thine.
>
> . . . .
>
> That bucket down, and full of tears am I,
> Drinking my griefs, whilst you mount up on high.
> (182–90)

The tableau presents the two men frozen in the liminal moment, equal and opposite.[5] The language of the next ten lines, exchanged between Richard and Bolingbroke, is the "stichomythia of ritual tragedy," wherein "the symmetry of the tragic dialogue is perfectly mirrored" (Girard, *Violence* 44):

> If we want to understand the nature of the ritual crisis, we must pay heed ... to those aspects of rituals and prohibitions that suggest

fierce mimetic rivalries and a reciprocal alienation that is constantly reinforced by a feedback effect until separate perceptions become jumbled together. If we observe the constant fascination with mirror effects and enemy twins in primitive ritual as well as in primitive mythology, we will have to conclude that the undifferentiated has something to do with the symmetry of conflict, with a circular pattern of destructuration that must constitute a real threat. This would explain why primitive societies are . . . loath to think these matters through. . . . Their purpose is . . . to redifferentiate the identical twins, to stop the crisis, and to replace the fearful symmetry of mimetic rivalry with . . . reassuringly static and manageable binary patterns. . . .

. . . the world of reciprocal violence is one of constant mirror effects in which the antagonists become each other's doubles and lose their individual identities. (Girard, *Double Business* 164, 186)

Shakespeare ensures that we will see the binding symmetrical patterns of the rival brothers at the beginning and end of the play. When Mowbray charges Bolingbroke at the start, "and let him be no kinsman to my liege," Richard answers that he would be impartial "Were he my brother, nay, my kingdom's heir, / As he is but my father's brother's son" (I.i.59, 116–17), although he later confides to Aumerle that he suspects Bolingbroke feels a little less than kin: "He is our cousin, cousin; but 'tis doubt, / When time shall call him home from banishment, / Whether our kinsman come to see his friends" (I.iv.20–22). Meanwhile Bolingbroke vows to avenge the Duke of Gloucester, whose "blood, like sacrificing Abel's, cries / . . . To me for justice" (104–6). By the end of the play, in perfect structural symmetry, Bolingbroke is associated not with Abel but, via Exton's enactment of his regicidal wish, "With Cain [to] go wander thorough shades of night." He pledges to "make a voyage to the Holy Land, / To wash the blood off from my guilty hand" (V.vi.43, 49–50). As with the other restitutive rituals in the play, this one too will be aborted by the continuing civil strife.

The mirrored relationship of Richard and Henry is set forth once again in V.ii, this time by verbal recitation. The Duchess of York reminds her husband to "tell the rest / When weeping made you break the story off, / Of our two cousins coming into London" (1–3). Besides the immediate pairing of "our two cousins" as kin and equals, the narrative relates the double royal *entrée* as the last formal ceremony in the play. Since there cannot be two kings, the description images appropriately York's—and England's

—crisis in witnessing and recording it, and completes the redifferentiation of the royal pair:

> Then, as I said, the Duke, great Bolingbroke,
> Mounted upon a hot and fiery steed
> Which his aspiring rider seem'd to know,
> With slow but stately pace kept on his course,
> Whilst all tongues cried, "God save thee, Bolingbroke!"
> (7–11)

In grotesque contrast, there is the mirrored reverse:

> As in a theatre the eyes of men,
>
> . . . .
>
> Did scowl on gentle Richard. No man cried, "God save him!"
> No joyful tongue gave him his welcome home,
> But dust was thrown upon his sacred head—
> (23–30)

Undoubtedly the sight of a monarch so degraded and abused by the citizenry was too painful to be enacted, and so we have it narrated. It was also, "in the language of the Tudor law derived from a statute of 1352" [i.e., Edward III's reign], treason even to imagine it (Kastan 473). The verbal recreation crystallizes York's own crisis of partisanship so that weeping chokes him off. But York saw it; his narrative underscores the painful paradox of what cannot be and nonetheless is. In the exchange between the Duke and his wife, the audience hears it twice, in York's line and in the Duchess's recall of "that sad stop, my lord, / Where rude misgovern'd hands from windows' tops / Threw dust and rubbish on King Richard's head" (4–6), and knows that it was said a third time, when the Duke broke off. The imagined/actualized scene also constitutes a third deposition, the public witness and approval of Richard's disgrace. The unthinkable has come to pass, "But heaven hath a hand in these events" (37). The issue has already been foretold, and now is told again: "To Bolingbroke are we sworn subjects now, / Whose state and honour I for aye allow" (39–40). It is easy to catch the homophonic "eye for eye" of retribution, and indeed in the next lines we learn that Aumerle has been stripped of his title by Henry for supporting Richard, though allowed to remain Earl of Rutland, recreating in part Henry's position in the early scenes of the play.

In his degraded state, Richard's passage through liminality is momentarily frozen; he is stuck in a nameless, faceless, uncreated condition, neither what he was nor what he will be:

> I have no name, no title —
> No, not that name was given me at the font —
> But 'tis usurp'd. Alack the heavy day,
> That I have worn so many winters out
> And know not now what name to call myself!
> O, that I were a mockery king of snow,
> Standing before the sun of Bolingbroke,
> To melt myself away in water drops!
>
> (IV.i.260–63)

He has assumed, in Girard's terms,

> the role of the unworthy king, the antisovereign. The king then unloads on this inverted image of himself all his negative attributes. We now have the true pharmakos: the king's double, but in reverse. He is similar to those mock kings who are crowned at carnival time, when everything is set topsy-turvy and social hierarchies turned upside down . . . when, in short, the throne is yielded only to the basest, ugliest, most ridiculous and criminal beings. But once the carnival is over the anti-king is expelled from the community or put to death, and his disappearance puts an end to all the disorder that his person served to symbolize for the community and also to purge for it. (*Violence* 109n.)

Richard's carnivalization of himself as "a mockery king of snow" condenses an extended narrative in Holinshed which begins: "Thus was king Richard deprived of all kinglie honour and princelie dignitie, by reason he was so given to follow evill counsell, and used such inconvenient waies and meanes, through insolent misgovernance, and youthfull outrage, though otherwise a right noble and woorthie prince," and ends "[Yet] hee was a prince the most unthankfullie used of his subjects, of any one of whom ye shall lightlie read" (Bullough 3:408–9). His sins are enumerated by Holinshed as prodigality and lasciviousness, in which he was not alone: "speciallie in the king, but most cheefelie in the prelacie . . . " (3:409). These are hardly high crimes and capital treasons; Holinshed's Richard was more a Lord of Misrule than a criminal. His implication in Woodstock's death is barely mentioned in Holinshed, and however much is made of it by Shakespeare, it is likewise forgotten after act I.

The seriousness of identifying an anointed monarch as Misrule would not have been lost upon Shakespeare's audience. For clearly political reasons, "as awe of man for master diminished, . . . a decline is apparent in the discontinuance of the Lord of Misrule at court under Mary and Elizabeth—after most elaborate ceremonies at court and in the city under Edward VI and occasionally under Henry VIII" (Barber 26). Although Elizabeth promoted and supported various seasonal festivities in and out of court, Misrule was not one of them. "The Queen's presence inevitably made for constraint: though she herself could be wonderfully downright and spontaneous, she was not one to suspend her majesty—misrule had to keep well clear of that" (ibid., 30). Even a temporary release of control is fatal to the monarch in unstable times. Elizabeth knew that; Richard learned it in a shower of dust and rubbish.

The carnivalization of Richard, first by himself and then by his trash-throwing subjects, prepares him, as Girard notes, for the role of *pharmakos*, for it is only as his own double, not as his kingly self, that he can take on the sacrificial function of the scapegoat. Scapegoat rituals are often fertility rituals, and these, in turn, are often sun rituals (Holloway 133); Richard wants to see Bolingbroke, not himself, as the *roi soleil*. But Bolingbroke has already identified himself inversely with rain, not sun, in the lines quoted earlier from III.iii. It is Richard who is linked with the defeated sun (II.iv.21). Richard accurately thinks himself not quite up to the role of sun; he is the sun's son (or, if "sun" signifies an anointed king, the sun's grandson): "Down, down I come, like glist'ring Phaeton" (III.iii.178); in that image is his own confession of his failed potential. The mockery king of snow is, in Girard's terms, the inverse and alter-ego of the sun-king; in those terms, as sun turns to snow, Richard undoes himself. But snow is also the frozen, rigid form of rain, which is Bolingbroke's symbol, and rain melts and washes away snow. Moreover, both sun and rain, depending upon intensity, are either destructive or restorative elements. The ambiguous or double-sided meanings of these meteorological images, read deconstructively, complicate the way we understand the action of the play and prevent facile conclusions about Richard's sins and Henry's heroism.

Commenting on Richard's humiliation, Michael Bristol writes, "These images of royal abjection and victimization do not have the purely redressive and exemplary features of an actual ritual. The violent uncrowning of the royal martyr or royal villain is invariably accompanied by a more generalized, pervasive social violence or civil war. . . . The relationship between victimized king and victimized kingdom is complex and elusive" (197–98). For

Richard's deposition and Henry's accession to have those redressive features, the ambiguity of his alternately conservative and destructive behavior would have to be resolved as preeminently negative, and the matching ambiguity of Henry's restructuring of the monarchy would have to appear as salvatory. But Shakespeare does not allow us such an easy and comfortable resolution; as such New Historicist studies as Kastan's and Stephen Greenblatt's have ably demonstrated, the sugar-coating of the "Tudor Myth" did not entirely disguise, for Shakespeare at least, the bitter taste of Richard's deposition and the continual outbreaks of rebellion during Henry's reign. The restorative function of uncrowning followed by new crowning is absent from the play because the redressive capabilities of such rituals had long since been lost to medieval and Renaissance England, leaving only the outward forms of ritual actions. Rituals evacuated of meaning cannot work, and historically they did not work; the restoration of England's political stability took longer than the unquiet reign of Henry IV. "We always view the 'tragic flaw' from the perspective of the new, emergent order; never from that of the old order in the final stages of decay.... The real issue is the fate of the entire community" (Girard, *Violence* 43–44). Against the backdrop of an England whose rituals had turned from religious to secular to spectacular, and from purgative to political to *pro forma*, the "fate of an entire community" in *Richard II* is the "movement from ceremony and ritual to history" (Kernan 247) of the rest of the Henriad. In its attention to the changes during Richard's reign in the way ritual was variously honored, aborted, subverted, debased, and ignored, *Richard II* dramatizes the inevitable cost of secularizing a ritual-centered political ecology. As "history" marks a society's progress, ritual anchors that society's movement and protects its original social, political, and religious structures. The story of Richard II provided Shakespeare with the material through which he could explore with his audience their collective relation to the old and older values that appeared, as the Tudor reign drew to a close, to be permanently past.

NOTES

1. Edward Muir notes in *Civic Ritual in Renaissance Venice* (Princeton: Princeton University Press, 1981) that in sixteenth- and seventeenth-century Venice, jousts were part of the Sensa festival (celebrating the marriage of the sea) that marked the beginning of the theatrical season (121n.) and lent an element of structure to the course of the more topsy-turvy processes of Carnival (177).

2. This historical situation is analogous to the Roman one that occurs at the start of *Julius Caesar*, where the forms and function of the Lupercal have been subverted to the service of Caesar's political and superstitious nature, and the populace, represented by carpenter, cobbler, and tribunes, argue confusedly about the nature of the holiday and its proper observance. I explored this aspect of the Roman play in " 'Thou Bleeding Piece of Earth': the Ritual Ground of *Julius Caesar*," *Shakespeare Studies* 14 (1981): 175–96. A similar ambiguity of ceremony occurs in *Coriolanus*, at the moment when the protagonist offends the populace about to elect him consul by refusing to follow the tradition of public disrobing to display his bleeding wounds.

3. In *The Political History of England*, C. Oman makes the following point about Henry's accession: "His real claim rested only on conquest, and on the assent of parliament which was about to be granted him. For without a moment's delay the Lords spiritual and temporal and the Commons voted that they would have him for their king. . . . It is notable that no one said a word in favour of the young Earl of March, whom Richard had designated as his heir. . . . It cannot have been forgotten that there was good precedent for regarding the crown of England as elective, and for passing over March, even as Arthur of Brittany had been passed over in 1199. Henry of Lancaster, therefore, was for all intents and purposes an elective king, who came to the throne under a bargain to give the realm the good governance which his predecessor had denied" (4:153).

4. The contrast in this regard between Richard and Bolingbroke is most evident when the latter addresses the land at the moment of his departure into exile: "Then, England's ground, farewell; sweet soil, adieu, / My mother, and my nurse, that bears me yet!" (I.iii.306–7). Henry relates to the land in terms of himself, not as an externally and independently potent locus for respect as Richard does.

5. In a Royal Shakespeare Company production of the play some years ago, the actors did in fact freeze the moment for several seconds in a tableau. The image of that scene stays with me. Moreover, to underscore the reciprocal identification of the two kings and kinsmen, the actors playing Richard and Henry switched roles on alternate evenings throughout the run of the play.

WORKS CITED

Barber, C. L. *Shakespeare's Festive Comedy: A Study of Dramatic Form and its Relation to Social Custom*. Princeton: Princeton University Press, 1959.

Berger, Harry, Jr., "Psychoanalyzing the Shakespeare Text: The First Three Scenes of the Henriad," in *Shakespeare and the Question of Theory*, ed. Patricia Parker and Geoffrey Hartman. New York: Methuen, 1985. 210–29.

Bristol, Michael D. *Carnival and Theater: Plebeian Culture and the Structure of Authority in Renaissance England*. New York: Methuen, 1985.

Bucknell, Peter A. *Entertainment and Ritual: 600–1600.* London: Stainer and Bell, 1979.

Bullough, Geoffrey, ed. *Narrative and Dramatic Sources of Shakespeare.* 8 vols. New York: Columbia University Press, 1960. 3: 423–30.

Chaucer, Geoffrey. *Works*, ed. F. N. Robinson. Boston: Houghton Mifflin, 1957.

Girard, René. *Violence and the Sacred*, trans. Patrick Gregory. Baltimore: Johns Hopkins University Press, 1977.

———. *"To Double Business Bound": Essays on Literature, Mimesis, and Anthropology.* Baltimore: Johns Hopkins University Press, 1978.

Greenblatt, Stephen. "Invisible Bullets: Renaissance Authority and its Subversion." *Glyph* 8 (1981): 40–61.

Holloway, John. *The Story of the Night: Studies in Shakespeare's Major Tragedies.* Lincoln: University of Nebraska Press, 1961.

Kastan, David Scott. "Proud Majesty Made a Subject: Shakespeare and the Spectacle of Rule." *Shakespeare Quarterly* 37 (1986): 459–75.

Kernan, Alvin B. "The Henriad: Shakespeare's Major History Plays," in *Modern Shakespearean Criticism*, ed. Alvin B. Kernan. New York: Harcourt, Brace, and World, 1970. 245–75.

Liebler, Naomi Conn. " 'Thou Bleeding Piece of Earth': The Ritual Ground of *Julius Caesar." Shakespeare Studies* 14 (1981): 175–96.

Muir, Edward. *Civic Ritual in Renaissance Venice.* Princeton: Princeton University Press, 1981.

Oman, C. *The Political History of England.* 12 vols. London: Longmans, Green, 1906; reprinted New York: AMS, 1969. Vol. 4: *The History of England from the Accession of Richard II to the Death of Richard III (1377–1485).*

Saccio, Peter. *Shakespeare's English Kings: History, Chronicle, and Drama.* New York: Oxford University Press, 1977.

Strong, Roy. *Art and Power: Renaissance Festivals 1450–1650.* Berkeley: University of California Press, 1984.

Turner, Victor. *The Ritual Process: Structure and Anti-Structure.* Ithaca: Cornell University Press, 1969.

———. *From Ritual to Theatre: The Human Seriousness of Play.* New York: Performing Arts Journal Publications, 1982.

9

Ritual and Identity:
The Edgar-Edmund Combat
in *King Lear*

GILLIAN MURRAY KENDALL

GON. An enterlude!

Broken rituals complicate the action of many of Shakespeare's plays:
Ophelia's already "maimed rites" are further marred by an impromptu
performance on the part of Hamlet; in *Much Ado About Nothing*, Claudio
turns on Hero and puts an end to the marriage ceremony; in the scene of
ritual combat in *Richard II*, King Richard throws his warder down and
interrupts the action. *King Lear*, too, employs broken ritual as drama,
opening with a scene steeped in what are apparently ceremonial exchanges[1]
—exchanges that are broken down by the intrusion of spontaneous
and unexpected language ("Nothing, my lord." "Nothing?").[2] Such a disruption of ritual, of events meant to be patterned and ordered, foreshadows what is to come. In the world of *King Lear*, all concepts of order
and justice, whether human or divine, are shortly to disintegrate into the
vision of a mad king battered by an indifferent tempest on a wild heath.
And yet, in the final minutes of *King Lear*, the play returns to an extreme
form of ritual in the trial by combat of act V, scene iii.

No interruptions mar the confrontation between Edgar and Edmund.
Curiously, just before the play produces an apocalyptic vision of injustice
in the deaths of Cordelia and Lear, the action pauses. The consequences
of the (brief) battle for England, the question of the fate of Lear and
Cordelia, these things are set aside. Instead, the audience must pause in its
contemplation of images of horror and view from beginning to end the
uninterrupted workings of a ritualistic trial by combat.[3] The conclusion of
the play must wait; the audience is distracted from the plight of Lear and

Cordelia ("great thing of us forgot!"). The characters consent to the enactment of a ritual that will hold the play in thrall until one or both of two combatants is released by death. And in the trial by combat we witness precisely what the rest of the play negates: a vision of deep order, a working out of natural and, of course, poetic justice.

In this scene, the scripted language of ritual—a language that in itself acts as an emblem of order and culture, a negation of chaos—displaces the spontaneous exchanges of the squabbling victors of the battle. The characters reverse the movement of the first scene of the play, replacing the unexpected, the disordered, the impromptu, with a script. The combat really is, to use Goneril's word, an "enterlude," a brief play (in this case one that asserts a powerful vision of order) that, ironically, is contained within a script (*King Lear*) that undermines all visions of order. In the context of the larger play, this enterlude seems, I think, curiously displaced—a relic from a world that no longer exists.[4] The descent of *King Lear* into chaos and inarticulate despair is being interrupted by a mini-drama so morally pat and so old-fashioned (even to a Renaissance audience) that, in the end, it fails to satisfy—even given that trial-by-combat might be the modus operandi of the *King Lear* world.[5] This sudden obsession with ritual—seen in the calling of heralds, the ceremonial trumpetings, the concern with traditional wording and the rules of combat—finally becomes an empty and distorted assertion of order in a world that has already stripped ritual of meaning. The elaborate concern with rules, with scripted language, with rank and degree plays itself out to the end, only to reveal, finally, its essential meaninglessness. Naturally the way the combat is staged would have a profound impact on the way an audience might come to perceive this lack of meaning. Marvin Rosenberg notes that traditionally the combat has been staged as something formal, and directors have engaged in "such cliches as Edgar knocking Edmund's sword away and letting him retrieve it."[6] More recently, however, "the savagery of both fighters has been emphasized, they are in to kill—in the Dunn *Lear*, Edgar knifed the fallen Edmund repeatedly, and had to be dragged off."[7] A more formal staging would enhance the emptiness of ritual in the context of the *Lear* world; a savage battle—a choice in staging I would strongly favor—would exhibit the enormous gap between the language of ritual and what it supposedly represents.[8] Either extreme of staging indicates that, in some sense, this trial by combat begins what becomes a final movement away from ritual and ceremony at the end of the play. It is an enterlude that, in calling attention to itself as artifact, reveals the fragility of all scripts, all artifacts of order, even the script of *King Lear* itself. Indeed, in the final lines of the play, Edgar directs us away from scripted language altogether.[9]

Justice has difficulty triumphing on stage in *King Lear*, not only because villains commit evil acts, but, more importantly, because they refuse to take law and the righteous pronunciations of other characters seriously. When Albany tells his wife "O Goneril, / You are not worth the dust which the rude wind / Blows in your face," Goneril responds by calling him "Milk-liver'd man." His moralism about women and evil ("Proper deformity [shows] not in the fiend / So horrid as in woman") earns him the epithet of "vain fool."[10] Goneril makes of Albany's schoolbook morality something stodgy, something learned, perhaps out of a book of emblems; her energetic evil (and Edmund's) invigorates and dominates the play.

Asserting any kind of moral framework or justice in the play seems first to require getting the serious attention of Goneril, Regan, and Edmund in order to reveal to them—as well as to the audience—evidence of a deep order that must finally thwart evil. And Edgar and Albany attempt to do this. Not surprisingly, then, Goneril's very contempt toward any law that might attempt to bring her to account serves to introduce the trial by combat—as if the ritual were to undermine her position. She scoffs at Albany's ironic words as he reveals her wrongdoing, and proclaims the interchange an "enterlude"—she means a comic entertainment. Her contemptuous response, however, ushers in what might well be called an enterlude—but one of the didactic, rather than comic, ilk:[11] the ritual confrontation of Edgar and Edmund:

> *Gon.*   An enterlude!
>
> *Alb.*   Thou art armed, Gloucester, let the trumpet sound.
> If none appear to prove upon they person
> Thy heinous, manifest, and many treasons,
> There is my pledge. I'll make it on thy heart,
> Ere I taste bread, thou art in nothing less
> Than I have here proclaim'd thee.
>
> (V.iii.89–95)

An "enterlude," indeed. The language and action have become stylized; *King Lear* retreats into a world belonging to a much older kind of play.[12] Once the challenge is accepted, both Albany and Edmund reinforce how separate this piece of ritual drama is from the language and events that precede it. Suddenly, new rules are in effect. And Albany[13] calls for the member of the cast necessary before the play can continue: "*Alb.* A herald, ho!" The herald, with his traditional language and station, makes this scene one of public ritual instead of private vengeance. And in Edmund's calling for sounding of the trumpet, and Albany's calling for the herald, they both, in some sense, subscribe to the ritual that will follow. Meanwhile, their joint focus on the niceties of a trial by combat turns us away from the action of *King Lear* as a whole (where Cordelia and Lear are in peril).

Rituals like the trial by combat imply by their very design that a kind of deep order exists in the world – an order inherent in nature, not imposed on it by human law.[14] But the very terms in which Edgar chooses to reestablish himself and take his place in this (supposedly) natural order are suspect, since ritual – to reflect some kind of underlying order – tends to define itself in its own terms. Once governed by the heralds, the participants in the combat (should it follow uninterrupted to its conclusion) belong to a world where there is no conclusion but a just conclusion. The gods may appear not to be watching over the characters of *King Lear*, but in this instance, the gods can be replaced with heralds, trumpets, rules of combat. Lear and Cordelia may, contrary to all sense of justice, lose a battle, and later their lives, but the rules of ritual combat create justice from its outcome – whatever outcome. The combat might prove Edmund not to be the traitor that we all consummately know he is, but this conclusion would not undermine the ritual itself – since according to such ritual the final result must be just. This enterlude of combat thus provides an image of order that is like a snake with its tail in its mouth – endlessly circular and self-contained. The result of the trial by combat cannot really affect the audience's vision of the bleak chaotic landscape of the play, nor will it provide a lasting endorsement of Edgar's legitimacy: the result of the combat is undermined by the terms under which it is created.

In the introduction to *Secular Ritual*, Sally Moore and Barbara Myerhoff write: "In the repetition and order, ritual imitates the rhythmic imperatives of the biological and physical universe, thus suggesting a link with the perpetual processes of the cosmos. It thereby implies permanence and legitimacy of what are actually evanescent cultural constructs."[15] The word "legitimacy" has, I think, a special meaning when this statement is applied to *King Lear*. For "legitimacy" on a very basic level is precisely what Edgar is attempting to establish; among other things, the very concept of legitimacy and illegitimacy – and, as a corollary, primogeniture – that Edmund challenges early in the play is on trial here.[16] Edgar, who has every reason to buy into a patrilineal ideology that privileges the first legitimate son, comes to displace the ideologically wicked Edmund.[17] What Moore and Myerhoff suggest by their analysis of ritual, however, is that legitimacy – any kind of legitimacy – is a cultural artifact, not a God-given constant or a fact of nature. Edgar, by engaging in the combat, attempts to re-legitimize the concept of the legitimate (a concept eroded by the action of the play), to re-create his name and identity in a ritual that is also a kind of macabre baptism in his brother's blood (I have seen one production of *King Lear* in which Edgar, rising from his brother's body, has blood on his forehead – clearly the mark of Cain). But as a means of validating an identity as something concrete and "real" (i.e., something that cannot be created simply by the pronouncements of Cornwall or the machinations of Edmund), ritual here proves inadequate. Indeed, the exaggerated nature of all the ceremony surrounding the combat suggests, I think, that there is something hollow at its core. Myerhoff and Moore write: "Through form and formality it [ritual] celebrates man-made meaning, the culturally determinate, the regulated, the named, and the explained."[18] Here, however, the form of the ritual begins to reveal the indeterminate, the unregulated, the culturally unstable nature of the identity – the name, the status – that Edgar seeks to regain:

> *Edg.*   Know, my name is lost,
> By treason's tooth bare-gnawn and canker-bit,
> Yet am I noble as the adversary
> I come to cope.
>
> *Alb.*   Which is that adversary?
>
> *Edg.*   What's he that speaks for Edmund Earl of Gloucester?
>
> *Edm.*   Himself; what say'st thou to him?
>
> (V.iii.121–26)

Identities here become part of formulaic responses – but what the formula at first establishes is the doubtfulness of the identity of the participants going into battle. Edgar makes no claim to any name. He has no identity other than that of mysterious combatant – he only plays a role; he cannot unselfconsciously be Edgar – nor has he been unselfconscious since first assuming the role of Poor Tom. His identity has been absorbed by the many roles he plays.[19] And Edmund, in this formula, can, in his answer, claim only to speak for Edmund Earl of Gloucester, not as Edmund Earl of Gloucester. Moreover, he refers to himself in the third person. Roles take the place of names; names (or the acknowledged lack thereof) are simply part of the ritualistic form that at this stage reminds the combatants not of who they are, but of what they are. Edgar and Edmund are both here at one remove from their names. The roles they take up, however, in turn have the potential to give renewed meaning and determinacy to the name and title "Duke of Gloucester." The initial questions that introduce the above exchanges, after all, are ones meant to determine who the combatants are:

> *Alb.*   Ask him his purposes, why he appears
> Upon this call o' th' trumpet.
>
> *Her.*   What are you?
> Your name, your quality? and why you answer
> This present summons?
>
> (V.iii.118–21)

Albany wants to know about purpose, but the herald asks first the ritual questions about name and station. The question that is, essentially, asked twice adds significance to the answer (which at the end of the combat will be an answer that establishes identity). The questions, of course, do not proceed from spontaneous curiosity, but are part of the form of the challenge.[20] Edgar's reply—or lack of reply—to the herald, artificially reinforces his later assertion of identity. The disguised knight who comes unknown to the lists is, after all, a very old literary convention. By participating in it, Edgar adds to the illusion that the identity that is going to be revealed and asserted is in some very deep sense "real." But at this moment, as Edgar and Edmund face each other, they risk a realization of the fragility of the very concept of identity—a realization Lear experiences when he tries to find a person beneath the title of King. While Edgar, unlike Lear, does not seem to feel the need to ask "who is it that can tell me who I am?" (he believes he holds the answer to the riddle), the ritual itself comes to reveal how tricky such answers, and such riddles, can be.

When Edgar confronts Edmund he risks more than the knowledge of how fragile a thing identity is (something he should already realize from his experience as Poor Tom); he risks a confrontation with as deep and profound a chaos as any that Lear encounters in his mind. For rituals like the trial by combat are necessary only because the workings of order are not in actual fact clearly stamped on the natural world. Just as the Renaissance insistence on the validity of the great chain of being suggests a certain lack of security about hierarchy, the very order of ritual serves as a reminder of the threat of chaos: "And underlying all rituals is an ultimate danger, lurking beneath the smallest and largest of them, the more banal and the most ambitious—the possibility that we will encounter ourselves making up our conceptions of the world, society, our very selves. We may slip in that fatal perspective of recognizing culture as our construct, arbitrary, conventional, invented by mortals."[21] Essentially, what happens in the course of the trial by combat is that we, as audience, can see that Edgar is encountering himself in the act of creating himself—and his place in the social hierarchy. In facing a bastard brother who has usurped his name and title, Edgar is, to some degree, facing a distorted reflection of himself.[22] Indeed, he equates himself with Edmund, saying that although his name is lost, "Yet am I noble as the adversary." In winning the combat, too, Edgar's language is suggestive:

> Let's exchange charity.
> I am no less in blood than thou art, Edmund;
> If more, the more th' hast wrong'd me.
> My name is Edgar, and thy father's son.
>   (V.iii.167–70)

He proclaims himself to be Edgar (and it has been noted how much less compelling this is than Hamlet's similar assertion of identity—which occurs as Hamlet disrupts a ritual). Edgar does so, however, by comparing himself to Edmund and claiming "thy father" as his own. Edgar, in reestablishing his name and status as the legitimate son and heir to the title of Gloucester, shows his act of assertion to be similar in nature to Edmund's seemingly false creation of himself as Gloucester's heir—as the legitimate Duke of Gloucester. Edgar needs Edmund in order to define himself, but by so using his bastard brother, Edgar reveals the fragility of the constructs of legitimacy. Indeed, Nahum Tate, in rewriting *King Lear* into a comic form that raises few, if any, questions about established social order, makes important changes in the combat scene. These changes are designed to allay any uneasiness we might feel about the battle over the Gloucester inheritance. First, the moment that Tate's Edgar enters, armed, Albany exclaims, "Lord Edgar!" (V.v.14),[23] thus instantly giving the legitimate son a title and name. Secondly, upon seeing Edgar, Edmund is immediately smitten with guilt. He has clearly internalized and accepted the patrilineal ideology of primogeniture and legitimacy. Thirdly, Edmund states he may well not be Gloucester's son at all, since his mother "disdaining constancy, leaves me / To hope that I am sprung from nobler blood, / And possibly a king might be my sire / ... Who 'twas that had the hit to father me / I know not" (V.v.49~54). The idea that Edmund is not Gloucester's son at all changes the terms of the combat entirely, and, of course, frees Edgar from the taint of having committed fratricide.

Legitimacy was, of course, an important social concept in Renaissance England, and The Bastard was a stock villain in literary works—one has only to think of Don John in *Much Ado About Nothing* and Spurio in *The Revenger's Tragedy*. But the very vehemence with which both society and literature condemned bastardy and the begetting of bastards indicates an unease with the subject—an unease perhaps out of proportion to the practical difficulties bastards might pose to questions of inheritance or social position. The reaction against bastards may have come partially, I think, from the possibility that by their very existence they might raise questions about the artificiality of concepts of legitimacy. To Angelo, for instance, in *Measure for Measure*, bastards are counterfeit, not "true made," and his language is excessive and violent in his assertion of this difference:

> It were as good
> To pardon him that hath from nature stol'n
> A man already made, as to remit
> Their saucy sweetness that do coin heaven's image
> In stamps that are forbid. 'Tis all as easy
> Falsely to take away a life true made
> As to put metal in restrained means
> To make a false one.
>
> (II.iv.42~49)

To Angelo, making a bastard is as bad as committing murder. Bastards are "false"—the implication is that they are made in an entirely different manner than the legitimate. Actually, of course, the difference between legitimate and illegitimate is not in the making, but in the exchange of words that constitute the ritual of marriage. But to acknowledge this is to come close to raising the insidious and subversive question that Edmund asks, and that Angelo's language (and imagery of counterfeiting) would keep suppressed:

> Wherefore should I
> Stand in the plague of custom, and permit
> The curiosity of nations to deprive me,

> For that I am some twelve or fourteen moonshines
> Lag of a brother? Why bastard? Wherefore base?
>
> (I.ii.2–6)

Edmund peers into the abyss that ritual and convention attempt to cover; he consciously flouts the artificial order that covers chaos.[24] Interestingly, once Edmund has achieved the position he covets, it becomes in his interests to establish it as a socially conventional position within a conventional moral scheme. Hence, perhaps, Edmund's willingness to fight Edgar even though he need not:

> In wisdom I should ask thy name,
> But since thy outside looks so fair and warlike,
> And that thy tongue some say of breeding breathes,
> What safe and nicely I might well delay
> By rule of knighthood, I disdain and spurn.
>
> (V.iii.142–46)

The trial by combat, should he win, would secure him in the social order. Edmund sounds, here, not unlike a social climber, as he shows himself to be even more chivalric than the "rule of knighthood" requires. He will use no loopholes to delay the combat, and he seems to embrace the opportunity to leave behind the shadowy status of the Renaissance illegitimate. For Edmund the outsider, conventions have little value; but once on the inside of society, his newly created self needs, and seems to crave, some way of establishing that that self was not self-created at all, but part of the natural universe.[25] We might see that Edmund's fall comes from a participation in the act of creation that Edgar is trying to bring about. Edgar absorbs Edmund into his plot—his scripted ritual of combat—and by so doing disarms Edmund, whose energy and ability to new-create himself came from the rejection of conventional scripts.[26] Goneril protests that Edmund's fall comes from trickery:

> This is practice, Gloucester.
> By th' law of war thou wast not bound to answer
> An unknown opposite. Thou art not vanquish'd,
> But cozen'd and beguil'd.
>
> (V.iii.152–55)

Albany, as much a conventional moralist as Edgar throughout the play, responds as though stung to Goneril's undercutting of an act that has just appeared to reestablish some kind of justice in the world: "Shut your mouth, dame, / Or with this paper shall I stopple it" (V.iii.155–56). Albany's angry reaction draws attention to Goneril's claim. Her refusal to accept the results of the ritual combat are as dangerous to established morality as her statement that "the laws are mine" is "most monstrous." This is especially true because, in some sense, by waiving his right to refuse combat, Edmund has been tricked by appearances into fighting his brother on his brother's terms. The ritual of combat, because it is conservative, traditional, should, of course, do just what it does here – lay bare the falseness of Edmund's assumed identity as Duke of Gloucester. Goneril, though, threatens to lay bare the artificiality of all tradition, ritual, and law.

Ritual, like law, only appears to be a part of the ordering of the universe. As mentioned above, the security of ritual covers a deep and fundamental insecurity about all of human artifice, culture, and order. In fighting Edmund, moreover, Edgar engages in the same kind of self-creation that his brother did (hence, I think, the reflective imagery within the dialogue concerning the combat). The legitimacy conferred by marriage, after all, is purely a cultural artifact, something created from nothing by going through a ritual – the marriage ceremony – that, like that of trial by combat, defines itself in its own terms. One is married when one has been married. Lear himself hints at the tenuousness of the kind of legitimacy (and legitimacy and morality become closely linked in the play) that marriage imparts to offspring:

> Die for adultery? No,
> The wren goes to't, and the small gilded fly
> Does lecher in my sight.
> Let copulation thrive; for Gloucester's bastard son
> Was kinder to his father than my daughters
> Got 'tween the lawful sheets.
>
> (IV.vi.111–16)

Of course, Gloucester's bastard son is not, as it turns out, very kind to his father, but no less kind than Lear's daughters. When Edgar says "Edgar I nothing am," he approaches the vision of the world that ritual and ceremony attempt to cover, the vision of the world where legitimacy, order, titles have no meaning. No wonder then that he uses the trial by combat to establish that his "name is Edgar." This ritual, by its very nature, is designed to turn Edmund's vision of the world – one that would have it that might is right (or, rather, that whoever has ability will triumph) — into Edgar's moralistic version of the same — that right has might. The conclusion of the combat between Edgar and Edmund reinforces the image of ritual as order, justice, completion:

> *Edg.*   The gods are just, and of our pleasant vices
> Make instruments to plague us:
> The dark and vicious place where thee he got
> Cost him his eyes.
>   *Edm.*   Th' hast spoken right, 'tis true.
> The wheel is come full circle, I am here.
>   (V.iii.171-75)

Edgar, like Albany, has found morals and meaning in many of the events of the play. Here, Edmund accepts Edgar's moralistic vision of the world and his version of events — a change that presages his change of heart about the murders of Lear and Cordelia. Like most of Edgar's moralisms, however, this one, which crowns the scene of ritual combat and completes it, finally proves inadequate, hollow, and just a little too pat. As many critics have noted, it is also an astounding thing to say of one's father.[27] Moreover, the gods do not, in the final analysis, seem very just. Ensuing events will reveal the inadequacy of the entire trial by combat, of Edgar's assertions of identity, and of ceremony and ritual in general. The completion of this morality play acted out between Edgar and Edmund is "but a trifle."[28]

For, despite Edmund's words, the wheel has not yet really come full circle. The ritual combat which has captured the attention of the characters onstage, which has come to a pat conclusion with a tidy moral, is not the completion of that larger moving wheel, *King Lear*. Something great has been forgot, and that something undercuts all the bulwarks against chaos that the ritual combat set out to construct. The death of Cordelia and finally of Lear take the play beyond the scope of pat moralisms or proclamations of innate justice. The hollow effort of Edgar to re-create himself — without acknowledging that he is so doing — is not only circumvented by the reflection of his act in the creative act of Edmund, but by a sudden vision of the hollowness of all ritual.[29]

The ritual combat of Edgar and Edmund is only an enterlude in the relentless spiraling of the play beyond the normal bounds of theater, beyond, in fact, anything that ritual can encompass. *King Lear* is itself in some sense a ritual, but one that ceremonially works to undermine all ceremony. William Frost notes of Cordelia and Lear that "these two personages have passed beyond ritual altogether at the close. They cannot be expressed or comprehended by any of its forms—this fact is their greatness and their tragedy."[30] Edgar is left behind, to close the play. And there is reason, I think, to prefer to have Edgar as the speaker of these final lines (although Albany, too, after all his pat attempts to find morals in the events of the play, might speak them effectively as well). Edgar says this:

> The weight of this sad time we must obey,
> Speak what we feel, not what we ought to say:
> The oldest hath borne most; we that are young
> Shall never see so much, nor live so long.
>
> (V.iii.324–27)

This is a different Edgar from the Edgar who announced his identity and asserted that his father's blinding was an action of just gods. This final speech is a statement that is as anti-ritualistic as it is possible to imagine. Edgar sees that it is time to pass beyond the script and "speak what we feel," not use the formulaic and deceptive language of ritual and order. The final two lines of the play, too, are a statement of the uniqueness of events: what has happened will not happen again.[31] Again, this is an statement of anti-ritual; these events cannot participate in the repetitions that give to the world an artificial sense of meaning.

And yet this movement toward anti-ritual, toward the undercutting of all order and hierarchy and meaning is only an "image of that horror," and an image that is itself ritualistic. For *King Lear* transforms the unique into the repeated, the chaotic into the ordered by the very act of being a scripted play. Perhaps ironically, it is through the ordered artifact of drama that the audience can come close to a vision of the void, and the very ritual that undoes itself finally contains itself.

The ritual trial by combat that seems to promise the restoration of a kind of order and justice may fail to do so, but the anti-ritualistic epilogue spoken by Edgar succeeds in reestablishing a sense of ceremony and order where words spoken in double script (the script of ritual combat and the script of *King Lear*) fail. Perhaps more than anything else, the enterlude of ritual combat prepares us to accept in the place of moralisms a simple expression of deep feeling.

NOTES

1. Lawrence Danson, in *Tragic Alphabet* (New Haven: Yale University Press, 1974), 164, notes that the "love-trial is staged with all the pomp and symmetry which is ritual's way of setting words and gestures apart from their ordinary contexts."

2. One can no longer write on *King Lear* without addressing the textual issues involved. While the jury may forever be out on the question of whether or not Shakespeare was responsible for the Folio revisions, the fact remains that we have two authoritative versions of the play. I have chosen the tighter, Folio version of the play to work with, although to use the Quarto would not substantially alter my argument. For ease of reference, all quotations are from *The Riverside Shakespeare*, ed. G. Blakemore Evans (Boston: Houghton Mifflin, 1974). Where this conflated text inserts material from the Quarto, I have deleted that material and noted the fact. For a discussion of the two texts and their effect on our reading of the play and our understanding of Edgar, see Michael J. Warren, "Quarto and Folio *King Lear* and the Interpretation of Albany and Edgar," 95–107, in *Shakespeare: Pattern of Excelling Nature*, ed. David Bevington and Jay Halio (Newark: University of Delaware Press, 1978); see also Stephen Urkowitz, *Shakespeare's Revision of King Lear* (Princeton: Princeton University Press, 1980), and *The Division of the Kingdoms*, ed. Gary Taylor and Michael Warren (Oxford: Clarendon, 1983). For a discussion of the implications of having two authoritative texts, see Jonathan Goldberg, "Textual Properties," in *Shakespeare Quarterly* 37:2 (1986): 213–17, and Marion Trousdale, "A Trip through the Divided Kingdoms," *Shakespeare Quarterly* 37:2 (1986): 218–23.

3. Stephen Booth, in *King Lear, Macbeth, Indefinition, and Tragedy* (New Haven: Yale University Press, 1983), discusses the way in which the ending of *King Lear* is consistently delayed. He notes that "Edgar's victory—the triumph of virtue—has the feel of dramatic conclusion, and the lines that follow it offer an anthology of familiar signals that a play is ending," 7. I agree, and view the combat as a play complete unto itself.

4. Rosalie L. Colie, in "*King Lear* and the 'Crisis' of the Aristocracy," in *Some Facets of King Lear*, ed. Rosalie L. Colie and F. T. Flahiff (London: Heinemann, 1974), notes that the trial by combat was an anachronism as far as the play's Renaissance audience was concerned, and that Edgar is to "prove himself by an old-fashioned and quintessentially aristocratic method, the formal trial-at-arms outmoded in the late sixteenth century as a customary proof.... The anachronism stresses the play's archaism.... With this episode we are back in the world of chivalry of which we have heard nothing in the play and to which, under normal circumstances, Edmund the bastard could never have aspired," 208.

5. G. Wilson Knight, in *The Wheel of Fire* (London: Methuen and Co., 1930),

views the scene somewhat more optimistically, stating that "It is Edgar's trumpet, symbol of natural judgement, that summons Edmund to account at the end, sounding through the Lear mist from which right and wrong at this moment emerge distinct," 194–95.

6. Marvin Rosenberg, *The Masks of King Lear* (Berkeley: University of California Press, 1972), 305.

7. Ibid.

8. Ritual, then, is a mediator in the same way that Howard Felperin sees morality and madness as being mediators. Felperin writes that "in the end, the play renounces its own mediations of morality and madness alike and redirects our attention to an undetermined reality that exists prior to and remains unavailable to both." *Shakespearean Representations* (Princeton: Princeton University Press, 1977), 104.

9. In Q, Albany speaks the final words of the play. For the implications of Edgar as speaker, see Warren, "Quarto and Folio," 105. For the idea that Edgar's name makes him, historically, a good candidate for the kingship, see F. T. Flahiff, "Edgar: Once and Future King," in *Some Facets of King Lear*, 221–37. In this article, Flahiff identifies Edgar with the King Edgar who drove the wolves from Britain. See also Donna B. Hamilton, "*King Lear* and the Historical Edgars," in *Renaissance Papers*, ed. A. Leigh Deneef and M. Thomas Hester (Raleigh: The Southeastern Renaissance Conference, 1983), 35–42.

10. These are the exchanges as written in the Folio. The Quarto version is longer: see IV.ii.31–49, 53–59, 62–68, in *The Riverside Shakespeare* for the Quarto dialogue.

11. Enterludes (somewhat old-fashioned entertainment at this time) came in two varieties, the entertaining and the didactic. Goneril refers to the former, but inadvertently introduces the latter.

12. Felperin, *Shakespearean Representations*, sees the Gloucester plot as closely related to the morality play tradition: "the air of contrivance that hangs about the Gloucester action is pervasive, and it smells of morality," 94. Felperin sees this motion toward the morality tradition as mediating between characters and "the confusion of raw experience," 101, and as gesturing toward a new kind of mimetic experience.

13. In Q, Edmund also calls for a herald. This emphasizes his interest in the socially accepted rules of combat, but the deletion of the line from the Folio makes Albany more central as a master-of-ceremonies presiding over the combat.

14. See, for instance, the introduction to *Secular Ritual*, ed. Sally Moore and Barbara Myerhoff, which discusses the ways in which secular rituals are created to reinforce the idea that order exists (Amsterdam: Van Gorcum, 1977).

15. Ibid., 8.

16. Phyllis Rackin, in "Delusion as Resolution in *King Lear*," *Shakespeare Quarterly* 21 (1970): 29–34, notes that Edgar challenges Edmund "dressed in all the formal splendour that the hierarchy can afford," 32, and hence, as I see it, as a kind

of force of order and legitimacy. She also states that "the representation is, at least from one point of view, a delusion," 32.

17. Lynda Boose, in *Approaches to Teaching Shakespeare's King Lear* (New York: The Modern Language Association of America, 1986), notes that "having been cast out by the father and displaced by the rival brother, each struggles violently to get back into the family enclosure and inherit the privileges of the father . . . the very privileges that, by the laws of primogeniture . . . set up the competitive, ultimately fratricidal rivalry that this drama plays out," 63.

18. Moore and Myerhoff, *Secular Ritual*, 16.

19. M. C. Bradbrook in *Aspects of Dramatic Form in the English and Irish Renaissance* (Sussex: The Harvester Press, 1983) notes of disguise on the Elizabethan stage that "there could be no such thing as a mere physical transformation. . . . A character could be really changed by the assumption of a disguise," 37–38. Clearly, Edgar is changed by, among other roles, that of Poor Tom. And Alexander Leggatt notes, in *King Lear* (Twayne's New Critical Introductions to Shakespeare [Boston: Twayne, 1988], 63), that "the sheer variety of his roles . . . makes him as much a chameleon as Richard III or Iago." Janet Adelman, in the introduction to *Twentieth Century Interpretations of King Lear* (Englewood Cliffs: Prentice-Hall, 1978), writes that "both of Edgar's decided actions—his killing of Oswald and his killing of Edmund—are performed in disguises that allow him to submerge himself in a role," 16. For an insightful discussion of Edgar's relationship to his Poor Tom role, see William C. Carroll, " 'The Base Shall Top th' Legitimate': The Bedlam Beggar and the Role of Edgar in *King Lear*," *Shakespeare Quarterly* 38:4 (1987): 426–41. Carroll notes that Edgar "far out-tops even his brother's histrionic genius," 485.

20. There is, of course, a parallel scene also using ritual wording in *Richard II*, I.iii.7–35. This trial by combat is broken off.

21. Moore and Myerhoff, *Secular Ritual*, 18.

22. Many critics, for example, have noted how interchangeable the names of the two brothers are. Carroll, " 'The Base Shall Top th' Legitimate,' " sees in the subplot a "doppelganger tale," 439.

23. All quotations come from *The History of King Lear*, ed. Nahum Tate and James Black (Lincoln: University of Nebraska Press, 1975).

24. Danson, *Tragic Alphabet*, writes that "Edmund reduces the traditional values of kinship to so many empty words—words without fixed meanings, but only the meanings we as individuals want to give them. . . . Edmund will define himself, choose his own words, and not accept society's evaluation," 169. In this sense, Edmund's language is anti-ritualistic—until he joins Edgar in the trial by combat.

25. Jonathan Dollimore, in *Radical Tragedy* (Sussex: The Harvester Press, 1984), makes the interesting point that "Edmund's sceptical independence is itself constituted by a contradiction: his illegitimate exclusion from society gives him an insight into the ideological basis of that society even as it renders him vulnerable to and

dependent upon it," 201. I would further argue that he is co-opted into the ideological society he initially rejects.

26. In some sense, we can see Edgar here as what Stephen Greenblatt might call an improvisator, as well as someone engaged in an act of self-fashioning. See Stephen Greenblatt, *Renaissance Self-fashioning* (Chicago: University of Chicago Press, 1980), 222–54.

27. This quotation and Edgar's behavior on the "cliff" near Dover have proven to be the loci for discussions about Edgar's character. Leggatt, in *King Lear,* calls Edgar's words "repulsive" and notes that "there is unexpected, self-satisfied cruelty in his reference to the way the gods have punished Gloucester," 62. Harry Berger, Jr., in "Text Against Performance: The Gloucester Family Romance," in *Shakespeare's Rough Magic,* ed. Peter Erickson and Coppélia Kahn (Newark: University of Delaware Press, 1985), sees Edgar as committing "symbolic parricide," 222–23. James Calderwood, in "Creative Uncreation in *King Lear,*" notes that "as a poete manque . . . he settles too readily for conventional forms and ideas," 11. Stanley Cavell, in *Must We Mean What We Say?* (Cambridge: Cambridge University Press, 1976), writes that "Edgar's capacity for cruelty . . . shows how radically implicated good is in evil," 283. Adelman, however, in *Twentieth Century Interpretations,* notes that "the absolute goodness and nobility of Edgar . . . has been assumed in much of the criticism of the twentieth century," 8. See, for example, Russell A. Peck, "Edgar's Pilgrimage: High Comedy in *King Lear,*" *Studies in English Literature* 7 (1967): 219–37, and John Riebetanz, *The Lear World* (Toronto: University of Toronto Press, 1977), who writes that Edgar is a "most selfless intriguer," 62, and "our Virgil," 126.

28. For *King Lear's* use of the morality play tradition, see Maynard Mack, *King Lear in Our Time* (Berkeley: University of California Press, 1964), 59–63, 78–79; Alvin B. Kernan, "Formalism and Realism in Elizabethan Drama: The Miracles in *King Lear,*" *Renaissance Drama* 9 (1966): 59–66; Bridget Gellert Lyons, "The Subplot as Simplification," in *Some Facets of King Lear,* op. cit.; Howard Felperin, op. cit. (and see also endnote 12).

29. Stephen Greenblatt, in "Shakespeare and the Exorcists," in *Shakespeare and the Question of Theory,* ed. Patricia Parker and Geoffrey Hartman (New York: Methuen, 1985), writes that "*King Lear* is haunted by a sense of rituals and beliefs that are no longer efficacious, that have been *emptied out,*" 177.

30. William Frost, in "Shakespeare's Rituals and the Opening of King Lear," 200, in *Shakespeare: The Tragedies,* ed. Clifford Leech (Chicago: University of Chicago Press, 1965).

31. David Scott Kastan, in *Shakespeare and the Shapes of Time* (Hanover: University Press of New England, 1982), writes that "in Shakespeare's *King Lear* time proceeds with a vicious linearity. The past cannot be escaped, and the future offers neither redemption nor renewal. Youth will not be recalled, Lear will not be king again, and death is inescapable and final," 104.

10

Conjuring Caesar: Ceremony, History, and Authority in 1599

MARK ROSE

Julius Caesar opens with Marullus and Flavius rebuking the plebeians for transferring their allegiance from Pompey and making a holiday to celebrate Caesar's triumph. It is commonplace to remark that the plebeians in this scene, the cheeky cobbler who makes puns about mending bad soles and the other workmen, are more Elizabethan than Roman. But it is not usually noted that the tribune Marullus sounds strikingly like an indignant Puritan calling sinners to repent.

> O you hard hearts, you cruel men of Rome,
> Knew you not Pompey? Many a time and oft
> Have you climb'd up to walls and battlements,
> To towers and windows, yea, to chimney-tops,
> Your infants in your arms, and there have sat
> The livelong day, with patient expectation,
> To see great Pompey pass the streets of Rome:
> And when you saw his chariot but appear,
> Have you not made an universal shout,
> That Tiber trembled underneath her banks
> To hear the replications of your sound
> Made in her concave shores?
> And do you now put on your best attire?
> And do you now cull out a holiday?
> And do you now strew flowers in his way,

That comes in triumph over Pompey's blood?
Be gone!
Run to your houses, fall upon your knees,
Pray to the gods to intermit the plague
That needs must light on this ingratitude.[1]
(I.i.36-55)

Besides the emotionalism and rhetorical urgency that were characteristic of the Puritans and their "spiritual" style of preaching, we can note that the imagery of hard hearts, plagues, chariots, and trembling waters recalls that favorite Old Testament story of the reformers, Exodus. In 1599, when *Julius Caesar* was first performed, similarly styled calls to prayer and repentance might be heard from pulpits all over London.[2]

In the tangled world of Elizabethan England, religion and politics were more often than not indistinguishable, and we need not be surprised to find that Shakespeare, trying to understand the nature of the political contentions of ancient Rome as he found them described in Plutarch's *Lives*, should think of the contemporary struggle in the church. A crucial point of contention between Anglican conservatives and Puritan reformers was whether a clergyman's authority came from above or from below, from the crown or from the congregation. Anglican clergy maintained the importance of episcopal ordination, and thus also the principle of the monarch as the final reservoir of power. The reformers insisted that authority derived from the inward call of the spirit, confirmed by the outward call of the congregation. The prescribed role of the Roman tribunes of the people—the "tongues o' th' common mouth" as Coriolanus contemptuously calls them—was as spokesmen and defenders of plebeian rights. Furthermore, the tribunes were not appointed but elected by the plebeians themselves. Perhaps then the reformers' claim to an authority derived not from the crown but from God and the congregations of the faithful, led Shakespeare to conceive an analogy between the ancient tribunes and the Puritan preachers of his day.

That Shakespeare was in fact making this connection is only speculation of course, but the readiness with which this analogy might come to mind is suggested by the fact that a few years later King James made a similar association. Irritated by the independence of the English parliament, he asserted in 1605 that there were in the House of Commons "some Tribunes of the people, whose mouths could not be stopped, either from the matters of the Puritans, or of the purveyance."[3] Moreover, a number of details in the play suggest that some such analogy might be at work in Shakespeare's mind. Casca reports that "Marullus and Flavius, for pulling scarfs off Caesar's images, are put to silence" (I.ii.282–83), a phrase that recalls precisely the action that was commonly taken against a Puritan who had become a thorn in the side of authority. In a well-known episode in 1586, for example, Archbishop Whitgift intervened in the running debate at Temple Church between the orthodox Richard Hooker and his Puritan deputy Walter Travers by prohibiting Travers from further preaching, or, in Hooker's phrase, enjoining him to silence.[4] And in 1599 Laurence Barker complained that Londoners would rush to hear any preacher "that will not sticke to reuile them that are in authoritie, that his sectaries may crie he is persecuted when he is iustly silenced."[5]

Also suggestive is the exchange at the end of the opening scene when the tribunes go off to "disrobe" the images:

> *Flavius.*   Disrobe the images,
> If you do find them deck'd with ceremonies.
>
> *Marullus.*   May we do so?
> You know it is the feast of Lupercal.
>
> *Flavius.*   It is no matter; let no images
> Be hung with Caesar's trophies.
>
> (I.i.164–69)

The language seems to glance at the controversies over garments and the use of images; and in the word "ceremonies" — Plutarch speaks of "diadems" — Flavius employs a term of great contemporary resonance, one containing within itself practically the entire history of half a century of passionate struggle. Again and again the Puritans condemned what they called "superstitious" and "filthy" ceremonies, the "chains," as one put it, "whereby we were tied to popish religion."[6] With equal determination, the Anglican establishment insisted on the retention of those ceremonies necessary to maintain, in the words of the Book of Common Prayer, "a decente ordre, and godlye discipline."[7] Over the years the term "ceremony" had been used so often and had acquired so many associations that it had become, as W. Gordon Zeeveld remarks, "a word of extraordinary emotive power with verbal and conceptual values instantly resonant in the theatre."[8]

One form of ceremony that offended the Puritans was the keeping of holidays — the term still carried much of the old sense of holy day — other than those specifically appointed in the Bible. Flavius's dismissive attitude toward the feast of Lupercal may well have sounded Puritanical in the late 1590s when the reformers were making a point of refusing to stop work to celebrate such feasts as saints' days.[9] His comment here recalls the contempt with which he chastises the workmen at the play's start:

> Hence! home, you idle creatures, get you home:
> Is this a holiday? What, know you not,
> Being mechanical, you ought not walk
> Upon a labouring day without the sign
> Of your profession?
>
> (I.i.1–5)

From the first lines of the scene, then, even before Marullus's harangue, a certain aura of Puritanism hangs about the tribunes.

The confrontations between the Puritans and the Anglicans often focused on matters of ritual or ceremony, but as the phrase "decent ordre" in the Book of Common Prayer implies, the issues raised were felt to be fundamental and far reaching. The discarding of the symbols of religious authority might lead, as many understood, to the questioning of other images of social authority, and thus to a challenge to the crown itself. No bishop, no king. At stake ultimately was the matter of power in the realm—which is, of course, also what is at stake at the opening of *Julius Caesar* as the tribunes and then the conspirators seek to prevent Caesar from being crowned.

II

Although the tribunes themselves do not reappear after the first scene, the opposition between Puritanical anti-ritualism and a more conservative belief in the efficacy of ceremony is at work throughout the play. Caesar's first appearance shows him concerned about ceremonies as he enters speaking about the Lupercalian rite and his desire to have Antony touch Calphurnia. "Set on," he commands, "and leave no ceremony out" (I.i.11). Later Cassius remarks to the conspirators that Caesar "is superstitious grown of late, / Quite from the main opinion he held once / Of fantasy, of dreams, and ceremonies" (II.i.195–97). "Ceremonies" here may refer to portents or omens, as it does when Calphurnia comments that although she "never stood on ceremonies" (II.ii.13) they now frighten her, but the word's other sense is not lost. We can note, too, Cassius's Puritanical dislike of plays and music, pointed out by Caesar; and in this context

Casca's sour dismissal of the ceremony of the offering of the crown as "foolery" may also be suggestive.

In a general way, then, the anti-Caesar parties—both the tribunes and the bitter republicans of the second scene, Cassius and Casca—are associated with anti-ritualism. But Brutus, whom the play carefully distinguishes from the other opponents of Caesar, is no enemy to ceremony as such. Indeed, it is precisely because of his belief in the power of ritual that he comes to the conclusion that Caesar must die. As Frank Kermode observes, anachronistic assumptions about the significance of a coronation ceremony are at work in Brutus's soliloquy in his orchard. For Plutarch, Caesar is already a king de facto. But Brutus, thinking more like an Elizabethan subject than a Roman citizen, attaches great importance to the actual crowning: "He would be crown'd: / How that might change his nature, there's the question" (II.i.12–13). Crown Caesar and he will be put beyond reprisal. The ritual itself is what must be prevented.[10]

From the solemn shaking of hands in II.i to the bathing in Caesar's blood, the conspiracy is, under Brutus's direction, carried out in a conspicuously ceremonial manner. As Brents Stirling and others have noted, onstage the ritualistic character of the assassination is clear.[11] One by one the conspirators kneel to Caesar, begging him to repeal Publius Cimber's banishment although they know he will not. By arrangement Casca strikes first, rearing his hand over Caesar's head. Each conspirator then stabs in turn, after which they bathe in the blood. But long before the event, Brutus insists that the assassination must be conducted as a sacrifice. His well-known speech evokes both ritual slaughter and the notion of purging or bleeding a sick commonweal in a medicinal act that he conceives as a kind of exorcism of Caesar's spirit:

> Let's be sacrificers, but not butchers, Caius.
> We all stand up against the spirit of Caesar,
> And in the spirit of men there is no blood.
> O, that we then could come by Caesar's spirit
> And not dismember Caesar! But, alas,
> Caesar must bleed for it. And, gentle friends,
> Let's kill him boldly, but not wrathfully;
> Let's carve him as a dish fit for the gods,
> Not hew him as a carcass fit for hounds.

> And let our hearts, as subtle masters do,
> Stir up their servants to an act of rage,
> And after seem to chide 'em. This shall make
> Our purpose necessary, and not envious;
> Which so appearing to the common eyes,
> We shall be call'd purgers, not murderers.
>
> (II.i.166–80)

Interestingly, some of these motifs recur when Caius Ligarius enters dressed like a sick man and explicitly refers to Brutus as an "exorcist" who can give health: "Brave son, deriv'd from honourable loins! / Thou, like an exorcist, hast conjur'd up / My mortified spirit" (II.i.321–24). There is, however, an ambiguity in Caius Ligarius's speech, for in Elizabethan usage "exorcise" can mean to raise a spirit as well as to expel one, and this ambiguity perhaps foreshadows the ironic turn that events in Rome are to take. Is Brutus an exorcist or a conjurer, Rome's doctor or the means by which the spirit of Caesar is permanently established in the state?

Early in the play, Cassius rather sardonically introduces the notion of conjuration when he attempts to move Brutus against Caesar by speaking of the relative power of their names:

> Brutus and Caesar: what should be in that "Caesar"?
> Why should that name be sounded more than yours?
> Write them together, yours is as fair a name;
> Sound them, it doth become the mouth as well;
> Weigh them, it is as heavy; conjure with 'em,
> "Brutus" will start a spirit as soon as "Caesar".
>
> (I.ii.140–45)

Later, in his soliloquy over Caesar's corpse, Antony imagines civil war in Italy with "Caesar's spirit, ranging for revenge" (III.i.270). Antony no doubt is only speaking metaphorically, and yet, together with other allusions to exorcism and conjuration, his picture of the ranging spirit invites us to consider the play's action as an attempt at exorcism that turns into a conjuration, two rituals that are dangerously similar in that each involves the demonstration of power over spirits.[12] In any case, the play makes much of Caesar's spirit and at the end that spirit does literally range the world, manifesting itself to us as well as to Brutus before the battle of Philippi.

III

But to speak of *Julius Caesar* in terms of spirits and conjuration perhaps seems odd. We generally think of this play as a hard-headed political study, one that treats Brutus's attempt to ritualize and purify the assassination with scornful irony. Our approach tends to be in the skeptical vein of Cassius or in that of Antony, who regards the assassination as exactly what Brutus sought to avoid, a butchery. And yet though Antony, the cynical manipulator of the plebeians, may be disenchanted, *Julius Caesar*, with its ghost, its soothsayer, its prophetic dreams and supernatural prodigies, is not. The world of this play is fundamentally mysterious. Minor mysteries such as Cassius's death falling on his birthday are emphasized, and the play implies that Caesar was right to have grown superstitious, to have changed his opinion about dreams: the portents that prefigure the assassination are not daggers of the mind. By the play's end even Cassius has lost some of his enlightened skepticism and come to grant some credit to omens.

Of course we do not need to believe that Shakespeare himself had to be superstitious to write *Julius Caesar*. The Elizabethan stage was filled with supernatural beings: witches, fairies, conjurers, ghosts, and others. Purged from the church by the new enlightenment of the reformation, magic reappeared in the ostensibly circumscribed and make-believe world of the theater. If sixteenth-century English folk could no longer experience the real physical presence of God on the altar in church, they could still experience the pretended physical manifestation of demons and spirits in the theater. We are sometimes inclined to dismiss the Puritan objections to the theater as sour crankiness, but their antagonism can perhaps be sympathetically comprehended as part of their larger campaign against superstition and idolatry.[13] Moreover, there is a real connection between magic, ritual, and drama, and it is sometimes hard to say where the boundary lies between attending a play that is about ritual and participating in a ritual.

Julius Caesar is a case in point. The assassination is so conspicuously ritualized—the conspirators kneeling before Caesar, the repeated stabbing, the ceremonial bathing in Caesar's blood, the clasping of purpled hands when Antony enters—that an audience may well feel that it is not only witnessing but participating in a kind of ceremony. Indeed, in its dramatic self-consciousness, the play calls attention to its special quality as a kind of ritual when, immediately after the death, Cassius speaks of it as an event that will provide high drama in future tongues and states:

Cassius. Stoop then, and wash. How many ages hence
Shall this our lofty scene be acted over,
In states unborn, and accents yet unknown!

Brutus. How many times shall Caesar bleed in sport,
That now on Pompey's basis lies along,
No worthier than the dust!

Cassius. So oft as that shall be,
So often shall the knot of us be call'd
The men that gave their country liberty.

(III.i.111~18)

This ritual quality is directly related to the special historical status of this play's subject: for the Elizabethans as for ourselves, the assassination of Julius Caesar was probably the single most famous event in ancient history. It would have been quite possible for Shakespeare to have suppressed our knowledge of this history in the interest of illusionism, of making us forget that we are attending a performance, but in fact he does the opposite. For example, the soothsayer who appears in the second scene and again just before the assassination activates our own retrospective foreknowledge. Again and again, Shakespeare in effect reminds us that the story is famous and the outcome known. What does the night of prodigies signify? What is the meaning of the beast in which Caesar's augurers cannot find a heart? What does Calphurnia's dream portend? For the characters these are riddles, and indeed the difficulty of interpreting becomes an important motif in the play. As Cicero says on the night of prodigies, "men may construe things, after their fashion, / Clean from the purpose of the things themselves" (I.iii.34~35). But for the audience there is no difficulty in construing these signs because we are participating in a reenactment of an event whose most important meanings are already known. Why should the name Caesar be sounded more than any other? Because, as we know, this name will become a title greater even than king. Why should the ghost of Caesar range the world? Because, as we know, the assassination was not the end of Caesarism but effectively the beginning.

A few words about the play's structure as historical drama are necessary. *Julius Caesar* is built upon a tautology: Caesar becomes Caesar, the past becomes the completed past that we know. Much like ourselves, the Elizabethans seem to have imagined ancient Rome in architectural terms, thinking of pillars, arches, and statues; and Shakespeare's Rome is notably a city of statues: Caesar's images, Junius Brutus's statue, the statue of Pompey the Great.[14] Cassius warns Brutus that Caesar has turned himself into a Colossus, and indeed Caesar, who repeatedly suppresses his private fears in order to play out his historical role as "Caesar," does present himself as a kind of immovable monument. As a historical tragedy, then, *Julius Caesar* is built upon the tension between the present tense of dramatic reenactment and the past of history, between the ordinary flesh and blood of life and the immobile statues of antiquity. The play insists throughout upon Caesar's fleshly vulnerability: his falling sickness, his deafness, his near drowning in the Tiber and his fever in Spain. What Shakespeare shows us is—to employ the grotesque imagery of Calphurnia's dream—marble statues spouting blood; or, putting the point the other way around, it shows us flesh and blood aspiring to monumentality. Ironically, it is precisely because of his aspiration to a monumentality as fixed as the North Star, that Caesar is vulnerable to the conspirators' plot. "Hence! Wilt thou lift up Olympus?" (III.i.74) he exclaims the moment before the assassination. This is hubris of course, but in the different sense that the play's historical perspective provides, it is true. "*Et tu, Brute?*" As Caesar leaves behind the frailty of the flesh and enters history, Shakespeare gives him the one Latin line in the play, underscoring the transformation. The vulnerable man has been revealed as the marmoreal figure of history. Caesar has become Caesar.

What I am suggesting is that the play's mystifications, its magical elements, are associated with this tautological design. Couched in terms of prophecies and omens, our knowledge of events is represented in the drama as a magical necessity embedded in history. The result is that dramatic irony is raised to a metaphysical level and presented as fate. In this manner the play creates a feeling of necessity and persuades its audience that in witnessing Caesar's death and the collapse of the republican cause it has witnessed something inevitable.

IV

Why should Caesar's assassination and apotheosis as an immortal spirit be ceremonially repeated on the stage of the Globe? Why should Shakespeare conjure up Caesar? Considered not merely as a play about ritual but as itself a version of ritual, Shakespeare's historical drama becomes a ceremony of sacrifice and transcendence that I would like to term a kind of political Mass. As David Kaula has pointed out, there are eucharistic overtones in Brutus's ceremonial charge to the conspirators to wash their hands in Caesar's blood, an action that echoes the New Testament invocations of Christ having "washed us from our sins in his own blood" (Rev. 1:5). So, too, there are allusions to Christian sacrifice in Decius Brutus's interpretation of Calphurnia's dream, in which he claims that the statue spouting blood signifies that Caesar will be the source of renewal for Rome and that Romans will come to him, as to a saint, for "relics" (II.ii.83–90). And there are similar overtones when Mark Antony, speaking over Caesar's body, tells the populace that if they heard Caesar's testament they

> would go and kiss dead Caesar's wound,
> And dip their napkins in his sacred blood,
> Yea, beg a hair of him for memory,
> And, dying, mention it within their wills,
> Bequeathing it as a rich legacy
> Unto their issue.

> (III.ii.134–39)

"Behind all the oblique allusions to Christian sacrifice," Kaula remarks, "lurks the notion that what the conspirators produce is a disastrous imitation of the true redemptive action."[15] The assassination of Caesar is in other words merely a parody of Christian sacrifice. What I want to suggest by speaking of the play as a kind of political Mass, however, is an alternative way of understanding these eucharistic overtones. Brutus may be misguided in his conception of the assassination, Decius Brutus may be trying to flatter Caesar in order to persuade him to go to the Senate House, and Mark Antony may be a demagogue manipulating a crowd; nevertheless, like the Mass, *Julius Caesar* centers upon a sacrificial death that initiates a new era in history, the emergence of imperial Rome, and perhaps the association of Caesar and Christ is not wholly ironic.

Let us recall again the intermingling of religion and politics in the sixteenth century. The struggle within the church, glanced at in the opening scene, represents one aspect of this intermingling. Another is the way the crown penetrated the church. The penetration was literal; in place of the holy rood the royal coat of arms was erected in the chancel arch of English churches. At the same time, religious forms such as the figure of the double nature of the man-god Christ were systematically displaced onto the political sphere. Drained out of the official religion, magic and ceremony reappeared not only on the stage, but in the equally theatrical world of the court, where, for example, something reminiscent of the rejected cult of the Virgin reappeared as the cult of Gloriana, with its attendant rites and ceremonies such as the spectacular Accession Day celebrations. Particularly interesting, given the statues in *Julius Caesar,* the destruction of "popish idols" was paralleled by the rise of the sacred image of Elizabeth, forever young and beautiful. Shakespeare's Caesar turns himself into a monument of greatness; Shakespeare's Queen did something not altogether different, presenting herself as a living idol to be worshipped.[16] Moreover, the Roman imperial theme had immediate significance in sixteenth-century England, where Elizabeth, determined to maintain her independence from the threatening powers of Catholic Europe, dressed herself in the symbolism of an empress, the heir ultimately of the Caesars.[17] Even Caesarian triumphs were part of her style. In 1588 she marked the defeat of the Spanish Armada with an entry into London in the ancient Roman manner, and one of the most famous of her late portraits, the procession picture attributed to Robert Peake, is as we now understand a version of the triumph *á l'antique* with affinities to Mantegna's *Triumph of Caesar.*[18] Probably many in Shakespeare's audience would have been prepared to see parallels between the first Emperor, as Caesar was commonly if erroneously regarded, and the great Queen.[19]

I hardly mean to suggest that *Julius Caesar* is to be taken as an allegory, though some in Shakespeare's audience may have interpreted it in this way, as they evidently did *Richard II* a few years later. Nevertheless, the play does have political dimensions, and as a representation of the transformation of the Roman Republic into the Empire, *Julius Caesar* may be understood as yet another of the many originary myths of the Imperial Tudor State, a fable parallel in its way to that of the descent of true British authority from the ancestral figure of Trojan Brute or to that of the apocalyptic union of the red rose and the white. Furthermore, by transforming the historical fact of the defeat of Brutus and the republican movement in Rome into a metaphysical confirmation of the inevitability of imperial greatness, Shakespeare's play implicitly confirms the legitimacy of the Tudor state. And yet, even as it does this, *Julius Caesar* is far from univocal. Shakespeare's Caesar may be great, may even be the greatest man who ever lived in the tide of times, but he is also inflexible and pretentious. Nor is Brutus a foul traitor, like Dante's Brutus condemned to the deepest circle of Hell, but a patriot and an idealist, though a misguided one.[20]

In the last years of the sixteenth century it became increasingly difficult for the old Queen to play the role of Gloriana. Elizabeth was still of course a figure of awe and admiration to her people, most of whom, including Shakespeare, had never known any other ruler; nevertheless, many of her loyal subjects were impatiently looking forward to the end of her reign. Office-seekers were anxious for advancement and for the titles of honor that Elizabeth so rarely bestowed, and the Puritans were waiting for a monarch more disposed to continuing the reformation of the church. To make matters worse, the old Queen obstinately refused to name her heir.[21] Perhaps *Julius Caesar* incorporates, in significantly displaced form, something of the ambivalence and frustration with which many regarded the resident deity of England in her final years. In any event, a suggestive doubleness inheres in the play, which allows us at once to do away with Caesar and to submit to him.

Drama, like any form of narrative, has as one of its functions the mediation of contradictions that lie too deep in the culture to be resolved or, sometimes, too deep even to be effectively articulated. Two years after *Julius Caesar* was performed, there was a confused and traumatic revolt in England, the Essex uprising. But this was not a revolution—no general principles lay behind it—and it was pursued, significantly, in the form of loyalty to the Queen. In the last years of Elizabeth's reign we are still a long way from the Civil Wars and the public bleeding of King Charles. Nevertheless, the Puritan reformers, however loyal to the person of the Queen they might be as individuals, had made an important step toward the future with their subversive claim to an authority derived not from the crown but from the congregation. No bishop, no king. At stake in the controversy over discarding the ceremonies in the church and the attendant symbols of social legitimation was indeed the matter of power in the realm. In its strategic ambivalence, Shakespeare's play can perhaps be understood as mobilizing some of the contradictory feelings toward the absolute authority of the crown that were beginning to be felt even as early as 1599.

NOTES

This essay is reprinted by permission of *English Literary Renaissance.*

1. All quotations of *Julius Caesar* are from the Arden edition, ed. T. S. Dorsch (London: Methuen, 1955).

2. On the "spiritual" style of preaching, which developed in the 1580s and 1590s, see William Haller, *The Rise of Puritanism* (New York: Columbia University

Press, 1938), 19–34, 128–72. David Kaula in "'Let Us Be Sacrificers': Religious Motifs in *Julius Caesar*," *Shakespeare Studies* 14 (1981): 197–214, also observes the analogy between the tribunes and the reformers. Kaula develops the point rather differently from the way I do, suggesting that Caesar worship in this play is something akin to Roman Catholic worship and that Caesar himself can be associated with the Pope.

3. William Cobbett, *Parliamentary History of England* (London: 1806), vol. 1, cols. 1071–72. In the ensuing debates over purveyance reform, the principal supporters of reform became associated in the public mind with tribunes. See W. Gordon Zeeveld, "*Coriolanus* and Jacobean Politics," *Modern Language Review* 57 (1962): 321–34, who discusses the episode in relation to the tribunes in the later play.

4. Hooker, *Works*, ed. J. Keble (Oxford: Clarendon Press, 1863), vol. 3, 570.

5. *Christs Checke to S. Peter*, (London, 1599), sig. M8. On preaching as a crucial area for political control see Christopher Hill, *Society and Puritanism in Pre-Revolutionary England* (London: Secker & Warburg, 1964), 30–78.

6. Robert Crowley, *An Answere for the tyme* (London, 1566), quoted by W. Gordon Zeeveld, *The Temper of Shakespeare's Thought* (New Haven: Yale University Press, 1974), 25.

7. London, 1599, sig. D1.

8. *The Temper of Shakespeare's Thought*, 15.

9. By the 1590s an anti-holiday attitude had become virtually "official" Puritan doctrine. See Patrick Collinson, *The Elizabethan Puritan Movement* (London: Methuen, 1982), 436–37, and Hill, *Society and Puritanism*, 145–218, who reports that Puritans were regularly penalized for insisting on working on saints' days.

10. See Kermode's introduction to *Julius Caesar* in *The Riverside Shakespeare*, ed. G. Blakemore Evans (Boston: Houghton Mifflin Company, 1974), 1103.

11. See Stirling's influential "Or Else This Were a Savage Spectacle," *PMLA* 66 (1951): 765–74. My reading differs significantly from Stirling's in that I do not see the play as treating ritual with enlightened scorn. Naomi Conn Liebler, "'Thou Bleeding Piece of Earth': The Ritual Ground of *Julius Caesar*," *Shakespeare Studies* 14 (1981): 175–96, is particularly concerned with Shakespeare's use of Roman rituals. Her argument is that in the Caesarean period there was confusion about ritual practices as one social order was coming to an end and another was emerging. Brutus's desire to preserve ritual seriousness, to treat the assassination as a religious sacrifice, suggests, in her reading, his "impossibly idealistic conservatism" (180).

12. Exorcism, which was associated with the enemies of the Elizabethan establishment, was much in the news in the 1590s in connection with John Darrell, the famous Puritan exorcist whom the authorities put on trial as a fraud. For an account of this affair see D. P. Walker, *Unclean Spirits: Possession and Exorcism in France and England in the Late Sixteenth and Early Seventeenth Centuries* (London: Scolar Press, 1981), and for a suggestive recent discussion that is particularly

concerned with possession and dispossession in relation to *King Lear*, see Stephen Greenblatt, "Shakespeare and the Exorcists," in *After Strange Texts*, ed. Gregory S. Jay and David L. Miller (University: University of Alabama Press, 1985), 101–23.

13. Michael O'Connell explores the seriousness of some of the Puritan objections in "The Idolatrous Eye: Iconoclasm, Anti-theatricalism, and the Image of the Elizabethan Theater," *ELH* 52 (1985): 279–310.

14. Collections of engravings of Roman ruins such as Hieronymus Cock's *Romanae Antiquitatis Ruinorum Monumenta* (Antwerp, 1551) or Antonius Lafreri's *Speculum Romanae* (Rome, 1579) would give a sense of ancient Rome as a city of gigantic columns, arches, and statues. John W. Velz, "The Ancient World in Shakespeare: Authenticity or Anachronism? A Retrospect," *Shakespeare Survey* 31 (1978): 1–12, observes that "Shakespeare thought of Rome in architectural terms."

15. Kaula, " 'Let us be Sacrificers': Religious Motifs in *Julius Caesar*," 209–10. The pattern of eucharistic allusions in the play was also pointed out to me by Frank Burch Brown at the American Academy of Religion in 1985.

16. John Phillips comments on the parallel decline of images of Christ and rise of images of Elizabeth; see *The Reformation of Images: Destruction of Art in England, 1535–1660* (Berkeley: University of California Press, 1973), esp. 119. On the displacement of religious themes onto the monarch see Francis A. Yates, *Astraea: The Imperial Theme in the Sixteenth Century* (London: Routledge & Kegan Paul, 1975), 29–87, and Roy Strong, *The Cult of Elizabeth: Elizabethan Portraiture and Pageantry* (London: Thames and Hudson, 1977), passim.

17. See Yates, *Astraea*, esp. 29–87. On the emergence of Tudor imperial claims in the reign of Henry VIII, see Richard Koebner, " 'The Imperial Crown of This Realm': Henry VIII, Constantine the Great, and Polydore Vergil," *Bulletin of the Institute of Historical Research* 26 (1953): 29–53.

18. See Roy Strong, "Eliza Triumphans," in *The Cult of Elizabeth*, 17–55. The royal entry of 1588 in a symbolic chariot-throne surmounted by a "Crowne Imperiall" is described by John Stowe, *Annales* (London, 1631), 751, quoted by Strong, 120.

19. I have noted that Kaula in " 'Let us be Sacrificers': Religious Motifs in *Julius Caesar*" suggests that Caesar can be associated with the Pope. Some in Shakespeare's audience may well have made this connection. Others, however, might have been more interested in the analogy with Elizabeth.

20. Indeed, the play even treats Brutus's republican politics with some sympathy, though the anti-Caesarean voice as it speaks here is perhaps more the antithesis implicit in absolutist monarchy than it is classical republicanism. J. L. Simmons argues suggestively that the republicanism of *Julius Caesar* is colored by the radical ideal of "godly egalitarianism"; see *Shakespeare's Pagan World: The Roman Tragedies* (Charlottesville: University of Virginia Press, 1973), 80–84.

21. J. E. Neale discusses relevant aspects of the late Elizabethan court in "The Elizabethan Political Scene," in *Essays in Elizabethan History* (London: Jonathan Cape, 1958), 59–84.

11

Palisading the Body Politic

LINDA WOODBRIDGE

"That island of England breeds very valiant creatures."
— *Henry V*

To island-dwellers like the Elizabethan English, Shakespeare's description of Lucrece's death must have held a peculiar horror:

And bubbling from her breast, it [the blood] doth divide
In two slow rivers, that the crimson blood
Circles her body in on every side,
Who, like a late-sack'd island, vastly stood
Bare and unpeopled in this fearful flood.
  Some of her blood still pure and red remain'd,
  And some look'd black, and that false Tarquin stain'd.
                                                    (1737–43)

The goriness of those blood-rivers, the creepiness of their "slow" movement, even the chilling vision of blood turned black through pollution, might have paled, in those immediately post-Armada days, beside the specter of a sacked island. That the woman *is* the island provides a clue to the impact of the Lucrece story on Elizabethans. *The Rape of Lucrece, Titus Andronicus,* and *Cymbeline* offer vivid testimony to the truth of anthropological theories that treat the human body as an image of society. Viewing through an anthropological lens, these texts, and also that bête noire of colonial discourse theorists, *The Tempest,* also helps explain why England identified with Rome, why Shakespeare so favored the themes of seige warfare and threatened women, and why cartographers put so much water on Renaissance maps of England.

First let me sketch the anthropological theory and link it with some background material on England's love affair with Rome.

Implicit in Van Gennep's sweeping synthesis of territorial passage rites with rites of passage like initiations or weddings is that most cultures are receptive to analogies between the spatial and the temporal. Noting the "interchangeability of a temporal and spatial vocabulary" in Shakespeare, Berry notes that nearly half of Shakespeare's uses of "space" refer to time (139). Life's events can be plotted as on a map; a human life is like the land.

Anthropologist Mary Douglas, addressing the problem of why many societies guard the body's orifices so zealously that an unsanctioned penetration—a breach of chastity, eating forbidden food—is a pollution, argues that the body is "a symbol of society," and finds "the powers and dangers credited to social structure reproduced in small on the human body" (*Purity* 115). Philosophers and art historians have long recognized the body as a cosmic structuring principle: Panofsky concludes that despite "mathematical or philosophical foundations, perspective and proportional systems are still iconologies of space and of the human body" (Argan 298). Douglas sees bodily margins as Van Gennep and Turner see the no-man's-land between territories and the liminal phase between life-stages—as powerful, dangerous marginal states. Fear of bodily pollution expresses fear for the fabric of society: "Each culture has its own special risks and problems. To which particular bodily margins its beliefs attribute power depends on what situation the body is mirroring. It seems that our deepest fears and desires take expression with a kind of witty aptness. To understand body pollution we should try to argue back from the known dangers of society. . . . Symbolism of the body's boundaries is used in [a] kind of unfunny wit to express danger to community boundaries" (*Purity* 121-22). Among Douglas's examples are the Coorgs of India, ensconced in a mountain fastness, whose culture was deeply oriented toward fear of pollution.

The early American land-as-woman metaphor (see Kolodny's provocatively entitled *The Lay of the Land*) was a species of the Renaissance body/state analogy. In what Stallybrass calls "the geography of the body" (138), Donne calls his mistress "my America, my new found land," and Shakespeare calls Lucrece's breasts "ivory globes circled with blue, / A pair of maiden worlds unconquered"; Lucrece's smoothness is "like a goodly champaign plain" (407-8, 1247). Barkan surveys the metaphor of cosmos and commonwealth as the body (Plato saw the cosmos as a living creature, astrologers described Aries as the head, Libra the buttocks, Pisces the feet, of a great body). The body/state analogy "was already a commonplace in Plato's time not only among political philosophers using anatomical descriptions but also among physicians describing anatomy in social or political terms" (69), but Renaissance England saw "the heyday of the anthropomorphic image of the commonwealth" (75).

Anthropological notions of body and society, of pollution and dangerous margins, emerge often in Shakespeare, but with particular force in *Lucrece, Titus,* and *Cymbeline,* where women's bodies are metaphors for societies threatened. All involve Rome, which offered early modern England a potent symbol of invasion that spoke poignantly to England's sense of herself.

As the Romans Do

A binary image of Rome, almost Lévi-Straussian in its precise mirror inversion, haunted the European imagination for a thousand years: Rome the implacable invader, thrusting its masculine armies deep into the virgin territory of the Goths, its soldiers raping the Queen of Britain's daughters; and Rome the invaded, the sacked city, ravaged by Goths. But history offered a potent tool for deconstructing this binary opposition: the opposed images represented successive phases of Roman history, and poised between them, as a historical "time out" like calendric intercalary days, was a third Rome, Augustus Caesar's, a Rome which had finished its invasions, acquired its colonies, and was enjoying its empire in peace, a Rome yet unsacked. This compound image, its binary oppositions mediated by a liminal zone of history, fascinated Renaissance England partly because she spun from it images of herself. The ancient world was the setting for one third of the Shakespeare canon—"two of the comedies, both of the narrative poems, four of the five romances, and six of the eleven tragedies" (Velz 1). The many readers who have seen Elizabethan politics in Shakespeare's Roman politics (see Velz) confirm the link in Shakespeare's mind between England and ancient Rome. Besides the "ubiquitous presence of Rome in Elizabethan culture" (Miola 11), a classicism shared with all Europe, England often identified more specifically with Rome, as when Roman civil wars were compared with the Wars of the Roses (Barroll 328–29).

Titus and *Lucrece* display Rome in both aspects, as invader and invaded. Each opens with the typically Roman activity of soldiers invading someone's territory—Titus returns home from "weary wars against the barbarous Goths" (I.i.28); Lucrece's husband is among Romans besieging Ardea. Yet the sense of an invaded Rome predominates. In *Lucrece,* Tarquin, having seized power in a bloody coup, is reigning tyrannously; *Titus* opens on armed men battering the "city walls"; "Open the gates and let me in," cries

Saturninus (I.i.26, 65), who soon becomes emperor and rules tyrannously; his marriage to the Queen of the Goths and adoption of her unlovely sons creates a reconstituted family that brings the barbarian to the gates. *Lucrece* culminates in an army marching on Rome bearing Lucrece's body and ousting the tyrants; late in *Titus,* an army of Goths surrounds Rome; the tyrant is killed. Though the Rome of these texts is a complex mixture, part thrusting, martial masculinity, part woman in danger of ravishment — now invader, now invaded — the image of Rome besieged predominates. If Douglas's theory is correct and if Shakespeare has imaginatively captured the *episteme* of a siege-mentality culture, we should expect, for such a society, images of the human body threatened with unsanctioned penetration and pollution. This is exactly what we find. In *Titus,* where Rome's margins are threatened, a woman is raped and dismembered; Lavinia's invaded orifices and mangled margins are aptly symbolized by the horrifying "marginal stuff" (Douglas, *Purity and Danger* 121), blood issuing from her mouth. In *Lucrece,* tyrant and rapist are father and son; that coup and rape are parallel usurpations, the poem makes clear: Tarquin approaches Lucrece "like a foul usurper" who means "from this fair throne to heave the owner out" (412–13); debating whether to rape her, "now he vows a league [i.e., peace treaty] and now invasion" (287); he "march[es] on to make his stand / On her bare breast, the heart of all her land" (438–39). Military siege is the governing image of *Lucrece,* which opens upon "the besieged Ardea" and which imagines the rape as a siege. Tarquin fears Lucrece's husband will dream of "this siege that hath engirt his marriage" (220). When "the Roman lord marcheth to Lucrece' bed" (301), Shakespeare imagines a medieval or Renaissance city siege, with its scaling of turrets and battering rams: "her bare breast... / Whose ranks of blue veins, as his hand did scale, / Left their round turrets destitute and pale"; "His hand, that yet remains upon her breast — Rude ram, to batter such an ivory wall! — may feel her heart — poor citizen! — distress'd" (440–41, 463–65). "I come," he announces, "to scale / Thy never-conquered fort" (481–82). An analogue of the rape is a painted siege of Troy, again a Renaissance city siege: "The laboring pioner / Begrim'd with sweat" (1380–81). And in a Chinese box of siege/rape analogies, this siege was occasioned by a rape: the Greek army has assembled "for Helen's rape the city to destroy" (1369). (See Vickers 106ff., Dubrow 93–95.)

In *Lucrece* as elsewhere, Shakespeare envisions Rome as "the enclave of civilization ringed round with a protective wall, outside of which the dark forces of barbarism lurk" (Velz 11); Dubrow suggests that Lucrece "comes to represent the center of civilization that is threatened by barbarians" (94). "In a sense . . . violence is not really outside the wall," since Tarquin is a Roman (95); but so firmly is the siege trope attached to Rome that Shakespeare's imagination configures even Roman enemies as invaders. As in *Titus* we first see the Roman Saturninus arriving from foreign wars and beating on Rome's doors, so Tarquin, arriving at Lucrece's house from an outlying camp, has the air of an external invader: "Throughout the poem Shakespeare depicts Tarquin as the invading barbarian who comes to raze Lucrece's city. . . . Although he is a 'Roman lord,' " he is "alien and hostile" (Miola 27).

Heckscher notes, "The woman who had been dishonored was easily equated with a city or fortress that had been conquered by the enemy. . . . From classical antiquity onward, cities and fortresses had . . . been considered to be of the feminine sex. The Virtues of Prudentius's fifth-century *Psychomachia* were . . . maidens inhabiting and defending their *Tugendburgen*. . . . The classical *triumphator* entering a city was often greeted by a group of women, or a single woman, representing the city. . . . The daughter of Sion appears frequently in sixth-century representations of the Entry into Jerusalem" (26–27). As Dubrow notes, "Given the common association of gates with the vagina, the notion of rape is latent in the image of the attacked city" (94). And cities wear female attire: "outskirts" is a Renaissance coinage.

A Woman's Place Is in the Home

The invasion of defended territory may be domestic as well as national or civic—as countries may be invaded and cities besieged and sacked, a house may be burglarized. Among more specialized cases is illegal entry into a game preserve: "He is no woodman that doth bend his bow / To strike a poor unseasonable doe" (*Luc.* 580–81); "Hast not thou full often struck a doe, / And borne her cleanly by the keeper's nose?" (*Tit.* II.i.93–94); raped Lavinia is a poacher's deer (II.i.117, ii.26; III.i.91–92). Metaphors for Lucrece's body—house, fortress, mansion, temple, tree bark, "emphasize the protective and enclosing function of the body," which "surrounds the soul and wards off danger" (Maus 70). All territorial invasions invite literary analogues of bodily violation, and rape, in Shakespeare, calls forth comparisons with all kinds of territorial invasion.

Lucrece riots in images of sex as burglary.[1] In the rape scene, the analogy is explicit, as Tarquin burgles his way to Lucrece's bedchamber, forcing the locks of doors. Lock-forcing, analogue of the rape, calls forth a metaphor of rape: "Each [lock] by him enforc'd retires his ward" (302–3). Even more suggestive than this rape of the lock is the way Tarquin opens the last door: "His guilty hand pluck'd up the latch, / And with his knee the door he opens wide" (358–59)—why, unless to emphasize the parallel between such breaking-and-entering and the rape itself, should Tarquin open the door with his knee?

Stallybrass discusses conflation of body with enguarding house: "Surveillance of women concentrated upon ... the mouth, chastity, the threshold of the house.... Silence, the closed mouth, is made a sign of chastity. And silence and chastity are ... homologous to woman's enclosure within the house ... This 'Woman,' like Bakhtin's classical body, is rigidly 'finished': her signs are the enclosed body, the closed mouth, the locked house" (126–27).

As Douglas reminds us, "Van Gennep ... saw society as a house with rooms and corridors in which passage from one to another is dangerous. Danger lies in transitional states" (*Purity* 96). Turner's term "liminal" for such states comes from Latin *limen*, threshold. The bride carried across the threshold embodies the spatial/temporal analogy—spatially, she enters new territory; temporally, she enters a new phase of life. (A common superstition reflects the danger inherent in threshold states: "Men that stumble at the threshold / Are well foretold that danger lurks within" [*3H6* IV.vii.11–12; cf. *LLL* III.i.115].) Burgling his way towards Lucrece, Tarquin meets resistance in locked doors and threshold guardians reminiscent of myth's monstrous figures;[2] metallic threshold guardians seem animate:

> The locks between her chamber and his will,
> Each one by him enforc'd retires his ward;
> But, as they open, they all rate [berate] his ill,
> Which drives the creeping thief to some regard.
> The threshold grates the door to have him heard;
> Night-wand'ring weasels shriek to see him there;
> They fright him, yet he still pursues his fear.
>
> (302–8)

The paradox of the seemingly passive threshold grating actively against the seemingly active opening door foreshadows the paradoxical power of seemingly passive Lucrece to effect the ultimate downfall of her rapist.

Lucrece dies by creating, with a knife, a new bodily orifice leading to her heart. No orifice leads to Tarquin's heart; the orifices of his ear open on no passageways reaching that far. Though Lucrece pleads, "his ear her prayers admits, but his heart granteth / No penetrable entrance to her plaining" (558–59). But then, women have more orifices than men to start with, which may be why the female body offers the more frequent image of society endangered. If Tarquin begins, however, as an image of impenetrable body and soul, he ends invaded and sacked. He finally realizes that he has invaded himself, raped his own soul, a soul he imagines as a woman polluted:

> His soul's fair temple is defaced,
> To whose weak ruins muster troops of cares,
> To ask the spotted princess how she fares.
> She says her subjects with foul insurrection
> Have batter'd down her consecrated wall. . . .
> Ev'n in this thought through the dark night he stealeth,
> A captive victor that hath lost in gain.
>
> (719–30)

As Tarquin's invasions, first (as the usurper's heir) of the Roman political state and then of Lucrece's body, make him paradoxically a prisoner, a "captive victor," so the violent penetrations of Lucrece, first by rape and then by knife, paradoxically free her, restoring her to the safety of defended territory. The image with which I began captures this paradox in all its complexity. Lucrece's body becomes a sacked island—the ravished female body as an image of society not merely endangered but wrecked: "The crimson blood / Circles her body in on every side, / Who, like a late-sack'd island, vastly stood / Bare and unpeopled in this fearful flood." But symbols of encirclement mark the reintegrative *agrégation* phase of Van Gennep's rites of passage, and the river-ringed island suggests the liminal zone buffering defended territory. Lucrece has saved her reputation, even her soul, and the island is at least in part an image of safety and protection. Lucrece's death frees Rome from tyranny, as Lavinia's rape ultimately frees Rome from tyranny in *Titus*.

Trunks, Girdles, and Ears

The endings of the two early works, personally bleak if politically redemptive, contrast with *Cymbeline*'s comic resolution. In the early, invasion-obsessed texts, redemption comes through killing or expelling the invader.

Cymbeline still stresses England's danger from invasion, but suggests another way out, not expulsion but peacemaking; as I shall show, it is a distinctly Jacobean solution.[3] Invasion is averted partly because *Cymbeline* is comedy but partly because a new Jacobean ideology, as we shall see, was downplaying the threat of invasion. England throughout most of *Cymbeline* is still a nation under seige: the Britain which always identified with Rome here takes on Rome's identity as the besieged, while Rome wears its invader face. Rome's dual nature is thus divided between two societies, England adopting the aspect with which Elizabethans had most readily identified.

Lucrece's image of a "late-sack'd island" would strike a sympathetic chord in *Cymbeline*, where memory of Julius Caesar's invasion of the island Britain is still fresh. This invasion, however, was almost unsuccessful, for Britain was defended actively by its very surrounding liminal zone, the sea:

> Your isle . . . stands
> As Neptune's park, ribb'd and paled in
> With rocks unscalable and roaring waters,
> With sands that will not bear your enemies' boats,
> But suck them up to th' topmast. A kind of conquest
> Caesar made here, but made not here his brag
> Of "Came and saw and overcame." With shame —
> The first that ever touch'd him — he was carried
> From off our coast, twice beaten; and his shipping,
> Poor ignorant baubles, on our terrible seas,
> Like egg-shells mov'd upon their surges, crack'd
> As easily 'gainst our rocks.
>
> (III.i.18-29)

Britain courts Roman invasion again, as Cymbeline refuses to pay the tribute. The Queen's son defies the Roman emissary, declaring that if Rome invades Britain, "you shall find us in our saltwater girdle" (III.i.79-80). Though the image is unheroic for a moment of high patriotism, and its speaker *is* the lumpen villain Cloten, it is perfect for the play, conjuring the seawater protecting an endangered society, and comparing military invasion with getting inside a person's clothing — endangered society as a body protected by clothing against rape. My colleague James Marino suggests that Cloten's image hints at the magical virginity-protecting girdles of medieval romances like *Bevis of Hampton* and *Emare*. Clothing, like the body, can be an "image of society." In Renaissance plague time pores "needed permanent protection from attack," which "rendered the shape and nature of clothing in time of plague all-important: smooth fabrics, dense weave and close fit. . . . Men and women alike longed to have smooth and hermetically sealed clothes enclosing their weak bodies" (Vigarello 10); compare this with the storming-the-Bastille image of French Revolutionary times: "Our clothes are like fetters, they are the invention of the barbarian and Gothic centuries. You must break these fetters if you wish to become free and happy" (B. C. Faust, 1792 [Vigarello 140]).

When the Romans invade, they press into Britain at an inlet, Milford Haven, and try to penetrate through a lane whose narrowness is repeatedly emphasized. A stand being made at the cervix of this lane, British society, direly endangered, is saved. Here, the *attempted* invasion of a country is paralleled by the attempted invasion of a woman's body. One male character tries to seduce the heroine, another to have her murdered, a third to rape her. A fourth attempted invasion, through her mouth, is averted when the poison turns out to be a sleeping potion. She is also nearly poisoned through the ear, slanderously told that her husband has been untrue; a similar poison is poured into her husband's ear. Such ear-poisoning was a penetration like rape: the ear seemed vaginal; the Virgin Mary supposedly conceived through the ear (see below; cf. Cleopatra's "Ram thou thy fruitful tidings in mine ears, / That long time have been barren" [II.v.24–25]). Cloten's plan to penetrate Imogen's ear with music is fraught with double entendre: "I am advis'd to give her music o' mornings; they say it will penetrate. *Enter Musicians.* Come on; tune. If you can penetrate her with your fingering, so; we'll try with tongue too" (II.iii.11–15). The series of close calls which make Imogen's story so like The Perils of Pauline reiterate Britain's near-misses: the royal line is nearly wiped out by the kidnapping of the princes and near murder of Imogen; tyranny is averted by the Queen's timely suicide; the Roman army is fended off in the act of breaching Britain's maidenhead at that narrow lane. Imogen's perils are Britain's.[4]

Threshold crossings objectify this repeated pattern of danger averted. The seducer Iachimo is carried across the threshold of the chamber where Imogen sleeps. The would-be rapist Cloten is carried across the threshold of the cave where Imogen sleeps. (Pointing up the connection, in both chambers the unconscious Imogen is called a "lily" [see Skura, *Dream* 213–14].) But just as the threat of Roman invasion is headed off through the death of many soldiers at the neck of a lane, so the threat to Imogen from the sexual miscreants who keep being carried into her chamber is contained by images of death: the resemblance of Iachimo's trunk to a coffin suggests the ultimate death of his evil aspirations; and Cloten arrives in Imogen's chamber quite deceased, having recently been beheaded. Iachimo's conveyance is insistently called a "trunk": Cloten's beheaded trunk, a visual pun, recalls the earlier incident; of his body a character cries, "Soft, ho, what trunk is here / Without his top?" (IV.ii.354–55). Perhaps this is a species of that "unfunny wit" to which Douglas alludes. The constant danger threatening this young woman who spends too much time sleeping next to trunks is symbolized by the menacing penetration of domestic thresholds — a burglary which is an analogue of attempted seduction or rape, itself an analogue of military invasion. In Douglas's terms, danger to society is expressed by danger to the body; in Van Gennep's, different kinds of "passage" have a similar structure and vocabulary of symbols; in Turner's, the indeterminacy of a liminal state expresses vulnerability.

"God Breathed and They Were Scattered"; Armadas, Virgins, Pores

Shakespeare sees Lucrece's rape as a pollution: " 'To kill myself, . . . alack, what were it, / But with my body my poor soul's pollution?' "; her body is a "polluted prison" (1156–57, 1725–26). In tribal societies, pollution may be removed by simple purification rites, but for Shakespeare so severe a pollution is rape that its only purifier is death: "My blood shall wash the slander of mine ill," resolves Lucrece (1207), as Titus kills his rape-polluted daughter. *Lucrece* uses "stain" eighteen times, alongside "blot," "spot," "blur," "blemish," "attaint," "scar," and "pollution": Kahn argues that "though Lucrece uses moral terms such as sin and guilt, she actually condemns herself according to primitive, nonmoral standards of pollution and uncleanness" (49). (On guilt *versus* shame, sin *versus* pollution, Donaldson, H. Hawkins, and Dubrow have written perceptively.) It is startling to find in a Christian writer the pagan force of "some of her blood still pure and red remain'd, / And some look'd black, and that false Tarquin stain'd" (1742–43). Augustine, a thousand years earlier, seems more Christian, even more modern, in arguing that soiled flesh was irrelevant if Lucrece's mind was pure: Shakespeare's arresting image of blackened blood as a sign of pollution seems more at home amongst the Yoruba or the Ndembu.[5] Did something in his society make it hospitable to primitive pollution beliefs—even more so than the rest of European Christendom?

By Douglas's theory, a society bound up in pollution beliefs and obsessed with protecting orifices should be a society endangered, besieged, vulnerable at its margins. What could more accurately describe Elizabethan England, a second-rate military power in perennial danger from great powers like Spain, a Protestant country obsessed with the threat of papal takeover and nourishing a paranoid certainty that foreign Jesuit infiltrators were penetrating every available national orifice? Sequestered like the Coorgs in their mountain fastness, Elizabethan England had a sense of herself as an island, perpetually threatened with invasion but defended by her liminal zone, the sea.

Morgan sees the sixteenth-century boom in English map making as owing partly to "the international situation throughout the greater part of the century, with the recurring threat of invasion"; many royally sponsored maps were of coasts and their fortifications (136). The map on which Elizabeth stands in the Ditchley portrait emphasizes the south coast. The order of Saxton's county maps focuses early on the south coast. His map of England highlights its island nature: England occupies about half the plate; the rest is given over to seas with prominently lettered names—Oceanus Britannicus, Mare Hibernium, Oceanus Germanicus—and filled with some thirty-five ships, plus sea monsters, fish, crabs, and mermaids (Evans and Lawrence).

We can still say that England was last successfully invaded in 1066, but Elizabethans were not complacent—they saw the sea as rising up to defend them against repeated near-invasions, a real and constant threat. (Today's periodic outcries against a channel tunnel suggest that England's fear of penetration has not even yet wholly abated.) The historical moment when this sense was strongest, the 1588 defeat of the Armada, coincided closely with the beginning of Shakespeare's career. Although the Spanish fleet enjoyed particularly good weather during its progress through the English channel, encountering storms only during the retreat along the Irish coast, the great sea storm scattering the Spanish fleet quickly entered the mythology of this attempt on England's virtue: England protected by her saltwater girdle.

"God breathed and they were scattered," runs the legend on one of Queen Elizabeth's Armada medals. A Dutch medal records a similar sentiment, and the learned poets who celebrated in Latin verse the triumphant preservation of the Virgin Queen and the Protestant faith were so busy extolling the divine partisanship which drowned some thousands of Spaniards by a specially provided tempest that they scarcely had time to mention the English fleet. Of course, better ships and better guns had won the battle before the Spaniards had any trouble with the weather.... The great storm which destroyed the Spanish Armada joined the other legends. (Mattingly 390)[6]

A medal struck the year after the Armada defeat shows Elizabeth on one side, an island emerging from storm on the other (Strong 138); several portraits foregrounding Elizabeth feature a drowning Armada in the background. Of one of them, Louis Montrose writes, "The demure iconography of Elizabeth's virgin-knot suggests a causal relationship between her sanctified chastity and the providential destruction of the Spanish Catholic invaders.... The royal body provides an instructive Elizabethan illustration of Mary Douglas's cross-cultural thesis that the body's 'boundaries can represent any boundaries which are threatened or precarious.'... The inviolability of the island realm, the secure boundary of the English nation, is thus made to seem mystically dependent on the inviolability of the English sovereign, upon the intact condition of the queen's body natural" ("Elizabethan Subject" 315; see also Marcus 62).

Shakespeare often writes about England besieged, threatened at her watery borders, and sometimes saved by "our terrible seas." Elizabethans knew Caesar's invasions from the *Gallic Wars* and from many embellishing legends and pseudohistories (see Nearing); considering the many available elements of legend—from magical swords to Geoffrey of Monmouth's "admirable old Britons . . . ready to die for country" (Nearing 904)—Shakespeare's focus on the role of the sea is all the more significant. When in *King John* the French try to invade England, their ships are wrecked on the Goodwin Sands, a liminal zone Shakespeare returned to—one of Antonio's ships is wrecked there in *The Merchant.* John of Gaunt's classic description of England offers many familiar elements—the emphasis on England as an island, the island envisioned as a natural fortress, England imagined as naturally on the defensive (even the sea here an invading enemy), the besieged nation as walled house or moated castle, the land-as-woman trope, the idea that the England once conquering others has now conquered itself through tolerating tyranny—as Rome in *Titus* and *Lucrece* is both conqueror of foreign lands and conquered itself by tyrants, as *Lucrece's* rapist has raped his own soul. When England turns against herself, in

Shakespeare's many civil wars, the *Lucrece/Titus* phenomenon appears: subjects who turn against their monarch are configured as foreign invaders. To maintain the less disturbing fiction that the enemy is without, rebels are laundered by foreign travel, and appear as invaders from abroad: Bolingbroke invades from France, Hotspur (hailing from the perilous north) invades from Wales.

Recalling Shakespeare's passion for siege warfare, we might link it with his remarkable interest in sexually besieged women—the many raped or threatened with rape, the seduction attempts, the four plays in whose main plots a woman is falsely accused of sexual misconduct (*Oth.*, *Ado*, *Cym.*, *WT*). The biblical story of Susanna, sexually besieged by men who accuse her of sexual misconduct, thus combining sexual siege with siege of sexual reputation, attracted Elizabethans; perhaps reflecting his age's interest in this kind of female culture hero, Shakespeare had a daughter Susanna. Siege of body and of reputation are linked when Tarquin forces Lucrece to submit by threatening to accuse her of adultery with a servant if she does not. Shakespeare's preoccupation with slander may reflect its being a poisoning through the ear, another vulnerable orifice, subject to his culture's fear of danger to the opened body. A long tradition links ear penetration with vaginal penetration. Origen "suggested that Mary had conceived Jesus the Word at the words of the angel"; in medieval lyrics, Mary conceives through the ear, a way to preserve her as *virgo intacta* (Warner 37). Poisoning or wounding through the ear is common in Shakespeare, sometimes literal (as in Hamlet Senior), sometimes figurative, as in Iago's "I'll pour this pestilence into his ear" (*Oth.* II.iii.362). Shakespeare's concern with *sexual* slander recalls the link between ear and vagina, orifices vulnerable to sexual invasion.

Douglas's thesis that societies threatened at their borders obsessively protect bodily orifices suggests a profound link between two prominent concerns—with siege warfare and England embattled, and with the threatened female body. The link was not Shakespeare's alone: it was built into his culture.

Renaissance maps often identified England with the female body. The frontispiece figure Britannia in Drayton's *Poly-Olbion* is clothed in a map. Elizabeth in the Ditchley portrait stands on a map of England; jewels carbuncling her dress resemble in color and distribution the map's towns and forests, and the south coast below her feet disconcertingly resembles toes. In a portrait in Hardwick Hall (Strong and Oman 32) Elizabeth's petticoat is adorned with fish and sea horses like the sea creatures surrounding England in Saxton's country map. Elizabeth appears as defender against papist invasion in a Dutch engraving superimposing her body on a map of Europe (Strong 116).

Though this society officially lionized the masculine invader Henry V, its unease about Henry is suggested by Shakespeare's ambivalent treatments of him. And in a long passage in *Henry V* (anticipatory of James' "back door" argument) Henry hesitates to become invader because of England's traditional vulnerability to invasion, especially via Scotland, when her kings are away: "We must not only arm t' invade the French, / But lay down our proportions to defend / Against the Scot, who will make road upon us / With all advantages." The Archbishop of Canterbury minimizes the danger: England is a house walled against thieves ("They of those marches, . . . / Shall be a wall sufficient to defend / Our inland from the pilfering borderers"), but Henry sees threat of invasion as a condition of English history: "We do not mean the coursing snatchers only, / But fear the main intendment of the Scot, / Who hath been still a giddy neighbor to us. / For you shall read that my great-grandfather / Never went with his forces into France / But that the Scot on his unfurnish'd kingdom / Came pouring, like the tide into a breach, / With ample and brim fullness of his force, / Galling the gleaned land with hot assays, / Girding with grievous siege castles and towns; / That England, being empty of defense, / Hath shook and trembled" (I.ii.137–54). Here the great masculine invader himself describes England as a vulnerable nation always subject to sieges.

Even at its most invasive, as in its aggressive Irish policy, Elizabethan England expressed fear of invasion through an insecure border: "All over Catholic Europe, as well as in Ireland, Elizabeth was regarded as illegitimate, and unlikely to remain for long on the throne she had wrongfully ascended. Catholics were convinced that, when the time was ripe, Philip II of Spain, or some other powerful Catholic sovereign, would unseat her on the pope's behalf. With her position so weak, she saw a disobedient Ireland as a constant menace to her security. . . . Elizabeth could not allow Ireland to become a base for hostile fleets and armies" (Somerset Fry 116). Irish lords kept up "a continual correspondence with the queen's enemies in France, Spain and Scotland"; Ulster assisted refugees from the Spanish Armada, and a Spanish army landed in Ireland in 1601 (ibid., 117, 127, 134). Sir Philip Sidney warned in 1577 that the Irish "will turn to any invading force" (Myers 37), and the enclave of English in the Irish pale had the palisaded mentality of a surrounded minority subject to constant border raids.

The tissue of cultural signifiers I have been describing was not unique to the Elizabethan age. The island trope looks back beyond the Norman invasion to Julius Caesar's. Metaphors comparing siege warfare with the siege of a lady's heart permeate medieval literature in many countries, and besieged cities are compared with sexually embattled women in many cultures besides England and many ages besides the Renaissance. The siege mentality seems to have affected Europe to the point where even pores became vulnerable orifices, and people quit washing; bathing, popular in the Middle Ages, was almost completely discontinued in the sixteenth and seventeenth centuries. Vigarello attributes the new mentality largely to fear of the plague: the skin "was seen as porous, and countless openings seemed to threaten . . . The plague had only to slip through. . . . The body had less resistance to poisons after bathing, because it was more open to them. It was as if the body was permeable; infectious air threatened to flood in from all sides. 'Steam-baths and bath-houses should be forbidden, because when one emerges, the flesh and the whole disposition of the body are softened and the pores open, and . . . pestiferous vapour can rapidly enter the body and cause sudden death' [Houel, 1573, p. 16]. . . . The architectural metaphor played a central role, with the body seen as a house invaded and occupied by the plague" (Vigarello 9). But isn't there a peculiar intensity to the almost paranoid self-palisading of the *English* Renaissance psyche – something akin to what Canadian literati used to call a garrison mentality? And wasn't England, for a Protestant country, oddly obsessed with virginity? Countless literary examples spring to mind, from Spenser's Knights of Maidenhead to the virgins slaughtered during *Tamburlaine*'s city siege, and lingering as late as virginity's magical power in *Comus*. Who spurred on the army to meet Armada invaders? The Virgin Queen, ideal image of Invaders of England versus Embattled Woman. The Land as Woman, society as a body threatened at its orifices – such deeply ingrained ideas help explain why Elizabethans valued virginity, why England needed a virgin queen.

All Europe was influenced by what Douglas calls "the exaggerated importance attached to virginity in the early centuries of Christianity": "The idea that virginity had a special positive value was bound to fall on good soil in a small persecuted minority group," such social conditions encouraging symbolism of the body as "an imperfect container which will only be perfect if it can be made impermeable" (*Purity* 157–58). Warner documents the persecution (100,000 early Christians martyred) and virginity's growing centrality in medieval dogma, which stressed "technical, physical virginity, . . . the closed womb, . . . the 'fountain sealed,' an unbroken body, and not . . . a spiritual state of purity" (63). Though Augustine's view of rape was more spiritual than Shakespeare's, this architect of the original sin doctrine laid the foundations for the cult of sealed-up virginity: his belief that original sin is transmitted by male genitals during intercourse made sin a venereal disease; it linked sexual penetration with admission of evil to the human interior. Saint Methodius wrote: "Anyone who intends to avoid sin . . . must keep all his members and senses pure and sealed—just as pilots caulk a ship's timbers—to prevent sin from getting an opening and pouring in" (Warner 54, 73). Medieval belief that the hymen sealed off the uterus abetted the idea of a virgin as a sealed vessel. Medieval women's passion for fasting sealed the body from food and from the passage of other substances through orifices: fasting saints like Joan the Meatless ceased to menstruate and were believed not to defecate, urinate, sweat, or emit tears; of one it was said, "neither saliva nor sputum emanated from her mouth nor any mucus or other fluid from her nostrils"; another "discharged no filth or dandruff from her hair" (Bynum 91, 100, 122, 211). Here was truly one of Douglas's societies to "develop taboos and pollution beliefs around anything—from feces to menstrual blood—issuing from a bodily orifice" (*Purity* 115). But in most Protestant countries, virginity as an ideal was now yielding to marriage. England joined in this movement, as many cultural documents show (marriage sermons, romantic comedies); but in England virginity persisted as a potent ideal in the virgin queen cult and in works of many Protestant writers; and where married love emerged as the ideal, writers became obsessed, like Shakespeare, with sexually besieged *wives*. It is tempting to conclude that Douglas's theory is right and explains a lot—the Elizabethan mentality resembled the early Christian because similar political and social conditions of the two groups fostered similar anxieties.

Augustus, Brutus, and the Back Door

But the sky began to change in 1603. Forthrightly enunciating a new ideology in his first speech to Parliament in 1603, James promised to avoid wars, and declared the island Britain more secure from invasion than ever before. He also announced a policy of not persecuting Catholics, whose threat to the nation he saw as diminished: rather than demonizing them as would-be rapists, potential invaders of the national body, he minimized them as the last remnants of an amoebic dysentery lingering in the national alimentary canal, a "Sect, lurking within the bowels of this Nation" (274). His one reference to his predecessor did not mention her virginity (270–76). This speech put an ingenious spin on the island trope: union of England and Scotland would create a *true* nation-island immune to invasion. Abolishing its main landlocked border gave Britain sea on all its boundaries:

> These two countries being separated neither by sea, nor great river, mountaine, . . . but only by little small brooks, or demolished little walles; . . . And now in the end and fullness of time united, the right and title of both in my person, . . . whereby it is now become like a little world within itself, being intrenched and fortified round about with a natural, and yet admirable strong pond or ditch, whereby all the former fears of this nation are now quite cut off: the other part of the Island being ever before now not only the place of landing to all strangers, that was to make invasion here, but likewise moved by the enemies of this State by untimely incursions, to make enforced diversion from their conquests, for defending themselves at home, and keeping sure their back-door, as then it was called, which was the greatest hindrance and let that euer my predecessors of this nation got in disturbing them from their many famous and glorious conquests abroad. (272)

James thinks England's status as besieged island has long hampered its expansion into empire; the island of his beleaguered predecessors he sees as a house, the Scottish border its unsecured back door. The passage even hints at invasion as unsanctioned bodily penetration, given the Renaissance slang meaning of back door. (The trope persists to this day: in the 1989 European elections, the British Conservative Party campaigned on an isolationist platform; radio commercials threatened that closer alliance with Europe would bring left-wing policies to Britain "through the back door.") But his rule, James says, has changed all that; and well he *might* wish to minimize the threat from the north, having himself recently penetrated the inner chambers of the English monarchy through that same Scottish back door. But what *was* the change? Was the new Jacobean ideology a simple shift from fear of invasion to joy in the prospect of invading others? I think not: James's pacifism, stressed in this speech, undermines talk of "famous and glorious conquests." As the address deconstructs, by introducing pacifism, its own opposition Besieged Nation/Conquering Nation, so James's ideology deconstructed Rome's opposed images as invader/invadee, by focusing on the historical liminal zone of Augustus.

Elizabethan England conceptualized herself mainly as the "feminine" society, vulnerable to invasion. In Jacobean England, official ideology played down the threat of invasion, comparing England with Rome the possessor of empire, enjoying the golden age of Augustus. James's first speech to Parliament heightened his peacemaking efforts by painting the Wars of the Roses, then more than a century past, as but recently ended; this helped create the desired Augustan atmosphere. Remember that there were always *three* concepts of Rome and of England: first, the "masculine" invader concept, whose frequent signifiers were Julius Caesar and Henry V; second, the "feminine" invadee concept, whose signifiers were Lucrece and Boudicca's ravished daughters; and third, the perhaps hermaphroditic "peaceful empire" concept,[7] symbolized by Augustus Caesar and King James. James's ideology belonged to the third concept. That he identified with Augustus rather than Julius Caesar is crucial: in focusing on the Augustan moment in Roman history, James emphasized peaceful possession, rather than acquisition, of empire. As the old binary oppositions invite the language of sexual difference I have here employed *sous rature*, James's deconstruction of this oppositional system invites the language of, as it were, sexual indifference: James's own bisexuality is as revealing a cultural signifier as Elizabeth's virginity.[8] James's ideology favored not the "feminine" image of endangered England, but not the "masculine" invader image either: it posited the peaceful colonial power.

The ideology's colonial side preceded and shaped reality, for at this moment in history the image of empire was premature: England planted its first American colony four years after James's first speech to Parliament. Early reports from the colonies are among the sources of *Cymbeline*'s close contemporary *The Tempest*, a play whose complexity and ambivalence have often been ignored in recent criticism, where it has gradually become a touchstone of the western colonial discourse, a central image of European invasion of the non-white world.[9] Prospero, be it remembered, finally abandons his colony, allowing it to revert to its pre-colonial state; if this mentality sadly did *not* shape reality, it remains unlikely that pacifist James would have conflated colonization and invasion; he found in colonization a peaceful *alternative* to invasion. His word "plantation" conjures more the fertility rites of an agrarian society than the invasion mentality's rites of war.[10]

Jacobean England expanding into empire fancied itself heir to the Roman Empire. The title of Speed's 1611 atlas, *The Theater of the Empire of Great Britaine,* alluded to Ortelius' *Theatrum Orbis Terrarum:* *"Orbis"* there means both "world" and "Roman Empire," and "the authority of the Roman Empire . . . attach[ed] by implication to the English Empire" (Harley 39). James carefully fostered the identification, especially in his "favourite self-appointed role of Peacemaker. *Beati pacifici* was his motto, and he loved to be called, and poets duly obliged him, the second Augustus" (Jones 90); James was portrayed in Roman dress as early as 1590 (Goldberg 46). As Bergeron shows (*"Cymbeline"*), the popular mind linked the Jacobean era with Augustan Rome.

The ideology incorporated that traditional link between England and the ancient world, the Brutus-Trojan myth; significantly, Brutus was a colony founder. But this myth encoded a vulnerability more typical of the Lucrece than the Augustus paradigm: Brutus founded Britain because his own society was destroyed. Mythic common ancestor of Rome and Britain, Troy shared Rome's dual image of besieged city and empire-builder: Aeneas founded Rome after fleeing sacked Troy; his grandson Brutus dubbed the Ur-London New Troy. Jacobean ideology identified James with Brutus as well as Augustus, but as he downplayed England's "feminine," vulnerable image, James borrowed Brutus's nation-founding image without its vulnerability. Not only had Brutus come from a vulnerable society, he had created one, by dividing Britain—Lear-like—into three kingdoms. Appropriating the title "new Brutus," James created himself as an anti-Brutus: uniting England and Scotland reversed Brutus's dangerous division. Image-makers promoted the theme: Munday's *Triumphs of Re-united Britania* (1605), notes that *"England, Wales, & Scotland,* by the first *Brute* severed and divided, is in our second *Brute* reunited" (7). But so entrenched are a culture's semiotic codes, even in times of change, that image-makers could not entirely forget Brutus's vulnerable side: Heywood's *Troia Britanica: or, Great Britain's Troy* (1609), rejoicing that in James "three kingdoms, first by Brute divided, / United are, and by one scepter guided" (437), also develops a parallel between Troy's sack and the rapes or near-rapes of Helen.

Throughout a poem and five plays about Rome, Shakespeare "makes continual reference to Troy, the city that gave birth to Rome" (Miola 17).[11] Since he most often represents Troy as a besieged, sacked city, this identification underlines the basic vulnerability of Shakespeare's Rome. The ecphrasis so prominent in *Lucrece* evokes Troy's destruction. Katharine Maus justly notes that "for Shakespeare the sack of Troy is a culturally primal event" (81). Shakespeare's return, in works early and late, to the

Rome/Troy complex of ideas suggests deep resonance between the Rome/Troy culture he imagined and the English culture he experienced. Across his career he more typically represents that culture in its vulnerable aspect, at risk of invasion, than in James's imperial aspect; but his treatment does shift during his Jacobean phase.

Elizabethan Shakespeare typically imagines a "feminine" embattled society, like Douglas's Coorgs–the Lucrece paradigm; but in Jacobean works like *Cymbeline* he shifts toward the Augustus (not the Julius Caesar) paradigm. This reflected, I think, his culture's changing sense of itself. The change did not occur overnight; it was a subtle shift, a tilting rather than a revolution–jaundiced views of virginity emerge in works before 1603, jaundiced views of Augustus Caesar in works after 1603 (witness *Antony and Cleopatra's* Caesar). The change was not universally applauded: James's pacifism and bisexuality disturbed many; transvestism in the streets disturbed even James. The change did not flow down from the top, the sole creation of Jamesian ideology: like most social change, it welled up from many sources. The ideology was not innocent: the bad faith behind pacifist pronouncements was only too clear in Ireland's continuing agonies. But the vision held great potential; it offered much to women, to the New World, to relations between sexes and between nations, to England's sense of herself. Like Wordsworth's spots of time, the Jacobean intercalary period offers one of history's shining worlds of possibility.

Of Salamanders and Hermaphrodism: Life in the Interstices

Purity and Danger, in a neat piece of puzzle-solving, decodes the Hebrew abominations of Deuteronomy and Leviticus. To two thousand years' efforts to solve the puzzle of what a pig shares with a salamander that both should be abominated, Douglas adds her solution: abominated animals are those that fail to fit one clear category. "Any class of creatures which is not equipped for the right kind of locomotion in its element is contrary to holiness. . . . Anything in the water which has not fins and scales is unclean" (55). Pigs, with cloven hooves but non-cud-chewing, fail to conform to the category of cattle, "the model of the proper kind of food for a pastoralist" (54). As Turner encapsulates this theory of Douglas's, the unclear is unclean.

Fear and avoidance of creatures that stray out of class boundaries is symptomatic of that boundary-obsession that generates pollution beliefs–in a society that feels endangered, clear boundaries divide Jew from Gentile, as an invisible wall guards bodily boundaries, protecting orifices. "The discrimination of statuses obsessed the guardians of the Elizabethan social order" (Montrose 56), as sumptuary laws dictated dress for social classes. Extraordinary efforts during this period to maintain the line between man and beast recall Douglas's theory of boundary-blurring creatures: "It was bestial to work at night, for the same reason that burglary was a worse crime than daylight robbery; the night . . . was 'the time wherein man is to rest, and wherein beasts run about seeking their prey.' It was even bestial to go swimming, for . . . it was essentially a non-human method of progression. As a Cambridge divine observed in 1600: men walked; birds flew; only fish swam. . . . Even to pretend to be an animal for purposes of ritual or entertainment was unacceptable. . . . In the early seventeenth century the hobby horse seems to have largely disappeared from the morris dance. . . . Monstrous births caused such horror [because] they threatened the firm dividing-line between men and animals" (Thomas 39). Such *human* self-palisading is contemporary with other instances we have seen; it was during the early modern period that "most farmers finally moved the animals out of their houses into separate accommodation," and bestiality became a capital offence in England in 1534; bestiality was a "sin of confusion; it was immoral to mix the categories"; the many tales of monstrous human/animal births "show that, in popular estimation at least, man was not so distinct a species that he could not breed with beasts. It was because the separateness of the human race was thought so precarious . . . that the boundary had been so tightly guarded" (ibid., 39-40, 135). Also feared was whatever blurred the "categories of 'wild' and 'tame'. . . . The encroachment of wild creatures into the human domain was always alarming. . . . In 1593 it was feared that the plague in London would get worse because a heron perched on the top of St. Peter's, Cornhill, and stayed there all afternoon. In 1604 the House of Commons rejected a bill after the speech of its Puritan sponsor had been interrupted by the flight of a jackdaw through the Chamber—an indisputably bad omen. The attitude resembled that of those African peoples amongst whom misfortune is expected whenever the world of the bush encroaches upon that of human settlement" (ibid., 78).

The Israelites abominated some foods; Elizabethans abominated some women. Organizing women into clear categories—maid, widow, wife, whore—they abominated the unmarried non-virgin partly because she confounded the distinction between maid and wife (see my *Women*, 84). In Douglas's terms, such women would have been considered polluted, not because sex was inherently staining but because in a society that demands clear boundaries, to confound the line between categories is to become an abomination as sure as the finless salamander or the flying ant.[12] The raped wife, too, is decategorized. Because her extramarital sex is unsanctioned but unwilled, she is neither chaste wife nor adulteress. Her classlessness — or boundary-crossing double class — like rape's "stain," leaves her polluted, potentially contaminating to others. She inhabits a liminal zone between two classes.[13] All margins are dangerous.

But, Douglas says, to be in the margins is to be "in contact with danger, to [be] at a source of power" (*Purity* 97). Propp reminds us how many folk heroes disobey interdictions, transgress boundaries — dangerous but necessary for a hero to grow up and triumph. The dangers that boys in tribal cultures undergo in initiation, Douglas says, "express something important about marginality. . . . To go out of the formal structure and to enter the margins is to be exposed to power that is enough to kill them or make their manhood. . . , The danger that is risked by boundary transgression is power" (*Purity* 96, 161).

In *Titus* and *Lucrece*, rape and mutilation lead to the downfall of a tyrannical government and to Rome's political salvation. Like smashing an atom, smashing these women releases tremendous power. When bodily violence propels them into dangerous margins, when ceasing to be chaste wives they transgress confining boundaries, they release an uncanny power upon the world.

Releasing power through blood sacrifice is tragedy's ancient heritage from ritual. Modern female readers may prefer comedy's way of releasing power. All through *Cymbeline*, Imogen tiptoes along a chasm of rape and death, but escapes violation and murder, and England escapes invasion. Imogen transgresses boundaries in happier ways — eloping, running off to Wales, confounding sexual distinctions by dressing as a boy, transgressing theatrical conventions in being Shakespeare's only transvestite heroine who is not a virgin. This last, a break with her comedic sisters, signals a difference not generic but historical. That this symbol of Endangered Britain is a sexually experienced woman seems a sign of change. Are the orifices not to be so desperately guarded as before? Can Britain escape invasion without a royal virgin as a rallying symbol? Britain escapes here because the Britons trounce the Romans at the lane, but also because Britain pays the tribute and makes peace. Has the invasion mentality ebbed? This is the last invasion attempt in Shakespeare.

In *The Tempest*, Shakespeare's last globetrotting Italians, like the classical Romans before them, make themselves at home on what islands they come upon. The virginity magic of Prospero's "virgin knot" threat proves temporary: Prospero does not favor *perpetual* virginity, but wants his daughter to marry. The menace has bleached out of the invaded-island theme: the storm wrecking the intruders' ship, as storms defended Britain (at least in imagination) from Caesar's ships and the Armada, is here controlled by the island's sovereign, and the threat of rape, by the alien Caliban, is contained. The virgin will marry; the besieged island is abandoned. Prospero returns to the mainland to rule without aid of boundary-protecting magic.

We know, as Shakespeare did not, what lay ahead for the island Britain. The besieged virgin of Renaissance imaginings would become the thrusting masculine conqueror, threatening the New World with ravishment. As Rome moved from invader stage through Augustan liminal zone to invaded stage, so Britain would move from invaded stage through Jacobean liminal zone to invader stage. Colonization would reveal its brutal face, indistinguishable from invasion: the "plantation" James saw as a peaceful alternative to invasion soon displayed invasion's panoply of signifiers—rape, pillage, genocide. The British Empire, like the Roman, would thrust deep into the world's virgin territories; many read *The Tempest* as a document heralding that advance. But while Jacobeans helped invent English colonialism, the play does not fully inhabit that discourse; like Jacobean ideology, it dwells in a liminal zone. No longer an ideology of feminine endangerment, not yet one of masculine rapacity, James's ideology deconstructed a world view that offered only these equally unpleasant alternatives. *The Tempest* belongs to a *pre-colonial* discourse: to locate it fully within the discourse of colonialism, as do Brown or Barker/Hulme, is to miss the power accruing from its position in the interstices of literary history. The late comedies conjure a world poised between society as threatened virgin and as thrusting rapist, a world redeemable without rape and mutilation of women, where territorial integrity can fit comfortably—a loose-fitting salt water girdle—without being tested through invading other nations.

Cymbeline closes with peace, concluded without the need for purification rites: "Let / A Roman and a British ensign wave / Friendly together. . . . / Never was a war did cease, / Ere bloody hands were wash'd, with such a peace" (V.v.481–87).[14] Shakespeare had always identified England with Rome, and his last Roman play unites them; this union weds the "third Rome," which desists from invading, with the "third England," saved from invasion—Augustan Rome meets Jacobean England. Toward the end of his career Shakespeare, living in a charmed moment in a changing culture, envisioned a society neither invaded nor invader, neither raped nor rapist, neither polluted nor polluter, "this happy breed of men, this little world, / This precious stone set in the silver sea, / . . . This blessed plot, this earth, this realm, *this* England."

NOTES

This essay is reprinted by permission of *Texas Studies in Literature and Language.*

1. See lines 16, 33–34, 838, 1056, 1067–68; see Dubrow, 92–93. *Cymbeline,* too, imagines sex as burglary (see I.vi.15, II.ii.41–42).

2. Fineman notes that doors, wind, and glove objectify the rape (40).

3. Marcus's reading of the play as a "sustained political allegory" of Jacobean political concerns (*Puzzling*) is a more topical approach than mine.

4. The Roman emissary arrives in Britain to demand tribute just before the Roman seducer arrives in Britain to attempt Imogen's virtue. Imogen represents British womanhood against the claims of a Roman, Frenchman, Dutchman, and Spaniard that their own country-women are superior (I.iv). Told that her husband has been consorting with Roman prostitutes, Imogen replies wanly, "My lord, I fear, / Has forgot Britain" (I.vi.112–13), meaning "he has forgotten me," a natural identification of herself with Britain. Believing her dead, Posthumus repents of having commissioned her murder and joined the Romans invading Britain: " 'Tis enough / That, Britain, I have kill'd thy mistress [Imogen as the king's daughter]; peace, / I'll give no wound to thee" (V.i.19–21).

5. As Douglas argues elsewhere, however, it is a mistake to regard as advanced or civilized an "internalized" view of transgression as moral guilt, and as primitive or uncivilized an "external" view of transgression as taboo-violation. Instead she locates the taboo-like attitudes in claustrophobic societies obsessed with boundary-protection (*Natural Symbols* 102).

6. In the spate of books published in 1988 for the Armada's four hundredth anniversary, this verdict has stood. The most revisionary, Fernández-Armesto's (which has not been reviewed very favorably), tries to resurrect the weather as a determining factor, but mainly cites poor weather on the voyage from Spain; even he admits that twice during the battle itself the weather *helped* the Spanish (202–3, 205, 238; see also Hart-Davis 198).

7. I have elsewhere discussed the hermaphrodite symbol's centrality in Jacobean culture, including female cross-dressing in London (see *Women*, part two). Some Elizabethan women also cross-dressed—scattered references appear from about 1570—but the fashion blossomed in Jacobean times. Elizabeth's cross-dressing at Tilbury might tell against hermaphrodism as a typically *Jacobean* symbol; but Susan Frye notes a complete lack of contemporary evidence that Elizabeth *did* cross-dress at Tilbury: this image of Elizabeth was, tellingly, a Jacobean creation.

Determined to find hermaphrodism in Elizabeth, Marcus exaggerates from small hints—Elizabeth's holding a truncheon at Tilbury Marcus inflates into the "donning of male battle gear" (*Puzzling* 63).

8. Building on Mary Douglas's theories, Hastrup suggests "that the ambivalent feelings of most people towards transvestism, and to a lesser extent towards homosexuality, are founded on the fact that the people designated by these terms defy the normal categorisation of male and female. . . . If transvestism and homosexuality are concepts of danger, in the sense that they are notions relating to ambiguous areas of classification, then virginity and heterosexuality may be said to be notions of purity, in that they operate with distinct categories of men and women" (52).

9. Skura's recent essay ("Discourse") usefully gathers together (f.n. 1) and cogently criticizes the many "colonial discourse" treatments of the play. She argues that the English colonialism of later centuries has anachronistically colored readings of the play: in fact the play marked, in 1611, the very beginning of a colonial discourse which was significantly altered as early as Purchas's remarks in 1625. She questions whether "colonialism was already encoded in the anomalous situation in 1611," when "there were in England no literary portrayals of New World inhabitants and certainly no fictional examples of colonialist discourse. . . . Insofar as *The Tempest* does in some way allude to an encounter with a New World native, . . . it is the very first work of literature to do so. . . . If the play is 'colonialist,' it must be seen as 'prophetic' rather than descriptive" (52–58). For another perceptive recent critique of the "colonial discourse" interpretation of *The Tempest*, see Willis.

10. Jim Black drew my attention to this Jamesian usage.

11. Miola details many links among our three Roman works: the wager on the wife's chastity (*Luc.*, *Cym.*), Tarquin's and Iachimo's similar approach to sleeping victims, the configuration wicked queen/lustful son (*Tit.*, *Cym.*). Other readers too have noticed close affinities among these works: "The Lucrece story and the Titus Andronicus story look like alternative versions of the same archetype" (G. K. Hunter 184). The Rome/Troy works grew out of a discrete body of material, encoded to conflate harm to the state with bodily harm. That great Jacobean endangered heroine in endangered Britain, *Cymbeline*'s Imogen, bears the name of the wife of Brutus of Troy (see Goldberg 240).

12. An Ashanti girl who becomes pregnant before initiation is so decategorized that she is ostracized and driven into the forest: "Women denounce her for her intrusion into their territory; girls reject her for her treachery. She is without status: no-one calls her *eno* ('mother') and so she is not a woman, and she is not a girl because girls do not become pregnant" (Sarpong 76). Other boundary-blurrers: the leper is "a walking oxymoron; violating the sacrosanct boundary between life and death, he had long been a figure of anomaly and hence of pollution"; leprosariums were on the outskirts of the city (Mullaney 33); the actor "was a willful

confuser of categories" — as Gosson charged, "in stage plays for a boy to put on the attire, the gesture, the passions of a woman, for a mean person to take upon him the title of a prince . . . [is] to show themselves otherwise than they are" (Montrose 55).

13. As Dubrow shows, *Lucrece* "repeatedly describes ambiguous intermediate states, such as the sensation of being both dead and alive or the dilemma of being at once chaste and unchaste, and these examples of 'strange harmony' are mirrored by syneciosis," in phrases like "lifeless life" (82). Dubrow is interested in identity-loss in the rape victim; but such interstitial states can also be attributed to society's rigid categories.

14. Jones thinks that "the peace-tableau with which *Cymbeline* ends . . . pays tribute to James's strenuous peace-making policy" (89), and Wickham offers, "The drift away from revenge tragedy and towards regenerative tragicomedy in the first decade of James's reign . . . has its true origins in the political consciousness of the British peoples saved from foreign invasion and civil war by the peaceful accession of James I in 1603" (36).

WORKS CITED

Argan, Giulio. "Ideology and Iconology." *Critical Inquiry* 2 (1975): 297–305.

Barkan, Leonard. *Nature's Work of Art: The Human Body as Image of the World*. New Haven: Yale University Press, 1975.

Barker, Francis, and Peter Hulme. "'Nymphs and Reapers Heavily Vanish': The Discursive Con-texts of *The Tempest.*" *Alternative Shakespeares*. Ed. John Drakakis. London: Methuen, 1985. 191–205.

Barroll, J. Leeds. "Shakespeare and Roman History." *Modern Language Review* 53 (1958): 327–43.

Bergeron, David M. "*Cymbeline*: Shakespeare's Last Roman Play." *Shakespeare Quarterly* 31 (1980): 31–41.

Berry, Edward. *Shakespeare's Comic Rites*. Cambridge: Cambridge University Press, 1984.

Brown, Paul. "'This thing of darkness I acknowledge mine': *The Tempest* and the Discourse of Colonialism." *Political Shakespeare: New Essays in Cultural Materialism*. Ed. Jonathan Dollimore and Alan Sinfield. Manchester: Manchester University Press, 1985. 48–71.

Bynum, Caroline Walker. *Holy Feast and Holy Fast: The Religious Significance of Food to Medieval Women*. Berkeley: University of California Press, 1987.

Donaldson, Ian. *The Rapes of Lucretia*. Oxford: Clarendon, 1982.

Douglas, Mary. *Natural Symbols: Explorations in Cosmology*. New York: Pantheon, 1970.

———. *Purity and Danger: An Analysis of the Concepts of Pollution and Taboo*. London: Routledge and Kegan Paul, 1966.

Dubrow, Heather. *Captive Victors: Shakespeare's Narrative Poems and Sonnets.* Ithaca: Cornell University Press, 1987.

Evans, Ifor M., and Heather Lawrence. *Christopher Saxton: Elizabethan Map-Maker.* London: Holland, 1979.

Fernández-Armesto, Felipe. *The Spanish Armada: The Experience of War in 1588.* Oxford: Oxford University Press, 1988.

Fineman, Joel. "Shakespeare's *Will:* The Temporality of Rape." *Representations* 20 (1987): 25–76.

Fish, Lydia M. *The Folklore of the Coal Miners of the Northeast of England.* Norwood, Pa.: Norwood, 1975.

Fitz, L. T. "Humanism Questioned: A Study of Four Renaissance Characters." *English Studies in Canada* 5 (1979): 388–405.

Goldberg, Jonathan. *James I and the Politics of Literature: Jonson, Shakespeare, Donne, and their Contemporaries.* Baltimore: Johns Hopkins University Press, 1983.

Harley, J. B. "Meaning and Ambiguity in Tudor Cartography." *English Map Making 1400–1650.* Ed. Sarah Tyacke. London: British Library, 1983. 22–45.

Hart-Davis, Duff. *Armada.* London: Bantam, 1988.

Hastrup, Kirsten. "The Semantics of Biology: Virginity." *Defining Females: The Nature of Women in Society.* Ed. Shirley Ardener. New York: John Wiley, 1978. 49–65.

Hawkins, Harriett. *The Devil's Party: Critical Counter-Interpretations of Shakespearian Drama.* Oxford: Clarendon, 1985.

Heckscher, William S. "Shakespeare in His Relationship to the Visual Arts: A Study in Paradox." *Research Opportunities in Renaissance Drama* 13–14 (1970–71): 5–72.

Heywood, Thomas. *Troia Britanica: or, Great Britaines Troy,* 1609. Hildesheim: Georg Olms, 1972.

Houel, N. *Traité de la Peste.* Paris, 1573.

Hunter, G. K. "Sources and Meanings in *Titus Andronicus.*" *Mirror up to Shakespeare: Essays in Honour of G. R. Hibbard.* Ed. J. C. Gray. Toronto: University of Toronto Press, 1984. 171–88.

James I, King. *The Political Works of James I. Reprinted from the Edition of 1616.* Ed. Charles Howard McIlwain. Cambridge, Mass.: Harvard University Press, 1918.

Jones, Emrys. "Stuart *Cymbeline.*" *Essays in Criticism* 11 (1961): 84–99.

Kahn, Coppélia. "The Rape in Shakespeare's *Lucrece.*" *Shakespeare Studies* 9 (1976): 45–72.

Kolodny, Annette. *The Lay of the Land.* Chapel Hill: University of North Carolina Press, 1984.

Marcus, Leah. *Puzzling Shakespeare: Local Reading and Its Discontents.* Berkeley: University of California Press, 1988.

Mattingly, Garrett. *The Armada.* Cambridge: Riverside, 1959.

Maus, Katharine Eisaman. "Taking Tropes Seriously: Language and Violence in Shakespeare's *Rape of Lucrece.*" *Shakespeare Quarterly* 37 (1986): 66–82.

Miola, Robert S. *Shakespeare's Rome*. Cambridge, Mass.: Cambridge University Press, 1983.

Montrose, Louis Adrian. "The Elizabethan Subject and the Spenserian Text." *Literary Theory/Renaissance Texts*. Ed. Patricia Parker and David Quint. Baltimore: Johns Hopkins University Press, 1986. 303–40.

———. "The Purpose of Playing: Reflections on a Shakespearean Anthropology." *Helios* 7 (1980): 51–74.

Morgan, Victor. "The Cartographic Image of 'The Country' in Early Modern England." *Transactions of the Royal Historical Society*, fifth series, 29. London: Royal Historical Society, 1979. 129–54.

Mullaney, Steven. *The Place of the Stage: License, Play, and Power in Renaissance England*. Chicago: University of Chicago Press, 1988.

Munday, Anthony. *The Triumphs of Re-united Britania*, 1605. *Pageants and Entertainments of Anthony Munday*. Ed. David Bergeron. New York: Garland, 1985. 1–23.

Myers, James P., Jr. *Elizabethan Ireland: A Selection of Writings of Elizabethan Writers on Ireland*. Hamden, Conn.: Archon, 1983.

Nearing, Homer, Jr. "The Legend of Julius Caesar's British Conquest." *PMLA* 64 (1949): 889–929.

Oesterreich, Traugott K. *Possession and Exorcism among Primitive Races, in Antiquity, the Middle Ages, and Modern Times*. Trans. D. Ibberson. New York: Causeway, 1974. First published 1921.

Propp, Vladimir. *Morphology of the Folktale*. Trans. Lawrence Scott. Ed. Svatana Pirkova-Jakobson. Bloomington: Publications of the Indiana Research Center in Anthropology, Folklore, and Linguistics, 1958.

Sarpong, Peter. *Girls' Nubility Rites in Ashanti*. Accra-Tema: Ghana Publishing Corporation, 1977.

Shakespeare, William. *Complete Works*. Ed. David Bevington. Third edition. Glenview, Ill.: Scott, Foresman, 1980.

Skura, Meredith Anne. "Discourse and the Individual: The Case of Colonialism in *The Tempest.*" *Shakespeare Quarterly* 40 (1989): 42–69.

———. "Interpreting Posthumus' Dream from Above and Below: Families, Psychoanalysts, and Literary Critics." *Representing Shakespeare*. Ed. Murray M. Schwartz and Coppélia Kahn. Baltimore: Johns Hopkins University Press, 1980. 203–16.

Somerset Fry, Peter and Fiona Somerset Fry. *A History of Ireland*. London: Routledge, 1988.

Speed, John. *The Theatre of the Empire of Great Britaine*. Ed. John Arlott. London: Phoenix House, 1953–55. 4 vols.

Stallybrass, Peter. "Patriarchal Territories: The Body Enclosed." *Rewriting the Renaissance: The Discourses of Sexual Difference in Early Modern Europe*. Ed. Margaret W. Ferguson, Maureen Quilligan, and Nancy J. Vickers. Chicago: University of Chicago Press, 1986.

Strong, Roy C. *Portraits of Queen Elizabeth.* Oxford: Clarendon, 1963.

——, and Julia Trevelyan Oman. *Elizabeth R.* London: Secker and Warburg, 1971.

Thomas, Keith. *Man and the Natural World: Changing Attitudes in England 1500–1800.* London: Allen Lane, 1983.

Turner, Victor. *The Ritual Process: Structure and Anti-Structure.* Chicago: Aldine, 1969.

Van Gennep, Arnold. *The Rites of Passage.* Trans. Monika B. Vizedom and Gabrielle L. Caffee. London: Routledge and Kegan Paul, 1960. First published in French, 1908.

Velz, John W. "The Ancient World in Shakespeare: Authenticity or Anachronism?" *Shakespeare Survey* 31 (1978): 1–12.

Vickers, Nancy. " 'The Blazon of Sweet Beauty's Best': Shakespeare's *Lucrece.*" In *Shakespeare and the Question of Theory.* Ed. Patricia Parker and Geoffrey Hartman. New York: Methuen, 1985. 95–115.

Vigarello, Georges. *Concepts of Cleanliness: Changing Attitudes in France Since the Middle Ages.* Cambridge: Cambridge University Press, 1989.

Warner, Marina. *Alone of All Her Sex: The Myth and the Cult of the Virgin Mary.* London: Weidenfeld and Nicolson, 1976.

Wickham, Glynne. "From Tragedy to Tragi-Comedy: *King Lear* as Prologue." *Shakespeare Survey* 26 (1973): 33–48.

Willis, Deborah. "Shakespeare's *Tempest* and the Discourse of Colonialism." *Studies in English Literature 1500–1900* 29 (1989): 277–89.

Woodbridge, Linda. *Women and the English Renaissance: Literature and the Nature of Womankind, 1540–1620.* Urbana: University of Illinois Press; Brighton: Harvester, 1984.

Notes on Contributors

EDWARD BERRY is Professor of English and Dean of Humanities at the University of Victoria. He is the author of articles on Bacon, Shakespeare, and Sidney, and of two books: *Patterns of Decay: Shakespeare's Early Histories* and *Shakespeare's Comic Rites*.

MICHAEL D. BRISTOL is Professor of English at McGill University. He is the author of *Carnival and Theater: Plebeian Culture and the Structure of Authority in Renaissance England* and of *Shakespeare's America/America's Shakespeare*.

WILLIAM C. CARROLL is Professor of English at Boston University. He is the author of *The Great Feast of Language in "Love's Labour's Lost"* and *The Metamorphoses of Shakespearean Comedy*; his current project is a book on vagrancy and marginality in Tudor-Stuart culture.

PHYLLIS GORFAIN, Professor of English at Oberlin College, has published many articles on folklore and Shakespeare, particularly emphasizing riddling. She is finishing a series of articles on play and *Hamlet* and writes on topics in folklore in Africa.

GILLIAN MURRAY KENDALL is an Assistant Professor of English at Smith College. She has written mostly on Shakespeare and is currently at work on a book about non-Shakespearean Elizabethan and Jacobean tragedy.

NAOMI CONN LIEBLER is Professor of English, College Distinguished Scholar, and Graduate Program Coordinator for English and Comparative Literature at Montclair State College (New Jersey). She has published articles on Shakespeare, Pirandello, and Edward Albee, and is completing a book on the ritual foundations of Shakespearean tragedy.

MICHAEL NEILL is Associate Professor of English at the University of Auckland, New Zealand. His publications include *The Selected Plays of John Marston* and *John Ford: Critical Re-visions*. He has recently completed an introduction to *Hamlet* for the Folger Shakespeare and is editing

Antony and Cleopatra for the Oxford Shakespeare. His book on representations of death in Renaissance Drama is nearing completion.

JEANNE ADDISON ROBERTS is Professor of Literature at the American University in Washington, D.C. She is past President of the Shakespeare Association of America and author, most recently, of *The Shakespearean Wild: Geography, Genus, and Gender.*

MARK ROSE is Director of the University of California Humanities Research Institute and Professor of English at the University of California, Santa Barbara. He is the author of *Shakespearean Design* and other books on modern as well as Renaissance subjects.

DEBORAH WILLIS is Assistant Professor of English at the University of California, Riverside, where she teaches Shakespeare and Renaissance drama. She is currently working on a book about Shakespeare and the gendered history of witch-hunting. Her most recently published article is "Shakespeare's *Tempest* and the Discourse of Colonialism."

LINDA WOODBRIDGE is Professor of English at the University of Alberta. Her publications include *Women and the English Renaissance, Shakespeare: A Selective Bibliography of Modern Criticism,* and a number of articles, some under her former name, L. T. Fitz. She is President of the Shakespeare Association of America.

BRUCE W. YOUNG is Associate Professor of English at Brigham Young University, where he has taught Shakespeare, literary theory, and other subjects since 1983. Among his publications are essays on *Lear* and *The Winter's Tale* in two volumes of the MLA *Approaches to Teaching World Masterpieces* series. He is working on a book-length study of Shakespeare and Renaissance family life.

Index

2448